Challenge and Consequence

...forcing change to eCommerce

Dear Michael & Carol, Ralph W. Notto

I am always pleased to see you when we are in St. Paul. And thanks for your visits to Maryland.

To get a frame of reference for this book, see pages 21-29. To know what I think about all of this work, see pages 288-289. Also, look at the Preface and Dedication.

Ralph

July 11, 2005

Challenge and Consequence: Forcing Change to eCommerce

Published by Fenestra Books™

610 East Delano Street, Suite 104, Tucson, Arizona 85705 U.S.A.

www.fenestrabooks.com

Publisher's Cataloging-in-Publication
(Provided by Quality Books, Inc.)

Notto, Ralph W.
Challenge and consequence-- forcing change to eCommerce / Ralph W. Notto.
p. cm.
LCCN 2004115374
ISBN 1-58736-414-X

1. Electronic commerce. I. Title.

HF5548.32.N67 2005 658.8'72

QBI04-200514

Preface

By the year 2000, *eCommerce* was used around the world, changing all of our lives. How did this happen so fast? Most of us had never heard the term before 1995.

In truth, it was not fast at all. It has resulted from the interaction of legislative, educational, scientific, engineering, business, and entrepreneurial events over several decades beginning in the 1940s. It resulted from vision provided by people from many different professions.

Executives and other leaders must pay particular attention to this subject, especially if they assign tasks technical in nature, and the survival of the corporation or organization is put at risk if the tasks are not driven with sound objectives and completed with deliberate methodology. In particular, economies worldwide have shown surprising growth and strength due to appreciable productivity increases, a significant part of which are attributed to *eCommerce*. Therefore, future decision-making processes for some components of *eCommerce* are too important to be treated lightly. It follows that we need a historical reference when performing and evaluating the continuing *eCommerce* enhancement and implementation work.

Challenge and Consequence is a history of electronic commerce and the unfolding of a new era in the use and flow of data and information—why a change was sought, how it occurred, what impact it has had, and how success was achieved from vision, purpose, coordination, belief, commitment, determination, and an effective strategy. The emphasis is on one of the main components of *eCommerce*, electronic data interchange (EDI). How did it start, why is it significant, what principles were used, how does it relate to the growth in national economies, are there other benefits, how is this related to the Internet, are any future changes recommended?

Although EDI was introduced as a public standard in 1975, there were many events that preceded it that gave a breath of life to all of the *eCommerce* components. These events included a legislative event in the 1940s relative to making a commitment as a nation to the education and training of our people based on a belief that such a commitment would make a better and more stable quality of life for all of us. The event was the passage of the GI Bill, which enabled World War II veterans to earn university or college degrees. In turn, this provided for much of the educated talent required to start and continuously expand the computer industry and to dramatically enhance most of the communications industry. Both industries are essential for *eCommerce.* The GI Bill was repeated for Korean and Vietnam War veterans.

Another legislative event of similar importance in the 1970s extended to minorities new opportunities in the information and other industries. This was the civil rights legislation that did not pay for education, but now opened for minorities the doors that were previously closed. Without this, those companies seeking people with skills in short supply may have overlooked an excellent source of talent. A similar result in the fight for women's rights also helped to expand the source of talent.

Consider that the freshman classes of 1947 at United States universities and colleges across the nation included a very large number of World War II veterans. All benefited from the GI Bill, a significant piece of legislation that, among other benefits, paid the veterans for attending these schools. The schools responded to the massive increases in student populations by erecting temporary classroom buildings, increasing class sizes, and bending or changing some of their rules that were meant for younger people.

I watched this phenomenon from the perspective of a seventeen-year-old freshman. The group of older fellow students imparted on the rest of us a sense of determination, purpose, importance, and conduct that we may have missed in another era. Perhaps none of us sensed it at the time, but a large number of this class of seasoned veterans and recent high school graduates would eventually create the computer industry and a revised communications industry, or would work in companies applying the use of computers and data communications.

In 1947, students were not thinking about computers or data communications. Those of us in mathematics or engineering studies always carried a slide rule and book of logarithm tables and were required to use them correctly. That was still true by 1951 when we were graduated.

Somehow, however, the commercial computer industry was born in the 1950s, *and a requirement for connecting computers with electronic data communications became apparent for many applications.*

(Indeed, I was one of several people working on a "Sea Surveillance" project in 1957-1960 where we were tasked to write the computer programs required for keeping track of *all* surface, air, and submerged vessels in the North Atlantic. This meant keeping track of movement and vessel types for vessels of friend and foe—as well as the United States. We did, in fact, write working programs. The system was not put into active use, however, because the vacuum tube technology limited system meantime between failures to four hours.)

With vacuum tubes as major components, the computers of the 1950s were slow, unreliable, difficult to maintain, and lacking in software. They were also wonderful, because they permitted solving problems more quickly, or made it possible for new and more efficient methods and procedures in business and industry. As a minimum, these computers let us absolutely know what was possible, forced us to adapt to frequent change to achieve our goals, and continuously offered new exciting capability that was impossible to ignore.

The next generation of computers, beginning in 1960, used transistor logic. The resultant computers were twice as fast, provided twice as much memory, and supporting software included an assembler, sort routine, and real-time executive program; all this at half the price of computer systems of the 1950s, which had none of these three items. We adapted to short-term computer generations, each lasting about three years and providing similar changes in capability. From the vacuum tube to the transistor era, reliability increased from four to one thousand hours meantime between failures. Transistors were replaced with microchips later in the 1960s. Computer generations passed fairly consistently each three-year period, with similar rates of improvement until the late 1990s, when the length of a computer generation became less than one year.

EDI grew from this environment. To many people, the concept and value of EDI was not evident or even required or considered possible. For others, some computer tasks in the late 1950s and early 1960s were instrumental in providing learning experiences for those who would later define and initially develop EDI.

EDI requires computers and data communications. It is a major factor in improving productivity, control, accuracy, timeliness, quality, and customer satisfaction. EDI, by its very nature, is a treasure house of information required for management decision-making and operations excellence.

Challenge and Consequence identifies what operational strategy was employed, what was its impact, and how success was achieved.

A major change has evolved over the quarter century beginning in 1975. Directly or indirectly, this change has affected everyone worldwide. Multi-billion dollar industries were spawned specifically to service the needs of companies and organizations that use or will use EDI.

This book is written from the perspective of an eyewitness and participant in the development of *eCommerce.* The intent is threefold-to show how people involved in creating EDI interacted with each other and made a difference in EDI's ultimate success, to indicate the foundation on which the EDI technology is built in order to provide credible evidence of its solid base, and to impart an understanding of EDI's current and potential impact on companies and people.

My preparation for writing this book also dates back to the 1940s. I sought to become a systems engineer before the skill was defined. I studied not only to be a mathematician but to also have significant training and experiences in history, journalism, statistics, electronics, actuarial science, computer programming, business, education, and economics. I accepted jobs primarily on the bases of experiences I thought essential for growth as a mathematician and systems engineer.

It is my hope that this book will help others to understand that *eCommerce* is the result of people working together, sometimes cooperating, sometimes confronting, sometimes cajoling, but always dedicated to the same primary objectives. It is important that executive decision makers understand the role of EDI in *eCommerce* and in business process reengineering, assuring that future decisions facilitate new growth and benefits.

For those people who are the current and future innovators in *eCommerce*, it is my hope that this book may provide new insights to assist in your work.

To my colleagues, I express my gratitude for the opportunity to have worked with you.

—Ralph W. Notto

Acknowledgments

Ed Guilbert provided me with the opportunity to work toward EDI development, invited me to participate in the creation of the first EDI standard, and to contribute my efforts toward EDI's implementation and enhancement.

Joe Carley and Buddy Bass read an earlier draft of this book and provided suggestions and encouragement. Joe Carley developed the strategy for creating EDI and chaired all of the EDI work groups during the late 1970s, ensuring success. Buddy Bass designed the first EDI standards manual in 1975. Both men had distinguished careers in EDI for a quarter century. Both wrote extensively about EDI, and some of their writings are quoted in this book.

George Klima sent me four letters to identify some of the early EDI pioneers. These are shown in Chapter 2 and provide insights revealing the far-reaching thought processes relative to use of EDI and its byproducts—ideas that were discussed in his company long before inter-industry *standard* EDI became a reality.

Dan Ferguson published several of my articles in the *EDI Forum* and granted permission to quote from these and articles by other authors. The *EDI Forum* has been a source for a broad range of information about EDI and *eCommerce*.

Fran Guilbert (Mrs. Ed Guilbert) and Peter Guilbert (Ed and Fran's son) provided some of the photos of Ed Guilbert and the references used in chapter seven. Peter has also worked in EDI and was a co-author of the *EDI Workbook* used by TDCC for some of its EDI implementation classes.

Ralph Berwanger wrote the *Security Focus and Products* topic in chapter four.

Richard Bort granted permission to use the email message in the *Use of Expert Opinion* example in chapter six.

Vegard Nervik of Norway wrote the *XML-Is it the future?* topic in chapter four.

Dr. Y.T. Lee of Korea granted permission to use the text in the *Another View* topic in chapter eight, pointing out that in addition to addressing standards, business, and technical issues, EDI also has an effect on social issues.

Soo Hong Noh (Daniel) of Korea worked with me on several EDI projects, traveled extensively in the US to participate in EDI discussions, and helped me to gain new insights into the interest and potential for EDI in other countries. He also reviewed a pre-publication copy of this book, and helped me to obtain additional information and photos from Korean sources.

Ray MacDougall recommended a style change in this book to make the EDI story appear less technical. This resulted in moving to the appendix more of the detail required for the historical record and revising paragraphs that contained bulleted lists.

Discussions with Susan Reamer led to changes or additions to some of the topics, all of which improved style and clarity. Susan was an EDI consultant for more than two decades.

Joan Gennaro and Elsa Lundgren Jackman, both librarians, helped to select the title and subtitle of this book. They also read the earliest draft and provided valuable suggestions for modifications and style. Elsa helped to find suitable quotes used at the beginning of chapters. Joan suggested use of text boxes to present acronyms and their meanings.

Bill Galitz introduced me to the principles of human factors engineering while we were both at Univac during the 1960s. This knowledge was extremely important when I had a role during the 1970s helping others to learn how the generalization of EDI software could easily be accomplished, even considering multi-industry and international communities.

Terry Schager read all of a "final" draft of this book and provided important and challenging editing comments. Terry has had early and continuing involvement in the EDI industry since 1984, making contributions on the X12 Legal and Audit Subcommittee, transportation EDI standards work, and X12 transaction development for the pulp and paper industry's *eCommerce* working group. He also noted that this book offers insight into what has been going on at both the micro and macro levels, as well as including significant historical detail.

Abdel-Kamel Imadalou also read a "final" draft of this book and helped to identify items requiring clarification.

Dedicated to Dorothy Notto

During a period approaching five decades, my wife Dorothy welcomed to our home visitors from thirty-four countries. This provided an informal setting for conversations with individuals and small groups about their interests, concerns, families, and homelands. Some of the guests were related to our work; some were not. This helped us to more deeply understand different points of view and to reflect this in our attitude and work. The countries were the United States, Canada, Mexico, Brazil, Argentina, Uruguay, Chile, Peru, Venezuela, Columbia, Italy, Germany, France, Switzerland, Spain, Sweden, Norway, Denmark, United Kingdom, Hungary, Algeria, Egypt, South Africa, Kenya, Rwanda, India, China, Taiwan, Korea, Vietnam, Cambodia, Japan, Singapore, and Australia.

Table of Contents

1. Challenge

"There comes a tide in the affairs of men,
which taken at the flood leads on to fortune;
omitted, all the days of their lives
are bound in shallows and despair."

William Shakespeare, *Julius Caesar*

INTO THE FUTURE

Each generation has its challenges and responsibilities. Some of us born during the period from 1915 to 1950 were challenged to invent electronic commerce and tasked to implement a major component of it. The component is called "electronic data interchange," or EDI.

In the evolution of this new technology, something wonderful has happened. For the quarter century following 1975, a worldwide cooperative effort has resulted in a global reach for communications and commerce never before thought possible.

People worked at this in a spirit of service to company, industry, country, world, and each other. Their work significantly contributed to the outstanding improvement in economies that was experienced during the 1990s, and will continue to be effective for many years to come, even considering a cyclic economic setback like that beginning in year 2001.

By the year 2000, we called this phenomenon "electronic commerce" or "eCommerce," terms not known or used with any frequency until the 1990s. Even the term "electronic data interchange" was not used until mid-1975, some months after the work to define EDI intensified. The term was first introduced by Donald Johnston of Phillips Petroleum Company in a speech he gave at a conference sponsored by the Transportation Data Coordinating Committee (TDCC). The term became "official" in July 1975 with the printing of the first U.S. public EDI standard.

While many company executives authorized funding for the developmental work by assigning talented people to TDCC work groups to help define the requirements and evolve a solution, even more executives thought that the work could not possibly bear fruit. Even if it were possible to define a viable concept for electronic commerce, they said that it would not be practical. In this context, those engaged in this work were possibly putting their careers at risk.

Visions and Mandate

The interest in EDI originated independently in several countries. Each had different visions for purpose and means of implementation.

In the United States, the vision was for a paperless environment for exchange of data between companies, computer to computer. In Europe, the vision was for efficient flow of international shipments through customs procedures at receiving countries, uninhibited by late arrival of required documents.

Both visions were valid for their environments.

The U.S. group had the mandate to use electronic methods to convey data from an automated process in one U.S. company to a complementing process in another. International shipments accounted for 10% of the U.S. trade.

With more countries and borders in Europe, the amount of international trade was much more significant, and streamlining it was a first priority. Their mandate was to insure timely availability of required paperwork at critical nodes in the transportation sequence.

Given these two mandates, the U.S. groups focused on a data-format standard for inter-company transmissions, and did not address printed documents. International EDI was addressed in all of their work, but the focus for initial tests and implementation was for intra-U.S. situations.

The European groups focused on a standard for documentation formats required for international shipments and on electronic data transmission to efficiently get data from one country to another, so required forms could be printed and processed before arrival of the corresponding shipment.

During the mid-1970s, the U.S. and European groups independently focused on standards, electronic data transmissions, and transportation environments. Eventually they would engage in more cooperative information exchanges, and a common international standard would evolve. Another decade would pass, however, before the results of that were put into practice, beginning about 1987. Before 1985, many other industries—grocery, chemical, electrical, steel, paper, retail—would join the U.S. transportation industries' EDI initiative. There were four transportation industries involved in the early EDI movement—air, motor, ocean and rail. Their customers belonged to other industries. So the initial transportation industries work included inter-industry cooperation. The subsequent non-transportation industry EDI initiatives built on this to create non-transportation transactions. Thus, the EDI standards movement became both international and multi-industry. Very nice, since all members of any industry buy from and sell to members of other industries.

Fundamental changes for the flow and use of data and the extraction of information from data resulted from this broad participation. These changes delivered favorable results relative to accuracy, timeliness, control, and efficiency. EDI became one of the major building blocks in the economic miracle of the 1990s, which was characterized by dramatic productivity increases, reduction in unemployment, stabilization of inflation, and increases in customer satisfaction.

While it may be argued that these changes occurred because "their time had come," the author's premise is that they occurred this early in time only because the people, companies, and organizations working toward these ends had a required mix of insight, skill, commitment, and attitude.

Creating and Implementing

Creating an information standard is a difficult task, requiring the skill and coordination of many people, long-term support from their companies for this endeavor, and research to determine the feasibility and effectiveness of possible solutions. A standards creation process of this type may take several years.

Implementing a standard like U.S.-focused EDI is considerably more difficult, because it involves changing the way people work in their companies, and requires coexistence of old and new methods for a significant period of time. In fact, the concept of eliminating paperwork was considered infeasible by many information processing "experts." Why then, did people persist with this view? Why did their corporate managers permit it, even mandate it? The paperwork systems were expensive and certainly not error-free, so corporate managers were looking for ways to improve accuracy and control. As a result, they hoped to benefit from an increase in customer satisfaction and enhancement of their competitive postures.

U.S. Organization and Roles

In the United States in 1975, those caught up with this task included four distinctly different, but cooperating, groups.

The first group included representatives from industry and government who concurrently and routinely used computer-processed data or directed the use of computers in their companies. This group represented users; those who would ultimately use whatever would come from this endeavor. Clearly, from the point of view of defining the content and functionality of what was to come, this group was in charge.

The second group included others from the same organizations that were specialists in solving computer science and data communications problems and completing the tasks required to implement the solutions. Whatever was to come, this group would be charged with its facilitation.

A third group included representatives from interested service industries like banking and time-sharing. The banking industry's interest stemmed from the understanding that the resulting information exchanges would include not only operational data exchanges but also payment exchanges (value transfers electronically rather than by actual currency or check transfer). The time-sharing industry provided a service involving the use of large-scale computers via time-sharing terminals (usually teletype machines) that connected to the computers via acoustic couplers (although modems may also have been used) and the telephone system. Thus individual users could randomly use the time-sharing service, independently write and execute their own programs, and pay for this on the basis of how much computer time and resources were used. The time-sharing companies' interest in EDI was natural in that they were almost ready to provide inter-company data communications service. The transmission speed of the time-sharing service was usually ten characters per second.

That speed did not seem either particularly slow or fast at the time. It was slow in the sense that responses were not immediate, but it was fast when compared with other means of getting information or data.

The final group included a few chosen to lead and coordinate the others. This group had eight people who were the total staff and consultants of TDCC. These were led by the organization's president, Edward A. Guilbert, who was a master at group motivation, and Program Director Joseph G. Carley Jr., who was a master at developing and executing involved strategies. The rest of the staff included two full-time and two part-time consultants, an expert in coding systems, and a secretary.[1]

Group Dynamics

The first group, users, was the ultimate authority for defining the subject and detail of all discussions.

The second group, corporate facilitators, used their combined knowledge of how systems were currently implemented and how proposed changes would affect implementation schedules to advise on the practicality of proposals.

About the first two groups, the 1975 EDI standards publications[2] stated: "The TDCC Shipper/Carrier Electronic Data Interchange Program is an undertaking of private industry for use primarily by industry to improve its ability to more effectively utilize and/or perform transportation services. It is therefore incumbent on the member corporations of industry to collectively define requirements, approve plans, undertake developmental efforts, comply with agreed standards, participate in test and evaluation programs, and support requirements for the maintenance of evolving systems. It is only through this philosophy of collective coordination and cooperation, and compatible methods of planning, definition, and development, that progress has been made and will continue to be made towards achieving the objectives of the transportation community."

---

[1] The consultants were Staff Systems Consultant Earl J. Bass, Systems Consultant Ralph W. Notto (author), Special Consultant (motor-carrier related) Lester A. Probst, and Communications Consultant Alexander Kreithen. The other two at TDCC were Director of Coding Standards Thomas DesNoyers and Administrative Supervisor Gina Forrest.

[2] TDCC, "Preliminary Functional Specification for a Prototype Electronic Data Interchange System," pages 1-4 to 1-5, July 1975, [Department of Transportation reference DOT-OS-50017-1].

Ed Guilbert

The participants comprising the third group were involved because of their belief that sales of their services to the first two groups were possible, but they were told at TDCC meetings that user companies, not vendors, would define requirements. Given this, it was clear that the users were heading toward a new plateau in the use of information automation and data communications, and did not want their work to be forced to conform to the capabilities of the current systems owned by those service industries they presently used. In fact, the original idea was that companies would communicate directly with each other with a computer in one company automatically placing a telephone call to a modem connected to a computer in another company. The receiving computer would then answer automatically and receive and process the incoming data. Data moving in the opposite direction would occur with the same processes, but with sender and receiver roles reversed.

The time-sharing companies believed that they had a potentially large communications market, so they persisted. Two types of communications followed in the next two decades: point-to-point and value added network services. The latter was a new role for the time-sharing companies. They accomplished this by simplifying and standardizing their data communications processes. They also agreed to process communications with their clients' trading partners, even when a partner did not subscribe to the same time-sharing service. This required that competing time-sharing companies had to connect to each other. So now, a frequent transmission flow was from the sending partner to its time-sharing service; then to the receiving trading partner's time-sharing service and to the receiving trading partner. But communication for any company became quite easy, since all data flowed between that company and its time-sharing service. The remaining communication processes were performed by the service company. In effect, the time-sharing company simulated the processes expected from an in-company data communications department, except that they were more cost-effective in most cases because they provided similar services for many clients. Companies did not begin the Internet for EDI until about 1995. The Internet, however, was effectively used for EDI at least two years before 1995 at universities and colleges for transmission of student transcripts in EDI format.

The fourth group, the complete staff and consultants of TDCC, had the primary job to keep the endeavor focused and on schedule. TDCC funding came from its member companies and a contract from the Office of Facilitation, U.S. Department of Transportation (DOT). William Myers of DOT administered the contract.

William Myers

The TDCC reference in the 1975 publication[3] was:

TDCC is a non-profit organization established in 1968 through the efforts of the Transportation Association of America. It is solely supported by private industry, inclusive of individual companies having a business concern with transportation as well as transportation industry associations such as the Association of American Railroads and the American Trucking Associations, Inc.

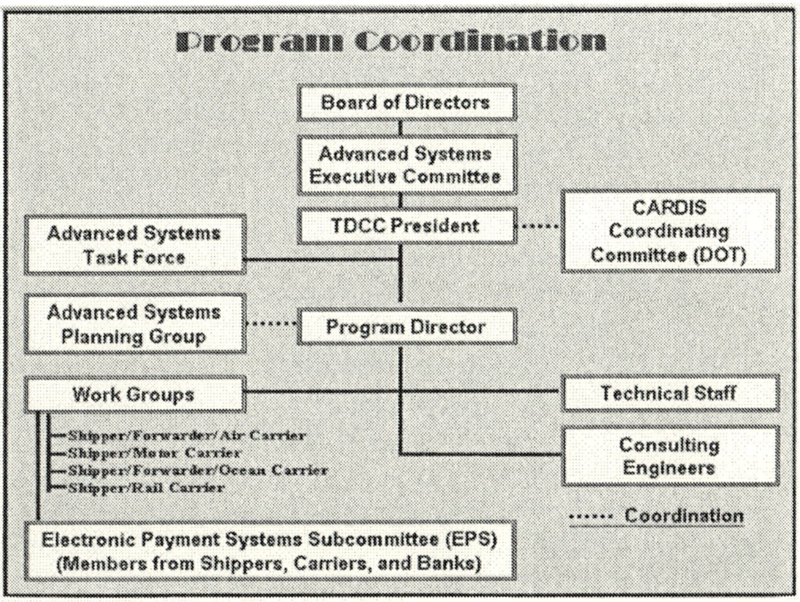

Figure 1. TDCC Project Coordination Structure

The organizational charter requires the TDCC to engage in research, developmental, and coordination activities addressing standard transportation codes, U.S. transportation tariffs, and transportation systems.

3 Ibid, pages 1-3 to 1-4, July 1975.

> The TDCC is a coordinating activity having no operational, administrative, or managerial responsibilities directly associated with the performance of transportation functions. In terms of transportation systems, the organization is a non-user. It maintains a strict coordinating posture in all aspects of development of the Shipper/Carrier Electronic Data Interchange Program. The TDCC staff concentrates its greater effort on the requirement to be fully responsive to the expressed needs of the representatives of the transportation community assisting in the effort. Special attention is given to the requirement for a balanced emphasis on domestic and international aspects of cargo movement, control, and administration.

TDCC: Transportation Data Coordinating Committee

EDI: Electronic Data Interchange

DOT: U.S. Department of Transportation

CARDIS: Cargo Data Interchange Standard

The government reference in the 1975 publication[4] was: "The official interests of the United States in transportation are wide ranging, involving all branches of government. Specific interests in the TDCC Shipper/Carrier Electronic Data Interchange Program fall into several categories. First, the program is associated with the research activity of the Cargo Data Interchange Standard (CARDIS) program of the Department of Transportation and therefore can have an impact on efforts to coordinate international agreements on standards and systems. Secondly, various departments of the executive branch of government are users of the U.S. transportation system and, as such, possess a significant operational interest. A similar degree of interest is maintained by those agencies of the government charged with regulatory, administrative, and control responsibilities for trade, transport, and communications. Most importantly, the federal government has a responsibility to provide leadership, support, and assistance towards the development of programs that may lead to an improved posture of the United States in transportation systems and services. It is in the latter role that the Department of Transportation is enabled to enter into research and development contracts with TDCC for purposes outlined herein."

---

4 Ibid, pages 1-5 to 1-6.

SENSING THE MOMENT

Did those involved really sense that they were heading toward a new plateau? Some did. In the July 1975 Standard, the Developmental Approach[5] was stated as:

> **General Structure of TDCC**—The TDCC performs its mission under the direction of an elected Board of Directors which is currently comprised of executives from twenty-eight companies. These companies provide a broad and balanced representation of industry and of the transportation community. Technical programs are developed and managed through and with the support and assistance of industry task forces. The Advanced Systems Task Force is the primary technical arm of the Board of Directors for transportation systems programs.
>
> **Program Coordination Structure**—This specification was developed under a system of work groups and special technical subcommittees. The work groups will be retained as a developmental and technical policy structure for the duration of this particular systems program. The purpose of the working group structure is to provide a means for focusing effort on the process of definition, and to assure a potential for maximum participation by members of the transportation community while maintaining a manageable production capability in terms of numbers of representatives. The functions of the work groups are to define requirements, coordinate and advise on technical policy matters, address a specific set of application subject areas for a particular mode of transportation, and provide a mechanism for coordination with the internal staffs of participating companies.

The overall definition of program parameters was developed by the TDCC staff in conjunction with the TDCC Advanced Systems Planning Group.

> **Philosophy of Development**—One of the primary charter tasks of TDCC was to develop a program to facilitate the electronic interchange of information between industrial, service, and governmental organizations of the transportation community. The extremely broad scope of the problem and complexity of subjects to be addressed presented a wide range of alternatives relative to developmental approach. In order to assure a basis for understanding the orientation of the concept adopted for the program, the following principles apply:

---

5 Ibid, page 1-8 to 1-12, July 1975, [Department of Transportation reference DOT-OS-50017-1].

Principles

The program only addresses the external data interchange environment as opposed to the internal activities of the separate companies and organizations involved. Internal procedures and methods are retained as internal prerogatives.

All modes of transportation have been addressed concurrently to enhance the potential for a common orientation and to stimulate a trend toward greater standardization within and between modes. The alternative of imposing four distinct modal standards and procedures for adoption by all other concerned agencies and organizations (including shippers and consignees) is not considered appropriate.

The program is structured around specific application areas of primary concern and interest to the transportation community.

Shippers and carriers are considered as the focal point for an expanding parameter in the scope, numbers and types of applications addressed and selected for development. The requirements of consignees are given attention in conjunction with those of shippers and carriers. (This is a logical conclusion due to the fact that shipments, shipment information, and a significant percentage of payments originate with shippers. Carriers represent the center of the transportation universe. Consignees are the target recipients of the transportation service. All other services, control, and regulatory organizations and functions are treated as support functions in the developmental scheme.)

The program does not address output transportation documentation standards as regards format, form, or content. This subject is considered beyond the scope of interest of TDCC and, further, probably should be retained as an internal prerogative of individual functions since the precedence of practice supports this view. Legislation, governmental rules and regulations, modal agreements, and transportation practices appear to satisfy requirements in the area as they relate to this program.

The program addresses dynamic, complex systems which could potentially involve, influence, or have an impact on the entire industrial base of the United States and its international trading partners. Therefore, the program is expected to be dynamic in character and must be developed and implemented in an evolutionary manner.

The program is approached from the perspective of paralleling current operations and procedures as regards the application of computers and communications to support the flow of shipment information.

The most legitimate sources for definitive requirements incorporated in this specification are the potential users of electronic data interchange procedures. More specifically, the recipients of the information in the current environment of manual data interchange are best qualified to stipulate informational requirements which should be incorporated in electronic data interchange procedures.

The information communicated through electronic interchange procedures has the purpose of enabling the performance of operational and administrative functions, and serving as basic information to which new information must be added for the same purpose and/or to reflect actions taken. Additionally, certain categories of information must be retained for "pass through" to the next user.

The program addresses the movement of shipments to, from, and within the trade environment of the United States. It does not attempt to establish standards for international dissemination procedures or for interfaces with the systems of other governments. However, a serious effort has been made to provide all necessary information to international carriers to enable them to comply with international ports of entry requirements and to perform other normal information dissemination tasks."

Scope

The Scope of Participation[6] in 1975 was recorded as: "The essential ingredient to the degree of validity achieved in this specification was the contribution made by representatives of private industry who participated in the planning group, work group, and subcommittee meetings. It was from these sources that the TDCC staff received the guidance, direction, and direct support necessary to perform the overall task of development and organization of the specification.

The scope of participation can be evaluated in terms of numbers of representatives present for meetings, numbers of companies represented at meetings, numbers of companies and/or representatives listed for documentation distribution for information purposes only, and numbers of representatives and/or companies contributing constructive staff time or resources towards the effort.

Adopting any particular basis for evaluation would potentially introduce assumptions of an invalid nature, positive and negative. It can be fac-

[6] Ibid, pages 1-12 to 1-14, July 1975, [Department of Transportation reference DOT-OS-50017-1].

tually stated that the effort generated growing interest and participation from companies and transportation associations. Further, work group membership and attendance records remained stable and consistent throughout the developmental period.

The companies, Planning and Work and Work Groups, and participants during 1975 are listed in Appendix II, which contains lists of representatives of companies and organizations who are participating members of the various groups and subcommittees. The lists also contain the names of personnel who requested and received copies of all appropriate draft documentation. Due to the depressed economic situation that existed during the period from August 1974 through July 1975, many corporations imposed severe restrictions on travel and on priority of staff effort. Therefore, it would be presumptuous to attempt to evaluate and qualify the interest and participation factors between the two categories of personnel. It is a significant fact that 90% of the personnel listed were active in the program through direct contributions of staff effort and/or during attendance at meetings.

Joe Carley

"It must be precisely understood that the development effort reflected in this specification and the list of names and companies provided in Appendix II cannot be interpreted to mean U.S. industry has approved the concept, validated requirements, or signaled an intent to be committed in any manner or form. This is, as stated before, designed to be a dynamic specification to be modified and adjusted as necessary to ultimately reflect the real needs of industry. The validity of the specification can only be proved through test and evaluation. Its applicability and utility will be proved by adoption and use.

At TDCC, Joe Carley wrote all of the previous quotes. It was Ed Guilbert's practice that all material to be included in the standards publication was to be reviewed by Guilbert, Carley, Bass, and Notto. All material, regardless of the author, was reviewed by each, discussed, and revised for several iterations before the final publication was released. Carley's writing skills were excellent. It was never the intent to question that. The focus was always to insure that all topics in the standards publication were coordinated.

About Electronic Commerce and EDI

Look at EDI as a component of eCommerce that is rapidly changing our patterns for work and other activities. Other components like email, facsimile, and shopping on the Internet are readily understandable and usable by the masses. EDI, by contrast, is more of a "back-office" function meant for communications between automatic and semi-automatic processes in different companies around the world.

EDI, electronic data interchange, requires timeliness. It demands an error-free environment. It requires communications with many trading partners, each with its own choices for standards versions, qualifying codes, formats, and communications linkage. For all such reasons, EDI is more difficult than most other eCommerce components. It is used because it is a factor in improved productivity, decreased cost, favorable changes in customer satisfaction, and improved data quality. All of these measures are influenced by the timeliness, accuracy, and completeness of the data. And with proper implementation, the data may also be efficiently and quickly changed into information required for management decision-making and operations excellence.

On local and worldwide bases, EDI's scope includes data communications among computers of different companies for purposes like connecting the purchasing process of one company to the order entry process of another, or connecting the invoicing process of a seller to the payment process of the buyer. In its full implication, these processes are completed automatically without paperwork and with a superior system of control. People, however, are not meant to be excluded. They are, in fact, required whenever they are part of any company's implementation of the process or sub-processes within it.

The EDI concept generates excitement because of the resultant impact on control, efficiency, quality, cost, customer service, and competitive advantage. With electronic commerce in general and EDI in particular, technology helps to bring society to a new plateau for data communications efficiency and accuracy worldwide. In fact, without electronic commerce technologies in general, some common processes today would not be economically feasible. Without EDI in particular,

> **ANSI**: American National Standards Institute
>
> **X12**: Code name for the ANSI EDI standard
>
> **UN**: United Nations
>
> **EDIFACT**: EDI For Administration, Commerce and Transport

many of today's automated (hands-off) processes would not be implemented.

But EDI is not only about purchasing and payment. It has penetrated many industries and addresses subjects as diverse as multiple credit advice, customs declaration, delivery schedule, medical service request, reinsurance settlement, vessel departure, multilevel railcar load details, student educational record, motion picture booking confirmation, healthcare services review information, cryptographic service message, payment order/remittance advice, specifications/technical information, electronic filing of tax return data, and notice of power of attorney. The transaction set and message lists in Appendix III include a list of over 400 titles for the combined EDI transactions defined in the ANSI X12 and UN/EDIFACT standards.

EDI is ...

This definition is adapted from the Society of Management Accountants of Canada report, Implementing EDI.[7]

> EDI is the transmission of data in public standard formats, computer-to-computer, process-to-process. In its total scope, the term 'EDI' may refer to format standards, inter-company data communications, computer-to-computer linkages, and/or localized interfaces.
>
> Depending on the industry, the following six factors are the driving forces behind the spread of inter-organizational systems:
>
> Customers are increasingly determining business activities: Across virtually all industries, customers (not dealers and suppliers) are determining which products and services will be successful. Customized products are replacing mass-produced goods of the past.
>
> Quick Response is becoming the retailing practice: Time is increasingly being recognized as a barrier to business. Quick response methods are redefining the way business is transacted by shortening the time periods around which commercial activities are arranged. The quick response orientation is to eliminate non-value-added paper-based information exchange practices.
>
> Just In Time (JIT) manufacturing techniques have gained popularity: Manufacturers are revising their strategies so that sufficient materials are on

[7] Holst, Jenkins, Notto and others, "Implementing Electronic Data Interchange," published by Society of Management Accountants of Canada (SMA), Hamilton, Ontario, 1994, pages 2-4.

hand and the materials arrive in time for manufacturing, but not so far in advance that they accumulate as inventory.

Essential information technology is available: Hardware, software, and communications networks enable organizations to hook up with other organizations and transmit business information electronically. The level of information technology needed for inter-organizational systems is generally available, with readily acceptable component reliability and cost levels.

Standards have been formulated: For customers, suppliers, and other business partners wishing to be linked, standards have been established and are available for many industries.

The global nature of business requires rapid, reliable communications and data: The capability to transmit and receive business communications over long distances between distinct time zones is increasingly becoming important.

EDI:

Format standards—Format standards ensure that the data is received and properly understood. Format standards specify the order of data items in a transmission and the characteristics of each item. These transmissions are referred to as transaction sets in a common standard (X12) used in North America or as messages in the United Nations standard (EDIFACT) and are functionally equivalent to items like purchase order, invoice, shipment information. With these standards, it is possible to transmit only data while conveying information because the information is derived from the explicit transmitted data and the implicit meaning and structure provided by the standard.

Inter-company data communications—EDI links to trading partners via an EDI value-added network (VAN), the Internet, or through point-to-point communications. (All of these communications options have independent standards.)

Computer-to-computer linkage—Data is exchanged electronically, in machine-readable form without the need for manual intervention. Data may be buffered in time and transmitted at any user's schedule when a VAN or the Internet is used, or it may be in real time through either a VAN or point-to-point communications.

Localized interfaces—Localized interfaces permit communications protocols and software packages used by trading partners to be chosen unilaterally by each trading partner. (This is accomplished through the use of Value Added Networks or the Internet and through a choice of software that conforms to the standards.)

Considering these driving forces, participants do EDI for strategic and operational reasons that vary.

Why do companies and organizations do it? Ed Guilbert of TDCC explained it in a very colorful and entertaining way. He was a very dynamic speaker. Many consider him the "Father of EDI." Charged with a drive to motivate corporate executives to embrace EDI, he had a favorite speech where he strolled down the isle in an auditorium talking about EDI and shouted, "What's it all about? It's about money!" While talking and shouting, he threw dollar bills at the audience. He certainly got their attention.

The author heard this speech only one time. It was at an EDI conference in London about 1987. At dinner after the meeting, Ed said that one of the attendees approached him to say he had done everything in public speaking that the attendee was taught not to do. "But," he said, "I just loved it. Please autograph my dollar."

In truth, it is not only about money. Figure 2 shows results of a 1994 survey conducted by the EDI Group for responses to the question, "What is the single most important reason why your company initially did EDI?" It is not only about money … it is about customer satisfaction and any benefits that derive from that (including money). Guilbert knew that, but his role was to motivate people into action, and he did it in his own dramatic and entertaining fashion. (How did he know it? He is famous for his earlier experiences as a U.S. Air Force Colonel during the Berlin Airlift in 1948-49, where he worked with the problem of rapidly moving the continuous flow of cargo from the airplanes to ground-based transportation and ultimate destinations. He was not interested in warehousing. The cargo was immediately needed elsewhere. He said many years later that more timely information would have made his operation even more efficient.)

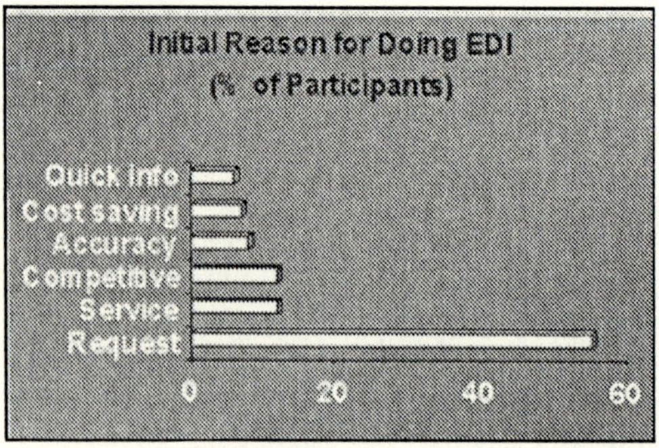

Summary:

Quick Access to Information 6%
Cost Savings 7%
Accuracy of Data 8%
Competitive Advantage 12%
Improving Customer Service 12%
Customer/Supplier Request 55%
Source: *EDI Forum*, Volume 7, No. 4 [1994]

Figure 2. Most important reasons why companies initially do EDI

Timeliness and accuracy lead to both economic benefits and customer satisfaction.

Information derived from data that passes through an EDI system is a source for information dearly sought after for executive and operational decision-making purposes. In the early 1990s, for example, an executive in a large grocery chain in Canada said that his problem was not about having too little data. It was about having too much. He needed to have the data processed into information when and how he wanted it and what he wanted it to address. He said that his computer staff could not deliver that in time to be useful. "Can EDI do this?" he asked. The reply was, "Yes, if you plan for it."

Those who recognize how to turn this data into accurate, timely, and pertinent information will have a competitive advantage–and so will their clientele.

In a 1991 survey,[8] respondents were asked to rate on a scale of 1 (not important) to 5 (most important) how EDI benefits certain operational issues. The highest three average ratings for issues rated as most benefiting from EDI were: improved accuracy of data, 4.37; improved customer service, 4.29; and faster access to information, 4.28. All three issues relate to customer satisfaction.I

Development Stage	Connection Points	Data Exchange Standards
Electronic Commerce	Application-to-Application Computer-to-computer Person-to-person Any combination of the above	National/International Standards
EDI II	Application-to-Application	National/International Standards
EDI	Computer-to-computer	National/International Standards
edi	Computer-to-computer	Proprietary

Figure 3. States of EDI Development

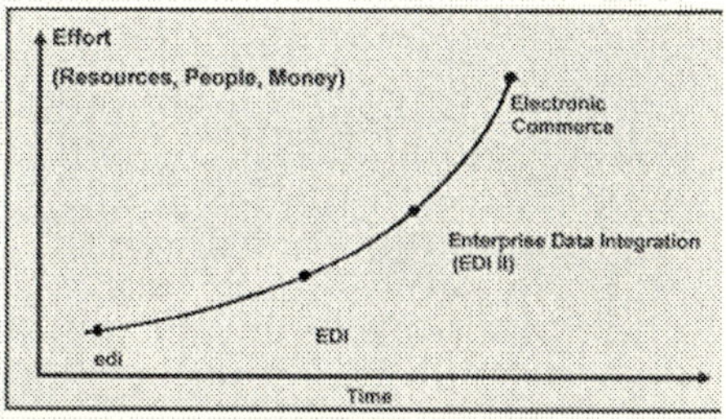

Figure 4. EDI Evolution

Evolution

Norman Barber stated[9] that the EDI concept is continually evolving, and that the situation in 1998 was as shown in Figure 3. Further, he stated

[8] The EDI Group, "Trends In EDI In North America," page 44, 1991.

[9] Norman F. Barber, "The Strategic Shift to Electronic Commerce from EDI," *EDI Forum*, Vol. 11, No. 1, 1998, pages 54-63, EDI Group, Oak Park, IL.

that all development stages currently exist, depending on the participant or participating community.

What Really Happens—Comparative Scenarios

What role does EDI have in productivity improvement? Consider the sequence of events (simplified for example purposes only) when one company buys products or materials used in the assembly of its products. These are repetitive events since, hopefully, the assembly of products continues indefinitely. The events at the ordering company (buyer) are ordering, follow-up, receiving, verifying, (perhaps warehousing), and paying. At the supplier company, the events are order entry, inventory management, transportation scheduling, invoicing, payment receipt, and reconciliation.

In the following table, look at the events from the buyer's perspective for scenarios when EDI is employed and not employed. Since EDI is not a unilateral choice, presume that the supplier receiving the order is also EDI-capable. What new benefits are introduced after implementation of EDI and the introduction of new processes only doable because of EDI?

A comparative summary follows:

Event	With EDI (Buyer's Perspective)	Without EDI
Ordering	Orders marked in the company's computer system as "released" are automatically downloaded as an electronic file to its EDI system. In the EDI system, the file is translated to EDI format and transmitted automatically. (The process is automatic.)	A purchase order is printed (from the ordering company's computer) and mailed or faxed to a supplier; or a purchase is ordered by telephone (voice), or picked up by a salesperson.Copies of the order are generally saved in a file cabinet or on microfiche. (The process includes manual activity.)

Event	With EDI (Buyer's Perspective)	Without EDI
Follow-up	The supplier's EDI system receives the EDI transmission, translates the data from EDI format to the supplier's internal format [checking for format errors during this step], creates an acknowledgment message and sends it to the buyer, and uploads the reformatted data to the supplier's order entry system.At the ordering company's EDI system, the acknowledgments are received and reconciled automatically. A status report is prepared for on-screen viewing or printing.[Each acknowledgment is an automatic event.]	After allowing time for the order to arrive at the supplier's office, The purchaser verifies receipt of the order via a telephone call to the supplier. (In older systems, the buyer may have specified that the supplier be required to send a printed acknowledgment to the buyer. In that case, the returned acknowledgment serves as the verification, but in some cases, follow-up action is required by the supplier to verify that the acknowledgment was received.)[Each acknowledgment is an individual manual event.]
Receiving	On the day of shipment or a few days before, the supplier automatically sends an advance shipment notice to the buyer via an EDI transmission. The buyer receives the EDI transmission, acknowledges it, and compares the notice with the order-all automatically.The delivery is scanned with a bar code reader to record what was received. [Automatic checking.]	The order is received, and manually checked off a list.
Verifying	The order, ship notice, and bar code scans are compared electronically.	The order list, acknowledgment, and received list are manually compared. The list is provided to accounts payable as part of the authorization for payment.[The comparison process is manual.]

Event	With EDI (Buyer's Perspective)	Without EDI
Paying	Presuming that all verification is satisfactory, payment is released electronically on an agreed scheduled. This is sent as an electronic funds transfer to the buyer's bank. The transmission includes reconciliation data. The buyer's bank completes a funds transfer to the supplier's bank, which adds the funds to the supplier's account.	When an invoice for the order is received (in the mail), the verification is referenced. If all is ok, a check is printed and mailed.The processes are manual or semi-automatic.The cancelled check is subsequently reconciled manually.
Event	No invoice is required.	

Process Improvements

When the steps in the order/payment cycle are compared for EDI and no-EDI, it is evident that several efficiencies and enhancements are possible with EDI and EFT (electronic funds transfer): 1) A clerical data entry department is not required. 2) The ordering lead-time may be decreased, since communications between buyer and supplier is electronic and automatic. 3) The amount of "safety stock" warehoused may be decreased, since the order cycle time has been decreased. (If with pre-EDI the order lead-time was six days vs. three days with EDI, the related inventory amount of the buyer may be cut in half. If two million dollars of inventory was on hand before EDI, half that amount may now be used as available cash for other purposes.) 4) With EFT, payment on dates-certain is possible, and may be used to negotiate better discount schedules for the buyer. The supplier benefits from estimating available cash on dates certain rather than estimating with empirical methods that are not consistently correct. 5) Accuracy is increased because of decreased manual processes. 6) The EDI acknowledgment process is superb–automatically created and sent by the supplier, and automatically received and processed by the buyer. 7) The invoice is replaced with something that has additional functional value (Advance Ship Notice). In fact, a lot of benefits happen when trading partners automatically exchange complementary transactions like purchase order and purchase order acknowledgment, request for quotation and response to request, transmission and automatic acknowledgment of the transmission sent after the receiver has identified the source of data and has automatically checked the transmission syntax...

INFLUENTIAL EVENTS

Many important decisions, accomplishments, and events contributed toward the definition and evolution of eCommerce. Some of these are identified in the following topics for the quarter-centuries preceding and following the publication of the first U.S. EDI public standard in 1975. The EDI purpose and dream or motivation is presented in the section "And Why?", which follows at the end of this section.

Glance Back, 1950-1974

The first general U.S. EDI standard was published in 1975. Its introduction was facilitated by social and technological events during the previous quarter century. We were armed with experiences where previously non-solvable problems began to be routinely solved. These pertained to both the infinite and the microscopic—reaching the moon and creating the computer microchip.

Influential events during this twenty-five-year period:

The Marshall Plan was implemented. It was a brilliant strategy following the aftermath of World War II that lead to Western European countries becoming more friendly and cooperative with each other and with North America. This, in turn, lead to a meaningful sharing of ideas across borders and continents, resulting in a more rapid pace of discovery and invention.

Jet aircraft for commercial airline use was introduced, making intercontinental traffic around the world practical, leading to the formation of personal friendships across borders and further sharing of information.

A computer industry was born, first with vacuum tube technology, then transistors, and then microchips. Reliability of computers measured as mean time between failures changed from four hours in 1957 to forty days in 1960 to several years at the beginning of the twenty-first century. What never seemed practical three years back was suddenly now being implemented.

During this period, punch cards and magnetic tapes became major facilities for storing data. A job skill in constant demand was that of keypunch operator. Computer speed originally measured in microseconds changed to nanoseconds. Computer experts fought over concepts like "batch" vs. "real-time" processing. A new major course of study in colleges and universities, beginning about 1965, was named "Computer Science." With this, there were both a significant number of computer scientists and an academic environment for educating others.

Technology began to "take off" as a result of space-age efforts, significantly increasing the number of available components for new products and imposing relevant new theories and ideas.

A computer generation was three years. Each generation produced computers twice as fast as the previous generation, at half the price, with more available memory, and with better and more comprehensive software. Computer users adapted to this phenomenon by finding valuable uses for the new capabilities, thus encouraging investment toward following generations.

There was always a shortage of computer programmers. Companies trained people in the skills of programming. These were usually people experienced in the manual processes that needed to be automated in their companies. Training in programming and training in computer science or mathematics are not the same. This class of company-trained programmers could get the job done and reflect their experiences in the finished work. Scientists and mathematicians working in this environment had to understand the manual processes requiring automation. They also challenged the processes, looked for generalized solutions, and considered maintenance issues. There was harmony in this mix of talent.

The communications industry changed dramatically. At the start of this period, Teletype machines required paper tape or keyboard for the input medium, and paper tape or printer for the output medium. Transmission speed was 10 characters per second. A time-sharing industry was born and offered use of large-scale computers interactively via a Teletype machine in a user's own office. Use of acoustic couplers was common in the time-sharing industry. Modem technology increased in parallel developments with the computer industry. Transmission speeds increased from 10 to 300 and to 600 characters per second. Modems and communications protocols used were not standard, so data communications was confined within a single company or a single cooperating industry (like the airline industry, for example).

The Transportation Data Coordinating Committee (TDCC) was formed in 1968. Its purpose was to create standards so that computers in different transportation companies and the industries they served can "talk" to each other.

This period saw no limit to what was possible. The period ended, however, in deep political and social crises.

In this twenty-five-year period, we also witnessed the equal rights movement and the resulting equal rights legislation that eventually increased the population of our group of highly educated–but also practical–people. We suffered through a serious recession in 1970-71, where even some of those who create work for others became unemployed. We struggled twice through an oil embargo in the mid-1970s that significantly affected the consumer price index and limited travel. The period also included the Korean Conflict and the Vietnam War.

This was a period of opposites: introducing wonderful social legislation like the Marshall Pan and equal rights vs. engaging in two wars; achieving enormous technological advancements vs. dismissing many who create jobs for others from the workforce (in 1970-71); showing an attitude of seeing no limits to what can be achieved vs. not setting priorities for addressing social problems needing attention; recognizing benefits from the interdependency of nations vs. not being able to get this point across at home and abroad; seeing the effect of events like the oil embargos vs. not making efficiency adjustments when the crisis was over.

From the significant positive advances achieved during this period, we know that education, experience, and attitude are equally important for success. Social and technological agendas both benefit when there is harmony between the two.

Look Forward, 1975-1999

The first U.S. EDI standard came at the beginning of this period. The ANSI X12 EDI standards defined today grew from the TDCC work. The process of arriving at a standard moved slowly at first. By 1980, Ed Guilbert asked why EDI was not in significant use. The reply was that companies needed the EDI standards publication to begin their planning processes, but the implementation schedules had to fit into the corporate budget processes.

The 1975 EDI standard was eight years before compatible modems and the personal computer (PC). It was eighteen years before business and industry seriously looked at the Internet. It was twenty years before Microsoft's Windows 95. In 1991, 33 megahertz was considered a fast computer, and 250 million bytes were considered a lot vs. 800 megahertz and 27 billion bytes by year 2000. While we entered the period with the length of a computer generation stable at three years, we left the period with the length of a generation down to less than one year.

In this twenty-five-year period:

Personal computers (PCs) were introduced about 1982. They initially had simple software applications, like text editors, and limited software tools for programmers. That changed rapidly. In fact, several entrepreneurs during the mid-1980s created EDI software products to operate on PCs. This suddenly made EDI practical for many companies, including small companies that never previously used computers for any purpose.

Very capable word processor software became a quick success, and completely displaced the typewriter in a few years. It also replaced machines that were manufactured and sold for the single-purpose of word processing. Within this quarter century, all companies became computer-literate. So did all schools. Apple Computer's introduction of its computers into all classifications of schools was instrumental in youthful students becoming comfortable with and competent in computer usage, laying the groundwork for a super-skilled workforce in the next generation.

Data communications speed jumped to 7,000 characters per second. File compression software was introduced, saving up to 90% of data storage space. Such efficiency extends to transmission time as well. All this, combined with the increase in communications channels facilitated by the launching of satellites for use by the communications industry, indicated that the communications and computer industries were in lock step for providing the resources required for new developments.

Now, at the end of this twenty-five-year period, PCs are used extensively throughout business, industry, homes, and schools. Most EDI systems are implemented on PCs, but mainframe and mid-range computer systems are also used. EDI service communities for communications, software, and consulting evolved. Having started in 1982, these became multibillion-dollar industries by the year 2000. Companies reengineered their processes, using EDI as one of the cornerstones employed for implementation. The EDI population grew to at least a half-million user sites worldwide, starting from about one hundred user sites in 1984.

Most companies and people generally became aware of the Internet during the 1990s. The Internet is one of the eCommerce technologies. In a very short time, it rapidly became an enabler for EDI and other eCommerce components, and now it is indispensable. Considerably more international trade is now feasible because of the Internet in conjunction with other technologies.

In this quarter century we learned to cope with rapid change and progress. Typewriters, Teletype machines, punch-card equipment, and the time-sharing industry have all disappeared. They were completely wiped out! The unemployment rate decreased, however, since people working at related jobs were transferred to new jobs created from new opportunities related to the effects of electronic commerce. While it was previously the norm for smaller companies to not have a computer of any type, all companies of all sizes now have at least one quite powerful computer. The end of this quarter century saw a half-million EDI users, the Internet, super-fast computers and data communications, computer-literate populations worldwide, and a very broad understanding of technology and its role. A new century begins with eCommerce firmly established on a global scale. Time barriers for the flow of data and information have disappeared. Security problems relative to protection of these data/information flows have been addressed. Verifiable data accuracy has been proven by transmission of billions of EDI transactions since 1982.

AND WHY?

The following text appeared in the TDCC General Systems Guide first published in 1976 and subsequently published under the title EDI Volume I, Concept.[10] In response to Ed Guilbert's concern to find ways to motivate companies into putting EDI implementation on their development schedules, Ralph Notto was looking for some way to stimulate executive thinking on the subject and wrote a list of points to imagine after implementation is completed. Joe Carley said we needed the list, but also needed to introduce it in a way that related to the then-current cor-

[10] TDCC, "The United States Electronic Data Interchange (EDI) Standards," Volume I, Concept, pages 1-3, 1977.

porate environments. He wrote that introduction. The two parts, introduction and list, are:

> Everybody uses business connections of one sort or another to get orders, send bills, make collections, determine and pay what they owe, move goods, and control their money. The business connections used historically to perform these operations have been the Postal Service and the telephone. A relatively new link is electronic data communications facilities.
>
> In all probability, your company has already installed a computer or computers to help run your business operations to keep track of orders, receivables, payables, equipment, schedules, people, facilities, and company money.
>
> Although everything may be satisfactory, there may be a couple of computer problems you want to overcome. One problem pertains to the wall of people kept around the computer to feed it data. Some of the people do their feeding with terminals. Others do it with magnetic devices or punched cards. All of them have one thing in common—they receive information brought to the company by its business connection links and transcribe it into a form convenient for the computer.
>
> The second problem has to do with the business connection links themselves. By comparison with what the computer can do at electronic speed, the Postal Service and the [voice] telephone are really bottlenecks. Both require human intervention to get the information they deliver into the computer. This slows down the computer feeding process and retards the speed and flow of operational data. In other words, orders, status reports, and other information vital to business operations are delayed days in route by mail before your company can begin to react. In fact, even though it costs more, you collect some of the more important operational information by telephone to overcome the mail bottleneck. The Postal Service recognizes the problem and is working on methods to speed up service. But no mater how fast the mail is moved or how much you use the telephone, the problems are still there because neither terminates with information directly usable by computers. The flow is brought to a halt while the information is transcribed and, during transcribing, errors may be introduced. The penalty for error is potentially wrong business decisions.
>
> Now you have a complete picture. Your links to business connections are limited to the mail and the telephone. Both are slow. Both terminate with that wall of people who feed the computer and who may make errors. Inbound operational information that is produced at the speed of light in

somebody else's computer gets to your computer, relatively speaking, at the speed of the turtle!

What your company needs is a better link to business connections and that is what electronic data interchange is all about. To appreciate what electronic data interchange (EDI) means, think about all those orders, invoices, freight bills, shipment instructions, tracing requests, payment instructions, government reports, and the like that your company sends out or receives every day. Think about each as a single transaction. And, think about how you send them and get them! Then:

> Imagine—Inbound transactions recorded for action in seconds after they are released by the originator—with no paperwork or intervening people ...
>
> Imagine—Getting operational data so early that planning is no longer an estimation process ...
>
> Imagine—The elimination of clerical transcribing errors ...
>
> Imagine—Current status reports even when the information source is another company ...
>
> Imagine—Positive control over operational information from origin to destination—from the time of ordering raw materials until payment for delivered finished products ...
>
> Imagine—An information system adaptable for expansion as your needs and capabilities change ...
>
> Imagine—A single computer "window" to the world—a single set of computer programs to interface your system with the system of any other company—on any business subject!

Your imagination has conceived the system for EDI, a system which connects your company's computer to that of a business associate only when and for only as long as required for each of you to exchange pertinent operational and status information.

And the system is not a complement of new equipment and dedicated communications facility! Rather, it is a means for interlinking present computer systems by employing standard information structures, standard com-

> munications protocols, and a limited number of special EDI interface computer programs.
>
> Incidentally, EDI is also a means to snap the paperwork chain ... a means to use electronics as a medium for recording information for inter-company transactions.

By the year 2000, it was only five years since the business/industrial community became actively engaged with the Internet. In the mid 1970s, we were using punch cards, magnetic tape, Teletype, and non-standard data communications with speeds up to 4800 baud (600 characters per second) for transmitting data.

Had we reached in 2000 what had been imagined in 1977? To some extent. About a half million companies and organizations did EDI for some of their information exchanges in 2000. But in 1977, there were no standard EDI users.

In 1977, many companies did not have computers. In 1985, the author personally delivered PCs to two such companies to be used for EDI. In year 2000, the 800-megahertz PC with its complement of equipment had considerably more power and capacity than most of the computer systems used in companies in the mid 1970s.

Does the Internet with its magnificent global outreach eliminate the need for EDI? Consider the definitions: electronic commerce is the application of advanced information technology to increase the effectiveness of commercial practices between trading partners.[11] EDI (a component of electronic commerce), by contrast, is more of a "back-office" function meant for communications between automatic and semi-automatic processes in different companies around the world.

In this context, EDI is one of the advanced information technologies used in conjunction with other information technologies—EFT, bar coding, email, bulletin boards, FTP, smart cards, electronic forms, facsimile, VAN, Internet ...

EDI may use the Internet to accomplish the communications function. By the year 2000, two Internet alternatives were already in use: File Transfer Protocol (FTP) and Simple Message Transfer Protocol (SMTP). Both permit security options when required. Use of SMTP for EDI indicates that an EDI-formatted data file is attached to an email message, and

---

[11] Roger Cadaret, "Electronic Commerce Handbook Preface," published by the EDI Council of Canada.

the message is addressed to a trading partner's EDI software. The receiving computer passes the file to the EDI processes. This may occur on a worldwide basis. In addition to FTP and SMTP, some companies sponsor Web-based forms for data entry and retrieval by some trading partners and EDI interfaces by others.

No, the Internet does not replace the need for standard EDI and its process-to-process orientation. The Internet, however, may be used to facilitate the flow of EDI data among companies around the world.

Can other kinds of software on the Internet replace EDI? People are working on it, but it will be several years before EDI stops growing, because its purpose was to replace company-to-company paper-based systems with process-to-process, company-to-company electronic data flows, addressing issues like functionality, timeliness, accuracy, security, and responsibility. The data originates or terminates in a company's computer processes. Because EDI data arrives from external sources, extensive data editing capability has been built into EDI systems to be able to "trust" the data. That the scheme works is attested to by the fact of several hundred thousand EDI participants worldwide. Leading companies based the reengineering of some of their internal processes on EDI and therefore intend to keep using EDI for some time (years), and will continue to increase their number of EDI trading partners.

2. Turning Points

"We must take the current when it serves,
or lose our ventures."

Wm. Shakespeare, *Julius Caesar*

"So, first of all, let me assert my firm belief that
the only thing we need to fear is fear itself."

Franklin D. Roosevelt, *Inaugural Address (1933)*

DEFINING MOMENTS

Success is never guaranteed. For endeavors involving many people, statesmanship greatly increases the likelihood of a beneficial outcome. So it was with EDI.

Although the first publication of the EDI standard was in 1975, it was not until 1983 that the author believed we had reached a point of no return, such a point where the developments would not be discarded and a new path sought. The eventual conclusion was based on many discussions with relevant people from industry. It was much like conducting a person-to-person poll during the period 1976 through 1982. What was sought was an indication that corporate representatives had identified significant benefits from EDI based on actual experiences and analysis.

There were many chances to fail during that period. Fortunately, many people continued working together to address the issues, understand various perspectives, and evolve acceptable resolutions.

This did not come easily.

> **EDI:** Electronic Data Interchange
>
> **EFT:** Electronic Funds Transfer
>
> ***EDI Forum: Journal of EDI***—The name was later changed to *EDI Forum: Journal of Electronic Commerce.*

In the autumn of 1975, a few months following publication of the standard, Bill Myers at the Department of Transportation asked TDCC what is needed next. Ed Guilbert called Joe Carley, Buddy Bass, Alex Kreithen, and Ralph Notto to a meeting. He asked the same question of them. Based upon discussions we all had had with the potential EDI user community, Notto said that it was clear that publication of the standard alone was not enough to insure standardization. Arguing from the role of systems engineer, he said that we needed to impose a software discipline on future implementers. We needed a general systems specification, a general programming guide, and a general communications guide.

This resulted in more questions than argument. Can we do that, and will the community accept it? Is publishing a programming guide straying from the mandate for deriving standardized formats and structures for business data (which had already been accomplished)? We collectively answered our own questions and drafted a proposal. Ed Guilbert presented the proposal to Bill Myers, and shortly afterwards the proposal was accepted by the Department of Transportation. Work on that began early in 1976 and was finished in 1977.

Other issues were coming up at the same time. Was this work applicable for other industries? Should we be thinking in terms of an American standard accredited by the American National Standards Institute (ANSI)? What about international application?

This chapter includes six topics about key events. The topics were originally published in the *EDI Forum* during the period 1988-1993, several years after the events occurred.

The *EDI Forum* began when Dan Ferguson and Ned Hill founded The EDI Group in 1987. Both men were pioneers in EDI and Electronic Funds Transfer (EFT). The EDI Group initially had three divisions: *EDI Forum*, EDI Education, and EDI Research.

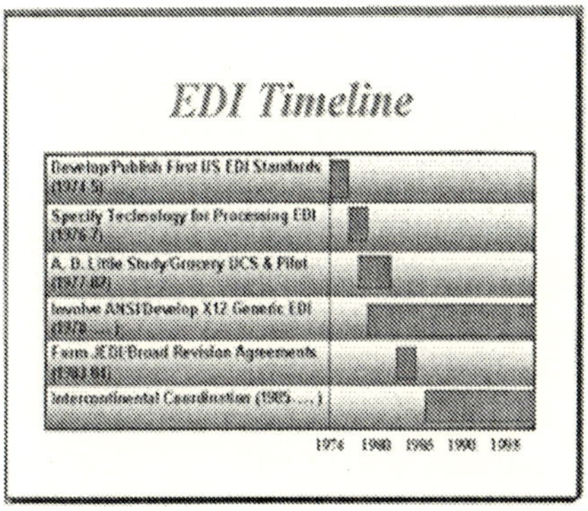

Dan asked his colleagues in the EDI industry what articles they might provide for the *EDI Forum.* Notto replied that there were six very significant events in the history of EDI from the North American perspective in which he had participated and had thought of often and was ready to document. These were the development and publication of the first set of U.S. EDI standards (1974-5), specification of a technology for processing EDI transmissions (1976-7), the A. D. Little study for the feasibility of electronic data interchange in the grocery industry and resultant grocery industry standard and pilot project (1977-82), the involvement of the American National Standards Institute (ANSI) and the development of X12 generic EDI standards (1978 and continuing), the formation of the Joint EDI (JEDI) Committee and the broad agreement reached for revision of the EDI data element dictionary (1983-4), and the intercontinental coordination (1985 and after).

To be sure, there were other important events—the development of the warehouse, freight claims, tariff and United States Customs EDI standards, the pilot projects in other industries, the conformance to EDI (X12) and the detailing of interchange conventions by the chemical, electrical, apparel, office products and paper industries, the coordination between EDI standards and encryption standards, the emergence of EDI network and software vendors, the international EDI standards development and publications, the introduction of a supporting journal (*EDI Forum*), and many others notable advances.

Dan Ferguson accepted the suggestion. This chapter includes adaptations of those six articles. The orientation of the text is from the perspective of a participant in the related events.

A CAST OF HUNDREDS[12]

Many people worked toward the development and publication of the first U.S. public EDI Standard during 1974-75.

In 1975, the excitement about EDI concerned its potential for the quality of information in terms of content, accuracy, timeliness, and the resulting impact on control and operations.

There had been many company-to-company, computer-to-computer data format standards created in the recent past. Some of these were in fairly wide use, but they all individually addressed the same subject in such a way that users were forced to become participants in several *proprietary* standards that often had conflicting definitions or specifications for the same elements.

The EDI *standards* provided a syntax definition and set of rules that made it possible to combine data communications requirements for several industries and users into a common standard. The result is efficiency in implementation, maintenance, control, and enhancement.

The EDI standards *environment* provides a framework, community, database of elements, and procedure for coordinating the development of standard formats for an endless number of subjects. By the end of the twentieth century, "endless" includes the over four hundred titles listed in Appendix III.

By year 2000, an estimated half million private and governmental organizations participate in the use of these standards for various subjects.

From a historical perspective, the concern is not about what the EDI standards are. Rather, the concern is how they came to be what they are, because an understanding of this will help others to enhance the standards for everyone's mutual benefit.

Think about it. With all the electronic data interchange format standards invented, why has this one, EDI, survived and grown while many others have already phased out? The answer lies in the issues addressed during the beginning period 1974-5, the interaction of the people involved, the methods used for working together, and the significance of the achievement.

The Scene

During the first half of 1975, 173 people were working in some coordinated fashion with the common goal to lay the foundation for the inter-

---

[12] Adapted from Ralph W. Notto, "EDI Standards: A Historical Perspective," *EDI Forum*, Founding Issue, 1988, pages 120-127, EDI Group, Oak Park IL.

change of transactional information electronically on both national and international scopes. The anticipated environment for their results was computer-to-computer data exchange among peer companies and organizations, each with a private schedule, each with private objectives, but all with a common purpose for exchanging information.

Counting the 173 names of people listed in Appendix II and their supporting staffs (not named), there were indeed hundreds of people working toward this goal.

The notion that this was an environment for peers meant a significant departure from the "master/slave" electronic communications concept prominently in use at the time.

What were the purpose and issues? Who were the people and their affiliations? What did they coordinate?

Why recall this now? The EDI standards committees are more active at the end of the twentieth century than in 1975. Change in EDI standards is commonplace as the community of users matures in their use of information. In addressing this change, understanding how something came to be is important when formulating courses for future actions.

The author had the good fortune of being there in 1975 to help to synthesize these standards. The source material for this article is from a recollection of first-hand experiences, feelings, and interpretations of the time, a review of the 1975 publication which resulted from the work groups' efforts, conversations with people who were there, and analysis of a personal calendar for that period.

The author started as a systems consultant to TDCC in March 1975. TDCC was a non-profit organization that was formed for the purpose of defining EDI standards. Ed Guilbert, President of TDCC, called him in response to an announcement of a private consulting practice. All he had to do was "hit it off" with Joe Carley, Ed said, and the assignment was his.

Joe was program director for the standards development. It took just fifteen minutes to convince each other that they wanted to work together. Joe then presented the newly appointed consultant with an enormous amount of background reading material for the weekend. It was documentation from older air, motor, ocean, and rail transportation standards—a memorable but, with respect to the reading, hardly exciting beginning.

The standards work had started years earlier in 1968. It moved slowly at first. The theory was that agreement was needed for common codes; then everything would fall into place. Codes were completed for commodity, location, carrier, patron, and packaging information. Agreement for the codes was reached, but "falling into place" was not happening. Something else was required to inter-relate these information elements.

Joe Carley had started working with TDCC in 1973. He and Ed Guilbert had known and worked with each other in the U.S. Air Force on several major projects, and had already established a rapport. Joe, Notto discovered, was a master at taking an enormously complex problem and organizing it in such a way that many people can work on it simultaneously. Ed was a master at getting people's interest and motivating them into action.

New Definitions

We began the EDI development talking about information items using terms familiar to us; Invoice, bill of lading, arrival notice … in the business practices of the time, these terms generally referred to a document or form. So we also talked about the items on a form. After a few meetings with work groups, it became apparent that we needed new terminology to avoid confusion and to readily understand when one was speaking about new data formats or the older printed documents. Basically, three new terms were introduced to the work groups—transaction set, segment, and data element.

All three terms were first decided on during a terminology meeting in Washington attended only by the TDCC staff and consultants. The requirement was that each term had to be one that could not be confused with anything else.

The term "transaction set" was introduced to generically identify a data item that includes all of the information corresponding to an older form, document, or function. Each transaction set defined has a corresponding identifying number and name. Example: the function for a motor carrier bill of lading form is identified in EDI as "204 (Shipment Information, Motor)." The identifying code (204) is always included in a data transmission, but the name is never transmitted since it adds no new information in a computer-to-computer exchange. Notto introduced the term, which he derived from a combination of earlier work at UNIVAC where he was charged to analyze and predict response times in transaction-oriented real-time systems like airline reservations systems. The word "set" came from a mathematical discipline called "set theory," which was used in the analysis. Of course, no one outside of TDCC was told where the term came from since if he or she knew, the term most certainly would have been rejected. At the time, Notto was quietly thinking ahead about how we would write generalized computer programs for what we were developing. To him, it was apparent that set theory would be employed, but never identified as such.

The term "segment" was introduced earlier by John Nelsen of Missouri Pacific Railroad. It generically described a data item that includes an identifying code plus one or more data elements, each preceded by a one-character delimiter. An alternative term was "record." "Segment" was very clear, and its definition was readily understood, so that term was adopted. Each defined segment also has a unique name. Transaction sets are defined in terms of segments. The segment identifying code is always included in transmissions, but segment names are never included.

Buddy Bass proposed the term "data element" to generically identify a data item such as quantity, code value, date, time, name, address ... with an identifying number, name, and defined characteristics for data type, minimum length, and maximum length. An alternative was "field," but that was rejected. Segments are defined in terms of data elements. The data element identifier, name, and characteristics are never included in transmissions because all of these are implied by a data element's position in a segment.

The definitions indicate that efficiency of transmissions in terms of the amount of information conveyed was always a conscious concern. It was always understood that while data was being transmitted, information was being conveyed, and the design scheme focused on decreasing data flows while increasing the amount of useful information implied.

Following the meeting of the TDCC staff and consultants, the terms were documented and distributed at a joint work group meeting. After an explanation of intent and discussion with all work group members collectively, the terminology was adopted and added to the official documentation.

The Organizational Scheme and the Issues

The scheme that Ed and Joe had devised to move the standards activity toward fruition was to revise the subject and leadership of TDCC committees into five work groups: Air Carrier/Forwarder/Shipper, Motor Carrier/Shipper, Ocean Carrier/Forwarder/Shipper, Rail Carrier/Agent/Shipper, and Carrier/Shipper/Bank.

Ed appointed Joe to chair all work group committee meetings to ensure coordination among all groups. The older committees that were organized for definition of major code sets were now called "Task Forces" and continued with their current chairpersons to ensure that there was no friction with the work being completed by the new work groups. The Task Forces' role was to work toward improvement in the *standardized code sets* for commodity and the other coding lists mentioned. The work groups' role was to derive the *information structure* for data transmission.

In a short time, the greatest attention was with the work groups, and the influence of the theories of the older task forces became subservient. It then became apparent that the structure became the driving force and that the codes were addressed only as an item of detail when required in a specific structure. New standards development procedures and issues evolved.

Standards Development Procedure and Issues

Issue	Procedural Step
	1. Invitations for participation in the work groups were sent to TDCC members and other interested people, and general notices were placed in pertinent periodicals and with certain organizations.
	2. A meeting of the work group was called by TDCC.
Issue I: What was the purpose?	3. At the first meeting, Ed Guilbert stated the objectives, Joe Carley presented the ground rules, and attendees were invited to speak out on any issue. The objectives were a) to develop a set of standards for electronic data interchange between companies, and b) to invent a "living standard"—one that was organized to accommodate change as the needs of the user community changed concurrently with their maturing use of computers and electronic communications and with their growing sophistication in information processing.
Issue 2: What was the developmental process?	4. The "ground rules" were a) that the development of the standard be "top-down", starting with broad subjects such as shipping, billing, payment and query/reply and ending at the bottom level with data elements; and b) that all ideas be worthy of discussion so that no one need be fearful of the consequences for introducing a "dumb" idea since, by definition, there was no such idea.
Issue 3: Who was in control?	5. The work of the coding task forces became important in the definition of the content of some data elements, and other than that, had no influence on the top-down structure. (With reference to the work groups and the older task forces, the question of which was to wag what [analogous to the relationship of the dog and the tail] was discreetly resolved without any discussion.)
	6. A volunteer to develop a "strawman" for information structures was selected from each work group. The strawman was a starting point or "seed". "Strawman" was defined to be a definition or specification for starting purposes. With this approach, discussion within the work group was encouraged.

Standards Development Procedure and Issues

Issue	Procedural Step
	7. Criteria for structure and content of the strawman were discussed.
	8. The volunteer submitted the strawman to TDCC for distribution to the pertinent work group members.
	9. Work group members reviewed the strawman in preparation for the next meeting at TDCC.
	10. A routine was established: A meeting was called, the strawman was discussed, the TDCC staff took notes from which to revise the strawman, the revision (by the staff) was distributed within two weeks to be reviewed within another two weeks in preparation for the next meeting. (About three iterations were usually sufficient in order to derive an acceptable standard for any transaction set or item.)
	11. In 1975, all of the documentation was submitted to Gina Forrest in hand-written form. She typed it on paper. There was no word processor available. The consistency of the document considering the different topics and several authors was accurate because of Gina's capability to remember what she had typed in all parts of the document and her insistence on having the authors provide her with updates whenever she sensed a conflict.
	12. EDI transaction sets were related to information events required for transportation. Graphic example from 1975 document: 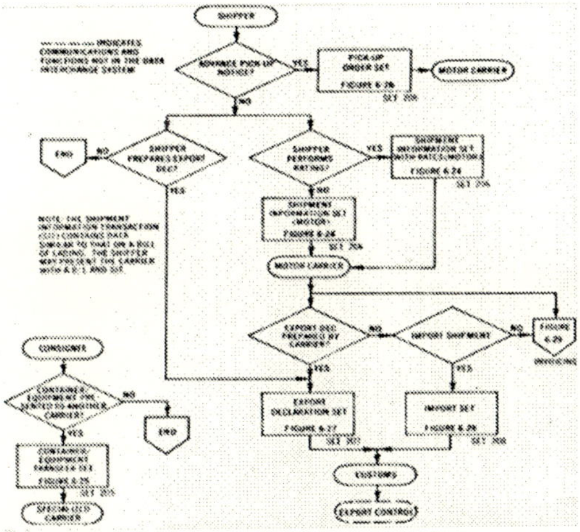

Standards Development Procedure and Issues

Issue	Procedural Step
Issue 4: How was consensus achieved?	13. Meanwhile, all of the work groups were reviewing and meeting independently. For each revision, the TDCC staff incorporated what they expected to be an inter-work group consensus. (Even though the work groups never met collectively, this consensus was discussed through the TDCC staff. Also, since shippers were part of each work group, there were common members among the various work groups. The consensus was easily achieved.)
	14. Finally, an integrated standard for air, motor, ocean and rail transportation information was published in July 1975. It was the first time any of the participants had seen the standard in its entirety. Unique in the publication of the 1975 standard was its extensive cross-referencing. This was included at that time because the first standards were for transportation, and transportation was a regulated industry at that time in the U.S. (Transportation rates were filed with the government [Interstate Commerce Commission] in printed documents called "tariffs". These documents stayed in the file indefinitely because no one knew which tariffs were no longer needed.)
Issue 5: How were the EDI standards to be maintained?	15. The intent of the cross-references in the EDI publication was to facilitate the coordination of change when change was thought necessary or beneficial. In upward or downward directions, the publication cross-referenced: Industry (banking and air, motor, ocean and rail transportation) with transaction sets · transaction sets with segments · segments with data elements · and data elements with code lists.

The purpose for electronic data interchange as stated in the 1975 publication of the standard, and with reference at that time to only the transportation function, is to "... provide such informational support as required to enable the members of the transportation community to appropriately process, move, protect, service, administer, control, monitor, and audit shipments moving in trade and commerce, and to facilitate the performance of associated payment and banking functions."[13] With such a broad purpose, the new standards development procedure was correct in its "top-down" approach.

[13]TDCC, "Preliminary Functional Specification for a Prototype Electronic Data Interchange System," page 3-1, July 1975, [Department of Transportation reference DOT-OS-50017-1].

People, Affiliations and Other Issues

Issue 6: What were the roles?

There was a four-way interaction among distinct groups. Government generally does not dictate a standard in the United States. A standard is something developed by its user community and becomes standard by its willing adoption and use by this community. Therefore, government was not directly one of the groups. The Office of Facilitation of the United States Department of Transportation (DOT) was a catalyst, but not a participant at the meetings.

There were four active groups: the first in this interaction was the user community, and the five work groups and the several task forces represented it in the standards-making process. This user group included users of the data. The second group included the software and data communications experts from the user companies. The third group included the banking industry representatives who participated in decisions relative to payment transactions. Participants from time-sharing companies were there for informational purposes. The means for communicating data was not a subject for the 1975 publication. The fourth group was the coordinator, TDCC. This was the group organized into being in 1968 by the user community for the purpose of EDI standards development.

The work group members and their affiliations are identified in Appendix II in Planning and Workgroups.

The TDCC staff and consultants included Ed Guilbert, Joe Carley, Earl (Buddy) Bass, Alex Kreithen, Lester Probst, Tom DesNoyers, Gina Forrest, and (author) Ralph Notto. Ed and Joe had the leadership roles, and Joe developed the master concept. Buddy's role was to invent the structure for the standard's documentation with respect to ease of use, inter-industry coordination, and conformance with standard cross-industry syntax. Alex addressed the technical and implementation issues of how to communicate. Les, in staff discussions, represented the interests of motor transportation, and he also compiled the first EDI integrated data element dictionary. Tom represented the coding task forces. Ralph was concerned with the integration of all of the definition into a single coordinated system addressing structure and flow of information. The maintenance of these standards today is automated. In 1975, the printed standard was typewritten, and accuracy was achieved from the work and techniques of Gina Forrest.

Bill Myers administered the DOT role. The standards development was paid for as a joint industry-government activity. The participating companies listed in Appendix II paid for the salaries and travel expenses of work group members. TDCC expenses were paid from a research contract with DOT. To be sure, there were several competing activities that wanted that research money. DOT picked TDCC as only one of these. Subsequent to the publication of the 1975 EDI standards, DOT recognized the significance of the industry/TDCC contribution and granted subsequent research contracts that furthered EDI development and ultimate implementation.

Issue 7: What is the syntax for EDI to be?

In the acknowledgments that TDCC printed in 1975, special recognition was given to John Nelsen, system consultant, Missouri Pacific Railroad Company, for his outstanding contribution. John invented the basic EDI syntax using segments of information composed of segment identifiers and variable length data elements with delimiters. He constructed the "strawman" for the rail industry standard. Actually, there were several "strawmen" since at least one was required for each application.

When Notto joined the activity in March 1975, Joe Carley asked him to make the strawman standards for the ocean and air transportation industries. In response to a request for guidelines, Joe asked that it be patterned on John's work.

There were other patterns besides John's. Tony D'Anna of Western Electric proposed one for motor transportation, which was very workable. It included segments such as those used for rail, but had the most frequently used data elements at the beginning of the format in fixed-length style. Tony, the second chairperson of X12, was a participant at all advance-planning meetings for EDI in 1975.

Eventually, all four transportation modes adopted the same basic syntax as that proposed by John Nelsen.

Nothing was left to chance. When it appeared that we were near a consensus on some major point, the TDCC staff, after careful and deliberate analysis, reflected this expected consensus in the next strawman issue. More importantly, there was a constant series of phone calls initiated by Ed and Joe to ensure the support required to be able to close an issue and to move on to another. The purposes of the calls were to identify issues, explain scope and significance, ask for opinions, and solicit support. Shipper representatives were asked to influence carriers. Carriers were asked to consider the broad context and potential of the standards. But many compromises on technical aspects were made at the time, strictly adhered to for about three to five years, before some were finally dropped as the community matured or the need for the compromise faded.

One such compromise involved the maximum length of a segment. In 1975, this was set at seventy characters, chosen because it represented the length of a line on a typed document.

Such a limitation was eventually dropped. In 1975, Cliff Buys representing the American Trucking Associations argued strongly for the seventy-character limit because tens of thousands of Teletype and Telex machines were in use, and with this limit, computer-to-terminal transmissions could be supported. We argued that the compressed format used in EDI transmissions does not lend itself to being understood when read by people (rather than by computer). Today, in fact, the EDI definition explicitly states "computer-to-computer transmission." And, in enhancing the standard during the period 1975-1978, the seventy-character limit made it awkward to achieve some desired effects.

Issue 8: Who was in the EDI community?

But 1975 was nine years before the personal computer revolution, and participants in the standards wanted it explicitly clear that the small companies were not to be excluded because they could not afford the equipment necessary to enjoy the benefits from EDI.

Consequently, the kinds of transmission that the 1975 standards claimed to support were: computer-to-computer, computer-to-terminal, terminal-to-computer, and terminal-to-terminal.

Actually, some parties did use the standards in all of these ways during the late 1970s, but the earnest use of the standards did not begin until about 1980.

Issue 9: What subjects were to be included in EDI?

Another compromise involved transaction sets for inquiry and reply. The rail transportation group had a standard in use called "Car Location Method" (CLM). Motor transportation had one that was just completed at that time called "Shipment Status and Reporting System" (SSRS). Neither group intended to drop these standards even though they were of different structures than EDI. The ocean and air transportation communities, however, used EDI to define inquiry and reply transaction sets. The advantage of total EDI involves ease of use, ease of maintenance, and efficient use of equipment, communications, and software facilities. The disadvantage pertains to changing something that is already working. Consequently, change was slow but persistent.

Citing...

Others who especially impressed the author in 1975 were:

Howard McKenna of General Motors who worked forcefully to make the standards practical and who called Notto following the first publication to exclaim, "We did it!" And indeed we had—all 173 of us.

Fred Lynch of the Flying Tiger Line whose idea it was to make the name/address segments generic. This led to several other simplifications in EDI syntax and maintenance.

Vernon Mendenhall of Chemical Leaman Tank Lines who became one of the first to implement the EDI standards.

Hans Wieting of Atlantic Container Line who participated in the Ocean Work Group and who helped Notto to get the user operational insight required for his first EDI assignment.

All of the people who participated are important. The complete list of names that are included in the 1975 publication is shown in Appendix II. Note the many different functions they represented within their companies.

Accomplishments

The committees and the TDCC staff and consultants produced an open-ended information standard. This became the foundation for a North American standard that would begin to come into wide use approximately ten years later. With respect to the standard, the accomplishments are: open architecture, multiple industry orientation, readily maintainable, and cross-referenced

Significance

The significance and lessons of the EDI beginning are:

The procedures of 1975 are still valid today, especially the technique that states that the receiver of the data should have the primary influence for defining the content of a transaction set, since the receiver is expected to act on the data.

The importance and role of a coordinating and supporting staff such as TDCC is still valid.

The nine issues for 1975 identified in this topic—purpose, developmental process, control (leadership), consensus, standards maintenance, roles, syntax, community, and subject—are not different from issues today.

Several of the leaders in the 1975 community are still leaders in EDI standards groups in year 2000, and they should be asked to explain why something is the way it is instead of only what it is.

Progress is made through the interaction of people via discussion, argument and compromise.

An enormous task can be completed through a large group of peers provided that a need is positively identified and that the solutions fit the technology or anticipated technology of the time.

EDI has the foundation and momentum required for the flow of sufficient, accurate, and timely information between companies. By 1990, exciting changes in control and operations became the ultimate result!

ENABLING TECHNOLOGY[14]

The definition of the technology for processing EDI transmissions was significant because it proposed in detail a set of software functions and techniques that were expected to eliminate ambiguities in the construction and interpretation of EDI transmissions.

While the first EDI standards publication was reported as having been the accomplishment of a "cast of hundreds," the proposed software technique was based on aspects of the author's work going back as far as 1958 plus important contributions by Earl "Buddy" Bass. With only four advocates (Ralph Notto, Buddy Bass, Ed Guilbert and Joe Carley—the core TDCC team), we expected that it would take a while for the technique to gain the acceptance of the EDI community, and it did.

Nonetheless, the table-driven technique described below eventually gained acceptance; its significance was proven in subsequent practice as it accomplished its objectives. Virtually all *generalized* EDI translation software eventually used the technique.

---

[14] Adapted from Ralph W. Notto, "Table-Driven Computer Programs for EDI," *EDI Forum*, 1989 Issue, pages 99-103, EDI Group, Oak Park IL.

The Requirement

The first EDI standards were produced in 1975 as a result of committee and staff work at the TDCC without benefit of any automated support. These standards were good enough to withstand the test of time because of the attention to detail as well as the "big picture" on the part of the committees and TDCC. The standards development was partially funded by the United States Department of Transportation (DOT).

This topic describes the origin of the TDCC general programming specification, the principles upon which it was based, and the effect and significance of its use.

The Action

DOT then funded TDCC to develop three proposed specifications: concept, programming guide, and communications guide. They were completed in 1976. The general systems specification was enhanced in 1977 and was published as the "TDCC Volume I—Concept." The general programming specification was left largely untouched and was first published in 1977 as "TDCC Volume II—General Programming Guide." It was maintained and published for several years to report changes and additions to the EDI standards tables. On the other hand, part of the volume pertaining to functional specifications and special processes was not changed.

The general communications specification was later republished as "TDCC Volume V-Communications." This became background information used in the publication of a revised Volume V, which specified the communications protocols for EDI transmissions for the UCS (reported in the next topic) and WINS standards (Warehousing Industry) as well as part of the TDCC transportation community and some of the industries using the X12 EDI standards.

The Principles

The principles governing the development of the table-driven computer programs as stated in TDCC Volume II are:

> **Generalization—**Show how the attributes of data interchange data units—transaction set, detail segment, and data element—may be general-

ized and described in table form. Show how a generalized program may be used to edit or construct transaction sets defined in these tables.

Modularity—Use a basic design from which new applications may be added without requiring redesign or duplication of functions.

Applicability—Specify only those modules that apply directly to data interchange.

Maintainability—Divide the program into modules performing specific non-overlapping functions.

Consistency—Provide clarity of definition to assure a common interpretation by all participants.

Completeness—Identify all major building blocks and specify those that several participants may require.

Conciseness—Present definitions for exact interpretation.

Directness—Avoid over-specification.

The principles were written *first.* The detail came second! The principles and reasons for them became part of the standard documentation that TDCC distributed. There was good reason to be this explicit, since we were aware that some of the participants considered it an accomplishment to complete the "programming" for all of the segments for a given transaction set. Indeed, it was TDCC's aim to quietly imply that programming individual segments would never permit the total community to achieve the benefits of the standard, since such a technique would mean a future of risky maintenance procedures and ultimately a commitment of large personnel resources for maintenance functions, thus "robbing" future budget dollars that could be spent for program expansion and new innovations.

"Risky maintenance procedures?" Consider that a company may implement a dozen types of transaction sets, all inter-related in the total scheme of intended progress. Consider that they write twelve related computer programs to accomplish this. Consider that they assign three transaction set types to each of four programmers under the supervision of the same person. Do you now think that their work is coordinated, and there is no need to worry?

Your company then engages in operational EDI tests with one or two trading partners. The trading partners' programmers did the reverse actions of what your programmers did. (For example, their programmers wrote EDI software for outgoing purchase orders; your programmer's software is for incoming orders.)

With the EDI programming for incoming orders complete, you proceed to a testing phase, receiving orders from your two EDI-capable trading partners, sending them acknowledgments, and ultimately sending EDI-formatted invoices.

Some discrepancies show up between your company's software and that of the two trading partners. Fix that. Now all is well? Did these changes affect the work of the other three programmers? Were the two trading partners in complete agreement with the changes, or were you required to insert program snippets to accommodate each in its own way? It doesn't matter. You now have "live" operations with two trading partners for incoming orders and outgoing acknowledges and invoices. This is a significant achievement. But wait! Imagine the same scenario as you strive toward ten EDI trading partners ... to a hundred ... perhaps after all, there is some point to generalization, modularity, applicability, maintainability, consistency, completeness, conciseness, and directness. Surely this is a good reason to be able to address most maintenance issues by simply changing values in a table. As new EDI transaction types are added to your operations or your company upgrades to a new standards version, it is comforting to know that the new definitions are defined in the same table structures, and the same EDI software will perform those tasks.

EDI is not practical without a standard. That implies a formatting standard, a documentation standard, and a software standard. The table-driven computer programming technique helped to achieve that. Imposing a discipline on software construction and maintenance is not only efficient, but is mandatory for success.

By the 1970s, we knew that the software maintenance tasks consumed over 90% of the software budgets of many companies. We thought that we could suggest a better way. Some considered this a threat. We considered it necessary in order to achieve the overall long-term objectives of EDI activity.

Accomplishing the Objectives

The original intent at TDCC was only to suggest a technique for programming that the TDCC staff thought would lead to common construction and interpretation of EDI formatted data. A lot of work was done to prepare, check, and publish the tables. A computer was not available for checking the functional specifications, so we simulated the action of a computer by writing computer statements on a deck of three-by-five-inch cards and manually processing through the cards recording data and parameter changes and following the logic path that a computer program is expected to take. Joe Carley called it Ralph and Buddy's "cardboard computer."

It was enough to establish credibility of the work. When the specification was distributed, the comments ranged all the way from "Why didn't you give us the programs, too?" to "Why are you doing this? It's not standards work." Writing the program, however, was eventually funded. In 1981, the programs partially finished were given as COBOL source code to each member company of the UCS Grocery Industry Pilot (thirteen companies in all). At the same time, the software was given to several transportation companies, including Chemical Leaman Tank Lines, which provided invaluable service by beta-testing the programs in an operational environment involving transmission of freight bills to trading partner E.I. du Pont.

After two months with the software at the grocery companies, we met to discuss progress. Several companies had already constructed data in the UCS formats and had exchanged this in magnetic tape form with trading partners in the pilot (communications tests were scheduled for a few months later). Some participants complained about the incomplete software. Ralph Chaney of Giant Food stood up to ask, "Why are we complaining? Two months ago we did not have the slightest idea of how we were going to write these programs and stay on schedule, and already we are constructing and interpreting EDI without problems." When the pilot was over, a UCS meeting was held to explain the results to an assembly of 350 people. During the meeting many statements were expressed or written about the use and effectiveness of the table technique.[15]

---

[15]Related presentations and quotes—1981: TDCC National Forum on Electronic Systems for Trade and Transportation, "A Uniform Communication System for the Grocery Industry," Arthur W. Woelfle, pages 22-24; "Electronic Data Interchange Standards and Applications," Ralph W. Notto, pages 52-57.

Comments on Use and Effectiveness of Table-driven Technique

Arthur W. Woelfle, President and Chief Operating Officer, Kraft, Inc., at the TDCC National Forum Proceedings, 1981	"We are confident that UCS will provide significant benefits to any manufacturer, distributor, or broker. Already we know that: "UCS can improve the productivity of all parties involved by reducing data entry and coding. "It expedites the receipt of purchase orders and invoices. "It is expected to improve production scheduling and inventory management, shipment tracing and tracking, cash planning and cash application to receivable open items. "It reduces errors in the ordering and invoicing process."
Patrick J. Hlubik, Director, Staff Support Systems, Nabisco Brands, Inc., at the TDCC National Forum Proceedings, 1982	"The interface essentially is based on the TDCC tables. They are not only descriptive of each one of the data elements, each one of the segments and the relationship thereof, but another important aspect of those tables is that they are utilized and are input to the software that prints the standards. The tables are directly synchronized with the standards [documentation]. This allows for flexibility. As the standard changes, the software is going to adjust to the change. By "change", it is going to improve and expand. Any users of UCS should at least use the TDCC tables even if they decide to build their own software."
Paul A. Lemme, Sales Force Companies, Inc., at the TDCC National Forum Proceedings, 1982	"In the past, we supported some 29 different standards with our customers. Eventually, UCS will allow us to use one set of standards. "Let me stress that the TDCC tables are vitally important in the expansion of such programs as UCS and the warehouse industry's WINS program. These same tables can also provide a means for us to track railcars involved in our shipments. We are continuing to grow with UCS and the many applications that can be handled electronically."

Comments on Use and Effectiveness of Table-driven Technique

James J. Muenz, Director, Systems Development, Kraft, Inc., at the TDCC National Forum Proceedings, 1982	"As a point of interest, we had several meetings with Safeway personnel where our technical staff sat down and went over formats and data fields in great detail. When we started with Ralph's [Grocery], we had only one brief meeting. By the time we got to Giant, the entire interface for installation was conducted by telephone and correspondence. "A few weeks ago, we implemented UCS with Super Valu in their Minneapolis Division, and plan to roll out to their other divisions as soon as possible. "I would say that one major key to the success of UCS is that all companies went through UCS implementation as a group under the guidance of TDCC. We all used common TDCC software to get started, and we all had a common understanding of the standards and an opportunity to discuss technical issues with other companies in the group at our monthly coordination meetings."

It took a year during the late 1970s before EDI groups began to understand the table concept and purpose. Eventually, we demonstrated the process with seven large charts and movable pointers. A narrator read the list of processes while assistants moved the pointers and data in conformance with the process being discussed (Figure 6). The technique became clear, and with it the purpose of the general table-driven solution became evident.

Want More?

TDCC taught several "startup-classes" to EDI implementers from several grocery industry companies. At the end of each class, Ed Guilbert asked what the students thought of the class teaching and content. The reply was usually satisfactory. One time, however, the first respondent said that the technique with the charts was not good at all. "How would you show it?" Guilbert asked.

"With transparences and overlays," he replied.

"I don't know," offered Chuck Kosi of General Foods, "Before I came, I was wondering if I would understand this. After seeing the charts and "animation" with the pointers, I believe that I won't ever forget it." That happened in 1983, long before we had the comprehensive graphic tools we now have on personal computers. In fact, the IBM PC was just introduced in 1983.

Figure 6. We demonstrated the process with movable pointers on seven large charts for SOURCE, TABLES 1 to 5, and RESULT. A narrator read the list of processes while assistants moved the pointers and data in conformance with the process being discussed. — Drawing by Kevin Reamer

It was not until 1985, eight years after the "table-driven" concept for EDI was introduced, that the author believed that finally the significance of it was generally understood. In that year, he was a developer of EDI software. A potential buyer visited his company and stated that he was interested in buying their EDI software product, but only after he could tell him that the software was "table-driven."

"Yes," I said.

(In the 1970s and early 1980s there were relatively very few database systems in use. Eventually the tables were moved to databases, and EDI programs were changed to process database records instead of sequential fixed-length text records when retrieving EDI specifications used for transaction set construction and editing. Tables that provide the standards details are available from the Data Interchange Standards Association (DISA) in a structured format with information units separated with a delimiter character. These formats can be read by a program to create database records for the EDI software tables each time a new version is added to the standard. Thus, the EDI software and DISA's automatically prepared documentation use the same source data, and therefore the software and documentation controls are coordinated.)

The requirement that a method be devised to eliminate ambiguities was met. In fact, EDI translation software written by competing companies routinely interacts without any dialogue required by the software authors.

The objectives were met. The software is stable and accurate; maintenance is easy; definition of new transaction set details is facilitated.

Significance

A broadly used national or international data format standard is required to insure that interacting automated processes in a community of trading partners do not interpret the same data differently. The EDI standards provide that assurance. It is equally important that the computer software that operates on the data is also "disciplined." The table driven logic described is an example of such a discipline, and it was proven in many automated environments for several years.

The EDI tables were a product of the 1970s. Programs to print the TDCC and other EDI standards also used the tables, ensuring that the operational EDI translation software and the EDI standards documentation were in a controlled link.

In the beginning, only TDCC offered the tables and associated software. Now, commercially priced EDI software is available from several competing companies. The tables are still in use, but software functionality and speed have been greatly enhanced.

The tables also paved the way for the development and implementation of software tools to compare different versions of EDI standards and identify differences, facilitate data mapping between user applications and EDI standards, and write application and documentation generators.

An underlying message in this topic is that technology has a role in the implementation and use of EDI standards. For the longest time, X12 committees used the expression, "That is an implementation issue, not a standards issue." One would hope that, in the future, we recognize that standards must stay in balance with the operational and technical environments, and vice versa.

THE ROLE OF UCS AND THE GROCERY INDUSTRY[16]

Synopsis

In the late 1970s, six grocery industry associations united to investigate the feasibility of EDI for their industry. These associations were Cooperative Food Distributors of America, Food Marketing Institute, Grocery Manufacturers of America Inc., National-American Wholesale Grocers' Association, National Association of Retail Grocers of the United States, and National Food Brokers Association.

The A. D. Little consulting firm was retained to investigate the feasibility of electronic data interchange for this industry; the principal A. D. Little investigator was Dr. Richard C. Norris.

The term "UCS" refers to Uniform Communication Standard, the name used by the industry to refer to both EDI standards and a separate data communications standard. Following the release of the A. D. Little *Electronic Data Interchange for the Grocery Industry Feasibility Report*, a pilot project was launched with thirteen companies.

The report was significant because it had a unifying purpose, was based on a thorough and objective investigation, presented a quantitative analysis of the effect of EDI if it were adopted and implemented by the industry, made far-reaching recommendations, and proposed a plan of action.

The action proposal included development of the UCS standard based on work at TDCC for EDI as applied to the transportation industries, and implementation of a pilot project to test the standards in operational environments.

The report, published April 1980, predicted a potential industry-wide savings of $324 million per year. This was very significant to industry executives whose companies were not known at that time for high profit ratios.

Beginning of Association of TDCC and Grocery Industry

Dr. Norris called on TDCC in the late 1970s. The TDCC standard was one of the five existing standards he was evaluating. His report included a

---

[16] Adapted from Ralph W. Notto, "The Grocery Industry UCS/EDI 1980 Report and the Initial Grocery EDI Pilot, *EDI Forum*, 1990 Issue, pages 90-94, EDI Group, Oak Park IL, 1990.

recommendation that the grocery industry adopt the TDCC standard. Although the report was exceptionally favorable toward TDCC, neither TDCC nor its staff solicited it. At the time, TDCC did not see any role in the grocery industry other than perhaps to coordinate the grocery and transportation EDI standards documentation and maintenance.

Essence of the Report

As noted in the report, the overall study objective was to evaluate the economic and technical feasibility of replacing the present manual and paper-based information flows among food/non-food manufacturers and distributors with an integrated electronic data communications network. The report addressed the economic and technical issues; any direct considerations of legal issues were excluded. The report also predicted that with a 50% EDI transaction penetration, the industry has a potential savings of $324 million per year.

Excerpt from the Executive Summary[17]

The executive summary in the UCS/EDI report included the following list of findings and recommendations:

> In order to achieve the full benefits offered by modern information processing technology, an Electronic Data Interchange system is needed that links together the computer systems operated by manufacturers and distributors.
>
> Both the direct and the indirect benefits offered by EDI are substantial.
>
> Each industry segment—manufacturer, distributor, broker—benefits, making EDI participation attractive to all.
>
> The EDI system we recommend does not require large capital costs to get started.
>
> The large net savings realized through direct benefits alone should encourage EDI participation to grow rapidly throughout the industry once EDI is introduced.
>
> Realization of indirect benefits will take longer and will be largely dependent upon how effectively individual firms act to seize them.

[17] Arthur D. Little, Inc., "Electronic Data Interchange for the Grocery Industry—Feasibility Report, April 1980".

Nevertheless, indirect benefits will ultimately exceed direct benefits.

Electronic Data Interchange in the grocery industry is technically feasible.

The major impediment to widespread development of EDI is the absence of industry-set standards.

Industry-set message standards are the key to getting EDI started.

While a set of standard communications protocols is needed as well, their selection is not as critical a task.

A large and expensive dedicated network is not needed to make EDI work.

The critical next step for the industry is to undertake a program directed at developing, testing, and demonstrating the use of a first-generation set of message standards."

The report's detailed recommendations on standards were:

This program requires active joint sponsorship by industry leaders, coupled with broad representation of all interested firms within a standards-setting working group. Included in this group should be a set of firms taking part directly in actual data interchange experiments. These pilot program participants should be limited to no more than twelve and should be selected to provide good representation of different kinds of firms. The first step, which can be completed in the next three months, is to establish the needed policy committee and working group. The next is the development of a trial set of message standards and selection of pilot test participants. If this can be accomplished in six more months, we estimate that pilot tests can be completed after a total of fifteen; general grocery industry participation in EDI using standard industry message formats could then begin after twenty-one months. Electronic Data Interchange is already starting to take place. Joint industry action directed at setting meaningful standards is needed now so that EDI can develop efficiently, expeditiously, and without the need for subsequent retrofit from parallel, incompatible systems.

Based on the examination of message format standards explained in this appendix, we recommend that the grocery industry data exchange adopt the TDCC electronic data interchange standard. We compared it to similar formats designed for other application areas, and we found it to be suitable for the grocery industry data interchange. Although certain details of the TDCC standard might be tuned in an attempt to tailor it more closely to the grocery industry's particular application needs, the added benefit of such tailoring does not outweigh, in our opinion, the benefits of using an existing well-developed and tested standard format.

This recommendation is based on the following key aspects of the TDCC standard and the grocery industry data interchange needs. The TDCC message format standard was specifically designed for the computer-to-computer exchange of routine business information used in certain application areas in the transportation industry. Because the scope is limited, the standard is easy to use and understand. Because the applications are varied, the standard includes an adequate variety of data types for most business applications.

The TDCC message format is general enough that the addition of new data elements, segments, and transaction sets would make it suitable for most routine business data interchange needs. In contrast to more specialized message format standards, such as the Library of Congress MARC-II format for biographic data interchange, the TDCC format is very easy to encode and decode by computer (or manually for testing or error detection). The extra complexity of the MARC-II code makes data transmission more efficient, but for the moderate amount of message traffic anticipated by users of a grocery industry data interchange, this is not as important as the simplicity and ease of understanding of a slightly more redundant message format.

Finally, the documentation of the TDCC standard and the interface programs that have been developed to use its message format standard are excellent. Since the grocery industry needs for data interchange are met by this existing code structure, it would be a poor use of resources to develop another similar, but slightly different, message format standard. It is desirable, but not necessary, to merge the table of standard grocery industry data elements with the TDCC data element table. Similarly, the grocery industry segment and transaction set definitions could be merged with the TDCC segment and transaction set definitions. Whether the tables are merged or not, the same TDCC message format syntax and computer programs can be used for grocery industry data exchange as well as for the transportation applications."

Development of the Standard

Following the A. D. Little report, the grocery industry retained the consulting firm of Touche Ross to help prepare the grocery industry EDI standards. They did a considerable amount of detail work, a standard was printed in May 1981, and the industry was ready for its pilot project. The standard included two volumes that independently addressed formats and communications: *UCS Volume I-Draft UCS Message Standards Manual*, and *UCS Volume II-Draft UCS Communications Standards Manual.* The Touche Ross standard followed the syntax of TDCC, except that graphically on paper it looked different.

The significant part of the work by the grocery industry, A. D. Little and Touche Ross is that it recognized the importance of inter-industry considerations for information format standards. At about the same time, other industries were investigating EDI. (Two of these—banking and insurance—developed EDI standards unique to themselves. Years later, however, both became active participants at X12 EDI standards meetings.)

To be sure, the grocery industry had those who proposed individual standards. The author was at some of those meetings and noted (with relief) that someone always spoke up for coordination and put the discussion back on track.

Before the Pilot

Following the Touche Ross standards involvement, the grocery industry sought out TDCC to possibly manage its pilot. TDCC agreed to do so and was accepted after it was emphasized that the industry was as much, if not more, interested in project management as it was in coordination. It took TDCC some time to get to that point, since its purpose had always been coordination.

The TDCC report on the pilot project made this statement regarding the standard:

> In the A. D. Little report, it was suggested that the UCS data elements, segments, and transaction set definitions could be merged with those for EDI maintained by TDCC. The UCS committees concurred that it would be beneficial since it presented an opportunity to use the same standard information structure and possibly the same computer programs to extend beyond the grocery industry environment into interchange with the transportation and other business communities at a later date.
>
> TDCC was designated to accomplish this merging. It entailed integrating the UCS standards database with that for EDI previously developed by TDCC. It required reassigning some identifying numbers for UCS data elements and representing the associated formats and specifications in TDCC computer-stored tables. This made available a set of standards maintenance programs that operated from the tables, checked for inconsistencies, calcu-

lated cross-references among data elements, segments, and transaction sets, and generated a digital image of the UCS standard for processing and reproduction on a laser printer system.

The draft standards were presented to the Industry Review Committee, which studied and analyzed them concurrently with and independently from the pilot project.

The significance of this was: Automated assists for preparation of the standards assured a minimum of errors for the draft publication. This is especially significant considering that the standards include thousands of individual detail specifications. Standard procedure for representing the standards in EDI tables also opened the possibility for the pilot project to use TDCC software to implement the standards. The industry review procedure enabled non-pilot companies to influence the contents of the standards.

In practice, the process was not quite this smooth, and the initial attempt at merging was rejected. The second try, however, was successful, and this work was completed in June 1981.

The UCS/EDI Pilot

The following is extracted from the TDCC report Pilot Project Startup—*June 1981*

As recommended in the ADL report, the pilot project was initiated to validate the message format and communications standards. The pilot participants agreed to implement the message standards for purchase orders and invoices, and to use the common communications protocol specified in the UCS standard (Volume II).

To facilitate planning and testing, company pairings were made so that each could communicate with their pilot partners 'one-on-one' using the UCS standards. Subsequent activity would expand the communications orientation from six 'one-on-one' environments to include several 'one-on-many.' The pairings were:

Chesebrough-Pond's/RMI/Giant Food

Dow Chemical/Sales Force/Super Valu

Kraft/Safeway

Nabisco Brands/Giant Food

Procter & Gamble/Wetterau

Quaker Oats/Ralph's Grocery.

Actually, the pairings were not exactly 'one-on-one,' since pairings involving brokers included three companies, and Giant Food was a member of two pairings.

:

The thirteen companies that particpated in the pilot group were:

Manufacturers	Distributors	Brokers
Chesebrough-Pond's, Inc.	Giant Food Inc.	RMI, Inc.
The Dow Chemical Company	Ralph's Grocery Company	Sales Force Companies, Inc.
Kraft, Inc.	Safeway Stores, Inc.	
Nabisco, Inc.	Super Valu Stores, Inc.	
The Procter & Gamble Company	Wetterau Incorporated	
The Quaker Oats Company		

Mainframe computer equipment employed by the pilot participants varied. It included at least four major brands and variations of model, configuration, and software systems.

Communications techniques also varied since some participants communicated directly from the computer mainframe, some used a communications front-end computer, and some used a service bureau.

Significance of UCS Standards

A true validation of the standards meant that the pilot project had to:

Involve more than one company from each group (manufacturer, distributor, broker) in the overall project.

Test more than one message type.

Orient a company's communications in both directions (outbound and inbound).

Involve representation of geographically dispersed points in the country.

Involve both large and small companies.

Involve companies with both centralized and decentralized orientations.

Test communications with more than just unique pairings.

Involve a multiplicity of types of computer systems.

Involve alternative choices for implementing communications.

The pilot project met all of these criteria.

Common Interface Software Initiation—July 1981

TDCC managed and coordinated the pilot project according to a plan that included already available TDCC interface software and documentation, and pilot software and implementation seminars.

The common interface software is 'called' [invoked] by a user's software system to construct transaction sets in UCS/EDI format for transmission to another company. It edits received transaction sets and 'explodes' them into fixed format records for internal processing.

In the information structure, transaction sets are composed of segments, and segments are composed of data elements. In the common software, the attributes of each information unit (transaction set, segment, data element) are identified and described in table form. Generalized software routines for set generation and set interpretation operate on the tables and user data in order to perform required functions related to the use and interpretation of the standard.

Since the standards are defined in tables, a table-driven programming technique is used. This allows for generalization of programming functions and commonality of procedure and interpretation from application to application. It also means that since every detail of the UCS message formats is specified in the tables, every detail is checked in a consistent programmed pattern. A transaction set is validated in terms of its segments, assuring that all required segments are present and that there are no extra segments. Each segment, in turn, is validated in terms of its data elements, assuring that all required data elements are present, considering both baseline and conditional requirements. Data elements are validated in terms of their attributes (type, length, special characteristics). Tables and software include elements called 'special processes' that identify processing to be performed relative to either the standards or the user's unique requirements. [Note: Present tense is used in this paragraph, since once programmed, the processes continue to be used.]

At the start of the pilot project, the interface software was written in ANSI COBOL 74 and had been tested with the generation and interpretation of thousands of transaction sets for transportation applications. The software program was expanded to accommodate UCS transactions.

Software modifications during the course of the pilot project included generation of UCS transmission header and trailer segments, modification to control programs, generalized special processes to edit for the conditional relationships among data elements within a segment, processing multiple transmissions from or to one file, processing nested loops (repetition of segments within a transaction set), acceptance/rejection criteria, and procedures (automatic acknowledgment function).

All programming relative to the standard was accomplished by TDCC in order to maintain UCS/EDI compatibility. Changes were issued to the pilot participants in the form of ten software memos during the pilot. Pilot companies were responsible for incorporating the changes into their own systems."

Significance of Table-Driven Software

EDI tables assured a common interpretation of the standards, allowed the pilot users to concentrate on internal programs and databases, provided for a maximum level of editing for both pre and post-transmission, and enabled the pilot project to maintain its schedule.

Ed Guilbert, Buddy Bass, and Ralph Notto wrote the pilot report from which this report was taken. After testing during during August 1981, the pilot participants began actual data communications in November 1981, and the project was completed on schedule in April 1982.

Achievements and Milestones

June 3, 1981	Introductory meeting with the Joint Industry Committee when TDCC was selected to manage the UCS program.
June 24	TDCC provided each company with EDI software to perform interface data transactions.
July/August	A series of pilot company meetings were held to coordinate programming and implementation.

Achievements and Milestones

September	Companies began sending test data on magnetic tapes to TDCC for editing.
October	Companies began sending test transmissions to each other for test purposes only.
November	By the end of November, some pilot companies were in operational data interchange for purchase orders and invoices.
December	All companies had indicated that the UCS/EDI capability for transmitting and receiving purchase orders and invoices was complete.
January, 1982	Expansion and improvements were added to the UCS/EDI software to accommodate such transactions as acceptance/rejection (acknowledgment) and other features.
February	Pilot companies indicated acceptance of the UCS Message and Communication Standards as a result of operational experience. Many companies had already expanded from one-on-one to one-on-many locations for interchange with their pilot partner company.
March	Final review of the Message and Communications Standards was completed and the Phase III Pilot Implementation Report was completed for review by the pilot companies prior to publication.
April, 1982	The Pilot Implementation Report and the UCS Standards were published.

Summary

The pilot implementation phase has been acclaimed by all pilot companies as being a thorough and valid evaluation of the UCS message and communication standards for purchase order and invoice electronic transactions. The success of this phase of the program is reflected in the adoption of the standards, not just for pilot testing by the participants, but also in the action taken by the pilot companies to implement UCS for long-term operations.

Since this was both a development and implementation project, it was necessary to reach an accord on definitions, procedures, conditions, and policies while operational capability was being designed. Future startup programs have the advantage of using these established standards and procedures to significantly reduce the cost and resource allocation necessary to implement UCS.

Although the introduction of the TDCC interface software was a new concept to some of the participants, it greatly reduced implementation time and assured that all companies were transmitting and receiving the same formats following the UCS message standards.

The volume of transactions accomplished during the pilot was more than adequate to evaluate the UCS standards. The Pilot Implementation Phase did not attempt to validate the cost savings that were forecast. However, it was the opinion of many of the pilot company participants that such savings are feasible and, in some cases, may be even greater than originally estimated.

The focus of attention during this phase was on purchase order and invoice applications. The pilot project has validated these transactions. Several other transaction sets have been formatted and published in the UCS standards documentation. The complete list was: purchase order, purchase order change, purchase order adjustment, invoice, credit memo/debit memo, shipment advice, receiving advice, item maintenance information, promotion announcement, prepayment adjustment advice, remittance advice, administrative message, and acceptance/rejection advice.

During the pilot, the purchase order, invoice and acceptance/rejection formats were evaluated under operational conditions; the others were not. As the project expanded, all transaction sets were scheduled for operational validation.

Conclusion

The UCS standards that were validated during the Pilot Implementation Phase are recommended for adoption and use by manufacturers, distributors, and brokers.

The work of the grocery industry was significant because it coordinated its information standard with that of other industries, made a quantitative analysis of EDI's effect on its industry, tested in pilot operations the message formats before releasing them for general use, tested on a broad basis the table-driven computer software, kept its message formatting and communications standards independent, opened its EDI community (and pilot) to small as well as large companies, executed a plan for follow-up, and publicized their results.

The grocery industry pursued EDI on both a businesslike and statesmanlike basis. For that, they are to be commended. Their example exists for other industry groups to follow.

Focus and Delivery

Key contributions during this critical period of EDI history were made by:

George Klima, Super Valu	... who was a focal point for much of the discussion about the purpose, significance, controls, and details for putting the standard together.
Burton Millard, Proctor & Gamble	... whose mature judgment and ability to persuade others kept the project on a progressive course.
Ralph Chaney, Giant Food	... who recognized early the importance of the unifying technology (table-driven computer programs reported in the previous topic) and got others to understand this and technology's role in keeping the pilot project on schedule.
Patrick Hlubik, Nabisco	... who introduced the concept of the transmission header and trailer, which at that time was an addition to the EDI syntax and included the data elements for communications ID and password.
Ronald Seger, Chesebrough-Pond's	... who argued convincingly for keeping the grocery industry and transportation industry EDI standards under the same "umbrella".
Richard Keener, Kraft	... who was instrumental in getting TDCC and the grocery industry pilot project together.
Jim Muenz, Kraft	... who led one of the earliest successful implementations of EDI during the pilot.
Norbert Ziegler and Donald Stanuch, Quaker Oats	... who worked with the TDCC software to convert it to non-IBM environments.
Kenneth Hite, Ralphs Grocery	... who also led an early implementation during the pilot.
Robert Olson, RMI	... who represented the points of view of the smaller companies implementing EDI.
Paul Lemme, Sales Force Companies	... who was a leader in quickly learning and explaining to others the TDCC software used in the pilot.

Key contributions during this critical period of EDI history were made by:

Peter Steinmetz and John Schmidt, Safeway Stores	… who implemented the pilot on the basis of regional requirements for the company.
George Garrett, Dow Chemical	… who quickly expanded the use of EDI for his company.
Robert Livsey and Syl Duncan, Wetterau	… who helped to uncover and resolve many of the roadblocks encountered during the early EDI implementation.
Gene Nelson, Dry Storage	… who coordinated the warehouse industry EDI requirements with those of the grocery industry.
Arthur W. Woelfle, Kraft, Inc., and Leonard Lieberman, Supermarkets General	… who were co-chairpersons of the grocery industry EDI implementation committee and who ensured top management direction and support for the initiative.
Paul Kelly, Grocery Manufacturers of America	... who was the administrator for the coordination between the grocery industry and TDCC.

George Klima Letters

After a chance meeting at an EDI conference in 1997 and a discussion of this book, George Klima, a forceful leader in getting EDI started at Super Valu and in the grocery industry, sent the following four letters to recall early EDI initiatives. His contributions toward the success of UCS and EDI, his interest in the author's writings, and his contribution of these letters are very much appreciated. Here, George recalls the EDI activity in the grocery industry in the 1970s, prior to involvement with TDCC.

We met for lunch again in June 2000. The social meeting is reason enough for getting together, but this time the author was also interested in George's recollections about a comment he made during an interview with *EDI Forum* in 1988 when asked about his initial encounter with Ed Guilbert. He said that his first impression was that the TDCC approach was "too informal." He explained this at the meeting and followed that with a "Letter 4," also included in this topic.

Letter 1

March 5, 1997: George Klima to: Ralph Notto

It was great to see you in San Francisco and to have lunch with you.

I was glad to hear that you are writing a history of EDI that, I assume, will include the history of EDI in the Food Industry.

If you do include the history of EDI in the American Food Industry, then Super Valu's involvement should play a prominent role in your write up.

George Klima

Super Valu started inter-company EDI well before anyone else in the Food Industry. We know this because when we tried to expand our EDI partner base and traveled around the country to do so, we were successful in a number of instances but met much resistance from many (some currently considered EDI pioneers). We were told, for example, that "We will never see EDI, our kids will not see EDI, and their kids will not see EDI," or "We considered EDI, but it did not look feasible to us," etc. Of course, we were practicing intra-company EDI before inter-company EDI.

With partners we engaged in inter-company EDI, we used standards developed jointly by Super Valu and the partners. At Super Valu, Curt Hanson was responsible for coordinating the development of the standards. Curt is now retired.

One of the organizations interested in working with us on EDI was AT&T (the only communication company in the U.S. at that time). AT&T suggested an approach, which required no standards similar to (I suspect) what Ken Steel is advocating today. Ken Steel's idea is well known among the standards developers (and accepted by many) and I certainly would like to hear your opinion on his idea.[18]

Eventually, the Food Industry could no longer ignore (we were told) Super Valu's successful deployment of EDI and we were invited to present our idea to the joint technical committee of SI (predecessor of FMI [Food

[18] The author's opinion is that a standard was absolutely required for us to achieve the results reported in this book.

Marketing Institute]) and GMA [Grocery Manufacturers of America]). The meeting was held at Chicago.

Next, the joint SI/GMA committee formed a task force that was charged to conduct a study to determine the practicality of EDI. I was a member of both the joint committee and the task force. The members of the joint committee were Bill Bishop representing SI (Bill is a well known Food Industry consultant), Dick Keener and Bill Reidy (Dick's boss) both from Kraft Foods, Bob Koenig from Super Valu, Les Lieberman, president of Super Markets General (very much responsible for acceptance of EDI in the Food Industry) and Schnuck Company. I believe Marsh Blackburn and others whose names I forgot, because this has been a long time ago, were also present and, I suspect, some of the names above are misspelled.

I chaired the distributor Study Task Force and Dick Keener chaired the supplier group. The distributor group consisted of Super Valu, Schnuck Co., and the Acme Co. The supplier group consisted of Kraft Foods and two others but I forgot the names of the other two companies. The results of this Joint Industry study were positive and, as a result, the Joint Industry Group suggested that the Industry should pursue EDI further.

Consequently, still another task force was formed (again I was a member of this task force) which recommended that another study should be performed this time by an independent consulting company to reconfirm the results of the first study and to provide "independent and impartial" validity of the results. This became the so-called Arthur D. Little Study, of which I know you are familiar.

During this time, Super Valu kept expanding its EDI partner base

Besides Dick Keener, there are others still around that can confirm the above. I am not sure if Marsh Blackburn [Sales Force Companies] was in this process right from the beginning, but I know he was in at the early stages of this process. Marsh Blackburn and Paul Kelly, for example, were not present at the GMA meeting at the Breakers at Palm Beach, one of the stepping-stones toward convincing the Industry to accept EDI, and I am not sure that Paul Kelly participated in the initial Joint Industry EDI study because Bill Reidy represented GMA at that time. In any case, with the exception of Paul Kelly, Marsh Blackburn, and myself, the original members of the Industry EDI effort did not continue when the EDI/UCS pilot was started (I am not sure if Dick Keener participated in the pilot). Of course, I might have overlooked someone.

I feel fortunate to have been a part of the EDI process and to be the chairman of the Standards Development Committee (UCS) during the EDI pilot phase. This gave me the opportunity to make sure that the conditional elements became programmatically enforceable instead of a "shake of hand," that the principle of mandatory and optional data elements was clearly defined and programmatically enforceable, and Functional Acknowledgement became mandatory in UCS standards.

Subsequently, Super Valu helped to pioneer development and implementation of many transactions (sets) where at Super Valu the incoming data were fully and programmatically integrated into the internal systems.

I do not know if any of the above is of interest to you but if you should have a question give me a call. Also people like Bob Koenig, former VP of MIS at Super Valu, deserves a lot of credit for the birth of EDI in the Food Industry and I am sure he would be willing to talk to you.

In conclusion, it was great to participate in development of a process like EDI.

The greatest thing about EDI, however, was meeting friends like you.

I hope to see you someplace sometime.

Best regards,

George Klima

Letter 2

June 24, 1997, Re: EDI history

Recently, some historical facts were brought to my attention regarding Super Valu's early 1970s work on EDI with Levi Strauss.

Super Valu, through its County Seat Division, was the second largest customer of Levi's at that time.

The EDI work did not come to fruition because the "serious problem" EDI was going to solve was eliminated by a change in the accounting procedure.

People involved at Levi's were James Assing, operations research manager, and Jerry O'Shea.

So the early EDI history marches on.

I am pretty sure I will be reminded of other early EDI development events and, of course, I will drop you a note.

Best regards,

George Klima

Letter 3

June 6, 1998, Re: My letter regarding EDI history in the Food Industry

During a recent trip, I met one of the "forgotten" EDI Pioneers who refreshed my memory regarding the names of the original start up EDI companies, long before UCS. These were Continental Coordinators (a large and innovative freight consolidator), Jeno's, Morton Foods, Banquet Foods, and Rich's.

The names of the later EDI Pioneers (but still before UCS) were Pillsbury, Green Giant, Ralston Purina, Kimberly Clark, Best Foods, and Fairmont Foods.

There are still others but we were unable to recall additional names. I am sure, however, that I will run into still another "forgotten" EDI Pioneer who will refresh my memory even further.

Best regards, George Klima

Letter 4

July 25, 2000

I certainly enjoyed our lunch. It was a very good lunch and great conversation recalling the old EDI days.

I read those areas of your book that you marked for me.

EDI (beginning) has been very long ago and, as I said to you at the lunch, I am hoping I did not leave anyone out in my recollections or misspelled somebody's name. It certainly would be unintentional.

About my statement, "TDCC's approach was too informal," I was referring the number of trading partners we had and planned to communicate with—the "shake of hands" principle for conditional data elements would be impractical and would not allow us to programmatically process incoming data which was the primary objective for entering into electronic data interchange. Consequently, I insisted that the conditional data elements become programmatically enforceable by defaulting to a predefined enforceable data element. The Functional Acknowledgement was also specified as an optional transaction. Again, this was inconsistent with the objective of processing incoming data programmatically.

In addition, a basic concept was missing; that is the sender of the data was responsible for making sure that the addressee did receive the transmitted data. I, therefore, insisted and got a statement included in the UCS Standard Manual that stated that fact. This was a lesson we learned in our electronic interchange long before UCS and, I believe, also before TDCC.

The inclusion of this principle, by the way, saved us hundreds of thousands of dollars in earned discount when a large supplier, for example, ignored reconciliation of functional acknowledgements, and, therefore, did not know that the invoice data he was transmitting to us never reached us and, therefore, could not have been paid.

This statement in the UCS standards manual protected us well in a number of instances.

Finally, TDCC standards included notes; i.e. narratives (as supplements to the numeric data elements) to be transmitted along with the numeric data–narratives, which, in effect, negated any effort to achieve programmatic processing of such transactions.

There might be other examples, but that is all I remember at the moment.

Again, it was great to see you. We must have another lunch when you visit St. Paul.

Best regards, George Klima

INVOLVEMENT OF ANSI IN EDI AND DEVELOPMENT OF X12[19]

X12: Name of the EDI standard accredited by ANSI
ANSI: American National Standards Institute
EDIFACT: United Nations standard EDI For Administration, Commerce and Transport
COMPORD: The U.S. steel industry EDI standard
NACHA: National Automated Clearing House Association

Synopsis

In the course of EDI work, the most difficult task during the period 1983-85 had been to fight off the tendency of new industry groups joining the EDI movement to make substantial changes to the standard before understanding the impact on the current user community. The X12 group was no exception to this tendency. An example of what can happen is reported here.

---

19 Adapted from Ralph W. Notto, "Involvement of ANSI in EDI and Development of X12 EDI Standards, *EDI Forum*, 1991 Issue, No. 1, pages 101-104, EDI Group, Oak Park IL.

The effect, however, must be measured in terms of its impact on time required to achieve the ultimate objective of converting the world from non-standard paper-based to standard electronic-based data and information interchange.

This topic describes how X12 originated as part of EDI, what emphasis and decisions were made by those in control, how well X12 was coordinated with the other open EDI standards, and what was the effect of interaction of groups, organizations and issues.

X12—First, "A Gleam in the Eye"

It seemed, during the formative EDI standards period in 1975, that Joe Carley was in a tireless pursuit to address every link in the information chain for trade and transportation. The discussions leading to the addition of the purchase order and invoice transaction sets to the TDCC's EDI standards took place between 1975 when the transportation EDI standards were first published, and 1977, when the EDI activity with ANSI began. Ed Guilbert of TDCC was the promoter during this period and Joe Carley was the strategist. Proactive companies involved during the early period included Procter & Gamble, Super Valu, U.S. Steel, PPG, Chrysler, Mellon Bank, AT&T, and Fisher Price.

Other Alternatives Were Pursued

During this same period, the banking industry was pursuing activity that led to the NACHA standards, and the insurance industry was pursuing development of another unique standard. By no means was it considered a foregone conclusion that other industries would follow transportation into adopting the same open syntax for EDI as that published by TDCC in 1975.

Driving Forces

Ed Bronder of U.S. Steel reported that the steel industry already had an EDI standard which they called "COMPORD" and which was satisfactory from the point of view of defining steel industry requirements for specifying and purchasing steel. He was looking for a way to possibly use this standard imbedded in a broader standard, and to work under ANSI rather than TDCC. The reason for this, he said, was because the steel industry had recently finished fighting allegations of collusion by steel companies and did not want any steel company EDI meetings to be considered any endeavor other than standards activity.

George Klima of Super Valu said that his company had proprietary formats for EDI in purchase order and invoice applications, but his company was interested in a public standard for EDI because they did not want to have to maintain their own standard, considering all of the ramifications for documentation and training of the users.

Burt Millard of P&G said that his company was interested in a broadly based standard because it viewed participation in several proprietary standards as having a potential negative effect on P&G considering maintenance, operations, and quality control of the different standards.

Organizing

TDCC was not sure that it wanted to pursue the standards activities on behalf of ANSI and its procedures, but agreement was finally reached whereby Credit Research Foundation was appointed secretariat for the standards activity under ANSI, and TDCC was retained as the technical coordinator and advisor.

There was considerable discussion during this period as to whether or not this activity would follow the TDCC syntax of 1975. At a standards meeting at P&G in Cincinnati early in 1977, strong statements were made by both P&G and Super Valu representatives that the TDCC standard was well thought out, would serve the purpose, and that there was no point in inventing still another format. Nevertheless, there was a period of time devoted towards evaluating the adequacy of the TDCC standard. This came about because companies came together in response to a call by Credit Research for an organizational meeting in December 1978. Ed Fisher of 3M was appointed chairperson of a committee addressing the purchase order format, and Ron Liss of Fisher Price for the invoice format. Following that, for several meetings, the committees met separately except for an administrative part of the meeting held jointly.

On the purchase order side, Ed Fisher placed a lot of emphasis on reevaluating the requirements, starting with the basic purchase order data element requirements of the various companies participating on the committee. Ed also emphasized putting together an organizational structure including by-laws and method of operation. Considering that committees only met three or four times per year, the process of getting the standard together took at least another year.

ANSI designated these activities as "X12," and Ted Johnson of Mellon Bank was the first chairperson of the combined purchase order and invoice group. At the end of his term, Ed Fisher was elected chairperson. Other highly visible participants were Jack Hunter of General Electric in the invoice group, Tony D'Anna of Western Electric in the purchase order group, Tom Jones of Western DataCom active in both groups, and Dave Torma of 3M, who participated in another committee that addressed communications. Tony D'Anna was elected chairperson of the purchase order group after Ed Fisher's term ended, and he was subsequently elected to succeed Ed Fisher as chairperson of the full ANSI Accredited Standards Committee (ASC) X12.

Technical Support

On the technical side, TDCC appointed Buddy Bass to work with the invoice group and Ralph Notto to work with the purchase order group. After we got through the organizational period, Ralph felt that the purchase order group was beginning to make significant progress. We had even resolved the Ed Bronder issue of how to imbed the steel industry COMPORD standard inside X12 and how to include transportation data that had to be included with a purchase order.

To accommodate COMPORD, a new segment was designed and labeled "J2X." It was a standard data segment that included a data element with up to eighty characters in length that might be used for any purpose. The purpose was specified by a code that was another data element in the segment.

EDI: Electronic Data Interchange

TDCC: Transportation Data Coordinating Committee

SMC: TDCC Standards Maintenance Committee

ANSI: American National Standards Institute

ASC: Accredited Standards Committee

X12: ANSI ASC for EDI

UCS: Grocery industry's EDI standard compatible with TDCC and X12 standards

WINS: Warehouse Information Network Standard, also compatible with TDCC, X12, and UCS standards

JEDI: Joint EDI committee subsequently formed to achieve consensus among TDCC, X12, UCS and WINS

One such code in a list of possible values was used to indicate that the eighty-character field was formatted according to some other standard. Finally then, a third data element in the segment indicated which standard this was. The J2X segment appeared in the line item loop in the purchase order, and with this capability could address COMPORD or any other standard requirement.

Feeling pretty good about this and somewhat competitive, Ralph told Buddy that he should "whip" his group into shape because we were way ahead of them. And he replied that they were soon ready to go to press with the standard invoice and, therefore, they were way ahead of us.

Issues

Timeliness

None of this impressed George Klima, who thought the whole process was taking too long, that the grocery industry had identified hundreds of millions of dollars of savings possible once the industry began using EDI, and, therefore, there was no point in waiting around. So, at this point, it became clear that the grocery industry would develop the Uniform Communications Standard (UCS) and use it long before X12 would be available. On the other hand, the grocery industry also maintained its representation on X12.

Burt Millard coordinated the flow of information between the X12 and UCS groups. TDCC also kept coordination between X12 and transportation as well as UCS and WINS (Warehouse Information Network Standard).

The issue then was timeliness. Once a user group identifies a need, it does not want to wait forever to address it before implementing solutions. Ironically, the length of time that it takes to complete something under ANSI, considering the thorough consensus process for approvals, is also one of ANSI's strong points because it lends stability to the standards process. In latter years, ASC X12 began to publish *Draft Standards for Trial Use* to meet the requirement for timeliness. The grocery community with UCS had a three-year head start over X12 on implementation buildup and had a critical mass of experienced users in its community by the end of 1983. (This was the time when the author finally understood that EDI had reached a "point of no return.") The X12 group achieved a similar critical mass by 1986.

Organizational Control and Coordination

The theme in EDI, as promoted by TDCC, was that each item of information in the standards, regardless of how many places in which it is used, would be maintained in one and only one place. This applied not only to segments and data elements, which are the building blocks for

EDI transaction sets, but also to definitions, code lists, and definitive and explanatory notes. TDCC had this data in computerized tables and had companion programs that constructed standards manuals completely from the explicit and implicit information in the tables. This was certainly used by the UCS committee and also, for a while, by X12. To be effective, it required that the tables and programs be controlled by a single source, TDCC. The various user groups worked together effectively, at least for a while.

TDCC had organized a Standards Maintenance Committee (SMC) that controlled changes to the standards (and by implication, changes also to the tables). Different groups were participants in the SMC. These included air, motor, ocean, and rail transportation, UCS (grocery), WINS (warehouses), and users of transportation services. X12 was not included by choice as a member, but attended SMC meetings with observer status.

In time, pride set in and this became too much to bear. X12 went its own way and TDCC offered no reconciliation. After a year, the two sides had made several conflicting assignments for identification codes, definitions, and other code values.

X12 used a word processor to prepare its standards documentation, and that caused other problems related to accuracy and control.

Finally, someone or some group (not identified) offered some sense in the process. EDI, they said, was too important for this kind of a rift, the rift was not in the best interest of American business, and the two sides must bring the standards back together under common control. This led to the formation of the Joint EDI Committee (JEDI).

Effectively, it took one to two years and a lot of difficult detailed work to put everything back on the right track. This was not only an expense for standards organizations but for the user community as well, since they were required to make changes to already operating programs. In the short run, this rift caused a snag in the process of creating a critical mass of users in an EDI community. In the long run, it may not matter and may even be helpful as the whole world studies and implements EDI and learns from and uses this experience.

Program Control and Coordination

EDI is a task meant for computer programs, and therefore the syntax includes items for computer program control since EDI transmissions are meant for the inter-organizational flow of data. The process demands that both the sender and receiver of the data understand exactly the source and meaning of the data. Part of these program control items include control segments which are included in the transmission and are made up of data elements which identify or specify trading partners, control numbers, date, time, passwords, and numeric quantities used to check the validity of the transmission.

The rift described above for organizational control also led to differences in the construction and use of control segments. Control segments include "headers" and corresponding "trailers." Today these include transmission or interchange header, functional group header, transaction set header, loop header, loop trailer, transaction set trailer, functional group trailer, and transmission or interchange trailer.

Long before the formation of JEDI, the groups representing X12, UCS, transportation, and WINS met to standardize control segments. This was in 1982. At that time, the control segments were not as nicely defined as they were a decade later. X12 and UCS had different transmission or interchange headers and trailers and transportation had none. The functional group header had many different identifiers. Regarding the control segments, agreed-changes were 1) to standardize the functional group header and trailer with common ID values and structure, and 2) to standardize the length and data type of the transaction set control number.

The committee did not address the transmission or interchange header/trailer or loop header/trailer.

The work was tremendously important because it simplified program control. Not going "all the way" to include transmission of interchange header/trailer in its agreement has caused many of today's EDI users to have to construct and interpret more than one type of control segment for the same purpose. It caused all of the EDI software vendors to have both capabilities for any transaction set since some industries using X12 for the body of the transaction set also use the UCS transmission header. But, most significantly, it requires users to have the capability to specify by trading partner which transmission or interchange header to use. Although today that is not difficult, it implies that the receiver rather than the sender may specify the detail of a transmission. Regarding headers, that is explicitly what the early EDI organizers wanted to avoid when they looked at migrating from a multiplicity of proprietary EDI formats to a single open standard.

Orientation and Results

TDCC had the theme for air, motor, ocean, and rail EDI standards that transaction sets reflect the requirements of a transportation mode. Thus, where each mode had similar transaction sets–freight invoice, for example–each mode's invoice was similar in some parts but tailored to the specific mode in others. UCS transaction sets were composed of standard data elements and segments, but designed for the needs of the grocery industry. X12 transaction sets were generic. The purchase order transaction set, for example, was meant to serve cross-industry.

This was a bold new and very useful concept. Perhaps more than one class of purchase order transaction set may be designed in the future for material purchases, service purchases, built-to-order purchases, and purchases of catalog items only, but nevertheless the generic contribution by X12 is significant.

In spite of the problems, in spite of the quarrels, in spite of the duplication of effort, X12 continued to grow and prosper. This must be taken as a sign of its importance and the potential of EDI and also a sign of the importance of the reputation and methods of ANSI. ASC X12 in 1990 took control of X12, UCS, Transportation, and WINS standards coordination.

Finally, standards maintenance is under a single control procedure. Hopefully, those in charge of this procedure will now continue to consider the effect of their decisions on the stability of the standards and on the rate of growth of the EDI user community.

Some on X12 committees wondered whether freight invoices ought to be brought under the X12 generic "umbrella." This began to be defined in X12 in 1990 but with an invoice class specifically for freight rather than attempting freight invoicing through use of the all-purpose X12 invoice.

JEDI—HEALING THE TDCC/X12 RIFT[20]

Rift?

This topic reports on the formation and work of the Joint EDI Committee (JEDI) that was created in 1984 to correct the situation where TDCC and X12 committees were assigning conflicting elements of definition and identification for critical items in the EDI standards documentation. This is important to recall because it shows the impact of a rift between two such important organizations in the evolution of a national EDI

[20]Ralph W. Notto, "JEDI—Healing the TDCC/X12 Rift in 1984-1986," *EDI Forum,* Issue No. 2, pages 69-72, 1991 The EDI Group, Oak Park, Illinois.

community, and the potential hazard should the scenario repeat on the worldwide scene.

Some detail related to this topic is included to indicate the extent of detail required for a computer-to-computer, process-to-process standard and related implementation. Standards are required for all of *eCommerce.* As it should be, the user public does not have to be aware of them. However, it is risky to allow anything to drift from the current standard in an uncoordinated manner, since the ultimate underlying purpose and implementation of the standard is compromised. That is why the work of the JEDI committee was so important.

This topic describes the work required to correct such a situation—the time it takes, the effect on the present user base, the influence on the EDI growth timetable, the issues, the roles of committee members, and the ultimate effect of the work.

Setting the Stage

TDCC had the difficult task to derive an EDI standard for four transportation industries while they were still regulated industries. This was accomplished by 1975. The work became noticed beyond transportation because of the interest of the grocery industry, the feasibility study for EDI in the grocery industry, and the recommendation by Dr. Richard Norris of Arthur D. Little in the study final report that the grocery industry would be well served to expand on TDCC rather than invent another standard.

Some companies, notably those in the steel industry, wanted the standard under the American National Standards Institute (ANSI) because it gave steel companies a forum to meet together for standards purposes with no possibility of being cited for price fixing.

The TDCC Board of Directors was looking at its transportation role and was not ready to "tackle" all industries.

Ultimately, the X12 committee was set up under ANSI with Credit Research Foundation as the secretariat and TDCC as a paid technical advisor. It is the reason that the X12 and TDCC standards are related with almost identical definitions and structure. It is also the reason that led to the rift. ANSI members felt their role was too large to be dominated by a TDCC Standards Maintenance Committee where they were outnumbered.

The rift continued for at least a year before the JEDI was formed.

Prominent Players

The participants at the first JEDI meeting were:

Ed Guilbert	TDCC President and JEDI Secretariat
Dennis McGinnis	Phillips North America, JEDI Chairperson, future EDIFACT Rapporteur
Burton Millard	Procter & Gamble and JEDI Vice Chairperson
Tony D'Anna	AT&T Technologies, future X12 Chairperson, representing X12
Paul Lemme	Sales Force, future Director TDCC Operations, representing UCS
Buddy Bass	Consultant to TDCC, Future X12 Chairperson, representing TDCC
Tom Jones	Western DataCom, a prominent contributing member at all X12 committee meetings, representing X12
Jack Hunter	General Electric and future prominent contributor for payment and finance related X12, representing X12
Gene Nelson	Dry Storage, representing WINS
Ralph Notto	Consultant to TDCC, representing TDCC

The First Meeting

The inaugural meeting in Washington, DC on July 23, 1984, started with a statement of cause and purpose. One major issue besides the alignment of data element dictionaries was that TDCC was publishing a standard called "BUSAP," EDI Business Applications—a TDCC answer to the dictionary alignment problem, but something that obviously infringed on what X12 considered its turf.

Tony D'Anna and Ralph Notto argued hard on the correction for the problem. Tony wanted BUSAP discontinued, and Ralph said that the easiest solution was to use BUSAP with a different cover. That way, he said, all of the automation behind the TDCC documentation will remain in tact. Tony, of course, was furious with such a suggestion. All of that was for starters to set a tone for the discussions.

The real problem was that alignment of data element dictionaries was not enough; when it was decided that the alignment would include the segment dictionary and rules as well, progress began.

When it was over, Jack Hunter said that they would report back to X12 that the TDCC group was "hard-nosed" to start, but an agreement was reached on how to proceed.

Several meetings followed in which data element definition variations were identified and decisions made for resolution. About a year later, the preface to the JEDI document was settled, which indicated the degree to which the JEDI work would extend.

The Committee Purpose: *The Preface*

As stated above, the committee was originally called to get the data element dictionaries into realignment and this was expanded to include the segment dictionaries and rules as well. To understand the depth of the work, consider a memo from Ed Guilbert to all members, JEDI Committee, that said, "Attached is the approved preface for the JEDI dictionary as agreed to at the JEDI meeting on March 26, 1985."

The *preface* included the following opening statement:

> **The Organization of EDI:** The need for any information movement originates with a business function to be communicated from one organization to another. For electronic data interchange to occur, each function must be defined in terms of an EDI transaction set which breaks the function down into segments of related information, and finally to the smallest element of detail, the data element.
>
> This document gives the definitions for three levels of EDI information units: The transaction set, the data segment and the data element. When a transaction set is constructed, it is from the bottom up.[21] [Author's note: The 'bottom up' statement was a compromise. It is, however, impos-

[21] "Bottom up" vs. "top down": A transaction set is constructed from segments (mid level) and data elements (bottom level). The determination of which segments to use is based on the transaction set (top level); determination of which data elements to use is based on the segment. This is "top down" orientation. It would be very difficult, if not impossible when considering software and standards maintenance, to program for all "bottom up" possibilities. The wording in *The Organization of EDI* paragraph was made that way as a compromise, since one side insisted on it, which was holding up progress. *Absolutely none of the TDCC writings or software was "bottom up."*

sible to design something as massive as EDI from the 'bottom up.' That is what TDCC committees were doing from 1968 to 1973 when they concentrated on agreeing on standardized codes. Significant progress toward EDI began when Joe Carley joined TDCC in 1973, changed the orientation to 'top down' and focusing first on subject.]. Data elements are grouped together to form complete pieces of information such as a quantity ordered and the unit of measure used with that quantity. Similarly, data segments contain pieces of related information such as the price and product ID number. Where groups of related segments must repeat (such as a name and address), repeating loops of segments are used.

Many assumptions have been built into all *private* databases which affect the interpretation of the data. As an example, all quantity fields might be assumed to be in cases and all length fields in millimeters; or all organizations might be identified by their UPC corporate ID number. Such interpretations must be included in transactions between unrelated organizations so that each may get the same meaning from the data. EDI transaction set definitions force these interpretations to be clearly defined and included with the data transferred.

This document is organized with the highest level structure (the transaction set) at the beginning; the intermediate level structure (the data segment) in the middle; and the lowest level structure (the data element) at the end. Each section contains abbreviated definitions of the structures used.

As with all standards for use in a wide range of applications, the EDI standards require only the minimum of information for each transaction. Each industry that requires information beyond that specified in the transaction set standards is encouraged to develop conventions for use of the standards in their own area. These conventions may make optional elements mandatory or specify a preferred code set to use, but they must not add new elements or codes except through the procedures of the appropriate maintenance committee.

Suggestions on this document are always welcome and may be addressed to the committee through either the TDCC Standards Maintenance Committee (SMC) or the ASC X12 Subcommittee B on Maintenance. In either case, the secretariat will forward the comments to the appropriate member.

The *preface* continued with descriptions of *transaction set listing, segment directory,* and *data dictionary.*

Unresolved Issues

Between the lines in the preface, the indication is that some issues were left unresolved. For example:

> No mention is made of the interchange or transmission control header, so even at the turn of the century there were two headers, ISA and BG, in common use.
>
> The word "document" used in reference to transaction sets is frowned upon today, but in 1985 it was commonly used by X12 ... in 1975, however, TDCC specifically "coined" the term "transaction set" to begin to lead away from the concept of merely making an electronic equivalent for paper documents of the day.
>
> The note after the definition of "time" to acknowledge a possible future extension of seconds (instead of only hours and minutes) is now in the current standard.
>
> Transaction set design is described as "bottom up," *but that has never been the case.*
>
> The requirement indicators for data elements are listed as mandatory (M), conditional (C), and optional (O)—no similar mention is made for segments because X12 allowed only M and O, while TDCC allowed M, C, and O.

Whatever compromises were made, the work of the committee was in depth, extremely important, and with considerable attention to detail and timeliness.

Technical Support

All of this work required a database to keep things straight. In the beginning, a decision was made that the dictionary comparisons would be completed without much effort. Because of that, no programs were written to control the database changes and maintenance was accomplished with a text editor. In retrospect, a set of programs would have been worth the investment, because the realignment could have been faster.

The Aftermath

At the conclusion of JEDI, there was a common database for items of EDI standards definition, TDCC was the keeper of the database, and X12 agreed to coordinate its additions and modifications. This continued until X12 assumed all of the standards maintenance functions in 1991.

The Message

Effectively, it took one to two years and a lot of difficult detailed work to put everything back on the right track. This was not only an expense for standards organizations but for the user community as well.

The message from this experience is that it is better to apply the correction rather than to save it for a later date. During the JEDI period, companies continued to implement EDI since it was better to get the experience and benefits rather than waiting until a standards issue is resolved.

Is this unlike the X12 to EDIFACT challenge?

INTERNATIONAL EDI DEBATES AND COORDINATION

Since many of the U.S. companies that worked to make EDI a reality had international as well as national interests, it was both reasonable and not reasonable to consider the international application of EDI in 1975.

It was reasonable because benefits expected relative to domestic business extended to international business as well. The ocean carrier industry was always represented at TDCC, and their focus is primarily international. Air carriers also have both domestic and international segments for their services. Rail and motor carriers have direct international interests at Canadian and Mexican borders. For transportation to and from overseas locations, these two carrier modes are part of the international service in that they provide the transport between ports and inland locations.

In transportation, a major time delay for international cargo transport in 1975 was due to documents required by customs agents at receiving countries. A practice at the time was to get documentation to customs ahead of the cargo so entry would be fast and efficient. EDI could accomplish that if it was accepted by trading countries. It was not uncommon for ocean transportation companies to send the paperwork by air courier to arrive several days before an ocean freight vessel.

However, other than for ocean transportation, it was not reasonable to think "International EDI" with respect to first U.S. implementations. Many thought that problems on just a national scope would be sufficiently overwhelming. Example—when working toward a joint Korean/North American EDI pilot in 1988, one person asked how we expected to get EDI data to and from Korea when she was having a problem doing EDI between Minneapolis and Duluth, Minnesota.

The United States was not the only country working toward achieving EDI. In Europe, Singapore, and Sourh Korea, for example, it was practical, even demanding, to consider international EDI implementations early. Europe, consisting of several countries, has a considerably higher percentage of international trade than the United States; Singapore is a transshipment[22] port in the Pacific, and becoming EDI capable was a strategic initiative; South Korea was working aggressively to become a major exporting nation.

So EDI in the U.S. progressed with a focus on significant early national successes and an eye toward eventual international coordination.

Early Steps and Dialog

The Department of Transportation Office of Facilitation (DOT) represented the U.S. at international EDI meetings held periodically in Geneva. Consequently, DOT issued contracts for study and development on the subject. Bill Myers at DOT administered the contracts. Two contract recipients were TDCC and the National Committee for International Trade Documentation (NCITD).

DOT: U.S. Department of Transportation

TDCC: Transportation Data Coordinating Committee

NCITD: National Committee for International Trade Documentation.

COSTPRO: Canadian Organization for Simplifying Trade Procedures

SITPRO: United Kingdom Simplification of International Trade Procedures Board

TDI: Trade Data Interchange

EDIFACT: United Nations standard EDI For Administration, Commerce and Transport

Initially, NCITD's work centered on the standardization and format of (paper) documents used for international trade. The emphasis was on making it easier to type and to understand the documents. Further, considering that there were several different types of documents that used portions of the same master documentation, designing documents so similar information blocks appeared in

[22] Transship: to transfer cargo from one ship to another for further conveyance.

the same position of each document type was a goal for purposes of simplicity, user friendliness, and error reduction. Given this standardization, it was then possible to design multi-page forms with carbon paper inserts and cutouts in the carbon relative to pages that did not require particular information blocks on related pages. Now consider that a form set contained sixteen sheets, including various forms and multiple copies when necessary. With a special typewriter, all sixteen copies could be prepared at the same time, insuring consistency. Of course, except for the electric typewriter, none of this was electronic. Nevertheless, in 1975 this was a dramatic improvement. The endeavor was referred to as "documentation alignment."

TDCC's approach was quite different. The theme was, "I [the company providing the data] will send you [the company receiving the data] whatever data you require. It will be in a standardized format that can be processed in your computer. It will be sent directly from my computer to yours. It will be error-free. It will be timely." The receiving company's theme was, "Fine. I will send you an acknowledgment from my computer to yours after my computer has checked that all of your data is error-free and you have indeed sent all of the data I require." No mention is made of documentation formats.

COSTPRO in Canada in the late 1970s, with some help from TDCC relative to using EDI, made an effort to combine EDI with word processing. COSTPRO complained that the EDI formats were difficult to relate to document forms.

In Europe, SITPRO believed it had the solution. Their EDI standard, Trade Data Interchange (TDI), had segment and data element building blocks similar to TDCC, but the segments were constructed to relate to information blocks in forms. The U.S. companies participating in the TDCC development were interested, but facilitating and prolonging the use of paper documentation as a means for inter-company information exchange was not in their long-term interest. The subsequent United Nations EDIFACT standard includes a name and address segment similar to that in TDI but adopts the X12 technique for using a qualifier in the segment to indicate what kind of name rather than defining a unique segment for each class of name (shipper, consignee, ocean carrier, etc.).

Forcing a Coordination Issue

Don Trafford of SITPRO (United Kingdom) visited Ed Guilbert at TDCC on several occasions. The author first met him about 1977. He explained what they were doing with segments and data elements. What caught Ralph Notto's eye was the difference in the methods we used to determine data element lengths.

In the U.S., whenever we introduced a new data element, we determined its length by finding out what length was used in present computer programs at TDCC-member companies. TDI determined length by how much room was allocated on a form for a particular element. Thus, if half a page width was allocated, the corresponding data element length specification was set at thirty-five, considering ten characters per inch and seventy characters per line on a typed page.

The same was true for the address data element.

It so happened that the TDCC lengths for name and address specified in the 1975 standard were each thirty characters. Notto thought that it was not practical to have this difference internationally for such frequently used data elements, especially at this early stage in EDI development. By then, he had automated the maintenance of TDCC standards documentation, and it was all table-driven. So all he had to do was change the two numbers corresponding to lengths of name and address from thirty to thirty-five, and the next printing of the standard would be internationally compatible for these two frequently used data elements. So he discussed it internally at TDCC and made the change, thinking we could easily change it back if there were objections.

Only the railroad group objected. Therefore we accommodated them with a different data element specification for name and address segments used only in railroad transaction sets, and let the thirty-five-length specification stand for the others.

John Nelsen of Missouri Pacific Railroad complained to Notto for several meetings after that. Not long afterward, the standards change-control process became tightly controlled. Control is absolutely necessary for a standard. This thirty-five vs. thirty incident and its aftermath were possible only because the standard was still in an early stage of development at the time.

Spreading the Word

Representatives of different companies and organizations concerned with data and information flow talked with each other about EDI. Some companies had specialists call on trading partners to interest them in EDI. Others called trading partners to a meeting for the same purpose. This occurred on both national and international scenes.

Following the October 1987 EDI Seminar in Seoul, some of the DACOM Korean participants and the American speakers spent time together to learn more about each other: First row—In-Tak Hwang, Soo Hong Noh, Hak Jung Lee, Young-Kook Kim, I.S. Bae; Second row—Ralph Notto (EDI Inc), Dan Petrosky (McDonnell Douglas), Jim Oravec (AIAG), S. K. Kim, Joe Carley (EDI Inc), Young-Min Na.

Seminars were held at some countries to alert and inform local people. Experts from other countries were invited to speak in addition to national speakers.

The first of these seminars was held in 1987 at Seoul with Data Communications Corporation of Korea (DACOM) as the sponsor, and featuring invited U.S. speakers from the Automotive Industry Action Group (AIAG), McDonnell Douglas, and EDI Inc.

Some other early seminars: Sao Paulo, Brazil sponsored by SGA Sistemas e Serviços in 1989; Vancouver, Canada sponsored by the EDI Council of Canada (First International EDI Congress) in 1989; Tokyo, Japan sponsored by Global VAN Japan in 1989; Taipei, Taiwan, ROC sponsored by the Institute for Information Industry in 1990.

Some Initiatives

Singapore Tradenet

Singapore developed and executed a master plan to use EDI to enhance services at its transshipment port. Measured success indicated dramatic favorable effects. (See the "Pearleen Chan" topic in the "Consultants Play a Major Role" section of Chapter 4.)

EDICOM (Montréal, Canada)

EDICOM (EDI for Commerce) was a non-profit organization formed in 1990 by members of the Montréal trade and transportation community for the purpose of introducing and increasing the use of EDI by transportation companies and their trading partners. The endeavor was jointly funded by the private and government sectors.

EDIFACT Phase 1, managed by Paul R. Bélanger, and completed in mid-1992, used a two-track approach: track one addressed analysis of the industry in order to build a reference model for further design and economic analysis purposes. Track two was used to gain operational experiences to accompany the analysis and to provide some early operational successes. Ralph Notto was EDI consultant for Phase 1.

Paul subsequently became founding member of the EDI World Institute, which was based in Montréal and included twelve other EDI experts.

Korean/North American EDI Pilot

An EDI initiative sponsored by the Data Communications Corporation of Korea (DACOM), and using relationships with the EDI Council of Canada (EDICC), EDI Inc., and Martin Marietta, began in 1988. DK Kim of DACOM directed the project. Martin Marietta provided the data communications services for the project.

Ralph Notto wrote the white paper[23] for this project, working closely on project activity with Hak Jung Lee and Soo Hong Noh of DACOM, Marshall Spence of EDICC, and Ed Bartee and Butch Mills of Martin Marietta.

Objectives were to facilitate trade by decreasing barriers to the flow of information and data, to evaluate through operational experience the benefits to be gained from international standardization of data formats and timely electronic transmission of information and data, and to establish an EDI communications capability that can be used domestically within Korea as well as internationally.

Software and data communications links were installed, and EDI data were interchanged for a year, but the experiences were more for learning and testing purposes than for live operations.

In one transmission, Ralph Notto received a purchase order transaction from a company where "Daniel" Noh had demonstrated EDI. It was for purchase of a copy of Notto's company EDI software. Everything looked so perfect that he was ready to fill the order until he realized that companies that do not already have an EDI system are not able to order via EDI. He sent an EDI administrative message to Daniel complementing him on his perfection.

---

[23] Ralph W. Notto, *Korean/North American EDI Pilot, White Paper,* December 14, 1988.

Two observations and recommendations from the activity–*adjust for the state of readiness for the proposed user base.* (Potential U.S. and Canadian trading partners in 1988-9 were immersed in national EDI activities, and were not ready to commit to intercontinental EDI interchanges.) *Determine a natural application environment for the project.* In the Korean/North American project, the strategy was to communicate purchase orders and invoices first and at a later date to begin ocean transportation data interchanges, as was the successful case domestically in the U.S. and Canada. Subsequent experiences showed that the reverse order would have been more practical for the given environment.

First International EDI Congress

The First International EDI Congress was called and organized by Marshall Spence of the EDI Council of Canada and Jerome Dreyer of EDIA (formerly TDCC). Their motivation was to bring internationally proactive EDI people together to discuss what they were doing with EDI, why they were doing it, and how. Spence and Dreyer's hope was to provide a forum for users of EDI to ensure that EDI technicians properly address user requirements.

Underlying all EDI requirements is the requirement for a data syntax standard. It may eventually be transparent to the user group, but during this formative period in EDI, much discussion centered on exactly *what* the standard is (or what *they* are, since at least three EDI syntax standards were used internationally).

At the congress, five speakers addressed the subject from different points of view:[24]

Jeff Sturrock of Texas Instruments, chairperson of the North American EDIFACT Board, told about the many different data standards his company must use and what he sees evolving with EDI syntax.

Colin M. Hill, manager, EDI Contingency and Planning, Mitsubishi Motors Australia Ltd., spoke about the need for EDI in Australia and how they expected to evolve toward a common standard.

Ray Walker, chief executive of SITPRO and UN/EDIFACT rapporteur for Western Europe, listed seven challenges for establishing EDI in the world community and described where we stand in relation to these challenges.

[24] See "The EDI Standards Debate," 1989 Issue, *EDI Forum*, pages 117-128, The EDI Group, Oak Park, Illinois.

Earl J. Bass, chairperson of ASC X12, vice president of EDI Inc., and one of the original developers of EDI standards in 1975, explained the process in place for X12 for coordinating development with EDIFACT, and said that the initial X12 coordination with EDIFACT did not follow proper procedures for consent of the users, but that controls are now in place to ensure this in the future.

Joseph G. Carley, Jr., president of EDI Integration Corporation and the person responsible for developing the strategy used during EDI's inception in 1973-6, disagreed with the current direction of EDIFACT. Carley argued that the status of the present (1989) EDI user community of 10,000 companies and the effect of EDIFACT on their currently functional and stable EDI operations is not desirable.

Jeff Sturrock

Jeff Sturrock (United States), speaking first, opened with:

> Today's EDI environment for multinational, cross-industry users many times appears chaotic. Today's multi-national, cross-industry EDI users must comprehend a multitude of EDI standards that vary according to the nation, region, industry, application, or trading relationship at hand. However, these EDI relationships vary primarily according to business-driven requirements.
>
> It's hard enough dealing with X12, TDCC, UCS, WINS, ODETTE, TRADACOMS, and EDIFACT [all names of EDI standards]. We also must deal with clones of these standards, conventions, interpretations, multiple releases, and, yes, the ultimate dirty word—proprietary formats. At the other end of the spectrum, we must decide what method of communication transport is to be used. Do we utilize direct or VAN communications methods, or both? Are vendor-specific protocols or open communication protocols utilized?
>
> Today's EDI environment demands that multi-national, cross-industry users comprehend all of the standards mentioned. Texas Instruments' business environment places us in the multi-national, cross-industry user group category."

He continued explaining the complexity of the data exchange environments his company addresses. Then:

> We, and several others, see the following events occurring in the EDI standards community:
>
> North American EDI standards alignment is happening.
>
> EDIFACT and X12 development in North America is occurring in the same arena—the ANSI ASC X12 committee.
>
> Development of more 'non-typical' EDI transactions sets is rising, particularly those relating to quality reporting, specification exchange, and real-time EDI methods.
>
> Most domestic X12 transaction sets are being recast into EDIFACT, offering functional equality in both standards.
>
> Activities are under way to align EDI syntaxes both regionally and globally.
>
> Efforts are under way to provide globally aligned data dictionaries.
>
> Open systems interconnection (OSI) and VAN efforts are complementing these EDI standards activities.

Jeff concluded with:

> We feel that EDIFACT will be used internationally, X12 domestically with some crossover. Implementations, various conventions and subsets within industries will define subsets of these "families," and all of this will be transported through the use of OSI-based protocols.
>
> In summary, the choice of EDI standards is based on market-driven business decisions. They are not emotional decisions, political decisions, or philosophical decisions. Multiple EDI standards can co-exist; one standard does not preclude another. Most multinational corporations use more that one standard, and multiple standards alignment is occurring. Modular EDI systems design will survive in this environment, and global EDI standards alignment is a necessity.

Collin M. Hill

Collin Hill (Australia) said:

> Australia is relatively new in its experience with EDI; whilst there is a great deal of interest in EDI, there is not much operational EDI. Therefore my views will be based upon a situation where Australia has virtually no changes to make but rather the opportunity to adopt the 'right way' from the start."

He followed with facts about Australia and then explained the need for EDI in Australia:

> Australia is a trading nation of some significance in respect to the size of its population; unfortunately, we are trading at a large deficit, a situation that cannot be allowed to continue.
>
> With only 16.5 million people, we cannot possibly economically manufacture anywhere near our domestic and industrial requirements. Until recently, many of our industries have been protected by high import tariffs; these are being progressively reduced.
>
> Most of our export income is obtained from raw materials; we have very large deposits of most major metal ores, almost limitless amounts of coal, and we are able to grow more cereals and harvest more wool than we need for domestic requirements.
>
> Unfortunately, most of the value is added after export; we should be exporting aluminum saucepans, not aluminum—this is a result of a small domestic market and fairly high labor and other costs. There are, however, markets for manufactured goods that require less capital investment and do not rely on the domestic market. I am referring to generally high-tech or niche market items.
>
> Whatever we export or import, it must be done in the most efficient and economic manner, for, with our relatively high labor costs and no government subsidies, we must increase our competitiveness by using every available technology and process. EDI is one that is very appropriate in improving the import/export process.
>
> EDI is particularly suitable in Australia for a number of reasons: because of the larger distances between business centers, because it assists all sizes and types of businesses, and because we have excellent nation-wide communications."

He described Australia's national challenge for making EDI work, and concluded by addressing the international challenge:

> That sounds like a pretty confident, smug scenario. It is not meant to be—it is meant to show that Australia takes EDI seriously and sees its use as a strategic priority. We might be a big country, but in world trading terms we are not so big and therefore must try to remove all possible disadvantages.

We will play our role in trying to implement international standards, at the same time ensuring that our requirements are catered for. Whilst we have attempted to make sure that we can respond to those wanting to use international standards, every country must ask its traders to encourage and promote their use, if only for commercial advantage.

I realize that other countries have a much more difficult task than Australia because of the large operational EDI base that would have to convert to another standard. It will be a long process that may never be totally completed. Many will see no value in making the change; others may take a compromise approach and use internal and external standards. I believe that the EDI translation software suppliers can and must play a significant role in easing the pain of conversion; EDI users must make sure that they do.

I believe that if we commence implementation of international standards in the trading interchanges that can most benefit from their use—such as customs and shipping—we will have started to roll the snowball.

Finally, the standards, above all, must serve the user. We must be pragmatic and not set aims that are so high that they require considerable expertise and money to implement. EDI and international standards will only be successful if the widest possible range of commerce, industry, and government can use them.

We look forward to interchanging with you.

Ray Walker

Ray Walker (United Kingdom) opened with a question:

Let me start by asking a simple but perhaps contentious question: Why is implementing international EDI standards a challenge? Isn't it obvious that we live in a global economy and that therefore in our world of EDI, we need global and international standards?

I do not think that any of us can deny that we already live in a highly integrated global economy—an economy which is becoming more integrated by the minute and which spans all commercial activity and nearly all the countries of the world.

Ray then offered examples and followed by offering seven challenges, giving examples for each:

Challenge Number One: Getting folks to trust each other. This is probably the biggest challenge of all. We come from different cultures and backgrounds, we live in different political environments, and it is not easy, at first, to place your trust in an international process and international people.

Challenge Number Two: Allowing for and coping with different business practices in different parts of the world and doing it in a way that does not bog down the process.

Challenge Number Three: Developing rational and disciplined procedures to control EDI message development and especially to control changes within the EDI message standard. This is particularly important in a generic standard, which by its very nature allows for flexibility in application.

Challenge Number Four: Developing the organization required to support a global EDI standard and ensuring and encouraging user input in the different regions of our world.

Challenge Number Five: Getting across the concept and objective of international EDI standards.

Challenge Number Six: The obvious one, that of delivering usable international EDI standards, openly accepted by all, within a reasonable time frame.

Challenge Number Seven: Why should I implement generic international EDI standards when my own local regional EDI standards are perfectly satisfactory?

Regarding challenge 7, Walker said:

This is not an easy challenge because, in all cases to date apart from EDIFACT, EDI has developed in response to local requirements, demands, and pressures, and the longer term international approach may appear irrelevant to existing users.

However, if EDI is really going to fulfill its promise in a global economy, not just at a regional level, it has to have a clear statement of direction and one which will ultimately benefit all users.

This does not mean that we throw away our existing EDI standards, or stop developing them, but it does mean that we commit, following the procedures, to contribute these developments to the international EDI standard—the clear statement of direction.

Ah, you say, but that means we will have to cope with two EDI standards, so what is the advantage?

Well, let us look at reality today. The reality today and tomorrow is that we all live in a multi-standard environment. Whether it is WINS or UCS and ANSI, or ANSI and EDIFACT, or EDIFACT and TRADACOMS, we live in that environment now. We are used to dealing with a number of different EDI standards and, within those, different versions and releases.

In my opinion, the key issue is that the number of different standards we use should be as small as possible and that our long-term direction and commitment to action should be clear. We need one global EDI message standard.

Once that decision has been made and it is a decision to support, understand and implement both *regional and international* EDI standards—the EDI standards challenge and the EDI standards issue will have been met. Thereafter industry and economic developments will dictate which particular EDI standard will be used to meet our particular requirements. And, of course, provided we commit to working within one global framework, in the medium term, unnecessary standards differences will disappear."

Ray continued by stating there were more challenges, and he presented the seven he considered major. He added:

I would like to give you my opinion of where we are in that five-year [transition] process. 1) The basics of EDIFACT are in place and we have an International EDI Standard that is whole and complete and usable, with over thirty messages under development. In many cases those messages build on experience gained in North America but now meet full international requirements. International cooperation for EDIFACT development is of a high order. 2) The organization required to support implementation, the EDIFACT Board, is beginning to mature in North America, Western Europe, and Eastern Europe. Major initiatives are underway in the South and North Pacific. In the South Pacific, a new EDIFACT Board for Australia and New Zealand has just been formed with the full support of the two governments. Developments are also underway in the North Pacific, including Japan, which has made it clear that it would wish to nominate an EDIFACT rapporteur. 3) Some problems remain with EDIFACT, which is not surprising. But the EDIFACT rapporteurs have agreed to proposals on all of the outstanding issues that have been submitted for approval at the UN in September 1989. Once those proposals have been approved—and I am personally very hopeful that they will be—then we will need to ensure that they have the widest possible distribution so that we can explain the real power of standard international generic EDI messages.

Having given you some of the reasons behind the development of UN/EDIFACT and some of the challenges we face, I would like to finish with a few comments on the perceptions that a number of people in North America hold.

Firstly is the perception that UN/EDIFACT is a European standard. That perception is absolutely wrong, as anyone who cares to analyze and compare TDI-based messages with UN/EDIFACT messages will soon find out. In the process of developing EDIFACT all participants accepted the need for convergence of the existing national EDI standards and, therefore, change to their existing positions.

For the sake of global trade facilitation, the Europeans accepted the concept of generic messages and of the qualifier approach. That was not easy for them and has slowed down the implementation of EDI in Europe considerably. But it was accepted because taking one step backwards in the name of a truly global standard was far, far better than a "standards war," which was a distinct possibility before the EDIFACT initiative was taken.

Having North America, Europe, Japan, and the Asia Pacific region all using different standards and competing, head-to-head, did not and does not make sense in our global village. Trade needs to be facilitated, not constrained, and common EDI standards are an essential goal for both efficient traders and trade facilitation."

Ray commented on perceptions about the United Nations Economic Commission for Europe and the International Standards Organization.

His closing statements were:

I believe that EDI is doing more to create the environment for an effective and efficient global economy than almost any other initiative—technical or political. All of us and all of you are privileged to be part of that process, but that privilege carries a responsibility. It requires recognition of a greater goal than perhaps individual goals or corporate goals or national goals or even vested interests.

That is the real challenge. Many others and I believe it can be met. We believe that in a global market we have no option, and being negative about international EDI developments and standards is tantamount to being an ostrich. So I ask you to join me in facing the challenge and helping us to develop, promote and nurture our global economy through promoting the use of EDI and one global EDI standard, UN/EDIFACT.

Earl J. Bass

Earl (Buddy) Bass began with:

The challenge of implementing international standards on the EDI world community is to accomplish implementation as smoothly as possible without disrupting the over 8,000 current X12 EDI users or the over 1,500 TDI users in the world.

The X12 committee is supporting the development and maintenance of both the X12 EDI standards and the international UN/EDIFACT standards. Having each of the functional subcommittees handle both standards does this. The North American EDIFACT Board was created with the help of our Canadian counterparts to oversee and direct the activities of submitting the North American positions to the other UN/EDIFACT international groups. It must be emphasized that X12 EDI is also an international standard, since 'international' is determined by its actual use rather than its syntax or political considerations.

To meet this international implementation challenge, we must provide for compatibility, or at least substantial similarity, between X12 EDI and UN/EDIFACT in order to protect current users.

Some form of compatibility is a must. Simplifying EDI, not complicating it, should be our goal.

X12 EDI was designed as an international standard and is being used that way at the present time. UN/EDIFACT should be structured to be compatible, allowing for an easy switch if a company wished to convert to UN/EDIFACT or wanted to function with both standards from the same database.

X12 EDI is being used in many countries of the world. I just returned from Australia and New Zealand, where I was on a UN/EDIFACT public relations mission along with members from the North American and Western European EDIFACT Boards. Although the U.S. team was instructed to advance only UN/EDIFACT and to avoid advancing any objectives conflicting with the main objective, I did have private conversations with business associates and others from the audiences. I was asked about the over one hundred Australian X12 retail and automotive users, the over twenty New Zealand X12 users and all the others who have software and are waiting to get started. What are they to do? Throw away a working system for questionable promises of a new and better system? My response was that it is wise to continue to expand their implementations and not wait three or more years for UN/EDIFACT to reach maturation with a critical mass of users and a stable maintenance process.

We, the X12 standards-making body, should and will assure that UN/EDIFACT is compatible with X12 EDI. Potential users should implement now, get the operational experiences and benefits, and then change to United Nations' Standard Messages (UNSMS) only if business needs warrant it. If compatibility exists, switching the software should be transparent to the operating personnel. Right now, the syntax is different, maintenance is different, data elements and segments are configured differently, but hopefully the meaning is the same.

UN/EDIFACT must consider adopting the over 900 data elements that are in X12 EDI use and have had the benefit of being used in literally millions of transmitted transaction sets. This will assist in any required data base conversions. Reinventing the wheel seems to be a fruitless exercise that only serves to confuse existing users and only benefits the new players.

Both X12 EDI and UN/EDIFACT are of such importance to users that, once implemented, the typical user is reluctant and unlikely to implement any changes that threaten the stability of an operational system.

Buddy went on to restate the goals of EDI established in the early 1970s:

Facilitate the flow of information from company to company, computer to computer, and database to database.

Establish a single standard for inter-company electronic data formats.

Decrease processing times related to inter-company information flow.

Establish a system for significantly decreasing data errors in the exchange of information.

Eliminate inter-company paperwork.

These EDI goals are an extension of the goals and objectives of the individual users. They want to improve customer service, improve competitive positions, decrease costs, increase accuracy, tighten controls, and decrease time delays.

Buddy talked about the standards EDI, TDI, TRADACOMS, ODETTE, and EDIFACT. He discussed purpose, responsibility, and said that compatibility is the greatest obstacle. He said that we have to make users of these standards comfortable.

Continuing, he summarized the ANSI ASC X12 position for cooperation in EDIFACT:

> Integration of UN/EDIFACT into X12's mission must have no impact on the existing EDI user community.
>
> The ASC X12 Committee will continue to support existing X12 standards.
>
> Practical international maintenance procedures must be developed that conform to all existing X12 procedures.
>
> The ASC X12 Committee will develop positions on international messages, maintenance, data elements, and syntax in similar fashion to the procedures being used for X12 EDI transaction sets.
>
> The long-range goal is convergence to a single set of standards encompassing domestic and international needs."

Buddy talked more about the conversion issue. He said that ease of use and stability are requirements, and that users will address this as a business issue. He talked about how more control aspects were added to X12 maintenance procedures.

He ended with:

> You are here because you are users or potential users of international standards. What are your thoughts? What would you like to see happen? After this conference, please let X12 know. Send your comments and questions to me and I will make sure that they are properly coordinated and sent to the appropriate organization for action and answers. You have to air your concerns now during the infancy of UN/EDIFACT.
>
> And remember that the ultimate challenge is not how we move the data, but the operational use of the electronic data once it's there!

Surprise!

Before the meeting started, Joe Carley had read his speech to Marshall Spence, Buddy Bass, and Ralph Notto. We all agreed that it was an excellent speech. However, that was not the speech he gave. He spoke from his heart about what he really thought. The three of us were as surprised as everyone else, not necessarily in disagreement, but surprised.

Joseph G. Carley, Jr.

Joe Carley immediately got everyone's attention with his opening statements:

> Is there any doubt where I come down on this question?
>
> You have it right! EDIFACT is wrong, but not for any particular parochial U.S. reason. It is wrong (in my opinion) for very important reasons associated with business operations of U.S. and Canadian companies and industries. It is wrong for the U.S. Department of Defense, the world's largest buyer, which has fully endorsed and adopted the North American EDI standards (X12) for implementation in a wide spectrum of activities in operations, logistics, and finance. I also feel it is automatically wrong for any other nation other than the European community of nations (they invented it) if EDIFACT is accepted purely on the basis of the heavy publicity program and rather high-handed political "sales" pressure we are witnessing. In fact, if examined from a very broad international perspective, it may even be wrong for the Europeans.
>
> I expressed a desire to be present for three reasons. First, I have become somewhat disenchanted with the American National Standards Institute (ANSI) X12 Committee because there are too many vendors involved in the decision process. The ANSI approach calls for a combined user/vendor forum for standards development, which is a reasonable format for purely technological subjects. However, EDI is "user country"—it is an environment where buyers and sellers of goods and services in trade and distribution strive to employ electronic technology to solve business-operating problems and to streamline business operations.
>
> Vendors have a different agenda. They want to sell their goods and services to buyers and sellers ... the real EDI users! Therefore, in my opinion, this conference represents a golden opportunity for the operations side of industry to bring a coalesced body of opinion to bear on the problem of keeping EDI 'on track' strictly as user territory. I am here to encourage you to take firm control.

> Am I suggesting that you throw the vendors out? In a way, yes! In the development and management of EDI standards, there is no substitute for having the assistance of people with twenty years functional and systems experience from the various trade and distribution industries. (I include transportation as part of the distribution process.) A vendor representative serves as a marketing intelligence source for his or her company and, when in a standards meeting, is continually facing existing or potential customers. No matter how good the intentions are or how technically qualified, a vendor representative cannot compete with experienced user personnel in terms of contributing to the basic purpose of the standards.
>
> As you probably know, I chaired all of the TDCC EDI industry groups from 1973 to 1979. We excluded vendors of all kinds. The quality of the functional and systems expertise that participated in those groups has never been challenged. The success of the efforts of those 150 people is self-evident. You are here today!"

Joe went on to say that X12 had gone too far with their generic concept. He said that because transaction sets were too inclusive and therefore too large, they have little or no functional validity and are hardly more than optional templates (considering the ease for editing data previously conceived).

He gave examples from his experiences and made a second attention-getting statement:

> The EDIFACT Problem—my second reason for being here is expressed in the title of my contribution to this session: Is EDIFACT right or wrong? The evidence says loud and clear that it is wrong! Does this mean that I believe that we do not need an international EDI standard? Absolutely not! After all, I was the person who had the audacity to propose to the TDCC Board of Directors in 1973 that we could develop a single electronic data interchange standard for the U.S. While they doubted that it could be done; they nevertheless gave an approval to make the effort.
>
> I strongly believe that an international standard is essential and that it can be achieved. But please, let us do it the right way.
>
> My idea of doing it the right way means we need a clearly defined concept, a definition of objectives in some detail, and a plan for implementation. First and foremost, to get my support you have to define what you mean by international. If you mean *international trade* as distinct from domestic trade, you come out wrong on all counts in my book … and no matter

how you color it, that is what the EDIFACT proponents are promoting. Hence, EDIFACT is wrong!

What are the differences between domestic and international trade?

I say there are no operational differences. There are only procedural differences, and most of the procedural differences are influenced by the import and export laws of the various nations.

Please let me clarify by example. Trade and distribution is a sequential process of events profiling the movement of goods from origin to destination. Supporting information generally follows the same path. The process begins in an operational sense with the purchase order. Purchase orders are purchase orders regardless of whether they are domestic or international. The same description applies to invoices, order tracing, requests for quotations, and a host of other buyer/seller business transactions, including payments.

Orders are distributed (shipped) to both domestic and/or international customers. It is here that transportation enters and becomes a part of the unbroken sequential process of events. The same vehicular methods are used to deliver regardless of whether the movement is to domestic or international destinations. Ships, airplanes, trucks, and trains all operate both internationally and domestically. In fact, the same vehicle often carries a mix of international and domestic shipments on the same trip.

Now we come to the single difference between international and domestic. It is a difference imposed by the export control activities and customs services, which you find at all authorized border crossing points, airports and seaports. However, as I said previously, those differences are procedural in nature and were accommodated in the design of the EDI standards.

Here is my point: I personally resent the use of the term *international* as if it were the private territory of EDIFACT. In my opinion, all that we are achieving with the EDIFACT smoke and colored-glasses is to remove the ocean carrier industry from the sequential process of information flow I discussed before and the imposition of an incompatible standard in its place. If we allow it to happen, we will be permitting the introduction of incompatibility into a distinctly stable EDI environment that has over 8,000 active users in the U.S. and Canada."

Joe then talked about the scope of the international trade between the U.S. and Canada and the EDI standard used.

He said that we should not be "Giving up in the middle of success." He said that he had asked a U.S. representative for international EDI why he did not argue more forcefully on certain points. Joe said that the startling response went something like, "We had to give on some points to keep them from accusing us of demanding that they do it our way or not at all!"

Joe recalled early U.S. attitude toward international EDI, and related it to his current objection:

> It is important to note that TDCC did not attempt to get the EDI standards established as an international standard. Was that because we were domestically oriented? Absolutely not! We planned and designed to support both. What we have in this case is a serious diversion in perspective with the Europeans. We simply refused to glorify international trade over domestic trade as something special beyond the procedural considerations previously discussed." (See **Figure 5. A page from early documentation: Shipment Information Flow, Motor," page 26 for a referencc to "Export Declaration" in the 1975 TDCC work, for example.)

He talked about U.S. Customs EDI activity and his disagreement with their EDIFACT position. He closed with:

> Finally, let me revisit the EDI vendor problem. I do not want to leave the impression that I dislike EDI vendors. I am an EDI vendor myself and consider it a highly respectable endeavor. However, I could not afford and would not keep anyone on my payroll who was a perennial standards meeting attendee unless I saw an assured profit potential. We all know that many of the U.S. network and software providers in the EDI business are attempting to get up to speed on the expected 1992 business windfall in Europe. You get my point? I again emphasized that EDI is user country and should be managed that way. But it is you the user who has to impose the requirement on the organizations you support.

Subsequently

Immediately after the session, many people said to Ralph Notto, "Joe really made the conference come to life." Dan Ferguson asked Notto to ask each speaker for a copy of his speech. Dan said that the event was too significant to be left undocumented.

Some attendees were pleased that Joe brought these issues to the forefront, since alignment of the two standards was actively being pursued. Many of those already engaged in X12 EDI were not in favor of merging X12 into EDIFACT; many who favored the integration were not pleased with Joe's statements and felt it set their progress back.

During the conference week, The EDI Group sponsored a dinner and cruise. On board were DK Kim and S.H. Noh of the Data Communications Corporation of Korea and many people from several other countries. Many U.S. and Canadian EDI professionals knew Noh as "Daniel." Speaker Joe Carley is visible in the background wearing glasses.

A few years later, some participants thought that completing the merger of X12 into EDIFACT would be accomplished by 1993. However in 1993, the level of participation of U.S. companies in EDI is indicated by the amount of expenditures in EDI services and the reasons for theses expenditures. According to the EDI Group's research, the 1993 U.S. expenditures were one $1.25 billion; the reasons indicated were quick access to information, cost savings, accuracy of data, competitive advantage, improving customer service, and customer/supplier request. Most of the implementation was with X12. Consequently, the 1993 goal for one EDI standard, EDIFACT, was set aside.

Still, the idea of a United Nations EDI standard was appealing, and the two standards bodies, X12 and EDIFACT, continued to cooperate with each other. Many EDI software systems are "bilingual" and are able to process either standard "fluently."

In 1989, the speakers said that there were about 8,000 to 10,000 active EDI users worldwide. By year 2000, the community had grown to an estimated 410,000 users.

The conference also encouraged renewing and strengthening friendships among EDI users and suppliers worldwide. This was done through events like a cruise and dinner evening sponsored by the EDI Group. Over a period of several years, these friendships helped the EDI community to mature and grow.

International References

Many international EDI articles were published in the *EDI Forum* during 1988–1999. Countries and regions included in these reports were Asia Pacific, Australia, Canada, China, Europe, Finland, France, Global, Hong Kong, Japan, Korea, Mexico, Netherlands, Quebec, Singapore, South America, and the United Kingdom.

3. Charting the Course

"The secret of success is constancy to purpose."

Benjamin Disraeli, *Speech in London, 24 June 1872*

SEARCHING FOR DIRECTION

Customer Information Service Study

Reports on searches for direction relative to EDI for industries were included in chapter two's topics. This chapter summarizes the results of some searches made by specific companies. User reports were based on analysis, trial, and evaluation.

Not published outside the company was a "Customer Information Service Study" commissioned by United States Lines (USL) in 1982. USL, a company very active in TDCC ocean transportation EDI work groups in the 1970s and 80s, was a container ship company interested in knowing what their customers wanted most, considering the possibility of electronic data interchanges between USL and their customers. EDI, Inc was chosen to conduct the study; Ralph Notto was the principal investigator.

Thirty people at eighteen functional locations were interviewed. These were in three groups—six USL locations, seven shipper customers, and five forwarders and brokers.

During interviews with USL's customers in 1982, it was apparent that most had not previously heard of EDI, so it was required to clearly and concisely describe it before asking questions. The subsequent report revealed that at the top of customers' concern was, "The *arrival notice* is key to customer operational efficiency, and is required early enough to be useful." Many expressed that it was seldom early enough.

At that time, the arrival notice was a printed document sent from the ocean carrier to the receiver of the shipment. It was generally sent by mail or courier. In lieu of timely information, receivers searched the periodical *Commerce Business Daily* for schedules.

In EDI, the arrival notice is an X12 transaction set or EDIFACT message. Its abstract in the X12 standard is, "This transaction set can be used to provide all the information necessary for a consignee to receive a shipment including customs requirement, payments due, and estimated arrival date and time of shipment." In EDIFACT, "A message from the party providing forwarding and/or transport services to the party such as has been indicated in the contract, giving notice and details of the arrival of the consignment."

USL closed its company in the mid-1980s for reasons other than EDI. The study, however, indicated the value of EDI for improving customer service and EDI's potential application in marketing strategies. The executive summary from the study follows:

Executive Summary, USL Customer Information Service Study

November 30, 1982

The results of a study to determine the desirability of and requirements for a Customer Information System (CIS) are presented. Data was collected by interviews with a representative sample of USL customers and by observation and discussion of internal USL operations. Additional data was assembled through analysis of current and planned USL system developments, and by analysis of the state of technology.

The study shows clearly the existence of a demand for improved and timelier information to be provided to USL customers.

Several possible systems for providing improved customer information were analyzed and evaluated on a relative cost benefit basis. The analysis shows that a CIS can achieve an annual cost savings on the order $3,000,000 and provide a basis for attracting additional sales of ocean freight services. Cost for developing the recommended system is approximately $300,000.

The recommendations are:

The Customer Information System (CIS) should be implemented because it will produce a significant cost savings compared with the current system.

The EDI standards installed at USL and used for the ACI [Automated Carrier Interface] project should be extended to other applications such as arrival notices, status inquiries and replies, and other ocean documentation.

The CIS should be implemented for the arrival notice and status inquiries/replies as soon as possible; the other applications may have longer implementation schedules.

USL should reexamine the current database design to address timing and information requirements of customers (inclusion of key customer shipment-identifying-numbers, for example).

USL should develop a marketing strategy to exploit the sales potential of the CIS.

USL should drop consideration for charging the customer for the CIS because of negative market acceptance; the system is cost-effective without this factor.

EARLY INSIGHTS FROM OTHER TRIALS AND EVALUATIONS

In the period 1985-95, the techniques and findings from several corporate EDI initiatives were shared with others in the EDI community through articles published in *EDI Forum.* Summaries of seven articles follow, pointing out priorities, technique, recommendations, and results.

Systems Planning—The Key to Realizing EDI Benefits

(Rick Carlberg, Topco Associates, Inc., EDI Forum, 1990 Issue, pages 71-72])

Rick Carlberg stated that the key to satisfying management requirements for successful EDI implementation is in systems planning, which he defines as a strategic planning process that takes the business plan of the company and translates it into information requirements. In implementing EDI for processing 50,000 incoming purchase orders per year and integrating this with payment reconciliation, Rick's company achieved a cost savings of $650,000 per year. The EDI project cost was $300,000, and the payback period was less than one year.

He offered seven key points to consider when factoring EDI into a systems planning effort: focus on the EDI payoffs; survey your trading partners—what are their interests in EDI?; understand the EDI standards you plan to use—particularly as they affect your master file contents and application systems; recognize the need for strong controls in your EDI operation; recognize the barriers to effective implementation of EDI; address these barriers in your plans; factor into your management information system capacity plan the cost of EDI hardware and software; and obtain management backing and endorsement of your system plan.

EDI at Sears: Past, Present, and Future

(Lance Dailey, Sears Merchandising Group; Tom Douglas, Sears Technology Services Inc., EDI Forum, 1990 Issue, pages 81-89)

Sears had used proprietary format EDI for over two decades; it began aggressively implementing X12 EDI in 1988. The motivation for the change had been due to the nature of its trading partners, many of which are small companies. But both large and small companies hesitate to implement EDI to accommodate only one customer, even when that one customer is Sears.

Public EDI standards would also increase the types of business information Sears would communicate. These types related to three key business strategies: increase focus on customer service, reduce cost of operations, and enhance relationships with suppliers.

One of the revisions due to EDI and possible at Sears was that store floor space allocated to inventory would become only 20%, compared with 50% before.

Sears processed 540,000 purchase orders during fourth quarter 1990, representing 63% of the total volume and sixty-five EDI trading partners. At the same time, trading partners representing 20% additional volume were testing the system. This all happened since the first trading partner was brought into the system in June 1989.

850—Purchase Order: Each transaction set has an identification number [850] and a name [Purchase Order]. The identification number is always included in a transmission, the name is never included.

X12 transaction sets used by Sears at that time were 850 (Purchase Order), 856 (Shipment Notice), 860 (Purchase Order Change), 870 (Order Status Report), 869 (Order Status Inquiry), 810 (Invoice), and 997 (Functional Acknowledgment).

Sears also used the X12 820 (Payment Order/Remittance Advice) and rail and motor transaction sets.

Functionally, Sears used EDI in its management of all aspects for the business—merchandising support, order processing, payment, and logistics. It recognizes effective use of EDI as a requirement for providing better service.

EDI at Ciba-Geigy Corporation: A Catalyst for Change and Improvement in Purchasing

(Ralph Bufkin, Purchasing Superintendent, McIntosh Alabama Plant CIBA-GEIGY, EDI Forum, 1991 Issue, No. 1, pages 80-83)

At a very large chemical plant in McIntosh, Alabama, CIBA-GEIGY began implementing EDI in 1988 for purchasing and other transactions. They processed 50,000 purchase orders per year with a total of 200,000 line items. Orders were classified into five categories—raw materials and packaging, material release order (MRO) purchases, plant supplies and services, capital, and construction.

Bufkin wrote that several questions were pertinent to deriving a strategic plan for EDI: Which transaction sets will be utilized; in what order will they be implemented; what schedule is required or desired?

He said that the strategic plan was summarized on one page that listed the transaction sets to be implemented and the target dates. The plan was made available to the three interested groups—employee, company, and customer.

The transaction sets selected and direction of flow with respect to CIBA-GEIGY were the X12 850 (Purchase Order–Send), 810 (Invoice–Receive), 860 (Purchase Order Change–Send), 855 (Purchase Order Acknowledgment–Receive), 863 (Certificate of Analysis/Report of Test Results–Receive), and 848 (Material Safety Data Sheet [MSDS]–Receive).

> **MRO:** Material release order purchases

The MRO category was chosen for first implementation because the category accounted for 60% of the total orders. A group of the top seventy-five MRO suppliers were invited to a one-day meeting in October 1987. Of these, fifteen stated that they were already EDI-capable, and an additional thirty-five said that they would be able to perform EDI within one year.

He reported that they were EDI operational with one trading partner by June 1988, thirty-nine trading partners one year later, and sixty-four by June 1990.

He reported that in addition to benefits in speed, accuracy, and productivity, the benefits to the McIntosh plant were that it placed buyers in control, was user oriented, included a quality control process feature, and, most of all, was a sound business method.

He said that success factors involve: understanding the transactions, developing a plan with a timetable, identifying customers (to participate), communicating the plan to the team, documenting progress, recognizing efforts and plateaus, and making business decisions (as required).

Electronic Data Interchange in the U.S. Government: Active Ingredient of Electronic Commerce

[Bruce McConnell, Senior Policy Analyst, Office of Information and Regulatory Affairs, (Office of Management and Budgets), EDI Forum, 1991 Issue, No. 1, pages 77-79]

This article was an excerpt from "A Five Year Plan for Meeting the Automatic Data Processing and Telecommunications Needs of the Federal Government (November 1990)." McConnell summarized what federal agencies were planning to do in EDI, listed issues of electronic commerce, and presented the federal government's strategy for implementing EDI.

He reported that the percentages of federal government EDI projects by type were 49% business and contracting, 23% regulatory, 21% case management, and 7% transport.

He said that the Department of Defense is the government's biggest EDI implementer, making up about one third of total existing and projected applications. These involved such transaction sets as request for quotation, invoice, proposal evaluation, purchase order, price list, delivery order, and shipping instruction.

McConnell said that the key issues that federal agencies face when moving to electronic commerce are legal issues, EDI and computer security issues, and issues related to evolving standards.

He reported that the federal government had already received significant benefit by implementing electronic funds transfer (EFT). Non-financial business transactions would also be beneficial, he said. Targeted for early conversion to electronic formats were: material inspection and receiving report, purchase order, invoice, and progress payment.

He stated that federal agencies must be encouraged to move in concert with industry to save money and to promote progress.

A History of ASAP® at Baxter Healthcare: The Journey from Proprietary to X12 Standards

[Rachel Foerster, ASAP/EDI Market Manager for Baxter Healthcare Corporation, EDI Forum, 1991 Issue, No. 1, pages 96-100]

Baxter Healthcare Corporation, formerly American Hospital Supply Corporation, began EDI in 1981 with a proprietary standard and began using X12 in 1986. Rachel Foerster reported that the activity had been extremely successful and that her company was communicating electronically with over 4,000 hospitals. She said the key is that technology be utilized to support business objectives formulated to meet customer needs.

A significant point in her article is that finding the lowest price is not the only element of keeping costs down. Other cost elements such as inventory investment, lead time, order quantity, transportation, receiving, space, obsolescence, back order handling, etc. nearly equal the cost of the supplies themselves. (This, she said, was a theory of Admiral Lee of Stanford Medical Center that he verified by analysis.) She said that her company worked with Admiral Lee to develop an overall systems approach to address total costs.

She reported that orders that used to take five days to process were done in seventeen minutes with EDI.

Closing the EDI Loop at Baxter

[Daniel L Browning, Director of EDI for Baxter Healthcare Corporation, EDI Forum, Volume 6, No. 1 (1993), pages 42-45]

Dan Browning, also with Baxter, offered information about how to approach such an immense task as implementing EDI between an eight-billion-dollar corporation and its trading partners: "When I became responsible for Baxter Healthcare Corporation's EDI strategy, I dutifully went to an EDI seminar to learn the 'Principles of EDI.' I remember hearing many of the recommendations you hear so often from the sages in the EDI community: name an EDI champion; form a cross-functional steering committee; prepare a strategy; seek and maintain senior management commitment. Being an EDI rookie who did not know any better, I proceeded to follow this advice. And today I am happy to report that it works."

Baxter Healthcare sells to doctors, hospitals, and other healthcare providers many of the supplies they need to deliver healthcare services to patients.

Dan said that Baxter uses EDI with both customers and suppliers, and for many years previously had used proprietary EDI before shifting to EDI based on public standards.

Dan continued:

> The first stage was the EDI strategy. We already had an EDI champion (a top-level manager who believed in and promoted the use of EDI within the company), but we didn't have a steering committee. So we put together a high-level steering committee representing technology, marketing, international, finance, manufacturing, distribution, and treasury functions. Five of the members were corporate officers. Representatives from internal audit were added when we started installing EDI software.

Dan reported that in Baxter's "Mature EDI Stage":

> Measurements play a key role in the quality process that pervades Baxter today.
>
> We break the total cost into cost components and then measure the cost per kilo character, tracking it over time. All of these measurements tie into our quality objective of reducing costs, cycle time, and errors.
>
> Benchmarking the EDI process with other experienced organizations can also help identify the best demonstrated practice, and give the EDI manager a goal to achieve and then surpass. As in pole vaulting, you must constantly *raise the bar.*

Also very significant is Baxter's emphasis on EDI education:

> Our EDI organization put together internal educational seminars using both external and internal resources. In many cases we tailored the education to the appropriate organization level within the business unit. For instance, one message is suitable for a controller, while a slightly different message should go to the manager of an accounts payable function. In tandem with the education, we would also work on an individual cost-benefit analysis for each business unit.

We negotiated for discounted tuition at various public EDI educational seminars so that our suppliers could get the training they needed at minimum cost.

We used the relationship we had with our Value-Added Networks to educate suppliers.

EDI at Apple Computer

[Ann Marie Jasse, Apple Computer, Inc., EDI Forum, 1990 Issue, pages 59-61]

The Apple Computer Company experienced a reduction in its operational transaction cost from $1.07 per purchase order before EDI to $0.27 after introduction of EDI. This did not take into account further cost reductions expected from lowering inventory levels.

Ms. Jasse shared the following suggestions, drawing upon Apple's experiences with EDI:

Understand that EDI is business-driven and not technology-driven.

Keep the scope of a pilot narrow enough in order to accomplish goals within a relatively short time period.

"Have a tested (non-EDI) relationship with your first EDI trading partner.

Test with a partner that has implemented EDI with more than one trading partner.

Choose a trading partner that shares your long-term commitment to EDI.

Meet with your chosen first EDI partner's other trading partners.

Continually educate your stakeholders and your customers.

Clearly define your assumptions with your trading partner in terms of standards and technical issues as well as business issues and objectives.

Bring your stakeholders into the EDI implementation process at an early stage.

Do not underestimate the tweaking that will be required for the software.

Be aware of the many requirements necessary to fully integrate the application to the host system.

Understand that EDI is more than a piece of translation software.

Develop and obtain a consensus on a corporate EDI strategy that encompasses both technical and business issues.

PLOTTING THE TREND, U.S. AND CANADA

The EDI Group

From its founding issue in 1988, The *EDI Forum* annually included articles about the state of EDI. These were based on surveys conducted by EDI Research, Inc. Both the *Forum* and *Research* were products of The EDI Group.

The contributions of The EDI Group toward the advancement of EDI have been enormous since Dan Ferguson and Ned Hill founded the company in 1987.

Their EDI research, based on sound statistical practices, provided 1) The required analysis and related motivation for driving EDI by hub companies, and 2) Data used by companies in the EDI service community in their product definition, evaluation, and resource allocation processes.

They offered the first courses in EDI. Their "Principles of EDI" course included a segment about restructuring payment agreements between buyers and sellers in win/win scenarios where both sides received substantial gains.

Their *EDI Forum—The Journal of Electronic Data Interchange* (which in 1994 changed its name to *The Journal of Electronic Commerce*, offering a wider forum) provided in-depth articles by many authors. This is an absolutely mandatory service required by a professional community.

Their best practices workshops provided an environment and resources where synergism developed as participants learned from each other and from The EDI Group.

This topic quotes some of the finding of the research relative to the U.S. and Canada. For more information, see *EDI Forum*, issues 1989-1999.

The Canadian section in this chapter also quotes from the objectives and findings from early research performed by Canadians in 1992.

United States

In 1988, thirteen years after the publication of the first public U.S. EDI standards, the general EDI Research survey conclusions were: "EDI Is here to stay in the U.S.!" Out of 1,094 U.S. respondents, 348 are using EDI (users) or planning to use EDI (planners) within two years; a full 32% of the managers were surveyed. Further, U.S. EDI users and planners expect significant growth in 1) EDI trading partners, 2) EDI document volume, 3) EDI sites, and 4) use of EDI in international trade."[25]

Reported in the same article: the research showed that almost 47% of those responding to the survey stated their firm's decision to use EDI was for "quick response and access to information." Also high in the list of reasons were cost efficiency (20%), customer request (19%), speed up and reduce paperwork (12%), and accuracy (10%). These statistics were derived from the survey question, "What are the main reasons influencing your firm's decision to use EDI?" Two responses per respondent were permitted.

The researchers also found: "Evidence of Commitment to EDI—We find evidence that Fortune 1000 firms are committed to EDI at a significant level that will insure solid EDI market growth in four key areas: 1) Surveyed firms anticipate significant growth in the number of EDI trading partners they deal with over the next two years; 2) Surveyed firms expect significant growth in the volume of documents processed via EDI; 3) Surveyed firms expect the number of sites at which EDI is carried out will increase over the next two years; and 4) Surveyed firms believe EDI has the potential to replace documents in the paper-intensive area of international trade."

In the years following 1988, the EDI Group continued to confidently predict the growth of EDI in terms of number of participating companies, distribution of sizes of corporate participants, business functions addressed with EDI, number of EDI trading partners per company, reasons for participation, types of EDI installations, uses of the EDI service community, and other factors. Research subscribers used this information as a basis for enhancing EDI products and services, or to assess the state of readiness among potential EDI trading partners to expand the use of EDI. In 1989 these subscribers were: Ameritech, Applied Communications Inc, AT&T, Baxter Healthcare Corporation, First Chicago, GE Information Services, Harris Bank, IBM, McDonnell Douglas Corporation, Michigan National Bank, Sears Communications Company, Security Pacific Bank, Sterling Software (Ordernet), Tandem Computers Inc, and the Royal Bank of Canada.[26]

VANs: Value Added Networks

Also in the 1989 article[27], the researchers included a graph of the expected growth of EDI, expressed in

[25] Daniel M. Ferguson and Ned C. Hill, *EDI Forum*, Founding Issue, page 28, EDI Group, Oak Park IL, 1988.

[26] D.J. Masson and Ned C. Hill, "The State of US EDI in 1988," *EDI Forum*, 1989 Issue, "The State of US EDI: 1989," page 15, EDI Group, Oak Park IL, 1989.

[27] Ibid, page 24.

terms of sales expected for the U.S. EDI service community as shown in **Figure 7**. These revenues include per-transaction charges (included in the pricing scheme used by VANs and banks) and purchases for software, hardware, and consulting.

In 1989 and projecting four years into the future, the researchers predicted an annual compound growth rate of 26.3%, as visually indicated in **Figure 7**.

How close was the prediction? The 1993 figure ($880 million) is an estimate made in 1989. Continuing each year, the *EDI Forum* included a "State of EDI" statistical report. The estimate for 1993 was adjusted down or up, depending on the best information at the time. The "downs" related to downturns in the economy. The "ups" related to economic upturns. In 1993 when more accuracy is expected because the date of prediction is during the same year for the prediction, the estimate for the year was revised to 1,242[28]—one and a quarter billion dollars, so the estimate made in 1988 was conservative.

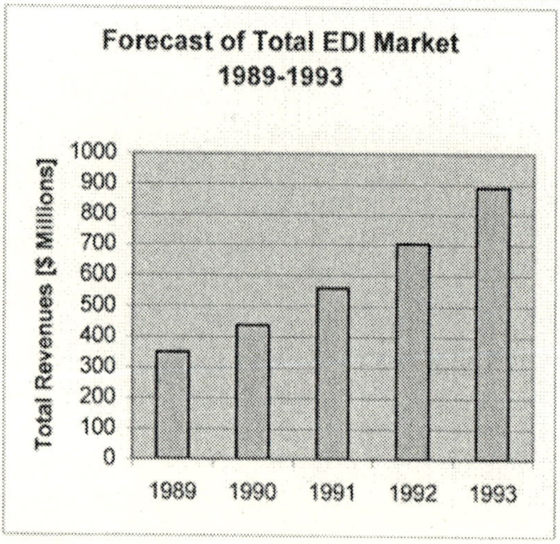

Figure 7. Forecast of EDI Market [1989]

[28]D.J. Masson and Daniel M. Ferguson, "The State of EDI in the US in 1993," *EDI Forum*, Volume 6, 1993, No. 4, pages 8-11.

The researchers had the following to say *in* 1993 about EDI:

EDI for many companies is well past the point of no return. EDI has become a mission-critical application tool, serving as a catalyst for the restructuring of U.S. business enterprises. The market for EDI products and services is growing at a rapid pace and promises to show continued growth in the future. We draw these conclusions from the 1993 U.S. EDI research data: The U.S. EDI market revenue growth is potentially explosive in the near term; EDI is becoming recognized as an important focus/discipline of data processing in most larger companies; the EDI market (users and vendors) is learning how to add EDI trading partners and transaction sets cheaper and faster; error rate and cycle time reductions are high priorities for EDI companies—EDI is playing a critical role in business process redesign intended to achieve those priorities; the pyramid of important EDI users is thickening at the top due to new hubs and an increased level of mid-level companies that have the potential to become hubs.

In the 1994 Research report, Dan Ferguson made the following summaries:[29]

Why are they doing it? Companies that are driving EDI, do it for the 40% cycle-time improvements, 30% error-rate reductions, and $5.00-per-document-converted cost savings.

Why are they really doing it? Two-thirds of all companies doing EDI initially were forced to do it. One-third of all companies doing EDI today still do it only because they have no choice.

What does it cost? The total cumulative investment in doing EDI is at minimum 1.0% of sales in a $250 million company. To drive EDI with your trading partners requires a staff of, at minimum, three to five people.

Where is it done? EDI is done at application sites, i.e., plants, sales offices, warehouses. EDI is generally not done at headquarters, unless the function doing EDI, such as finance, exists only at headquarters.

Why do it now? EDI is being driven by EDI hubs, which will continue to be the essential driving forces in the foreseeable future. EDI hubs see the competitive advantage of leading EDI.

---

[29] Daniel M. Ferguson, *EDI Forum*, "The Real Facts About EDI in 1994," Volume 7, 1994, No. 4, pages 8-11.

Who does it best? The best companies in EDI—those companies with the highest cycle time or error rate improvements—are those companies converting the most trading partners or business documents to EDI.

How do we win at doing it? The best companies in EDI have discovered or adopted business practices which help them do more EDI better, faster, and cheaper in the execution of business processes critical to the success of their business.

Since the 1970s, the motivation toward EDI was based on the desire to reduce or eliminate paperwork. A summary comment in Dan Ferguson's 1997 report[30] is especially important to absorb and understand, "If you invest enough dollars and people in EDI, you can expect to reap significant cycle-time, error-rate, and transactional improvements within your company. You will, however, have to convert a sizable proportion of your trading partners and paper documents to EDI before you can reap a substantial amount of these benefits. Further, the conversion to EDI requires that many documents, not just one or two, be changed to EDI exchanges and that the EDI exchanges end up computer-to-computer and not computer-to-paper."

Canada

EDI Use in Canada in 1992

To determine the extent of EDI use in Canada in 1992, Yvan Lauzon, EDI coordinator for the Quebec Department of Communications, and Carla Botting, a student in the Faculty of Management at the University of Manitoba, led a survey team that included the EDI Council of Canada, the EDI Institute of Quebec, and EDI vendors. The survey was nationwide.[31]

Context of the Survey

Given the increase in international trade and the U.S./Canada/Mexico Free Trade Agreement, EDI has become a necessity in Canadian business. Whether in multinational corporations or small businesses, Canadians are finding out that emphasis must be placed on efficiency and profitability in

[30]Daniel M. Ferguson, *EDI Forum*, Volume 11, 1998, No. 1, "The Real Facts About EDI in 1997," pages 18-25.

[31]Quoted paragraphs are from Yvan Lauzon and Carla Botting, "Just the Facts: 1992 Survey of EDI in Canada," *EDI Forum*, 1993 Issue No. 1, pages 18-23, EDI Group, Oak Park IL, 1988.

order to stay competitive. Strategic alliances, reinforced ties with business partners, and better customer service have become the rule rather than the exception. Fortunately, when used to full advantage EDI can help increase business effectiveness.

Since the early 1980s, EDI has been a part of the Canadian business landscape. EDI started out in the pharmaceutical and food industries—with the first Canadian EDI transmission between Drug Trading and Procter & Gamble—then spread to automotive manufacturing, transportation, and other industrial sectors.

From its inception in 1985, the EDI Council of Canada (EDICC) has endeavored to monitor the process of implementation in each industry segment within Canada. Accordingly, in April 1992 the council undertook a broad-based survey of EDI use, in close cooperation with the EDI Institute of Quebec and major vendors of EDI services. The objective was to obtain as accurate a picture as possible of the present use of EDI in Canadian firms, consistent with the time and resources available.

Objectives of the Survey:

The survey was designed to profile efficient EDI users and to determine the number of Canadian firms using EDI; EDI implementation status in each firm, including typical applications, implementation process, and types of trading partners; the relative importance of EDI in each firm in terms of overall volumes and types of transactions; EDI benefits, problems, and factors of success, in the opinion of the person in charge of managing the EDI implementation; the present technology base, including translation software, communication methods, processing platforms, and other related technologies used; the level of assistance required by EDI users.

The survey team concluded that:

With the globalization of the economy and a lingering recession, it becomes mandatory for firms to focus on competitiveness.

EDI is one of the most promising information technologies for enhancing the efficiency of firms by allowing rapid and economic transmission of business documents. With only 1,650 EDI users out of more than 800,000 companies, EDI is just starting in Canada. The same is true in all the other industrialized countries; the United States, for example, has only 26,000 EDI users out of more than 6,250,000 companies [1992].

EDI Research Report for State of EDI in Canada in 1993

Using a similar technique as for the research reports for the U.S., the EDI Group conducted surveys in Canada and made estimates of Canada's current EDI situation and predictions for the future.[32]

In the preceding Lauzon/Botting reference, the number of Canadian companies was estimated as 800,000 while the estimate for U.S. companies was 6,250,000, ratio: 1 to 7.8. The EDI Research reports shows the Canadian 1993 EDI investment as C$130 million and is in a similar ratio to the estimated U.S. dollar investment after adjusting for currency values.

In the same Ferguson/Masson 1993 Canadian EDI Survey report, the average ratings of respondents indicated on a scale of zero (no value) to five (very valuable) that EDI benefits to a firm are: improved customer service—4.31; improved accuracy of data—4.25; reduced clerical error—4.15; faster information access—4.07; decreased administrative cost—3.87; decreased delivery time—3.78; improved cash flow—3.70; ties into corporate strategy—3.67; and lower inventory cost—3.16.

For the 1993 *Canadian* report, the researchers concluded with:

> EDI for many companies in both Canada and the United States is well past the point of no return. EDI has become a mission-critical application, serving as a catalyst for the restructuring of North American business enterprises. The market for EDI products and services is also growing at a rapid pace, and promises continued future growth. We draw several high-level conclusions from our research: the Canadian EDI market shows signs of potential fast growth in the near term; EDI is becoming recognized as an important focus/discipline of data processing in most larger companies; the EDI market (users and vendors) is learning how to add EDI trading partners and transaction sets more quickly and at lower cost; the error rate and cycle time reductions achieved by EDI companies are impressive, and EDI is playing a critical role in business process redesign; and the pyramid of important EDI users is thickening at the top as new hubs and an increased level of mid-level companies (potential hubs) enter the community.

[32]Daniel M. Ferguson and D.J. Masson, "The State of EDI in Canada in 1993," *EDI Forum,* Volume 7, 1994, No. 1, pages 20-23.

4. Forging an EDI Service Industry

"We choose to do [these] things,
not because they are easy,
but because they are hard."
John F. Kennedy, *Address at Rice University, 1962*

COMPONENTS

There are four primary components of the EDI service industry: addressing products and services for communications, software, consultation, and financial EDI.

A fifth component is data encryption and authentication services, which are always essential for financial EDI and important for other applications as well, especially when the Internet is used for data communications.

There are other important components like specialized publications, EDI outsourcing services, EDI education, and EDI research.

This chapter focuses on the four primary and the encryption/authentication components. There can be no effective and practical EDI without standard protocols and ease of use for data communications services; there would be slow growth in use of EDI if each participant had to write its own EDI software; there would likely be unrealized potential without the vision provided by EDI consultants; and the electronic sequence of events would not completely match the corresponding business cycle if financial EDI were omitted. Encryption and authentication address the security requirement.

EDI VANS

Zero to Billion Dollar Industry in Fourteen Years[33]

> **VAN**: Value Added Network

Credit the EDI Value Added Network (VAN) as a major reason why EDI communications are as easy as they are. Credit the visionaries, salesmen, and technologists for taking technology quite primitive by current standards and changing it to build the connections that are making business more efficient around the world.

By 1984, leaders of data communications service companies understood the potential for a data communications service that had known objectives, but lacked the details of a specification or standard. Sensing a need and recognizing that EDI VAN service represented a natural outgrowth of services already in place, several companies independently committed resources for development, and assigned a "can-do" person to "make it so."

The ultimate result several years later was several competing, but also interlinking, EDI VANs. Customer needs were served, and a worldwide EDI VAN industry emerged. From its 1984 beginnings, EDI VAN service had become a billion-dollar-per-year industry in fourteen years.

To be sure, there were other enablers, like VANs, that just seemed to happen at the right time for the beginning EDI community. These included attractively priced items like microprocessor (PC) systems and software for developers, standardized modems, and competing EDI software systems that "understood" each other.

The VAN service linked the microprocessor-modem-EDI software combination at each user site to any other EDI-capable site. With VAN service acting as a buffer in time, the sender and receiver could work with independent communications schedules, enabling each to optimize equipment and personnel schedules. That helped to optimize both equipment and staff resources. Yes, there are also EDI sites that use point-to-point communications, but the VAN advantage is that all communications are done with a single telephone call from the user's system to the VAN. As a result of that call, the VAN forwards the user's outbound data to appropriate recipients even when any particular recipient is not a member of the same VAN. In the same telephone call, the user retrieves from the VAN any inbound data

[33] Adapted from Ralph W. Notto, "EDI VANs: Zero to Billion Dollar industry In 14 Years," *EDI Forum*, Volume 11 Number 1, pages 100-102, EDI Group, Oak Park IL, 1998.

ready from others. There are many additional services available from a VAN, and there are several competing VANs insuring that prices are competitive.

This topic offers some insight into the VAN beginnings and identifies some of the people that made this possible. The purpose is to document how such a significant service industry came to be, and what role individuals have in making something this enormous in scope happen. Eleven VANs and a key person at each are recognized. Six of these are described with some detail.

To visualize the significance of the accomplishment to introduce EDI VAN service by 1983-84, take note of the differences in technologies since 1983. Comparing with the turn of the century: The hard drives for PCs were introduced with only ten million bytes compared with the multi-gigabyte drives in this century; the random access memory (RAM) on PCs was 320,000 or 640,000 bytes compared with more than a hundred million bytes in 2001.

EDI: Electronic Data Interchange

VAN: Value Added Network

DOS: Disk Operating System [Subsequently replaced with Windows]—both are software products of Microsoft Corporation

Async: Asynchronous [protocol for data transmissions]

Bisync: Binary synchronous

Baud: Rate of transmission in binary digits per second

Byte: Eight binary digits, used to define characters and other symbols

Modem: A device used to connect a computer with a telephone line or other type of electronic service

UCS: Uniform Communication Standard (Grocery Industry EDI)

PC: Microprocessor (personal computer)

In the 1980s and 1990s, telephone lines were used. By the turn of the century, many participants switched to cable or wireless communications. Since EDI software and EDI communications are independent modules, each can be updated independently without affecting the other.

Many of the early installations (like today) used PCs for EDI installation, and PCs with MS-DOS operating systems were newly introduced in 1982-83. Without the availability of PCs, the growth of EDI would have been much slower, since mainframe and midrange software was not oriented toward the EDI requirement at that time, and programming costs were higher. Indeed, many companies (if not most) worked without computers before the introduction of PCs.

Pre-EDI communications technology and associated software were oriented toward time-sharing schemes that were different from the peer-to-peer requirement defined for EDI. Effective modem standardization was only beginning about 1984. Typical communications protocols were 600-baud async and 2400-baud bisync.

Some actions toward creating EDI VAN services were:

MCI

MCI's EDI*NET started from Tymshare in 1981. MacDonald Douglas acquired EDI*NET about 1984 and aggressively marketed it for several years. British Telecom (BT) acquired it from MacDonald Douglas, and MCI has it as a result of merger activities with BT.

Paul Olson, in the autumn of 1981, was a branch manager for Tymshare. At the time, the computer time-sharing business—Tymshare's expertise—was entering the classic "decline" stage of the product/market life cycle. This created urgency for new products to sell.

Tymshare already was selling and supporting an electronic mail product, OnTyme. Looking to his customers to gain an understanding of their future requirements, Olson was introduced to UCS by David Graves at General Mills. UCS is the grocery industry EDI standard, which is compatible with ANSI X12 standards, and it includes the transaction sets specifically used by that industry.

From that introduction he went on to work with Paul Lemme at Sales Force, a food broker company. Olson said that Lemme pushed hard for Tymshare to provide operational service by December 23, 1981, so that Sales Force would be on schedule for its participation in the UCS pilot. Olson, a former football professional, had the equivalent of a "two minute drill" in that he was almost ready, but had less than a day to tie everything together. He was charged to get the most from technologies not quite ready for EDI. With help from sixteen-year-old computer whiz Brent Geske and a Texas Instruments intelligent terminal (a forerunner to the microcomputer) and clever integration with Tymshare's standard services, success was achieved. In fact, it was achieved at precisely 3:45 p.m. December 23, 1981, fifteen minutes ahead of the absolute deadline.

EDI*NET went on to service many thousands of customers.

Paul Olson subsequently became president of the Network Services Group of Sterling Commerce, Inc.

Sterling Commerce

Bill Plumb

Sterling acquired Informatics, which had previously acquired ORDERNET Services.

Bill Plumb, president of ORDERNET, assigned Brad Sharp the task of expanding ORDERNET Services' repertoire to include EDI VAN communications. ORDERNET beginning in 1981 managed a proprietary VAN for service to the pharmaceutical industry. In 1982, they added a second proprietary VAN named Eagle and used it to service the hardware industry. Their first standard EDI VAN initiative, 1983-84, was to provide the EDI communications service for the North American Wholesale Grocers Association (NAWGA). The project included six pilot companies to communicate with already EDI-capable companies like Kraft and Brach Candy. Because this was the grocery industry, the EDI standard used was also UCS. The implementation employed two IBM (186) PCs equipped with modems connected to separate telephone lines and a cable linkage between the two PCs. One PC provided async communications power for the NAWGA companies, and the other provided bisync communications to larger companies. This scheme lasted one or two years until the PC arrangement was replaced with mainframe software. Thinking back about it, Sharp said that the 186s were equipped with 10 megabytes of hard disk and 320,000 bytes of RAM.

The NAWGA pilot was successful and ultimately resulted in many more companies joining the UCS/EDI community.

Brad Sharp later became president of the Interchange Software Group at Sterling Commerce.

General Electric Information Systems (GEIS)

General Electric had a time-sharing service prior to the advent of EDI that they offered with industry orientations. Because of EDI initiatives in Canada in 1983-84 involving a concerted effort in the grocery industry spearheaded by Provigo to link grocery distributors, manufacturers, and brokers, General Electric's standard EDI service began there when Jack Brooks sold many of the potential participants on using the VAN service provided by GE Canada and based on their time-sharing service in place. The technical fulfillment for this was managed by Don Quan. The service was named EDI XPRESS. As EDI XPRESS grew and because of the readiness of the X12 EDI standards and significant interest in the

United States, Dave Foster at General Electric in the United States (GEIS) coordinated with GE Canada to pick up and enhance the service to address the X12 standards and extend the service to other industries. They changed the name to EDI EXPRESS and began servicing other industries in 1985. At the turn of the century, EDI EXPRESS already services tens of thousands of EDI sites in the retail, grocery, automotive, and other industries worldwide.

GEIS created EDI PC and a mainframe EDI software product, and used these to implement EDI "hub"[34] environments. It also permitted connections to its VAN via other EDI software products and other VANs.

Don Quan of GE Canada and John Magnino of EDI, Inc preparing for an industry trade show–Don managed the technical fulfillment of GE Canada's EDI communication service; John provided hot line service for EDI, Inc's software customers that used EDI XPRESS.

IBM Global Services

Jim Crouse was the service administrator for the IBM Information Network beginning in 1982. That organization was formed in 1981 to provide network services for corporate clients that had multiple sites. The service managed user virtual networks for intra-corporate data communications. Crouse's role as service administrator included the responsibility to launch new services.

The first inter-company service was the Insurance Value Added Network Service (IVANS) for the insurance industry in the early 1980s. Its purpose was to electronically link the small insurance agencies with much larger insurance companies. This required an electronic mailboxing service and formatting standard specifically oriented toward insurance.

By 1985, IBM had operational all of the technology and facility needed for creating an EDI VAN. This was first accomplished with industrial supplier clients. Next, the IBM Information Network and Sears Communications Company (SCC) with its retail supplier clients jointly formed Advantis

[34] An EDI "hub" in this context is a large company or organization that is proactive in its use of EDI expansion and already has at least one hundred active EDI trading partners.

in 1992, forging a worldwide EDI VAN service. SCC was the vision of Gary Weiss, who had a role in the formation of Advantis. At the time of the joint venture, SCC serviced 10,000 clients with their VAN, including Sears and Anheuser Busch trading partners.

IBM Global Services includes all of the former Advantis. "Global" in the service name aptly indicates the vision for this service, since by the turn of the century they had over 1,000 points of presence worldwide.

Harbinger

Tyco Howle founded Harbinger in 1983 to service banking clients by providing cash management information to small business customers. The banks transmitted data to a Harbinger Tandem-based computer system, and Harbinger provided this data online to each pertinent bank client. This was a mailboxing service beginning about 1985.

By 1987, Harbinger provided PC software for reviewing this data by the small business customers. Also during 1987-88, banks asked Harbinger if EDI would have an impact on banking. After investigating it, Howle concluded that EDI would be procurement-driven rather than bank-driven.

By this time, Harbinger already had an established communications service with enabling software for small users. Howle sensed that the potential EDI VAN market had similar needs as those he was already providing. He has recognized and met the challenge to make pervasive solutions for companies of all sizes so that electronic commerce is a reality. During the 1990s, Harbinger grew at a compounded rate of 50% per year. By year 2000, it services over 40,000 companies. It continues to provide the VAN services implemented on Tandem computers and also offers an Internet Value Added Service (IVAS) implemented with Hewlett Packard and Sun equipment. This was started in 1994 in a venture with Bell South.

Kleinschmidt

Harry Gaples, president of Kleinschmidt, already had by the early 1980s an impressive data communications service specializing in rail-car location information gathering and reporting. In 1984-85, when looking for additional applications to use available capacity on Kleinschmidt's Tandem computers, he had two new clients who wanted technically similar but content-dissimilar data communications services. RCA wanted to send orders to suppliers and receive acknowledgments; Segrams wanted to receive sales data from distributors.

In both cases and also for car location, Gaples looked at the service as customer-defined data communications requirements between the customer and its trading partners. From that viewpoint, he said that he started implementing the EDI standard before he knew it was a standard. This is not surprising since there were not many EDI standards-capable companies in 1984-85. Gaples looked at Kleinschmidt's role to be the middle entity for data format conversion according to the varying needs of data senders and their trading partners.

The Kleinschmidt service is respected by clients for its reliability and the timely transmission of important and relevant information from source to user.

There Were Others

Other EDI VANs began during the same time period 1984 to 1986. These included the EDI VAN services offered by:

Company	EDI VAN Champion During Formative Period
ATT	Gary Dalton
Bell Canada	Bob Law
RAilinc	Association of American Railroads
Sprint	Michael Mansouri
TranSettlements	Hank Lavery

These VANs also grew from other communications services offered by those companies. They continue to offer EDI VAN service in 2000. They have participated in similar growth rates as the other VANs, their contemporaries in the beginning and today.

The Internet

The business community followed the academic community by a few years in use of the Internet for EDI. In response to a 1993 survey by The EDI Group, less than 5% of the respondents indicated any interest in employing the Internet in EDI communications processes. Interest changed rapidly, but implementation lagged. The concern was security and timeliness of delivery.

Hub: An EDI "hub" is a large company or organization that is proactive in its use of EDI expansion and has at least 100 active EDI trading partners.
XML: eXtensible Markup Language
EDI: Electronic Data Interchange
HTML: Hypertext Markup Language
SCM: Supply Chain Management,
CRM: Customer Relationship Management
ERP: Enterprise Resource Planning software

Relative to EDI in the academic community, the Internet is used almost exclusively for transmission of EDI-formatted student transcripts, but the data is encrypted.

In conjunction with EDI services, VANS have offered Web-based forms processing services connecting large (Hub) EDI users to their small to mid-sized trading partners. The concept includes form processing for the small users and EDI communications between a hub and the VAN. The concept is attractive for some small users while others consider it a duplication of effort, since they still are required to get data from the form to their internal automated processes.

Expect the Internet to have a larger role for EDI data communications in the business community as the hub companies gain confidence relative to the security and timeliness issues, VANs include more Internet services and innovations in their repertoires, and consideration is shown for the small to mid-sized companies' internal processing and control problems.

XML—Is it the future?

With the introduction of the Internet, another data formatting standard, XML, began to emerge, and it appeared to offer EDI some competition. Vegard Nervik[35] offered this topic to put the "competitors" in a proper perspective:

---

[35] This XML topic was contributed in year 2000 by Vegard Nervik, chief technical officer, Emanio, Oslo, Norway.

Yes, I believe XML is the future. I also strongly believe that EDI, HTML, SCM, CRM, and ERP are the future. All of this may be very confusing, because there are so many terms and so many different approaches.

Let me try to explain XML and its role by using a metaphor.

Imagine you are a young child again and you have just been sent to the corner grocery store to buy fruits and vegetables for your mother. Though you are very proud that your mother has trusted you with this important assignment, you are still too young to memorize a grocery list and you are not yet able to read. Therefore, your mother writes a shopping list that you bring to the store.

This shopping list is in English. As you walk to the store, you look at the shopping list several times, but you cannot make anything of it. It even seems to change every time you look at it. It contains only letters and numbers, you can't associate anything with it, and it is totally incomprehensible to you.

You get to the store, properly greet Shopkeeper Jones, and hand him the shopping list. He browses the list and assigns it to a clerk. The clerk hastens to get half a dozen apples from a shelf, picks tomatoes from another shelf, and weighs the tomatoes. They weigh exactly two pounds as specified in the list. The clerk brings the items back and puts them on the counter. Trips between the shelves and counter continue until all items have been retrieved. Finally, Cashier Smith records all the merchandise amounts into the cash register. You pay the appropriate amount, five dollars. You take all the bags and carry them home.

When you get home, you give the bags of merchandise and receipt to your mother who was anxiously waiting for you. Your mother checks the receipt and the merchandise and with a great smile she gives you a lollipop and a hug—to the best child who got it all right.

A series of events have happened here, and it is really important to distinguish them and relate them.

Does the shopping list tell the clerk where to find the apples? — No.

Does the shopping list make the clerk get the apples? — No.

Does the shopping list weigh the tomatoes? — No.

Does the shopping list calculate the price? — No (but it might stipulate it, so that enough money is brought).

Does the shopping list hand over the money? — No.

The analogy is that the shopping list is the XML document that your mother gave you.

Shopkeeper Jones is an experienced and talented man who is able to interpret the shopping list and assign tasks to his staff—the integrator.

The clerk takes care of finding the fruit and vegetables and fetching them—the supply chain management system or logistics system.

The clerk also weighs or counts items to insure that measurements and quantities are correct—the ERP system [Enterprise Resource Planning].

The shelves store all the fruits and vegetables—the database.

The shelves in the store are labeled so that they are easily found—the keys used in databases.

Cashier Smith calculates and receives the correct amount of money—the financial system.

Shopkeeper Jones gives you a receipt [shipment notice] that is the XML document you bring to your mother for control—the integrator again.

So traditionally, the shopping list and the receipt were formatted according to a standard called 'EDIFACT' or 'X12' (EDI). Now a new shopping list standard has emerged which is called 'XML.' It is a bit wider and longer than the old shopping list standard. Why add a new shopping list standard–i.e. XML–when there already is an existing shopping list standard, EDI?

XML has the advantage that it can be published on browsers so that people can read it and understand it. EDI does not have this. However, that functionality is not used by an application in a fully integrated process, so EDI is satisfactory and much more efficient.

The structure of XML messages is available on the Internet and can be retrieved by an application. The structure detail of an EDI message is determined between the trading partners themselves.

But the problem is still the same for both XML and EDI: you need to register the business rules for how you are interpreting the structure into a specific data model. That doesn't go away even though you can load the structure from the Internet.

EDI is more compact and uses more codes than XML, since it is designed to be interpreted by applications and not necessarily put on forms for people to read. For an application, moreover, compactness and codes are much more efficient since '2 bs tomato' or '6ea apple' are quicker for an application to read and understand than '2 pounds of tomatoes' or 'a half dozen apples,' since the application is more efficient when processing code. However, it makes XML more flexible.

So now there is a new shopping list standard, *XML*:

Do you believe it will render the clerk useless?
Do you believe there will be no need for the shelves?
Do you believe the child will not need the help of Shopkeeper Jones to understand and interpret the data in the new shopping list?

Interoperability, automation, and integration have been put at the top of the agenda.

Well, the merchandise is of no value if it cannot be moved somehow; it needs to be stored before it is purchased; all of the related process steps need to be integrated.

For that, we can thank XML. We still have work to do.

By the way, the proper greeting and handing over the shopping list to Shopkeeper Jones is the network handshake.

EDI SOFTWARE[36]

Another Billion-Dollar Industry in the EDI Service Community

The EDI software industry began about 1980 as a means to standardize EDI. By the year 2000, EDI software has become a billion-dollar industry.

The requirement was (and is) that EDI software made by competing companies must be compatible. This topic explains how that requirement was met and identifies some of the companies and people involved.

When this industry began, the intent was for all competing brands of software to be able to "understand" each other. This stemmed from the understanding at TDCC in 1975 that EDI standards would never be truly common to different software systems unless a software discipline was imposed on them. Towards that end, Bill Myers at the U.S. Department of Transportation funded a TDCC task force in 1976 to write a general programming guide for EDI. The result was a set of tables that completely defined the standards and a programming specification that described how to use the tables.

---

[36] Adapted from Ralph W. Notto, "EDI Software: From the Beginning to a Billion-Dollar Industry," *EDI Forum*, Volume 11 Number 2, pages 82-88, EDI Group, Oak Park IL, 1998.

Over seventy EDI software companies were founded in the U.S. between the years 1982-89. The EDI software market was predicted to show an overall annualized growth rate for total sales of nearly 16% between 1998 and 2001, according to research conducted by the EDI Group. With an estimated $1.58 billion in total sales in 1998, the EDI software market was projected to grow to $2.35 billion by 2001.

TDCC

TDCC initially intended that the tables and specification should be enough, and programmers could take it from there. Not so. Pressure came from various places to write the software, too. Ed Guilbert, president of TDCC and credited with being the "grandfather" of EDI, fully supported complying with the pressure.

The tables were designed and constructed in detail at TDCC by Ralph Notto using techniques and experiences he had devised and implemented for various purposes since 1958. Earl (Buddy) Bass, also at TDCC, worked with Notto and added significantly to the design by creating and defining the term "reference designator." Bass also devised a scheme for coding relational requirements so that the conditionality of data could be easily specified in a table with references to *reference designators* preceded by a one-character conditionality code that EDI software easily interpreted.

Bass and Notto simulated EDI software by creating a deck of cards, each card with a single program statement. By going through the deck in the same sequence that a computer would and performing programmed processes while referring to the detail specified in the EDI tables, the validity of the program and tables could be tested. Joe Carley, in charge of the development at TDCC, referred to this as "their cardboard computer" (see "Accomplishing the Objectives," page 33).

Using the tables and specifications, the software was written in COBOL by TDCC's software consultant, John Hon. the software did EDI translation, as we know it today, but was written for mainframe computers. The source code was distributed, and each user was required to link the coding into its own environment and compile the program. This was done five years before the introduction of the PC.

The initial interest in this work was at Chemical Leaman Tank Lines and E.I. du Pont. Howard McKenna at General Motors looked at the tables and specifications, tried some tests of his own, and concluded that the purpose and theory of operation were sound. The grocery industry used the software and tables for its thirteen-company EDI pilot project in 1981-82. They reported that the software and tables enabled the pilot companies to complete the tests they thought necessary to "prove" the EDI concept in (live) inter-company operational environments. This was accomplished according to a schedule specified two years earlier.

Railroad industry companies used the tables and concepts, but wrote their own computer programs to mesh with railroad software.

In 1984, Paul Lemme became executive director at TDCC, and, working with Ed Guilbert and John Hon, he extended the scope and usefulness of the software. According to Lemme, the software was sold as a source code product by TDCC for the purpose of getting people started with EDI translation. The TDCC software was intended for potential vendors and end users operating on a platform not supported by any particular commercial software vendor. It was licensed for $750 per year to TDCC members and $2,000 per year to nonmembers. There were over 700 subscribers to this software.

EDIFACT translation capability was added in 1987, and the software was rewritten for the "C" compiler in 1988-89. This software was designed to do translation and mapping directly to application formats in one step, which was one of the purposes for TDCC's distribution of source code. Because each user's application formats were different, the user was expected to incorporate their own record formats into the working storage definitions of the software, and identify the location of the beginning address of each data field through a (TDCC) table. The software would then move standards data to/from application records, thereby completing the mapping process.

Further, TDCC software was always intended to be functional as new transaction sets (or messages) were defined. All that was required for this extension was to add the new transaction sets or messages and related segments and data elements to the tables.

Commercially available EDI software for microprocessor systems came later. The importance of TDCC's work is that it made EDI software available for companies to begin implementing EDI, and it introduced new software concepts and tools to permit addressing with the same software all transaction sets in the standard, even those to be subsequently defined. These concepts were proven in working environments. EDI software companies that subsequently emerged each ensured, directly or indirectly, that their software was compatible with TDCC software systems already in place. This, in turn, ensured that the new software products were also compatible with each other.

To visualize the significance of both the TDCC work and subsequent commercially available EDI software at off-the-shelf prices (including TDCC's software), consider that: COBOL, the language for the TDCC software, was devised in the 1960s, and did not conveniently or intuitively address such generalization techniques; and that software used by companies, for the most part, was mostly designed to facilitate printing and archiving processes, not electronic transaction interaction with peer systems in other companies. (A notable exception was software for airline reservation systems.) The PC was not introduced until 1983.

Commercially Available EDI Software

Many of the early EDI software companies were formed around either a specific industry or a specific platform. The following profiles describe both the technical and business evolution of the EDI software industry. There were at least seventy EDI software companies in the 1980s and 1990s; this topic reports on eighteen.

APL Group

In 1983, Dan Codman and George Brigham founded the APL Group. APL introduced QUALEDI® as a complete EDI system, featuring full X12 compliance checking, a check for duplicate transactions, and data mapping facilitated through the use of data labels. QUALEDI included a single "To-Do" screen to provide users all the day-to-day functions and information needed to manage EDI processes. It also included a built-in tutorial and other functions.

APL's first customer was Colgate Palmolive, for whom APL facilitated communicating grocery industry UCS transaction sets. The customer base was extended to include distribution and transportation industries. Distribution included the warehouse WINS transaction sets; transportation addressed motor carrier sets. With sales to these three industries, APL's customer base quickly grew to 1,000 during the mid-1980s.

The consulting firm Cornerstone merged with APL in 1992, bringing with it Norman Barber, who had authored several insightful articles for the *EDI Forum*. Cornerstone also added education and consulting services to the enlarged APL's offerings.

The Computer Network, a Web-based technology company that was a certified VAN for U.S. government *eCommerce*, was acquired in 1997. This expanded APL's expertise to include the Internet.

In year 2000, APL had thousands of customers worldwide and offered a complete line of EDI software and EC/EDI professional services.

DNS

DNS started in 1979 as a consulting firm specifically oriented toward the railroad industry and performing such tasks as profitability and merger studies based on computerized mathematical modeling techniques. Founders Tom Dyer, Jim Newkirk, and Hugh Stewart knew each other from Dyer's work in engineering related to rail systems, Newkirk's work at the Federal Railroad Administration, and Stewart's rail consulting work at a Philadelphia-area consulting firm. Until the mid-1980s, they used a Prime 750 computer and FORTRAN to facilitate modeling based on detailed and extensive rail industry statistics.

About 1985, Conrail approached DNS with a request to develop a PC-based EDI system that would enable small freight forwarders to use EDI standards to communicate with railroad carriers. DNS seized on this opportunity as a companion business, since it occurred at a time when consulting activity had begun to decline.

The C programming language was chosen as the best tool for implementation. DNS decided to mirror electronically what is done in paper processes for small companies. Consequently, the application software was oriented toward "in basket," "out basket," "hold basket," and screen form.

For reasons not related to the software, Conrail's interest waned, but active interest from Pillsbury and E.I. du Pont followed. International opportunities opened up in Australia and New Zealand in 1988-89. The opportunities in this part of the world were for the use of X12 and EDIFACT in the banking industry.

DNS eventually changed its focus from specific clientele to industries (chemical, manufacturing, retail). They added new features and functionality, such as the warehouse (WINS) EDI standard. At the turn of the century, about 5,000 licenses for the product had been sold.

EDI, Inc.

Originally the idea of Buddy Bass, EDI Inc. was formed in February 1982 by Joe Carley, Ralph Notto, Bass, and Alex Kreithen. Work on the EDI software product began immediately.

Early in the design phase, Dale Sortland was added to the team. He was picked because he had significant experiences in the use of database systems at the National Marine Fisheries Service (NMFS) where Bass and Notto had earlier done consulting work. (EDI was actually implemented at NMFS with TDCC software, some additional FORTRAN programs, and the System 1022 Database system for DEC10 computers. The application was an ad hoc transaction set used by the U.S. Coast Guard to report to NMFS on any violations of NMFS regulations by commercial fishermen.)

Initially, the intent of EDI, Inc. was to implement the EDI software with database methods. After some research, the team concluded that PC database software at that time was too expensive for EDI and did not have all the functionality required for the task. The team then decided to use FORTRAN. Since the TDCC tables were matrices, FORTRAN's mathematical orientation was nicely suited for the task.

Although the software was created for use on a Victor microprocessor, a switch was made to IBM before entering the first EDI pilot, largely due to customer demand. (Still, the Victor compared very favorably with the IBM. It was about 10% faster than the IBM PC, and had a 1.2 million-byte diskette drive, compared to 320 thousand bytes on the IBM. The Victor FORTRAN had more features, the screen easily switched between 80 and 120 characters per line, and the "footprint" was smaller than that for IBM, which was important, because the early PC EDI systems were almost always placed on an already crowded desk.)

By 1983, EDI, Inc.'s software package, named TELINK, included EDI translation, communications, checkpoint/restart for error recovery, all of the TDCC tables, front-end software, archiving, audit trails, and a functional acknowledgment report. With TELINK, the company was able to deliver systems in 1983 for use in the North American Wholesale Grocers Association (NAWGA) pilot. It also delivered systems for ocean transportation and warehousing applications. When a series of X12 transaction sets were released by the standards committees in 1984, EDI Inc. added them to the TELINK tables.

The company sold systems for use in all industries as well as the U.S. Department of Defense.

In addition to direct sales, resellers of TELINK included McDonnell Douglas, GE Canada, ORDERNET Services, Bell Canada, and others.

After 1993, the company operated under the name Telink Systems, Inc.

EDI Integration Corporation

Following his key role as program director at TDCC in the 1970s and his work as president at EDI Inc 1982-87, Joe Carley and his family founded

EDI Integration Corporation (EIC). Rather than focusing on EDI software as a product, Carley thought it best to address the customer's EDI needs using a "one-stop shop" mentality. This enabled the customer to have full access to EIC's knowledge of EDI and their ability to place on site the most
efficient and technologically sound EDI environment available without having to "go to school" on the subject.

Since EIC's role is that of an integrator, it uses EDI software and EDI data communications services purchased from other companies and, in some cases, integrates it with its own application software written to the participant's specifications. The significance of the total service to the participants is that they have complete and coordinated electronic integration with trading partners and functions. The benefits to the user community are increased accuracy, better control over their individual processes, rapid access to relevant information, and transformation of cash management based on estimated payment dates to dates certain with an add-on application involving electronic funds transfer (EFT).

EIC has overseen and developed EDI operating scenarios in several industries.

In addition to Joe, Shirley, Dale, and Denise Carley, some of the 1990s EIC staff included Garrett Isacco, Dennis Brekhus, John Hon, Ralph Berwanger, and John Shultz.

EDI Solutions

Dick York and Associates formed EDI Solutions in 1986 initially to provide mainframe software to The 3M Company. Their software product GENTRAN was purchased and enhanced by Sterling Software in the late 1980s. St. Paul Software acquired EDI Solutions in 1995.

Electronic Data Systems (EDS)

H. Ross Perot founded EDS in 1962. It was acquired by General Motors in the 1970s, and created its EDI product, EDI*ASSET, in 1987 in Canada. Asghar Syed was in charge of design and development. The C programming language was used for development. EDI*EXPERT for UNIX operating systems was introduced in 1990. The software operates on PC and mid-range computers.

Emanio, Inc.

First appearing in the world EDI software market in the latter 1990s, EDITALK by Emanio Inc. is relatively new, but also very significant. It includes the capability to move data directly to or from application databases. Emanio was the leader in introducing this capability for EDI systems, which is an important innovation for EDI environments.

> **ERP**: Enterprise Resource Planning software
> **ASC X12**: [ANSI] Accredited Standards Committee X12
> **XML**: eXtensible Markup Language
> **EAI**: Enterprise Application Integration
> **B2Bi**: Business-to-Business Integration

The chief core competency of EDITALK is its ability to associate EDI data elements with application database fields. This addresses a general need for EDI software systems. Other systems have addressed this through exchange of flat files (text data) between the application system and the EDI system. While this does get the job done, it requires that the user write at least two programs: 1) For outbound data, extract data from the application system and create the flat file; 2) For inbound data, read the flat file and add data records to the application system. Most likely, the user writes these two programs for each message or transaction set type processed. EDITALK provides forms for accomplishing the same with techniques directly involving databases.

Emanio was founded by Vegard Nervik, Knut Øygardslia, and KG Charles-Harris in Oslo, Norway as Softcom Ltd in 1995. The name was changed to Emanio (the Latin word for "flow") in 2000. Vegard was first aware of EDI in 1988 as a result of the need for EDI messages for automated customs and excise treatment of goods. He headed up a project to integrate EDI into an ERP system. The ERP system used databases as its data store, and other pre-packaged EDI software could not provide an interface that fitted data models in databases. Knut was responsible for integrating EDI into Norwegian Telecom's systems in the early nineties.

Vegard and Knut conceived the schema for EDITALK based on their experiences with how business systems in general process data and how structured messaging works. They observed that EDI translators were not able to relate to database models. Knut had been researching such software for Norwegian Telecom who needed to integrate EDI directly into their database centric systems. Based on the fact that relational databases loop data within table relationships, they developed an algorithm aligning the looping structure of EDIFACT messages with row structures in related tables. Recognizing that messages and the business systems were dynamic to EDITALK at the time of compile, all messages and possible table relationships were designed to be handled dynamically. This created an extremely scalable and flexible model of integrating structured messages with business system data models. The model proved reliable both when they extended it to handle ASC X12 and later XML.

By year 2000, Emanio expanded its operations to include Europe and North America. It had added DATATALK and XMLTALK to its product line to address enterprise application integration (EAI) and business-to-business integration (B2Bi), thus providing a complete eBusiness integration solution including EDITALK, DATATALK. and XMLTALK.

Fortell

Barry Speilberg and Jim Parker founded Fortell in 1985 based on an opportunity with Sears. Fortell created systems for implementing EDI at Sears' trading partner companies. Using Sears' proprietary EDI format, the goal was to implement systems based on trading partner profiles, so systems were specifically created for each user. The scope was extended in 1986 to include Montgomery Ward's trading partners as well, based upon Ward's proprietary EDI standard.

(Use of proprietary EDI standards was the norm in the early 1980s. It took several years before the generalized, or generic, EDI became firmly established.)

This product was originally designed for "solution users" to support various proprietary formats used in the retail industry. When standard EDI was introduced, Fortell added EDI as a format, but the product was still designed to do partner-specific communications. Since small vendors used it almost exclusively in the retail business, Fortell was made to conform to the specific requirements of their customers. Because of this focus on retailer specifics, Fortell was chosen by Wal-Mart to develop the Retail Link product. This product was the only (Microsoft) Windows-based EDI software product on the market at that time. It was originally written in Clipper computer language, and later changed to C.

In the 1980s, Fortell became the first company to offer standard EDI software to use with the Windows operating system rather than DOS. About 1,000 companies implemented EDI in the 1980s with Fortell software. TSI International acquired the Fortell software in 1989.

Future Three

Walter Keyes founded Future Three in 1985 for service to the automotive industry. Its products specifically address EDI requirements for trading partners complying with OEM companies (General Motors, Ford, Chrysler, Caterpillar, and many others in the automotive industry). Future Three addresses integration of EDI with the user's own application systems for manufacturing, release accounting, and order entry. Their products operate on IBM AS400 computer systems. Their clients use Future Three for the total solution, considering individual OEM requirements, EDI system, communications, training, interface to MAPICS and other software, system maintenance, and help desk support.

Metro Mark

Metro Mark's EDI software product, designed by Gene Sedlock, implemented the TDCC software on the IBM System 38 computer. The work was for RMI, one of the thirteen companies in the grocery industry's UCS pilot program in 1981-82. Metro Mark's EDI product release in 1985 was as object code for either System 38 or the IBM PC. To complete the mapping process with this product, users were required to produce a "flat file" of records. Each record (line) in the file was in a format similar to EDI standards segments with the EDI control characters removed. All of the data fields were fixed length, equaling the maximum length of the data element as defined in the standards. Each record was basically the equivalent of an EDI segment. Users were expected to write interface programs to accomplish such things as product code conversions and reformatting to their own format.

Approaches of having users write interface programs became a common one for EDI translation software. It remained so until the early 1990s when products that performed translation and data mapping in one step were introduced. This simplified the data mapping processes through use of graphical user interface technology.

Metro Mark added IBM mainframe functionality by developing a relationship with a Canadian company that had developed their own mainframe translation product. Metro Mark was acquired by Sterling in 1991.

Premenos

The predecessor of Premenos, Apparel Computer Systems (ACS), was founded in 1978 by David Hildes, Lew Jenkins, and Manny Pasetes to address software needs for the apparel and retail industries.

In 1986, the company recognized the movement in the retail and apparel industries was toward connecting computers. Jeni Kandel joined ACS and brought to the company her experiences with EDI as a consultant to GEIS.

Kandel invented the Premenos EDI product. She focused on the data-mapping requirement to enable Premenos' users to specify any kind of data transfers between the application and EDI systems. The computer platforms for this software were the IBM mid-range systems 36, 38, and AS400.

The industry's acceptance of the product led to IBM becoming a distributor in 1988.

Later, the transportation and automotive industries were included in Premenos's sales strategies. By 1990, Premenos had about 1,500 systems installed at user sites.

ACS' application software for the apparel and retail industries was sold to KSA in 1990. The result after the sale was an EDI company called "Premenos," a name indicating, in Hildes' words, that the company was "based on a premonition of what is to come."

The Templar product was added in 1994 to provide encryption and authentication for transmissions via the Internet.

The company was acquired by Harbinger in 1998. Hildes noted the similarities between the meanings of the two names "Premenos" and "Harbinger."

SCT Corporation

EDI.Smart® was introduced in 1991 by Information Associates, a company acquired by SCT in 1993. EDI.Smart is used as an EDI front end to SCT's mainframe software for educational institutions. Although the introduction date does not match the time period 1984 to 1989 used for the other companies in this list, their developments are significant in early EDI software history, since SCT implemented student-related rather than commercial applications. SCT's first emphasis was on transaction sets like 130 (Student Educational Record [Transcript]), 131 (Transcript Acknowledgment), 189 (Application for Admission to Educational Institutions), and 190 (Enrollment Verification).

Although EDI.Smart offers a full EDI system in terms of X12 transaction sets and EDIFACT messages, the product's role in the education community is significant in that EDI.Smart was required to have an early interface between EDI and the Internet and data encryption processes included in the total EDI processing scheme. Therefore, the education community's experiences in the practical implementation and integration of EDI and the Internet precede by at least three years the business sector's interest in the Internet for that purpose. From the beginning, SCT offered the *complete* linkage—mainframe application databases *to* EDI *to* Internet *to* recipient, and conversely, including both application and functional acknowledgments.

Vice President Bill Mahoney led the early EDI.Smart initiative. The product was built completely on database technology. The work included technical support and assistance from R. W. Notto & Associates. The later assured continuity with prior EDI standards and software developments.

Regarding SCT's impact, people in the education industry (users of EDI.Smart in their institutions) said the following in 1995:

Edgar Chambers, associate executive vice president of San Jose State University: "Trading partners include junior colleges, community colleges, and East Bay high schools. Cost studies revealed $18 to $36 paper costs per transcript could be reduced to $1.50. Though EDI is a success at current levels, the future is even more exciting. The electronic approach is much more volume, staff, and student-friendly than the paper approach."

Herbert Chereck, registrar of the University of Oregon: "Seventy-three percent of our transcript exchanges are generated from in-state students. We have taken a big step with this technology to improve the quality of a key student service while reducing the costs."

St. Paul Software

Gary Anderson founded St. Paul Software in 1981 as a regional consulting firm in the Minneapolis/St. Paul area. Anderson was previously vice president for Northern Numbers, a start-up software development company that manufactured general accounting software. In 1984, St. Paul software developed and marketed an EDI package, and in 1989 developed the first UNIX-based EDI product. Anderson's brother, Roger, was the primary developer of the company's first EDI translator product. Many copies of the initial product were sold to trading partners of Burlington Northern for applying EDI to Burlington's purchasing and order acknowledgment processes.

St. Paul Software acquired EDI Solutions in 1995 to broaden its product offerings to include EDI systems for mainframe and midrange computers. By 2000, the company serviced about 10,000 clients worldwide with EC/EDI software, consulting, systems and software integration, custom programming, and project implementation.

Sterling Software

Originally, Sterling Software's EDI business focused on providing value-added networking (VAN) services. As part of the VAN business, the company resold PC products of EDI, Inc and ACS (Premenos). By 1987, the company saw a need to have a proprietary mainframe translation product and bought the rights to the source code of a product written by EDI Solutions. The GENTRAN family thus originated on IBM's MVS mainframe platform, under the direction of Brad Sharp, subsequently president of Sterling's Interchange Software group, and Robert Fisher, who later was president and CEO of FORESIGHT Corp.

The GENTRAN product developed from a mainframe translation product into a comprehensive EDI management system that began with a tool for creating data maps, which specified the relationships between data in a user's computer and its EDI formats, and ended with the tracking and routing of EDI messages throughout a company's network. In early 1990, Sterling Software acquired Metro Mark, one of their chief competitors. Sterling has since dropped the Metro Mark products from its product line, but has successfully converted the customer base to newer versions of GENTRAN.

In 1992, Sterling struggled with developing a UNIX-based software product. To increase its UNIX presence and broaden its product line to include comprehensive messaging functions, Sterling acquired American Business Computers (ABC) in 1994. ABC, started by Kimba Vasquez and Pat Davis, had a strong UNIX system and focused on the automotive business.

Following that, Sterling focused on the (Microsoft) Windows NT platform, with development and business headed by Bill Owen and Randy Harvey respectively. Sterling designed the NT-based system from the ground up to take full advantage of the graphical user interface and 32-bit PC technology.

At the beginning of the century, Sterling sees its EDI software becoming part of the movement toward enterprise-wide commerce systems. Sterling has been enhancing its software so that it translates messages in non-

EDI formats and manages the communication of all types of messages throughout an enterprise. The company also offers Web-based EDI solutions.

Supply Tech, Inc.

Supply Tech, Inc. began in 1984, offering EDI systems to the automotive industry. Gail Jackson, a cofounder and original president of the company, wrote the initial Supply Tech EDI software. The company's products included bar-code software interfaces.

Supply Tech introduced the concept of a "template" relative to addressing unique requirements by individual trading partners, thus enabling a user of the system to respond immediately to specific trading partner requests.

The company grew quickly, and became a major contender in EDI software sales during 1988-89.

Related to this growth is Gail Jackson's proactive participation with EDI standards processes since the mid-1980s. Active in both X12 and EDIFACT, she wrote the original implementation recommendation for the X12 material release (830) and advanced ship notice (856). She also authored the first draft of the EDIFACT CONTRL message (the EDIFACT equivalent of the X12 997 functional acknowledgment transaction set).

By 1995, Supply Tech had sold EDI systems in over forty countries and satisfied needs in over twenty-five industries.

Supply Tech was purchased by Harbinger.

TranSettlements

TranSettlements' EDI software, Translate, was developed in the early 1980s under the leadership of Hank Lavery. Based upon the TDCC software, Translate added capabilities to maintain trading partner profiles, reconcile acknowledgments, and address restart and recovery procedures. This product was sold until early 1990. At one time, it was the most popular commercially available IBM mainframe EDI translation product.

In 1990, TSI International bought the Translate product from TranSettlements, basically to acquire its customer base.

TSI International Software, Inc.

Founded in 1967, TSI was originally a Dunn and Bradstreet-owned Company. While many other companies created original EDI products,

TSI chose to build on its current product, KeyMaster, and enhance the product line by purchasing product rights and source codes from others. These were chosen based on a strategic plan and an accurate prediction of where the EDI market would move.

TSI created an EDI software product called Trading Partner intended for IBM mainframe environments. The product was different from its predecessors in that it was designed with built-in mapping functionality. The intent was to create data flows directly from EDI formats into application formats without the need for interface programming, and vice-versa. This was accomplished by joining together an EDI translation product purchased from National Semiconductor with TSI's KeyMaster.

Through KeyMaster, EDI data was translated and passed on to user-defined screens. Application edits were associated with each data field through the product's internal language, called Easy Logic. This internal language manipulated data in order to make it application-ready. Data could then be extracted from the product in a format that facilitated direct processing by the receiving application.

KeyMaster was later updated to operate in a real-time environment (Trading Partner Express), and then adapted for use in conjunction with Mercator, TSI International's "any-to-any" data-mapping product.

Trading Partner was used in high volume, high performance environments. Mercator is a data transform engine that permits enterprises to exchange information between internal systems; to implement and integrate advanced client/server applications, such as SAP's R/3 Enterprise Resource Planning (ERP) system, and to integrate EDI data and Web-based applications with their core business systems.

SAP: [SAP, AG] World's largest enterprise software company, headquartered in Walldorf, Germany.

Another product, TSI's Trading Partner PC, resulted from the purchase and subsequent enhancements of the Fortell product, which was the only Windows-based EDI package at the time. From this, TSI developed EDI kits, which were packaged solutions built to the specifications of a specific "hub." These "plug-and-play" solutions were designed to allow unsophisticated users to participate in EDI environments.

TSI is an aggressive worldwide contender for sale of EDI products, and by year 2000 had in excess of 10,000 users.

Unisys

Tom Costello

For its EDI product, Unisys focused on the UNIX operating system and data mapping. It contracted with EDI Inc for implementing EDI translation.

The Unisys mapper had the ability to map any-to-any data, using a script to control the mapping process. Tom Costello led the marketing effort and project direction; Gus Wing led the technical design and implementation.

Recap

The EDI software industry grew from a common origin based on the joint industry/government initiative in the early 1970s to create EDI standards. The initiative was coordinated by TDCC. The initiative's goal and objective was to facilitate the ability for companies to ultimately interchange data computer-to-computer, process-to-process.

To accomplish this, it was necessary for data created by one EDI software writer to be readily "understood" by software written by another. It was not expected that the software developers would need to coordinate their developments, given that the EDI standards were explicit in providing all of the detail required to complete the software implementations. TDCC devised a set of tables that defined the EDI standards in such a way that the software developers could incorporate the tables into their products, thus insuring compatibility. TDCC implemented the first such software. The concept was proven in pilot projects, and the beginning of the EDI software industry followed shortly. The introduction of the PC in 1983 made the implementation of EDI practical for all sizes of companies.

The founders of EDI software companies addressed the compatibility issue with their EDI system products. Part of the resultant success was due to the common beginning and testing environment provided by the TDCC development. Combining the compatibility requirement with ingenuity of developers created an EDI software industry that is highly competitive. The result is a choice for users of capable products at competitive off-the-shelf prices.

The conformance to EDI standards definitely did not imply that all the resultant software products were similar in design or functionality. In fact, they were all significantly different from each other, and reflected the ingenuity and experiences of the developers.

CONSULTANTS PLAY A MAJOR ROLE

EDI/*eCommerce* consultants provide insight and innovation for bridging application environments with EDI environments and bridging current reality with long-range goals. This has resulted in synergistic results in terms of opening industry eyes to the benefits of timeliness, accuracy, efficiency, and control available with EDI and what this means in a practical sense. It also has helped companies to prepare for change by understanding where all this eventually leads, and why companies will want to be part of the evolution.

Several consultants and some of their accomplishments and significance are identified in this topic. There were indeed many others as well that contributed toward EDI first establishing a "foot hold" and then continuing with gradual, but impressive, growth in terms of numbers of participating companies, importance of the transmissions, enhancement of concept, and success examples.

TDCC: Transportation Data Coordinating Committee

Preliminary to availability of any EDI consultants, there had to be a concept for EDI. Member companies and the staff of TDCC developed this during 1974-5.

First EDI Consultants

It is interesting that TDCC's first EDI standards manual was published exactly on schedule in mid-July, 1975. However, by March 1, 1975, Joe Carley reported to Ed Guilbert that the job would not be done on time without some consultant support. Guilbert approved two consultants. Carley chose Ralph Notto and Buddy Bass. Notto was chosen for his experiences and innovations in table-driven computer programs as applied to transportation and communications information systems. Bass was chosen because he was the only person among those Carley interviewed that immediately understood that a standard was required, and it was apparent to Carley that Bass had the knowledge in how to put together a comprehensive and efficient standards manual.

Buddy Bass

With less than four months to complete the assignment, Notto and Bass became the first two EDI consultants. Notto's role was to make all of the synthesis resulting from the work groups to "hang together as a single system" and to insure that all detail required for data flow among carriers, shippers, and banks were addressed. Bass' assignment was to insure that the project's result was a comprehensive and understandable standards manual. Of course, both assignments were completed during the allocated three-month schedule.

The main source of information was work groups composed of application and system specialists from air, motor, ocean, and rail transportation carriers; shipper companies that engaged these carriers; and banks that processed freight payments. The scope of the 1975 standards manual included forty-five transaction sets, sixty-eight segments, and 189 data elements. It included in its 427 pages all of the standards details in support of these forty-five sets, the concept, process flow diagrams, and seven appendices for references to related standards. The entire first manual was prepared without assistance from computer automation. The source information for the manual came from work group participants and writings by Guilbert, Carley, Bass, and Notto.

Other consultants contributed part time on the project: Alexander Kreithen relative to data communications and Lester A. Probst relative to motor transportation. Steven Bass helped to construct the first standards manual. Thomas DesNoyers provided required information about code lists and their sources. This information was used in the appendix of the standards manual as a reference to code lists used in EDI but not defined by EDI work groups.

The purpose stated in the July 1975 standards manual was "To define the procedures and standards necessary to enable a representative cross-section of the transportation community to undertake Phases II (Design and Development of Operational Prototype Facilities) and III (Test and Evaluation of Prototype Activities) of the program. The specification is further intended to facilitate the performance of appropriate development and operational cost analyses as a consideration towards a decision to directly participate in Phases II and III."[37]

[37] TDCC, "Prototype Electronic Data Interchange System," page 1-2, 1975.

Phase I was titled "Definition of Requirements," and was completed with delivery of the standards manual.

Notto and Bass continued their consulting relationships with TDCC until 1984. During that time the grocery industry opted to build on the TDCC concepts and detail, the grocery industry executed a thirteen-company EDI pilot, X12 was formed with TDCC and grocery industry participation in its standards meetings, other industry groups joined the standard EDI movement, and software for managing the standard and publishing standards manuals was created and significantly enhanced. With this software, a first draft of an EDI standards manual for a new industry could be created and printed within a few days, covering new and existing transaction sets of interest to that industry, the concept, all of the existing detail, and cross references. A final manual coordinated with industry work groups was usually created by the third draft. Notto and Bass worked on all of these activities.

Making this Practical

Overlapping the TDCC work and beginning in February 1982, Carley, Notto, Bass, and Kreithen founded EDI, Inc. for the purpose of creating and selling EDI software systems. Kreithen had previously written the "TDCC General Communications Guide" in 1976, and provided other consulting services at TDCC.

The early system sales at EDI, Inc. were in conjunction with consulting for pilot EDI projects. These were in the grocery, manufacturing, rail carrier, ocean carrier, banking, military, and motor carrier industries. All of the pilots required considerations for interfacing with current application systems. In doing this, it was always the attempt to create excitement by providing something users considered of value, but were doable only with a concept involving EDI. These included features like immediate reconciliation of orders and invoices, automatic acknowledgments, exception reporting, and code conversions.

Without the benefit of pilot projects, EDI, Inc. placed other systems in the retail and warehousing industries as well.

The significance of these consulting and system installation activities is that the concept of a single cross-industry EDI standard became firmly entrenched in participating companies, and the potential of EDI as one of the enabling tools for subsequent reengineering was beginning to be understood by the user community.

Shaping the Outcome

Some of the early EDI consultants are especially memorable because of what they advocated when industry, with reference to EDI, was searching for "The Way" and was especially vulnerable, because the data format definition phase of EDI was not accepted as being over, and a cross-industry standard was by no means universally considered to be necessary. One of the common experiences of the author at TDCC standards meetings during the early 1980s was to "fight off" the notion of revisiting the basic EDI format structures and concept each time a new industry group appeared at a meeting.

Richard C. Norris

The earlier EDI consulting work at TDCC needed a significant boost from somewhere. In an assignment completely independent of anything at TDCC, the work in the late 1970s by Richard C. Norris of the Arthur D. Little Consulting Firm provided that boost. It was especially important because Norris had an assignment to determine the feasibility of EDI in the grocery industry. The assignment was sponsored by six grocery industry associations and had high exposure with top executives in that industry. Norris was the principal investigator.

The project report, *Electronic Data Interchange for the Grocery Industry—Feasibility Report*, published in April 1980,[38] had an enormously favorable impact toward the advancement of EDI, getting the attention of executives from many industries in addition to the grocery and transportation industries.

Two of the actions Norris proposed in that report included: 1) Development of the UCS[39] standard based on TDCC's work with EDI for transportation industries. "Work" included standards concepts and detail, standards manual publication techniques, and implementation software concepts; and 2) implementation of a pilot project to test the standards in operational environments.

The pilot was significant, because it involved thirteen grocery manufacturer, distributor, and broker companies, and tested purchase orders, invoices, and acknowledgments. The pilot test was executed as proposed by Norris, was completed on a schedule also proposed by Norris, and proved

---

38 Arthur D. Little, Inc., *Electronic Data Interchange for the Grocery Industry—Feasibility Report,* [110 pages]. April 1980.

39 UCS: Uniform Communications Standard, the grocery industry's EDI standards manual.

many of the points in Norris's *Feasibility Study*, including the economic effect forecast.

The significance of this work is that it led the way toward other industries joining the same standards movement. The warehousing, chemical, electrical, metals, petroleum, defense, and other industries took note and began participating in standards discussions and in EDI implementations.

Other industries and companies discussing standards that were parochial in nature now had to pay attention to the trend. The concept of a cross-industry EDI standard finally became firmly entrenched about 1986. Norris's contribution was of enormous importance toward making this happen.

If that were the only EDI contribution by Richard Norris, it would be enough. However, the grocery industry went back to Arthur D. Little and Norris in the late 1980s for help toward applying EDI for direct store delivery. From this, Direct Exchange EDI (DEX/EDI) was defined. The ultimate result of this was data transfer between electronic units of deliverer and receiver at the store back door.

The significance of this is that EDI was extended from corporate computer-to-corporate computer transmissions to local events at the scene of inter-company product delivery and acceptance actions.

Paul Lemme

Another consultant effective in shaping EDI's outcome was Paul Lemme. In frequent (sometimes monthly) EDI standards meetings during the early 1980s, Lemme argued for the grocery industry building on the TDCC standard and concepts to implement its EDI plans, the usefulness of the TDCC implementation software for implementing the 1981-82 grocery industry EDI pilot, the significance of a cross-industry EDI standard, the role for *interaction* (rather than *integration*) between application and EDI software, the importance of timing, accuracy, and efficiency, and the modular requirements for EDI implementation,.

Initially, he represented Sales Force, a food broker in the grocery industry. Sales Force was one of the thirteen grocery EDI pilot companies. Paul Lemme was the leader of the Sales Force EDI implementation effort and a key participant for the general pilot.

At a time when it was more likely for an industry to independently define its own EDI standard, Lemme spoke out from several positions of advantage—as a member of a team of six experts representing the grocery industry for the purpose of evaluating TDCC's work, he argued for inter-industry cooperation; as a participant at UCS standards meetings, he consistently argued in favor of inter-industry interests; and as a grocery EDI pilot participant, he adhered to the published plan and completed implementation and testing on schedule while freely sharing discoveries and techniques with other pilot participants.

As EDI successes increased at Sales Force, Lemme was called on again to participate over a two-year period as a UCS representative on the Joint EDI Committee (JEDI). JEDI included a team of experts organized to correct the rift created in 1984 when TDCC and X12 committees where assigning conflicting definitions for critical items in EDI standards. The rift was corrected for the benefit of the entire EDI community. Lemme and the other JEDI members set aside narrow interests, offering statesmanship as well as technical expertise in order to accomplish this.

Later in the 1980s, Lemme became the executive director at TDCC, where he taught EDI to new industry groups, maintained the EDI standards database, and extended the usefulness of TDCC software.

Following the TDCC assignment, Lemme was an independent consultant before joining TSI International as a vice president tasked with development and delivery of professional services to the EDI community. Subsequently, he became a senior electronic commerce consultant at AppNet (now [2002] part of Connective Commerce Corporation), a firm dedicated to electronic commerce planning and implementation.

A pioneer is a person who initiates or takes part in the development of new areas of enterprise or research. Paul Lemme has done this well, and the EDI community has felt the effect of his work—this includes inter-industry coordination, adherence to software control of the standards database, and use of disciplined technology that led to availability of cost-effective off-the-shelf EDI software products.

EDI: Electronic Data Interchange
EFT: Electronic Funds Transfer
EC: Electronic Commerce [*eCommerce*]
NACHA: National Automatic Clearing House Association
GM: General Motors

Daniel M. Ferguson

When it comes to placing adjectives like "big," "important," "strategic," "secure," "cost-effective," "EFT/EDI," and "pilot" before a noun like "system," look to Daniel M. Ferguson, who put something like that together beginning in 1984. Working at the time as a vice president at First Chicago, he proposed an EDI system and service to General Motors (GM) that included: electronic funds transfer (in lieu of check),

EDI (in lieu of check stub, but containing much more detail), encryption and authentication (for security), audit controls (for safety), a pilot project that included eight banks and GM (as a practical test case and the beginning of a new type of funds transfer system), and a completely paperless system between companies (EFT/EDI).

Daniel Ferguson

This started when the U.S. Standard EDI population was about 150 sites, the 820 transaction set (payment order/remittance advice) was not even on the drawing board, no one else was discussing EDI and encryption together, and companies were only beginning to use the X12 EDI standards.

Ferguson was the concept originator, the organizer, the salesman, the team builder, the resource locator, the motivator, and the system engineer. Vice president … system engineer? Yes, considering an earlier Bell Labs definition, "Systems engineering is the planning and overall design of a new system and the follow through to insure its operational success in its working environment."

His First Chicago team included Ruth Andersen and Kathy Flynn. Starting in 1985, they put the details together for the 820, which they had ready for pilot testing later in 1985. In a special contract with EDI Inc, they added the 820 to the EDI list of X12 EDI transaction sets and added software interfaces for encryption and authentication. Tests between GM and banks began in 1986.

The pilot project was a success. The system became operational by 1987 and was expanded to include other banks. The payment process was completely automated with EFT/EDI.

The scheme was for GM to send 820s to the eight banks, authorizing release of funds and providing related detail to be used by the banks and payees; the banks determined if the funds recipient was a client in their bank–if not, a funds transfer and purpose was electronically sent on to the client's bank. A client's bank was responsible for recording the funds in the client's account and notifying the client of the transaction. All communications between GM and the banks were encrypted and authenticated EFT/EDI transmitted via point-to-point dial-up connections. The banks responded to GM with EDI 997s (functional acknowledgments).

Bank-to-bank communications was via 820/997 or the NATCHA banking standard. (Banks communicating with the eight primary banks had options for communications other than EDI.) Clients had options for payment electronically or by check; remittance detail was included in the transmission or printed on check stubs.

In one step, GM made all payments electronically. The significance of this accomplishment was: EFT and EDI were combined to provide payment and detailed remittance advice in the same transmission; other banks and payees were participants, directly or indirectly, even if they were not EDI capable; two communicating partners accomplished upgrading to EFT/EDI simply by changing preference values in a trading partner profile database; payment dates, from a payee's viewpoint, now changed from being estimated dates to dates certain; and GM and banks enjoyed a considerable costs savings from this process while improving payment service to GM suppliers.

With the system operational, Ferguson left First Chicago in 1987 and founded the EDI Group with Ned Hill. They concentrated on three needs for the new EDI industry—education, a journal, and research.

Their first course, "Principles of EDI," was a three-day event addressing EDI basics, data mapping, strategies, EFT, negotiating new terms between buyer and seller based on EFT/EDI, and Win/Win reasoning. For bonding purposes at dinner meetings, they even included singing EDI songs like: "O EDI, O EDI," based on the melody of "O Taunenbaum."

The founding Issue of *EDI Forum* published in 1988 included departments for the state of EDI, EDI user perspectives, EDI pioneer profiles, EDI standards, EDI vendor viewpoints, EDI global insights, EDI book reviews, and the EDI glossary.

Subsequent issues included similar departments. The *EDI Forum* is a journal with in-depth articles with research as well as news value.

The Group's EDI research is based on sound statistical techniques, includes surveys encompassing several hundred questions of significance to the EDI user and EDI service industry communities, is interpreted in statements of findings written by Ferguson and his associates, is used in EC/ EDI "best practices" workshops conducted by the EDI Group, and is a basis for some of the articles in the *EDI Forum* about the U.S. and Canadian state of EDI.

Craigg Ballance, also an expert in financial EDI, led the Canadian operations of The EDI Group.

The EDI Group was acquired in 1997 by Thomson EC Resources, and later became part of Faulkner & Gray.

The work of Ferguson and his associates is significant, because he addressed and combined issues of project scope and magnitude—importance, strategy, security, cost-effectiveness—with EFT/EDI together, and integrated all into an important part of *eCommerce*, providing all of that backed up by creditable research and publication.

Dennis McGinnis

Dennis McGinnis introduced himself to the EDI community about 1983 when he telephoned Ed Guilbert at TDCC to say, "My company's best customer told us that they like our products and services, but they will cease to do business with us if we do not become EDI-capable. They said that you could help us. Do you know what they are talking about?" Considering that McGinnis' company was Phillips North America and the best customer Western Electric, this telephone call was quite a significant event. McGinnis was the *first* of many to make that same statement and ask that same question.

It seemed like only a moment before McGinnis was totally emerged in EDI and TDCC activities. He quickly led a team to make his company EDI-capable. He contributed to the enhancement and promotion of EDI. He took leadership rolls on EDI committees.

He was chosen as the JEDI chairperson in 1984, and was a key participant in helping to resolve the TDCC/X12 rift at that time. (See "JEDI—Healing the TDCC/X12 Rift," page 53.)

He was the first EDIFACT rapporteur representing the United States. Working closely with Ray Walker, the European rapporteur, he guided the EDIFACT format structure into following schemes used in X12 and some European standards. This, in turn, made it easier and expeditious for EDI software companies to adapt their programs to include functionality for EDIFACT translations.

Subsequently, McGinnis joined the consulting firm of Price Waterhouse and led developmental teams that helped major corporations in the world to integrate EDI capability into their redesigned/reengineered information systems.

Even with such a demanding assignment, he found time to work in a leadership role with Dan Ferguson relative to the EDI Group's "best practices" workshops, helping to increase the effectiveness of EDI/*eCommerce* professionals, and increasing the value of the *eCommerce* systems they manage.

The work of Dennis McGinnis has been instrumental in EDI's role to standardize data format structures in information exchanges among countries worldwide and to make the use of this data essential in reengineered information systems and processes.

Norman F. Barber

During the late 1980s, when others were struggling to understand how to implement EDI, Norman F. Barber, president of Cornerstone, an EDI professional services organization, was analyzing research findings and statistics and reflecting on his own findings to determine what companies should do relative toward realizing the ultimate promise of EDI. He published his analysis and recommendations in a 1990 *EDI Forum* treatise on "Implementing EDI Beyond Connectivity."[40]

In the treatise, Barber's premise was that the vast majority of companies in EDI in 1990 remained in the early stages of EDI planning and implementation. He said that it was because the general case for those with a vision of the future with EDI had an incomplete understanding of vision. He stated that vision, as it relates to business, consists of three components: foresight, insight, and eyesight.

Barber's definition of foresight as it applies to EDI is that it is the ability to understand the role that technology will play in making the relationship among trading partners, even among some internal groups, as seamless as possible. He reported that most EDI visions he had seen stop there.

He stated that insight is the ability to understand the existing enterprise and how it really operates regarding people, organization structures, and corporate culture in relationship to trading partners, internal or external. He predicted that EDI would dramatically alter this vision.

Finally, he defined eyesight as the ability to objectively separate what we perceive about our companies from the realities in a structured and disciplined manner. The ultimate level of EDI implementation, he said, requires that we create realistic frames of reference from which we can build or modify specific elements of the business.

Barber indicated that the following traditional approach toward implementing EDI *is incomplete* with respect to gaining the full potential benefit: review current paper and data flow, identify potential benefits through EDI, develop EDI strategy and business case, identify technical steps, identify potential trading partners, run trading partner conference, implement a pilot, and move to production.

Rather, Barber stated, the implementation team must recognize that there are three distinct stages of EDI implementation:

---

[40]Norman F. Barber, "Implementing EDI Beyond Connectivity: The Management Challenge of the '90s," *EDI Forum*, 1990 Issue, pages 44-53.

Stage I EDI: Computer-to-computer integration

Stage II EDI: Application-to-application integration

Stage III EDI: Peer-to-peer integration.

Considering all three stages, he said that the implications are that skills must change, responsibilities may shift, patterns of communication may be altered, transaction processing time is decreased, number of transactions increase, work relationships with trading partners may change, and new organizational structures may evolve.

Barber wrote that the successful EDI professionals must learn three critical skills: figure out how to plan beyond EDI connectivity, determine what to change in the enterprise architecture, and understand how to manage the dynamics of change.

Finally, Barber offered the thoughts that efficiency is a prerequisite, but effectiveness is the goal; and the plan is to "re-architect" the business and not to demolish and rebuild.

Publication of this paper was a significant event in EDI history, because it organized thought processes required when analyzing the pre-reengineering situation in any company, was based on sound research statistics and techniques, provided a "must read" paper for those assigned to process-reengineering teams, and was timely in the sense that it was published in 1990, just prior to the initiation of process reengineering in many companies.

Norman Barber is a forward-thinking author of other *EDI Forum* thought-provoking articles, "Electronic Commerce: Toward the Virtual Corporation,"[41] "Electronic Commerce: Toward the Virtual Corporation Part 2,"[42] "Changing EDI Forever: The Federal EC/EDI Acquisition Mandate" (with Paul Lindoerfer), [43] and "The Strategic Shift to Electronic Commerce from EDI."[44]

In the first of these articles, Barber stated that in 1993 we were in a transition period from EDI as originally understood to something new. The article traces the evolution of EDI from simple proprietary file transfers to the

---

[41] Norman F. Barber, "Electronic Commerce: Toward the Virtual Corporation," *EDI Forum*, Volume 6 (1993) No. 3, pages 18-21.

[42] Norman F. Barber, "Electronic Commerce: Toward the Virtual Corporation Part 2," *EDI Forum*, Volume 6 (1993), No. 4, pages 18-22.

[43] Norman F. Barber and Paul W. Lindoerfer, "Changing EDI Forever: The Federal EC/EDI Acquisition Mandate," *EDI Forum*, Volume 8 (1995), No. 2, pages 9-15.

[44] Norman F. Barber, "The Strategic Shift to Electronic Commerce from EDI," *EDI Forum*, Volume 11 (1998), No. 1, pages 54-63.

emerging concept of electronic commerce. He believed that we needed to view technology in the context of larger strategic goals.

In the second article, he argued that the business case for implementing electronic commerce is strongest if the technology is coupled with an evolution toward two new business models: "extended enterprise" or "virtual corporation." He said that the business case for electronic commerce is stronger if the technology is placed within the context of an evolution, first toward the extended enterprise and ultimately the virtual corporation. "Extended enterprise," he said, has its roots in outsourcing where an entire business segment like logistics or data processing is segregated and run as an independent business; a "virtual corporation" has fewer and smaller full-time or permanent functions within it when compared to a traditional corporation, accomplishing much of its work through outsourcing.

In the third article, Barber and Lindoerfer pointed out how the presidential directive to fully implement EDI throughout the federal government will exponentially increase the EC/EDI technology's popularity, and predict that this signals the *end of the beginning period* for electronic commerce through EDI.

The fourth article further explained the meaning and implications of "virtual corporation."

All four articles are based on extensive research, experience, and analysis.

The significance is that these writings offer to both executives and managers a clear understanding and examples of the meanings, implications, and potential of EDI, electronic commerce, and virtual corporation.

Norman Barber also addressed the EDI/*eCommerce* "competition." In a 1998 article[45] he stated, "While EDI is ideal for large volume standard transmissions between trading partners, it has met with resistance among smaller organizations, in many cases proving to be too complex and too expensive. However, in the final analysis, it may be that the Internet has saved EDI instead of replacing it." He pointed out how and why the World Wide Web can and should be used to bring some of the smaller entities into the EDI community, and he reiterated that EDI provides the most benefit when more trading partners of all sizes are involved.

---

[45]Norman F. Barber, "Will EDI and the Internet Have a Happy Marriage or Fight to the Death?" *EDI Forum, Vol 10, No. 4, 1997, pages 7-10.*

Margaret Anne Emmelhainz

When sales people and purchasing agents were wondering what would happen to their jobs when EDI reached their companies, Dr. Margaret Anne Emmelhainz was busy finding the answers.[46]

Dr. Emmelhainz reported on the results of in-depth case analyses she conducted during 1986 with fifteen organizations that were in various stages of EDI implementation. The focus was on answers to specific questions: Does the use of EDI change the purchasing process, and if so, how? Does the use of EDI change purchasing workload, and if so, how? Does the use of EDI change buyer/vendor relationships, and if so, how? Does the use of EDI change the attitudes of purchasing personnel toward the purchasing process or toward their roles in the purchasing process?

Dr. Emmelhainz concluded that the purchasing process itself was not changed significantly due solely to EDI, but procedural changes resulted which allowed tasks to be completed by lower levels in the organization. The effect on buyers, for example, was to free them from some of the clerical aspects of the job and to allow them more time for professional purchasing activity.

Of the fifteen companies in the study, seven reported that EDI had no impact on buyer status because things that impact their job status are not affected by EDI, and buyers are not involved in activities directly related to EDI. On the other hand, three companies reported that EDI enhances the status of buyer assistants due to a reduction of activities associated with transmittal of orders, and some work previously performed by buyers has been allocated to assistants. Five companies reported that EDI frees up buyer time from routine activities for more challenging and more important activities.

For analysis of EDI's impact on buyer-vendor relationships, investigation centered on the buyer's perceptions of their relationships with vendors, the buyer's ability to resolve problems with vendors, and the number on contacts between buyers and vendors.

Findings indicated that thirteen of the fifteen companies strongly believed that EDI improves the relationship between buyers and vendors. Factors leading to the improvements include commitment and cooperation required by EDI, enhanced trust because EDI encourages the sharing of

---

[46] Margaret A. Emmelhainz, "Electronic Data Interchange: Does It Change the Purchasing Process?" *EDI Forum*, Founding Issue (1988), pages 49-54.

information, and elimination of nuisances (lost orders, errors) through use of EDI.

All fifteen of the companies *disagreed* with the statement that "since the implementation of EDI, relationships with vendors have or are expected to become more impersonal."

At the time of this study, Dr. Emmelhainz was an assistant professor of marketing at the University of Dayton. Her research is significant because it addressed fears held by a key employee group, and gave reasons for such groups to actively support and cooperate in EDI initiatives by their companies.

Steven Bass

While EDI consultants are one of the components of an EDI service industry, Steven Bass, founder of Washington Publishing Company (WPC) had another idea. WPC is also an EDI service company, but unlike the others in this group, many of WPC's clientele are the other service companies rather than companies in the EDI *user* community.

WPC provides consulting services relative to creating implementation conventions for industry groups or a specific user. These are documents that explicitly specify how data is to be mapped between a user application and EDI systems. Without such specification, the standard EDI formats may be somewhat ambiguous to a receiver, since it is possible to express data for a given transaction in different ways and still be within in a standard EDI format. This is similar to the use of language among people. Unlike people, however, software that receives EDI data even after it has been translated from EDI is not necessarily programmed to "understand" all of the variations possible. Hence the necessity for implementation conventions is apparent.

But a distinguishing capability of WPC, less known but extremely important, is a product that Bass designed during the mid-1980s and is distributed as a product by the Data Interchange Standards Association (DISA) on diskette. It contains all of the EDI standards detail for a particular X12 version. Included on the diskette are several tables (files) constructed in such a way that any item of definition or specification in that standards version is defined in a pertinent table and adheres to the principle that anything in the standard is defined in only one place, regardless of how often it is used. Thus, there are ten tables for: Transaction set names, transaction set details, segment names, segment details, composite names, composite details, data element names, data element details, EDI codes and values, and EDI text (definitions, abstracts, purpose, etc.).

Bass's work is especially important because these tables are used by EDI software companies and EDI standards publishers, and are significant because there is no room for variation in interpretation of an EDI standard format by any of the EDI translation products. Further, since they are composed from the same source, there is no difference in the meaning conveyed between the printed standard and EDI translation software.

Dan Petrosky

Dan Petrosky was with Tymshare when EDI standards were being developed in the mid-1970s. He subsequently had management positions with leading EDI service providers, where he provided EDI consulting to the governments of South Korea and Malaysia.

Dan then became one of The EDI Group's instructors for their Principles of EDI course.

Dan Petrosky, left, with Victor Almandoz, a proponent for EDI in Mexico, at an EDI industry exhibition.

He joined John Moriarty to form EDI Partners in the early 1990s, and continued to focus on EDI education. His significant contribution was to offer seminars at university sites and have seminar content in keeping with university rigor. The EDI "101" seminar, for example, focuses on understanding the business requirements that forced EDI into becoming a business trend worldwide, and includes topics on EDI standards, communications services, software products, trading partner EDI profiles, and key barriers.

The EDI Partners' curriculum also includes seminars for (advanced) EDI "201," financial EDI, introduction to knowledge management, and other related topics.

EDI Partners has alliances with more than ten universities.

And Around the World

Several people from other countries were recognized in *EDI Forum* as EDI pioneers. Examples cited in this chapter include Marshall Spence of Canada, Don Trafford and Ray Walker of the United Kingdom, Gunnar Sundblad of Sweden, Juletta Broomfield of Hong Kong, and Pearleen Chan of Singapore.

Marshall Spence

Marshall Spence,[47] president of the EDI Council of Canada (EDICC) during 1985-97, had a role in shaping the outcome of EDI not only in Canada, but worldwide. Effectively, from the vantage point of EDICC, Spence was everyone's EDI consultant.

The EDICC grew from a 1985 EDI pilot project in Canada for the food, grocery, pharmaceutical, and retail industries. Spence represented Nestle Enterprises Inc. during the pilot. He was later appointed to be the first president of the EDICC by representatives of the eight major trade associations that sponsored the pilot. The council was initially intended to provide EDI education, training, awareness, and implementation assistance.[48] Under Spence's leadership, EDICC's membership increased rapidly, growing from twenty members in 1985 to over 700 by 1990. The council's intentions were fulfilled through Spence's leadership and that of his assistant, Nigel Wood.

Recognizing the importance of global trade to Canada and the potential of EDI in facilitating this, Spence used his position at EDICC to sponsor global awareness of EDI. To that end, he set up the first International Congress of EDI Users that took place in Vancouver in July 1989 and included participants from sixteen countries. The congress continues each year with the host country changing each time. He continuously brought together representatives of Canadian and U.S. companies for discussion of EDI's role in cross-border trade. He was an active member of the Board of Directors of the EDI World Institute introduced in 1992.[49] And he accepted invitations to speak in several countries relative to assisting in the formation of national EDI associations similar to EDICC. These countries included Australia,

---

[47] Gordon R. Jenkins, "Marshall Spence [EDI Pioneer]," *EDI Forum*, 1990 Issue, page 77.

[48] Marshall Spence, "The EDICC: The Driving Force Behind EDI in Canada," *EDI Forum*, Volume 6 (1993), No. 1, pages 14-17.

[49] Pierre Lortie, "Going Global: The EDI World Institute Is Launched," *EDI Forum*, 1993 Issue No. 1, pages 94-96.

New Zealand, Korea, Japan, Italy, and the Netherlands. The EDI Associations of Korea, Australia, and New Zealand used the EDICC constitution and bylaws as models.[50]

The significance of the work of Marshall Spence and the EDICC is that it led Canada into being an early and successful participant in both domestic and international EDI, it helped other countries to organize effective supportive EDI infrastructures, and it routinely brought together EDI professionals from several countries.

Don Trafford

Don Trafford[51] of the U.K. had many experiences leading to his strategic involvement in EDI by the time he became director of EDP to the newly formed U.K. Government agency SITPRO (The Simplification of International Trade Procedures Board) in 1971. SITPRO published the first European rules for variable format trade data interchange in 1978. This consisted of syntax and a data element directory. Trafford led the UN/ECE (United Nations/Economic Commission for Europe) team to the publication of Trade Data Interchange (TDI) in 1984. TDI was an EDI standard that was universally accepted by all European countries. TDI went from there into operational usage. However, before TDI was processed by the International Standards Organization (ISO), the UN took the EDI initiative that led to UN/EDIFACT. Trafford had a leading role in that development as well. Trafford was awarded the Order of the British Empire in 1987.

During the late 1970s and early 1980s, Trafford visited TDCC several times. One of the results of a visit was that TDCC changed its data element specifications for names and addresses from thirty to thirty-five characters to agree with European specifications. Although this was a simple step, it was of enormous significance in the ultimate drive toward worldwide EDI standardization, because of the frequency of use of name and address data elements.

Trafford also led SITPRO into production of world-class software to facilitate international trade. He left SITPRO in 1986 to form his own consultancy company, but continued to be very involved in EDIFACT developments and use.

---

[50] Marshall Spence, "The EDICC: The Driving Force Behind EDI in Canada," *EDI Forum*, 1993 Issue No. 1, pages 14-17.

[51] Ray Walker, "Don Trafford: EDI Pioneer," *EDI Forum*, Founding Issue, 1988, page 101.

Gunnar Sundblad

Gunnar Sundblad[52] of Sweden was a prominent participant during EDI standards activities that preceded EDIFACT. These included early developments of the UN/Layout key, the Trade Data Elements Directory, and the Guidelines for Trade Data Interchange (GTDI). During the early development of EDIFACT, he spoke out and was respected for his broad view and knowledge on many issues. During this period, he was active for both the Swedish Standards Institute and the Swedish Trade Facilitation Organization (SWEPRO).

He continued to be active in EDIFACT. Even after retirement, he was still a major source in Europe for information about EDI in general, including EDIFACT.

Ray Walker

Ray Walker[53] of the U.K. was chief executive of SITPRO. He was nominated by UN/ECE to co-chair the team assembled to create UN/EDIFACT, and he served for five years as the UN/ECE Western European rapporteur for UN/EDIFACT, coordinating the EDI developments in the eighteen countries of the European Community and European Free Trade Association.

Walker received from the ANSI X12 community in 1986 an award for outstanding contribution to international data exchange. In 1988, he became the first person to hold the International Data Exchange Association's "Man of the Year" award.

Ray Walker was awarded in 1991 the Order of the British Empire in recognition for his services to export and international trade.

Juletta Broomfield

Juletta Broomfield[54] of Hong Kong from the mid 1980s worked to establish and lead the Tradelink Electronic Document Services Ltd. Tradelink consists of a group of leading Hong Kong organizations set up in 1988 to develop, promote, and educate local businesses in the use of

---

[52] Henk van Maaren, "Gunnar Sundblad: EDI Pioneer," EDI Forum, 1989 Issue, page 92.

[53] *EDI Forum*, "Ray Walker: EDI Pioneer," 1992 Issue No. 4, page 48.

[54] *EDI Forum*, "Juletta Broomfield: EDI Pioneer," 1992 Issue No. 4, page 46.

electronic trading. The Tradelink Board appointed Broomfield General Manager in 1991.

About the same time–and almost single-handedly–Broomfield created the event "EDI Asia '89." This became a popular annual event, and through her work, EDI Asia was established as the Pacific Rim's premier conference and exhibition for electronic trading.

Pearleen Chan

Pearleen Chan of Singapore has been one of her country's leading forces behind its impressive implementation of EDI strategies.[55] As managing director at Singapore Network Services (SNS), she led the efforts for the definition and implementation of Tradenet that became operational in 1989. Tradenet linked more than twenty government agencies and streamlined the movement of trade clearance documents. With Tradenet, a single document was processed electronically by all of these agencies for each shipment, rather than multiple forms used in the previous paper-based system. Singapore has a major transshipment port used in world trade.

SNS's mission was to be a world-class provider of quality communications and information services. Tradenet, the first service offered by SNS, was an "eye-catcher" before its three-month planned EDI pilot period ended. First, the pilot included fifty users, which is rather large for pilot projects; second, these pilot system users were experiencing fifteen-minute responses for government permits via Tradenet, while their competitors using the paper-based system waited two days for the equivalent response; and third, additional users were "clamoring to sign on as subscribers to the network."[56] Trading partners using the network include government agencies and both local and overseas companies.

Subsequent additions to SNS's services included electronic systems with EDI for use in healthcare, legal, manufacturing, retail, and finance communities.

The significance of the EDI successes in Singapore and Pearleen Chan's leadership are important worldwide; because Singapore is an important hub for world trade and transportation, the Singapore successes in electronic commerce were held as a model for others, and the requirement was proven

---

[55] *EDI Forum*, "Pearleen Chan: EDI Pioneer," 1993 Issue No. 4, pages 60-62.

[56] Pearleen Chan, "Singapore: Seizing Competitive Advantage with EDI," *EDI Forum*, Volume 7, No. 1 (1994), pages 39-42.

that maximum benefits through use of EDI must be accompanied by full integration of EDI with many facets of business operations.

Summary

The role of consultants is to listen, study, ponder, synthesize, and lead. The results of their work has special meaning when they are helping to chart an entirely new course which proposes to raise operational environments of their clients to a new plateau, bringing with it dramatic improvements in efficiency, quality, and customer service.

Such has been the case for EC/EDI consultants. They therefore have had the additional task to be convincing, since what they advocate is seldom easy. Consultants have a significant part in this evolution and comprise a significant segment of the EDI service industry.

FINANCIAL EDI

Financial EDI extends the capability to use EDI format structures and processes to electronically transfer money as well as data. In such environments, complete detail for reasons of the payment arrives simultaneously with the payment. Thus, the reconciliation process is simplified, unambiguous, and most likely automatic.

The first work with this was in conjunction with the pilot work of First Chicago Bank and General Motors. This included work by Ruth Andersen and Kathleen Flynn to define a new EDI transaction set, "820 (Payment Order, Remittance Advice)."

In brief, the 820 can be used to make a payment, send a remittance advice, or make a payment *and* send a remittance advice (same transmission). It can be sent as an order to a financial institution to make a payment to a payee. It can also be a remittance advice identifying the detail needed to perform cash application to the payee's accounts receivable system. The remittance advice can go directly from payer to payee, through a financial institution, or through a third-party agent.

Craigg Ballance in Canada had pointed out very early in financial EDI development that Canada was in an enviable position, since it had only ten major banks that serviced the country. All of these banks were EDI-capable by the early 1990s. That made it possible for a Canadian company to make a unilateral decision to do EDI/EFT regardless of what its trading partners were doing. This was accomplished with the company's arrangement with the bank where the company would transmit all fund releases and supporting data to its bank, and receive notice of incoming funds via EDI. The bank's function was to provide payment and data in a form specified by the funds recipient if the recipient used the same bank as the sender. If not, the funds and data were sent to the recipient's bank. How did the bank know how to do this? The EDI data included a code that identified the recipient's bank and account number. Craigg, working from his position at the Royal Bank of Canada, worked to make this happen. Craigg wrote many *EDI Forum* articles on Financial EDI.

Table 1: Other EFT Standards 1990

CCD, Corporate Concentration or Disbursements	"CCD is an electronic message used in the United States settlement system for the payment amount only. One payment can be sent using CCD for one invoice. CCD is the United States equivalent of the Canadian CPA005 with all its limitations, i.e. minimal data with payment details submitted separately. It has only 60 characters of information that can be transmitted along with the dollar amount. CCD is by far the most widely used form of the United States banking system [1990], but CCD is not EDI. No EDI payment and transmission information can be sent using CCD. It is a NATCHA payment format with no addenda record and therefore no remittance data can be sent.
CTP, Corporate Trade Payment	"CTP is an electronic message used in the United States settlement system. CTP is a fixed field of data with up to 4,990 invoice or addenda records of 94 characters each and 10 free-form characters of description for each invoice. CTP was supposed to be the successor to CCD but never really caught on in the United States because CTP is not EDI [X12]. Several invoices can be paid using one payment.

NATCHA: National Automated Clearing House Association

Table 1: Other EFT Standards 1990

CCD+, CCD Plus or Vendor Express	"CCD+ is an electronic message in the United States Settlement system. One 80-character EDI-compatible data string is in NATCHA format with payment record and therefore can carry a minimal remittance record. "CCD+ is a very innovative invention of the United States Federal Treasury to couple the traditional CCD non-EDI transmission with an EDI trailer of 80 characters. The beauty of this is that every one of the 20,000 United States banks has CCD and with minimum effort can receive an EDI payment from the United States government. Numerous United States government agencies are using EDI to one degree or another for some form of payment and they are to be commended for their efforts.
CTX, Corporate Trade Exchange	"CTX is an electronic message in the United States settlement system, and is a completely EDI payment with many payments and many invoices. CTX has variable data fields as developed by ANSI X12 utilizing the 94 character record convention of CTPs. The only trouble is that payment standards (CTX) have been developed between banks in isolation from standards developed on the business side (ANSI X12: 820). The result has been a banking payment envelope (CTX) in which a business payment (an ANSI X12 820) fits with difficulties."

Gordon Jenkins, also in Canada, summarized the EFT options:[57]Notice that only one of these options (CTX) is EDI, but depending on the bank involved, all options were possible.

The EDI/EFT implementation permits payers to send a single transmission to a bank covering many payees and invoices, and including the date for payment and details necessary for a payee to automatically reconcile payments with amounts due. The payer need not be concerned whether or not the payee is EDI-capable. The information route is payer to payer's bank. That bank moves funds on dates specified from the payer's account to payee's accounts for those payees that are also clients of the payer's bank. For other payees, the payer's bank transfers funds to appropriate payee

[57]Gordon Jenkins and Ray Lancashire, "The Canadian Electronic Data Interchange Handbook," published by EDI Council of Canada, Etobicoke, Ontario, 1990, pages 67-68.

banks with all of the detail. Notice that the scheme eliminates the need for printing and mailing checks, and that the payer's payment processes are automatic, electronic, and complete in terms of information provided the payee. Automation of the reverse processes by payees is up to each payee, independent of decisions of other payees.

Many exciting things began to happen in the business world after EDI and EFT were associated: 1) Terms of sale were reengineered in a "win/win" exchange by the buyer and supplier, permitting prompt payment on dates-certain by the buyer and more favorable discount terms offered by the supplier. 2) Processes were reengineered by the buyer to integrate automatic payment and eliminate need for an invoice. (This was based on receipt from the supplier of an EDI shipment advice, presenting details of what was shipped and when it will arrive. The buyer verifies the shipment advice against a check of what was ordered and what physically arrives, and releases payment automatically when assurance is established. This is referred to as "Evaluated Receipts Processing.") 3) Payment reconciliation by the supplier was made fully integrated and automated. 4) Cash flow estimates by the supplier were changed from empirical (statistical) methods to database inquiry methods. To this end, an always-current database used to record contracted amounts and receipt dates is automatically maintained with data extracted from EDI data flows. The automatic processes may be performed daily, or they may be linked to EDI processes if more timely updates are required. 5) Buyers began to specify a short window of time (sometimes as short as fifteen minutes) when the shipment is expected. This permitted dramatic decreases in warehousing costs.

Who is in the EDI/EFT service industry? To be sure, banks are involved. So are EDI communications, software, and consulting companies with specialized EDI/EFT knowledge.

Does this have anything to do with the phenomenal increases in productivity experienced by U.S. industries by year 2000? The affects regarding timeliness, decreased purchasing costs for the buyer, date-certain payments for the supplier, automation of reconciliation processes, and elimination of invoice reconciliation processes all indicate a significant effect on productivity. Combine this with controlled error-free environments, and expect very welcomed changes in productivity.

SECURITY FOCUS AND PRODUCTS[58]

Ralph Berwanger

ANSI ASC X12 Security

Security, as an EDI service, is a relatively new phenomenon. The ANSI ASC X12 standard contained no security services until the release of version 003011, and UN/EDIFACT provided no formal support for security until publication of syntax version four. Lack of security structures organic to the EDI standards was not an oversight by early standards developers. Rather, trading partner agreements or communications techniques satisfied initial security requirements.

> **ANSI:** American National Standards Institute
>
> **ASC:** Accredited Standards Committee
>
> **X12:** U.S. EDI standard
>
> **UN:** United Nations
>
> **EDIFACT:** EDI For Administration, Commerce and Transport
>
> **003011:** X12 versions are coded. The code structure, for example, is version 003, release 01, sub-release 1. Anew version-release is published each year; a sub-release may be published within a year.

Early EDI implementers created trading partner agreements containing information vital to successful electronic exchanges. The agreements not only codified delimiters and implementation conventions but also defined responsibilities and liabilities related to any information exchanged. Language within the trading partner agreements mitigated the need for digital signatures. Regardless of that language, they were not technically achievable. Also, the universe of transaction sets available to early EDI users was relatively small, and these transactions were viewed to have a relatively short lifespan. The EDI receiver could easily clarify any issues related to an EDI interchange while the data was still relevant. Who would have thought that EDI transactions would communicate mortgage information that must be maintained in its original form for the life of a thirty-year mortgage?

---

[58]This Security topic was provided by Ralph Berwanger, ambassador for standards and technology, BTrade.com, August 2000.

Communications processes were limited to direct dial-up connections or value-added networks (VANS) for the early EDI users. Both methods were perceived as "secure enough." These methods were not bulletproof. A nefarious party could masquerade as an EDI party, misrepresenting themselves as a valid trading partner. However, controls within the overall business process identified these activities before they caused damage to a legitimate trading partner. VANS used direct dial-up schemes to get the data from their customers to the networks. The direct dial-up approach coupled with password-protected mailboxes and multi-path packet routing satisfied security concerns of the early EDI users.

In the early 1990s the financial community began to craft a set of security standards specific for X12. The first security standards focused on providing confidentiality for EDI transactions from the point where the EDI was created to the point where the EDI was received and translated. The result of their work was published as X12.58. A companion standard, X12.42 was also published. This standard defined the 815 (Cryptographic Service Message) transaction set that supported the exchange of cryptographic keying materials.

> **DES:** Digital Encryption Standard
>
> **Non-repudiation:** Not able to deny
>
> **Disembodied signature:** Signature existing independent of the information that is being signed
>
> **Encryption:** Transformation of the characters in the transmission, so that the transmission may not be understood by either a software process or a person until the transmitted data is unencrypted, using tightly controlled (secret) encryption keys.
>
> **Authentication:** Creation of a code to be included in a transmission. The receiver re-creates the code and compares it with the value transmitted. If the transmitted and re-created values are not identical, it indicates that the transmission has been altered in some way. (Keys are also used for authentication.)

The initial version of X12.58, published in X12 version 003011, supported message integrity using a *message authentication code* and confidentiality using symmetric encryption (e.g., digital encryption standard, DES). This first generation of EDI security was approved when the concept of public-private (asymmetric) keys was still very experimental, so support for digital signatures was not available. Except for minor code value additions, the standard remained unchanged until the release of version 003052.

X12 version 003052 introduced some major changes to EDI security. The suite of security services incorporated message authentication support. Digital signatures provided a much-needed non-repudiation of receipt function. Additionally, the X12.42 standard was changed to permit EDI users to exchange digital certificates as well as perform some rudimentary certificate management functions.

The standard continued to evolve and improve. The final deficiency of the EDI standard was removed with the publication of X12 version 004030. This version included a new transaction set, 993 (Secure Receipt or Acknowledgment), which provided three discrete functions: non-repudiation of receipt, security error reporting, and delivery of disembodied signatures.

The non-repudiation of receipt allowed receivers of EDI data to acknowledge the receipt of the data in a way that could not be denied by the receiver. The data's sender was assured that the data received was the data that was sent and that the receiver was the party that was intended to get the message. The security model now provided a complete choreography between the two parties. The new transaction set also provided detailed security error information when required. Prior to this, all security errors were reported in the 997 (Functional Acknowledgment) transaction set. However, the types of security errors that could be reported were very limited. Furthermore, the errors could not—would not—be authenticated by the reporting party. The 993 provided security processes with authenticated, meaningful error reports.

Finally, the 993 also provided the capability to communicate a disembodied signature when the business process called for it. While no requirement for this functionality was ever stated, the service was present in the international community and carried into the ANSI standard.

UN/EDIFACT Security

> **ECE:** Economic Commission for Europe
> **WP:** Working Party
> **Non-repudiation:** Not able to deny.
> **ISO:** International Standards Organization
> **EAN:** European Article Number
> **PKI:** Public Key Infrastructure

The development of security services within UN/EDIFACT mirror those of X12.58. For reasons similar to those of early X12 versions, syntax versions one and two contain no security functionality. A set of security functions was defined for trial use within version three of the syntax by the UN/ECE/WP4. The proposed security services were never ratified for use as a part of the standard. Nevertheless, the simple fact is that strong business needs supersede standards. Several business sectors required immediate security solutions for their EDI so despite the lack of formal approval, many organizations built and deployed security solutions based on the trial proposal. These early trial standards were implemented by the Authentication/Acknowledgment Message (AUTACK). The AUTACK provided message integrity and message authentication services, as well as a controlled method of reporting errors within the security process. These are all functions that were later incorporated into the X12 993 transaction set.

There was an early attempt to define a message for confidentiality, called CIPHER. Standards developers were never able to obtain approval for this message, so it never progressed beyond its early proposal stage. Despite the inability of the development process to promote the CIPHER, it managed to become a component of a few EDI implementations—again business needs override standards. Syntax four of the EDIFACT standard was nearing completion when the trial period for the security services expired. A decision was made to forego any further development of security standards for syntax three. Syntax four was enhanced to include a full set of security services and was promoted instead of some "short-term" fix to syntax three.

Syntax four (ISO Standard 9735) was approved in 1998. Parts five, six, seven, and nine of the standard contained the security components. This standard provides a complete set of security functions for the UN/EDIFACT user. Message security services include confidentiality, message authentication, message integrity, and non-repudiation of origin. Additionally, the AUTACK message supports non-repudiation of either the sender or receiver of a message and security error reporting. A second security message is defined to provide cryptographic management support. The EDIFACT KEYMAN message allows security users to exchange cryptographic keying material and digital certificates.

There is one very important distinction between and X12 and EDIFACT communities that hindered adoption of the syntax four security services. The X12 community is accustomed to frequently upgrading their processes from one version/release of the standard to another to obtain new functionality. This migration is supported by the way EDI translation software providers produce their translation products. The majority of EDIFACT users cannot rapidly migrate from one version of the syntax to another. Many users have hard-coded EDI translation (converter) software making a migration effort very expensive. The migration problem does not eliminate the need for many EDIFACT users to have security services. Many organizations, unable to bear the expense of migrating to syntax four but needing security, devised "proprietary" or interim solutions. These solutions are attempting to incorporate the syntax four security structures within syntax three. The solutions are cleaver and functional. EAN International and the European financial community were just two examples of huge EDI user communities that produced a set of syntax three solutions. EDI purists and other critics of these non-standard solutions continue to lobby for these communities to adopt a standards-compliant security solution. At the same time, the purists acknowledge that many of the solutions that have been crafted work very well and are satisfying the business need.

The Future for EDI Security

The groundwork is in place to allow for the development of a secure EDI environment.

Government and commercial organizations have mandated the reduction of paper-based business transactions; also communications costs and technical availability are moving EDI users to the Internet. Initial investments have been made to implement EDI capability within many large and medium-size enterprises and distractions that forced spending of funds required to implement security are diminishing. Just as importantly, an infrastructure to support the security needs of the business world is now available. A mature standard (X.509) for digital credential and federal, state, and enterprise-level public key infrastructures (PKI) are in place. At least one international consortium has created a global infrastructure permitting business secure interactions between entities with minimal a priori knowledge of one another.

The result of these developments is that many EDI and communications software vendors are producing affordable software solutions. In the past, only large organizations could afford to deploy EDI security services, now small and medium enterprises can easily implement an interoperable, security solution.

Making It Happen—Security Products

It is absolutely necessary to have standards for encryption when transmissions are among independent companies and the communications processes are not completely under the control of the companies.

It is also necessary to have competitively-priced encryption software that can be linked with EDI processes. Early on, the lack of lucrative business opportunities kept the list of companies who produced security software very abbreviated. Prime Factors and Sterling Software were the most prominent suppliers. Both companies produced a security product that provided confidentiality compliant with the X12.58 standard. Later, Comm-Press Technologies (currently known as bTrade.com) offered a security solution that provided confidentiality and digital signatures. The significant thing about these products is that they were interoperable.

IEFT: Internet Engineering Task Force

S/MIME: Secure/Multipart Internet Mail Exchange, a capability for email messages to include more than one part (graphics, sound clip, video clip ...)

SSL: Secure Socket Layer

XML: eXtensible Markup Language

W3C: World Wide Web Consortium

Data Guard, the Sterling Software product, was withdrawn from the market but not before several other companies entered the market.

The migration of EDI communications onto the Internet spawned new interest in the security product market. Many of the solutions were not X12.58 compliant—they focused on the transport mechanisms. Rather than worry about X12 security structures, these vendors produced products that employed secure socket layer (SSL) technology. Others used a process defined by the Internet Engineering Task Force (IETF) to provide security using Secure/Multipart Internet Mail Exchange (S/MIME). The principal vendor of this technology was Harbinger. Additionally, Group 8760 provided S/MIME EDI security tools for the gas industry.

There is not, nor has there ever been, widely available EDIFACT security solutions. Several companies have produced security solutions for EDIFACT users, but the solutions were proprietary. Currently the Comm-Press Technologies security product provides syntax three and syntax four security services. Prime Factor is building UN/EDIFACT syntax four security functionality into their product. The product may be available before the end of calendar year 2000.

Conflict?

Why is there not greater interest in providing security solutions that are desperately needed by the business community? XML is the answer. A tidal wave of interest in eXtensible Markup Language business solutions has the software vendors believing that the real money is in XML, not X12 or UN/EDIFACT security solutions. The IETF and World Wide Web Consortium (W3C) have defined digital signature standards for XML, and groups like the ebXML Initiative are designing new business frameworks that rely on XML syntax. Already, vendors are building XML-based products.

Despite the focus on XML, traditional EDI users still want standards-based security solutions. Companies that make X12 and EDIFACT security products will have a rich marketplace for many years.

Why does interest in X12 and EDIFACT endure, and why does their use continue to grow? They provide efficient means to extensively edit the data by senders and receivers, a capability essential in process-to-process ("hands-off") environments. They also provide efficiencies in transmission file lengths, a factor which has a significant effect on data communications, computer processing speeds, and computer memory usage. In the year 2000, XML solutions do not offer equivalent extensiveness of edits and processing and memory efficiencies.

5. Forcing Change

"Don't talk of spring.
Don't talk of fall.
Don't talk at all.
Show me! Show me now."

Lerner and Loewe, *My Fair Lady*

ACTIONS

Drives for Experiences and Results

By 1980, TDCC was already age twelve, and the first U.S. public EDI standards document was age five. With all that was said and done about implementing EDI during that period, we were still only at the talking and theory stage. At the time, EDI had format standards, functional specifications, generalized software, and interested companies. And yes, we had some experimental initiatives. We did not, however, have broadly-based operational EDI experiences and success stories. Ed Guilbert at TDCC asked why were corporations putting all this effort into EDI and not using it. We needed action!

We needed some high-profile pilot EDI projects.

The challenge was to design pilots for proving (by actually doing it) the process-to-process, company-to-company, computer-to-computer (hands off) data transmission, verification, and processing concepts; proving the reliability and security concepts; indicating that the processes are economically viable; documenting results; leaving resulting systems in place to build on each; and increasing the number of trading partners and types of transactions.

From the point of view for getting started (getting the show on the road), the challenges were considerably more difficult. These required getting the attention and approval of top corporate managements; dissipating the fears of employees about termination of their jobs; getting EDI projects approved in corporate budget processes; having the good fortune that VANs, PCs, compatible EDI software, and compatible modems all became available at about the same time; and having access to an "EDI champion" within the proactive companies.

Several EDI pilots were already referenced:

Grocery Industry 13 companies, *The Role of UCS and the Grocery Industry*, page 37 [1981-82]	This project had high exposure, met its objectives, was completed on schedule, and proved that the significant financial benefits attributable to EDI were not underestimated.
Insights from six companies and a U.S. Government report, *Early Insights from Trials and Evaluations*, page 74 [1985-89]	These reports helped others to plan their own EDI initiatives and provided reasons for doing so.
Financial EDI General Motors / First Chicago [eight participating banks], *Daniel M. Ferguson*, page 108 [1984-86]	This work ultimately resulted in the electronic delivery of billions of dollars of payments to suppliers and the beginning of win-win scenarios in EDI/EFT environments.
Transmission of Student Transcripts, *SCT Corporation*, page 100 [1994-95]	This work was especially noteworthy because it dealt with sensitive non-commercial information that required security and timely and explicit proof of delivery. It also required that the data be encrypted.

In this chapter, seven projects are described in terms of purpose, scope, and some of the conversation that indicated the state of readiness for EDI in the mid-1980s. The first four projects are some in which the author had a role while serving at EDI, Inc. The fifth and sixth are from the author's experiences as an EDI consultant retained by EDI Integration Corporation; the seventh project was also from EDI Inc. experiences, but it is quite different from the other six events.

All seven projects are described from a participant's perspective.

To sense how rapidly technology is changing, compare the state of readiness for change relative to project environments in the 1980s and early

1990s with technology available at the turn of the century. In the past, we were comfortable with the arrival of a new computer generation every three years with each generation doubling the speed, improving and enhancing system software and dramatically increasing reliability, all this while cutting the price in half. At the turn of the century, a comparable computer generation passes in less than a year.

Similar Procedure and Goal

All of the following projects had a similar procedure and goal. The environment always included: 1) EDI investigators/implementers who were charged to understand a current environment and propose how EDI may be used to help accomplished defined objectives (improve service, increase reliability, cut costs, speed up processes); and 2) an operations staff who "owned" the current processes and who would be affected by introduction of EDI.

"Affected" did not mean elimination of jobs, but did mean a change in tasks. The investigators were from outside the organizations sponsoring the projects. The operations staffs were always insiders.

Generally, the procedure for the EDI investigators was to: 1) Meet with operational staffs to explain what was expected to be accomplish, what it meant to the staff, and why it was important to both staff members and their organizations; 2) Understand the current manual or partially automated processes where EDI was to be introduced or might be introduced; 3) Discuss or "walk" through the current processes with appropriate staff people; and 4) Learn how the current staff accomplished certain tasks, how their jobs "fit" into the work stream, whether any automation was involved, what controls they used, and what they might like from an automated system.

Tom Heard of Logistics Management Institute (LMI) gave the term "operating scenario" for "what they might like from an automated system."

As a result of a first meeting between EDI investigators and operational staff, the investigators returned to their own facilities to create a functional specification for a change in workflow involving the current operational objectives and EDI processes.

At this point, the functional specification was in a narrative form with talking points for specific key steps or focal points. The investigators (facilitators) met a second time with an operational staff to describe the concept and to get reactions, comments, and suggestions. It was imperative that operational staff members were enthusiastic and cooperated with the investigators, since these staff members were about to participate with the investigators in the implementation.

The functional specification was subsequently developed into a working plan. The starting point was always that operational objectives would persist. The resultant work flow would use readily available EDI software and value added network services (VANs), and additional software would be written to accomplish new functionality identified in the operating scenario.

When the additional software was written and tested, the EDI investigators returned to each participating operational organization to install, explain, demonstrate, train, and answer questions.

The operational team also had work to do while the investigators were away: explain to others in the company what was going on and why, respond to questions from the investigators, and write software (in some cases) that would facilitate moving data between their current computer and the EDI computer. The participating company appointed an EDI champion or coordinator as a focal point for these tasks. The EDI computer for the following examples was always a PC that was only to be used for EDI.

It was common in the early 1980s for small to medium-sized companies to not have computers. It was also common for large companies with mainframe computers having sophisticated software application systems to lack linkages among different applications. For example, an ocean carrier company may have had impressive software applications systems for tracking freight worldwide and for documenting the details and charges for each shipment; it may not have had the two applications linked or even operating on the same computer system.

The seven project examples were chosen for the following reasons:

Project	Reason for Inclusion
1. North American Wholesale Grocers Association [1984]	Show the limiting capabilities of PCs when they were first introduced and what was done to bring a project to "life" in spite of that; show the importance placed on executive attitude when initiating a project.

Project	Reason for Inclusion
2. Burlington Northern [1985]	Indicate what a large corporation did to become proactive toward EDI and how fast its EDI environment expanded; provide an example for automating a trading partner that used EDI as its first application for computers.
3. Automated Carrier Interface [1985-6]	Provide examples for "front-end" and "stand-alone" EDI systems and why choice was made for one or another.
4. Government Bill of Lading [1986-7]	Indicate how significant process enhancements become possible with incorporation of EDI into the process environment; describe some of the automation environment when EDI was getting into the pilot stage.
5. Shipbuilding Community [1992]	Show that ownership of a mainframe computer did not imply that likely applications were integrated, even given that a company specifically designed applications for itself; provide examples for the different approaches for initiating EDI.
6. Apparel Research Network [1996]	Provide an example in which a community of common interest came together to adopt a common standard and systematically began to use it for mutual benefits related to service, cost, and cash flow; show how and why EDI and Internet concepts were included in the same environment.
7. Barter [1985]	Show one of the means used to include a small company in the EDI community.

Operating Scenarios

North American Wholesale Grocers Association NAWGA (1984)

> In notation like **"880—Invoice,"** "880" is the identifying code for the type of transaction set. "Invoice" is the name of the transaction set. The code is required in each transmitted transaction set to identify the kind of transmission. A transaction set name is never included in a transmission, since a computer program does not require it.

The grocery industry pilot was implemented with mainframe and mid-range computers. NAWGA wanted to show that micro-computers (PCs) could be used to rapidly expand the EDI community within the grocery industry. They chose EDI, Inc. and ORDERNET Services to help with the pilot. The project scope was to implement EDI at six sites, be the first to use PCs for EDI, use EDI to facilitate automatic reconciliation of purchase orders and invoices, and use UCS transaction sets to send 880 (invoice) and send and receive 999 (acceptance/rejection acknowledgment).

The EDI, communications, and automatic reconciliation implementations were easy compared with moving data to and from a participant's internal computer. Software, equipment, and cables for doing this in a standard way were only beginning to be invented. In some cases we used a twelve-inch floppy disk drive to move the data. This required a special device attached to the PC and special software. Then, since we did not want to process the same data more than once, other new software was required to "remember" if the current diskette had new data or was re-inserted. In one case, Buddy Bass and Ralph Notto drove from Huntingdon, Pennsylvania to Pittsburgh (130 miles) because a wrong connecting cable was delivered, and it was needed for an important EDI demonstration two days hence.

One of the volunteers for the pilot wanted to be assured in advance that there would be no serious problem. We replied that he best wait until others had "paved the way."

But with perseverance, we delivered operational EDI systems to the extent that Jim Muenz of Kraft telephoned that the EDI purchase orders he received from NAGWA pilot companies worked perfectly the first time.

"Isn't that what you expected?" Notto asked.

"No," he replied. "It usually takes a month of testing and adjustment to get to that point." The EDI on PCs then became a serious contender for

EDI operations from that point forward. In fact, most EDI implementations used PCs. The EDI Group reported in 1996 that 85% of EDI systems were PC-based.

Burlington Northern (1985)

The railroad industry was a consistent contributor during formative EDI standards meetings. The early orientations were toward transportation transactions. By 1985, Burlington Northern (BN) had additionally implemented an EDI option for its purchasing processes. They intended to use X12 transaction sets to send 850 (Purchase Order–Receive) and 855 (Purchase Order Acknowledgment), and to send and receive 997 (Functional Acknowledgment).

They asked EDI Inc. to participate in vendor briefings and EDI demonstrations. In addition to the EDI system, this required software for responding on screen to purchase orders, indicating how and when the purchase order would be filled. Data communications was via an automatic direct dial to BN.

Over fifty companies ordered an EDI system within a few months of the vendor briefings. Some of these companies never previously had a computer.

One such company, Pick Industries near Minneapolis, manufactured doors for rail cars. The EDI system was installed in a PC on a table behind the receptionist/secretary's desk. The 1985 operating scenario was: swing around from the desk to the table; enter the name of the EDI system (Telink) from the PC keyboard, and press the enter key; invoke a menu choice to instruct the computer to automatically dial out to connect to BN and do a specified list of functions without further operator action or attention.

The specified list was: receive orders; automatically disconnect the communications; process the orders to create linkages to the reports modules and the purchase order acknowledgment file; automatically construct functional acknowledgments; connect again and send the acknowledgments; and automatically disconnect the communications again.

When the transmission was finished, the operator (receptionist) invoked a menu choice to: print the orders; make a subsequent menu choice to show an acknowledgment screen and, order-by-order, press a key to indicate that the order is accepted, or indicate on screen any variations necessary; and when responses for all orders are finished, make another menu selection to invoke the EDI translation and communications processes, and subsequently automatically disconnect the communications link.

During these communications processes, it was expected that both orders and functional acknowledgments might be received.

Mr. Pick looked at the first "live" session. About thirty orders were received. He looked over the printed orders, said that all would be filled as requested, and directed the secretary to acknowledge them that way. The entire scenario from getting the orders to acknowledging everything took about a half hour, including data communications at 150 characters per second. Mr. Pick was pleased. People at BN were pleased.

Automated Carrier Interface ACI (1985-6)

The U.S. Military Sealift Command (MSC) contracts with U.S. ocean carriers for transport of containers to military locations around the world. The transportation processes include ordering empty containers to be delivered to shipping points; scheduling transportation for shipping-point to port, home port to overseas port, and overseas port to receiving point; and tracking the shipments in route.

The Military Traffic Management Command (MTMC) provided the programs and computers relative to these processes as a service to MSC.

The project required installation of EDI systems at MTMC and several ocean carriers. For transmissions from MTMC to carriers, the TDCC 300 (Reservation Booking Request) was used. Carriers sending acceptance or change request notices to MTMC used the TDCC 301 (Confirmation/Counterproposal). To cancel an order, MTMC sent to carriers the TDCC 303 (Cancellation). The sending and receiving of acknowledgments were implemented with the X12 997 (Functional Acknowledgment).

The project included PC-based EDI systems connected to Honeywell computers at two MTMC locations. These are typically referred to as "EDI front-ends." That is, the computers are connected with a cable, and one computer is "in front of another" for purposes such as translating between internal data formats and EDI formats and sending/receiving EDI-formatted data communications with other organizations. MTMC added interfaces to existing container control software in order to send data to ocean carriers via the EDI front-end. This replaced the processes of printing and distributing reports. Data from ocean carriers was received via the EDI front-end, thus replacing manual key-entry processes with automatic processes.

Also required were EDI system installations on PCs at ocean-carrier sites. Each carrier had three choices: perform EDI tasks on its mainframe computer, use an EDI front-end, or use an EDI stand-alone system. The latter is a system that includes EDI and application software on the same computer. This was generally chosen in spite of the fact that the carriers had mainframe computers. The stand-alone system was then located in a carrier's sales support office, which serviced MTMC rather than in the carrier's central office. The application software facilitated creating the confirmation or counter proposal.

Data for several hundred containers per week were communicated this way for several years. Some ocean carriers replaced their stand-alone EDI systems with reengineered systems by the year 2000.

Government Bill of Lading (GBL) (1986-7)

Logistic Management Institute (LMI) does research and initial developmental work for the U.S. Department of Defense (DoD) on logistics matters. Their first EDI pilot project was to install EDI systems with application software at thirteen DoD sites for transmission of GBLs as EDI transaction sets.

For transmissions of GBLs from DoD to carriers and other DoD locations, the TDCC 204 (Shipment Information–Motor) was used. For invoices from carriers to DoD Finance Center the TDCC 210 (Freight Details and Invoice–Motor) was used. Acknowledgments sent and received were implemented with the X12 997 (Functional Acknowledgment).

Two examples for understanding the state of readiness for EDI type of automation in 1984:

1) Each site was required to have an outside telephone line installed before we arrived. On one occasion, everything worked except that we could not complete the communications session. Finally in desperation, Ledder asked for a phone set to test the line. He announced that instead of hearing a dial tone, someone said, "Operator."

2) During a training session, Notto wanted to emphasize how easy it was to use the system, so he asked one of those present to start the system just by typing the system name on the keyboard. "Certainly," was the reply. "Which piece is the keyboard?"

Contrast these with the state of readiness at year 2000 where millions of companies and homes are "wired" for access to the Internet, and millions of PCs at least fifty times more capable than those of 1986 are installed at millions of businesses and homes throughout the world.

Applications included automatic reconciliation of GBLs with freight invoices, management of inbound freight, and controlled modification of GBLs at time of dispatch.

The scheme was to use PCs for EDI and the new applications. The EDI systems were programmed for front-end capability as well.

The thirteen sites included Army, Navy, Marine Corps, Air Force, supply depot, and finance center locations.

Tom Heard and Bill Ledder of LMI and Ralph Notto of EDI Inc. were the EDI investigators. Much of our attention was focused on the Defense Finance and Accounting Center in Indianapolis and a supply depot at Mechanicsburg, Pennsylvania, but all sites were visited. A visit to some sites included bringing a PC (which was checked as baggage during the flight to the participating location). Software was installed onsite. Training was provided onsite.

A real challenge to automation showed up at Mechanicsburg. GBLs were prepared in advance of a truck arriving to pick up shipments. However, changes to what was to be shipped frequently occurred after GBLs were completed. In the old system, changes were written by hand or typewritten on an already printed GBL. The EDI environment required application software for this task, and the PC needed to be near the loading dock in order to record the changes.

The manual processes at the Finance Center in Indianapolis prior to EDI indicate some reasons why something like EDI was imperative. The pre-EDI environment was ready for change, because a few thousand freight invoices were received in the mail to the Finance Center each day. Each envelope was opened. The contents were manually entered into a log. The contents were placed on a numbered cart. The number corresponded to the day of the month that mail was received. Over a thirty-day period, the cart was moved from workstation to workstation (desk to desk, person to person) where tasks like validation, data entry, and crosschecking were performed. At the end of each thirty-day period, the required checks for payment were prepared by computer and sent via mail.

Problems? Something could get lost; logs were not automated at the entry point; the carts were open; personnel absence affected schedules and continuity; payments were not always on time.

For the GBL pilot, the reconciliation software used for the NAWGA pilot was revised to fit the freight invoice/bill of lading environment. Software for an automated log was written. Both the reconciliation and log software were installed on the EDI computer.

GBL: Government bill of lading

NAWGA: North American Wholesale Grocers Association

LMI: Logistics Management Institute

The result was that EDI transactions received in the pilot environment were immediately available in the log, data required for reconciliation purposes was extracted from incoming GBL copies received from the shipping points, incoming freight invoices from carriers triggered the reconciliation process, and discrepancies were immediately identified. If there were no discrepancies, data were transmitted to the finance processing system. Control was tightened; the processing cycle was changed from thirty days to match the transportation schedule; discrepancies were immediately reviewed; and payment delays were averted.

This, however, was a test environment. It was successful enough to warrant a drive for completely integrated payment authorization and release processes, control processes, and EDI-formatted data communications. Electronic payment processes followed. All became operational in the 1990s. Michael Bridges of LMI kept the conversion "on track" until it finally became fully operational in the early 1990s.

Shipbuilding Community (1992)

It takes up to seven years to make a military vessel like an aircraft carrier. The U.S. Navy contracts with companies in the U.S. shipbuilding industry to accomplish this. A necessary task for shipbuilders is to invoice the Navy every two weeks for work in progress. Spreadsheet programs were used to facilitate this. Every two weeks the spreadsheet programs were updated, invoices were printed from the updates, and printed copies were distributed internally and to the Navy locations for Supervisor of Ships (SoS), Defense Contract Auditing Agency (DCAA), and the Navy finance center. SoS and DCAA had offices at the shipbuilders' sites. The finance center was located near Washington. Copies of invoices were hand-carried to SoS and DCAA. They were express mailed to the finance center, or may have also been hand-carried. A typical invoicing day involved twenty to thirty invoices for each shipbuilding company totaling several hundred million dollars per company. The interest value per day of the money due in the event that payment was late was quite significant. Hence hand-carrying an invoice was in everyone's best interest.

Although the Navy may have worked with the spreadsheet programs to have some automation, there was no standard format used for each vessel being built. The Navy looked to EDI methods for standardization, timeliness, accuracy, and control, and chose EDI Integration Corporation as the EDI investigator/implementer. EDI sites were targeted for several Navy and shipbuilder sites.

Application software interfaced with an EDI system was required for invoicing, reconciliation, and status reporting. Electronic funds transfer was included in the scheme, and EDI was to be used to specify the transfer.

The EDI scope included several X12 transaction sets. For transmission of invoices from a shipbuilder to the Navy's SoS, DCAA, and Finance Center, the X12 810 (Invoice) was used. To report on an electronic funds transfer the Navy Finance Center sent to the shipbuilder, SoS, and DCAA, the X12 820 (Payment Order/Remittance Advice) was sent. Sending and receiving status information was accomplished with X12 824 (Application Advice). (This was added later in the project. The initial implementations used the 810 specifically adapted for this purpose.) Sending and receiving text messages was accomplished with X12 864 (Text Message). (This was also added later in the project.) Sending and receiving acknowledgments was implemented with X12 997 (Functional Acknowledgment).

During the initial investigative meeting at each site, we were trying to discover the proper entry points for inserting EDI interfaces. A significant insight first occurred at Newport News Shipbuilding Company. Someone said that the company wanted to participate but did not have anyone from the programming staff to assign to the project. We were standing at one end of a large room where the programmers worked. The other end of the room "disappeared" into the horizon. "Do you currently have any automation for these invoices?" we asked.

"Spreadsheets," was the reply.

"Can you download a print file from the spreadsheet to an EDI system?" we asked again.

The reply was, "Yes." That resulted in developing a generalized program to extract from any of the print file formats all of the data required to produce the EDI invoice. It was used at each participating shipbuilder site.

Another revelation at Newport News at the shipbuilder, SoS, and DCAA sites was that everyone who sent or received invoice copies kept a handwritten invoice log—what documents were received and when, the invoice amount, the contract number, what was the result of processing it, who was it sent to next, when was it sent? Finally we had something from which to insert quiet excitement into the project. So the implementation proceeded successfully and included an automatically created and maintained invoice log based on EDI data flows and data mapping based on data extracted from spreadsheet PRN (print) files. This log could be viewed on screen and was always current, since it included input from all of the EDI transaction sets as soon as they were sent from or received at a location. A line in the log identified the invoice, showed invoiced and approved amounts, had status information, messages, and other detail relative to each invoice.

One other major problem successfully addressed was that the involved communities were oriented toward printed reports, and all of the projects were somewhere in the middle of the six or seven-year building cycle for a relevant vessel. The need for reports had to be addressed. This was accomplished by putting the spreadsheet print file, automatically adapted for screen-width considerations, into EDI note segments for invoice copies sent to SoS and DCAA, but not included in the finance center copy. Then with a simple click on screen, the reviewer could see the report on screen and also print it if desired.

Apparel Research Network (1996)

This was the first of these six EDI pilots where the word "Internet" was spoken, indicating when the Internet began to be considered as a viable choice for EDI communications. Further, the Internet had to be only one of several communications options chosen on the basis of need at a participant's site. EDI Integration Corporation was also the EDI investigator/implementer for this project. Dennis Brekhus was the lead EDI investigator. Dale Carley designed and wrote application software for some sites in the project environment. Dennis Brekhus and Ralph Notto wrote the functional specification for the project.

> **ARN**: Apparel Research Network
> **DoD**: U.S. Department of Defense
> **DAM**: Defense Apparel Manufacturer

The Apparel Research Network (ARN) was a working group formed to address issues relative to ordering clothing expeditiously for military recruits and for other military personnel. The objective was to reduce the production and delivery cycle for an order from several weeks to fifteen days. Measuring personnel and issuing clothing may take place at a military base or at a school that has officer training. The total scope of the project included these points as well as other Department of Defense (DoD) and defense apparel manufacturer (DAM) locations.

It is important that measurements are complete and accurate to insure that personnel requiring special measurements do not lack required clothing. While most personnel are fitted with standard-size garments, the special measurement problem is relatively low volume. However, it is an issue in terms of cost, delivery time, and the possibility that a person may not be moved with a group, for lack of the correct clothing for the assignment.

The ARN included representatives from DoD organizations, DAM, universities, and companies with new technology to use in the apparel manufacturing process.

The pilot employed several X12 transaction sets. Invoices from DAM to DoD payer used 810 (Invoice). To notify a payee of electronics funds transfers, the payer sent a payee the X12 820 (Payment Order/Remittance Advise). For confirmation or discrepancy reporting, DoD and DAM used the X12 824 (Application Advice). For orders, DoD sent the 850 (Purchase Order). To report that something was shipped, the DAM sent to the recipient/location of garments the X12 856 (Ship Notice/Manifest). Sending and receiving acknowledgments was accomplished with X12 997 (Functional Acknowledgment).

The detailed ARN functional specification addressed all variations in the pilot environment: EDI front-end systems for mainframe locations; EDI stand-alone systems which included EDI, communications, and specially designed software screens to use at measuring sites for measurement data input, including reality checks based on statistical data pertinent to what is biologically reasonable; systems capable for both front-end and stand-alone processes; orientations based on the functions at the site; and availability of Internet-based forms for low volume measurement data entry. The low-volume locations were not expected to be EDI-capable. The total project scope included capability for the EDI systems to read *project-standard* flat files (non-EDI format) and to process these as though the data were received as EDI, and capability for the EDI systems to send project-standard flat files.

The pilot included all of the mentioned transaction sets. A hope of at least one of the DAMs was that the technology would transfer to the non-military market as well. However, the DoD EDI scope was subsequently narrowed to include only invoices, while orders and shipment notices were processed on Web-based forms.

Barter

At EDI Inc. in 1985, we received a telephone call from the owner of a small company that made barbecue sauce. A major customer of his was an Army commissary. He wanted our EDI software, he said, to receive commissary orders and to send back invoices via EDI. Considering the cost of a computer, modem, and communications service, he said that he had no money available for software. He asked if we would take a couple of cases of barbecue sauce in exchange for a copy of our EDI software product.

Thinking back to ten years earlier at TDCC when a theme was that EDI must be available to all sizes of companies, we said that we would.

We shipped the software to the company and distributed bottles of sauce among our staff.

A primary objective in 1985 was to get as many companies as possible into the EDI community. There were many hurdles to achieving this objective, so we were pleased with this event. The company owner was also pleased, because he achieved his objective to provide a requested additional service to a major customer.

WHAT WAS LEARNED

Transition

Pre-EDI applications implemented on computers at company and government locations around the world evolved over time and used technology resources available, given that costs for equipment, software, and data communications "fit" in the respective budgets. These application systems were very important for control and efficiency purposes. Still, there was something inhibiting the natural flow of data and information. Joe Carley stated it as "a wall of people kept around the computer to feed it data," and there were no universal standards for data formats and data communications. Indeed, companies and organizations sensed this and coordinated the development of data format and data communication protocol standards.

In spite of the desire and potential benefits, transition itself was a major problem that also needed to be addressed in a standard way. While this was happening, the current applications were being updated, technology was changing, additional equipment was being purchased and incorporated into the current application systems, corporate budgets were strained for unrelated reasons, and it was difficult for would-be EDI participants to assign people to help make their companies become EDI-capable. EDI was more difficult because it required adapting to a standard rather than making unilateral decisions in situations where the standard may be applied. Some of the computer systems that companies owned were not "nicely" adaptable for EDI processes. Even by 1990, many corporate decision makers had never heard of EDI or sensed a need for it.

Fortunately, there were "volunteers." There was also the introduction of the PC in 1983 that led to development of EDI software available from competing EDI software companies. About the same time, there was the introduction of compatible modems available for PCs at reasonable prices. Also, value added network services (VANs) oriented toward EDI addressing schemes became available. Although VANs competed for the same business, they also connected with each other to accommodate customers that had trading partners that used other VANs.

Even with seemingly everything we needed already available, we needed the imagination and success stories provided by the early EDI pilots.

The idea was not to automate with new standards, equipment, and services what we were previously doing; the idea was to question what we were doing in the light of what was now available.

This was called "reengineering." It meant forcing change! It meant:

> ... cooperating industry-wide as the grocery executives accomplished with the thirteen-company pilot—thereby dramatically increasing profits and improving customer service while not affecting customer pricing.
>
> ... spreading the good news about measurements of the effectiveness of EDI as reported by pioneering companies.
>
> ... changing payment procedures–as with the General Motors/First Chicago pilot–using EDI and EFT in a community of participating banks and suppliers to change strategies for payment terms and cash flow predictions, resulting in cost savings for both the purchaser and supplier while not affecting customer pricing.
>
> ... using EDI in non-commercial applications–as with transmission of student transcripts–tightening control of sensitive information, decreasing costs, and improving service for students.
>
> ... addressing environments where available equipment was limited–as in the NAWGA pilot–extending to the smaller companies similar benefits larger companies in the industry experienced like cost reduction and automatic reconciliation of orders and invoices.
>
> ... reaching out to non-computerized companies–as in the Burlington Northern/Pick Industries example–bringing exciting business methods and efficiencies to the smaller company while helping the huge company to also become more efficient.
>
> ... making changes in a defense agency and the ocean transportation industry–as in the ACI project–improving service even before industry had a chance to adjust its mainframe application computer systems.

... proving in a multi-source data-exchange environment–as in the GBL pilot–tested concepts leading to improvements in control, payment cycle, availability of information, cost reduction, and an always-current automatic reconciliation process.

... improving service, tightening control, improving cash flow, and reducing cost–as in the Shipbuilder project–long before a company's mainframe computer system can be adapted to support the change.

... broadening the scope of participation as in the ARN project to combine EDI and web-based options to enable all potential participants, large or small, to receive similar benefits from automation.

... accepting barter as a means of including a small enterprise in the EDI community–as in the instance of trading barbecue sauce for EDI software.

Learned

What was learned? Significant change is not easy. Executive attention has benefits. Imagination is an asset. EDI environments facilitate reengineering; the most dramatic benefits are associated with reengineering. Designs relevant to the EDI/Web-based form choices need to be addressed with broad system engineering principles, considering total impact on all participants. Customers benefit from the better service and product reliability that follow.

Internet and EDI Consideration

Although either can work independently of each other, the Internet and EDI working together show synergism in many situations. The challenge is to define the best of both worlds in general. Understand that EDI is a data formatting standard that specifically addresses process-to-process environments, meaning a process controlled from a computer in a company sending data to a process controlled by any kind of computer at another company anywhere else in the world. To be reliable automatic processes, it is necessary that the computer receiving the data has the capability to edit and verify the data received. EDI addresses this across industry boundaries. It has done this for several years for repetitive processes. Use it for that purpose. Use the Internet for communications (including communications of EDI-formatted data), for linking in sites with low data volume *and* with no EDI capability, or for business/individual-consumer data exchanges.

> **VAN**: Value added network
>
> **FTP:** Internet File Transfer Protocol
>
> **SMTP:** Internet Simple Message Transfer Protocol

During its first twenty years, EDI-formatted data was transmitted via VANs or via private point-to-point connections or dial-up connections. EDI is a data-formatting standard. To be of any use, the data must be transmitted, but the EDI and communications standards are independent of each other and mature independently. Therefore it was easy for EDI processes to adapt to the Internet for communications, using standard protocols like FTP and SMTP. EDI also requires software for translation of data to and from EDI format, and for invoking other processes like communications and data mapping. Such software is readily available and is competitively priced. (While writing software for data communications processes may not be a simple task, that task is independent from any of the rules for data formats, including EDI format. The EDI software creates files for outbound data and interprets files containing inbound data. These files have the same format, regardless of the type of network used.)

The format used in EDI is especially efficient, since all of the structural meaning in an X12 transaction set or EDIFACT message is conveyed by a three or six character code embedded in the data. Using this code, EDI software is able to accurately and efficiently construct or interpret EDI-formatted data. Data without structure has little meaning. This EDI scheme permits considerable efficiency for transmission, because all data specific to a transaction is transmitted, but the total meaning of the structure is implied by transmission of only a short code included with the data. Add to this data compression/decompression processes, and the efficiency increases dramatically. Internet schemes work in the opposite way. Instead of transmitting a short code to imply the exact meaning, the meaning as well as the data is transmitted. This is excellent in some scenarios, but inefficient in supply-chain process-to-process environments.

While communications capability seems to be a limitless resource, it is not. It is restricted by channels available, technological capability, and investment. Therefore, it is not a resource to be wasted, because we will require considerably more of it as we learn more about what is possible in this information age and act to make it a reality.

Example

In a transmission from a telephone company to a customer, visualize an EDI-formatted file for 2,000 invoice transactions totaling 2.7 million bytes.

Now visualize these 2,000 transactions in an earlier era when this information was conveyed via paper forms and consumed 2,000 pages. Think about these pages arriving on your desk in a box once per month. Consider putting that data on punch cards for entry into your company's computer.

Now consider the equivalent data being received in the year 2000 directly into your company's computer in EDI format, transparently over a seven-minute data-transmission session. Observe that your computer processed all of this data in less than a quarter hour. Finally, understand that the data was released to the Internet on a schedule set by the sender, and the data was retrieved from the Internet on a schedule set by your company. (This is accomplished via an EDI-capable communications service offering an Internet option for data transmission.)

What effect do you believe all of this has on productivity? Why does the number of jobs increase while productivity increases so dramatically? This productivity gain/job increase phenomenon has occurred consistently since the computer industry began in the 1950s. By the early 1960s, "experts" were predicting that the "bubble" would burst, and jobs would be scarce. It never happened. It is not happening now. Productivity gains permit a company to assign tasks never assigned before because of limited resources. Completion of these tasks results in product enhancements and new products, improvements in customer service, and increased reliability. Increased sales follow. More people are added to the workforce, and product demand increases.

6. Maturing Purpose

"When I was a child,
I used to talk like a child.
When I became a man,
I put childish ways aside."

1 Corinthians, 13:11

BEGINNING PURPOSE AND SUBSEQUENT ADJUSTMENTS

From the U.S. perspective before TDCC was formed in 1968, potential member companies knew that they needed something that would make data capture more efficient while leading to improvements in accuracy and customer service. They hoped that this might also facilitate cost reduction. At that time, some U.S. companies were sufficiently convinced that this was possible and sponsored TDCC as a new organization to coordinate the effort. Similar thoughts were discussed in other parts of the world as well.

The initial efforts were important and massive in terms of detail. The group achieved what it set out to complete. It also totally missed the point about putting everything together into an information processing and transmission system. TDCC changed its focus in 1973, and by 1975 had delivered the first U.S. EDI standards manual, complete in excruciating detail.

This chapter summarizes from the U.S. perspective how *purpose* evolved over time, building on experiences and vision.

Look at this chapter for evidence of consistency in upward trend of understanding and purpose. If there was a regressive action, reflect on how any successful counteraction took place, and the cost of the misstep in terms of time and delayed opportunity. Gain from this viewpoint a historical perspective to assist in plotting future direction.

Specific Events

Consider sixteen specific EDI events or periods that meant a revision in EDI purpose or progress. In this chapter, we review these events and assess whether each event represents an enhancement of purpose, a regression, a complete change in scope, or a milestone achievement.

The intent is to lead to a summary that shows how, if at all, EDI purpose has changed because of new insights or technologies. Does this, in turn, help us to expect anything new?

The sixteen events (chosen by the author) are identified in the following list. "Enhancement in purpose" events are in bold:

1968: Starting Point (TDCC is formed to coordinate the synthesis of a data-format standard to facilitate operational data transmissions between companies, and thereby eliminate the need for inter-company paperwork.)

1973: Joe Carley Chairs All Work Groups (TDCC's Ed Guilbert appoints Joe Carley to chair all committee work groups to insure coordination among four transportation industries—air, motor, ocean, and rail.)

1975: TDCC's First EDI standards publication (A standards manual is published complete in every detail. It is accepted by the TDCC work groups.)

1976: TDCC's General Systems Specification (The purpose and concept of the standard is published. It gives reasons for the standards initiative and surmises what to expect from it.)

1976-1977: American and European Views (Ideas are shared internationally. Some coordination effort begins.)

1978: Enter ANSI and X12 (The American National Standards Institute becomes involved in EDI.)

1980: Grocery Industry's A.D. Little Study (The grocery industry becomes proactive in EDI, and is supported by top industry executives.)

1984: JEDI Agreement (TDCC and ANSI X12 standards begin to drift apart, and then the necessary steps are taken to put the two on the same track again.)

1985: An EDI Service Industry Takes Shape (A new industry emerges to service EDI users. The industry includes communications, software, consulting, financial EDI, and security components.)

1986: Unnoticed (Additional international EDI discussions and exchange of ideas continues on a private level.)

1987: General Motors/First Chicago EDI/EFT Pilot (An enormous project undertaking including EDI, Financial EDI, encryption, and authentication is completed successfully and adopted for operational use.)

1989: First International EDI Congress (The congress is well attended. An international EDI debate takes place, pointing out status, challenges and differences. Attendees agree to make the congress an annual event.)

1990: Norman Barber's "Beyond Connectivity" (A new concept for EDI environments is published in time to offer guidance for process reengineering considerations.)

1994: Internet (Use of the Internet for EDI transmissions begins.)

1996: EDIFACT (A United Nations EDI standard is released.)

1998: Use of Expert Opinion (The Internet and email make it possible to share ideas and readily get expert opinion on EDI issues.)

1. 1968: Starting Point

The TDCC purpose was to create standards so that computers in different transportation companies and the industries they served could *talk* to each other."

The 1975 standards work had started years earlier in 1968. It moved slowly at first. The theory was that agreement was needed for common codes; then everything would fall into place. Codes were completed for commodity, location, carrier, patron, and packaging information. Agreement for the codes was reached, but "falling into place" was not happening. Something else was required to inter-relate these information elements.

Assessment: Even though the initial start did not produce the desired result, this event represented ***a complete change in scope***, since companies in general began to see a value in coordinating data formats with an eye toward eliminating inter-company paperwork and related recoding and data entry tasks. The work was very useful when subsequently defining EDI data elements.

2. Joe Carley Chairs All Work Groups

Ed Guilbert appointed Joe Carley to chair all work group committee meetings to ensure coordination among all groups. The older committees that were organized for definition of major code sets were called "task forces" and continued with their current chairpersons to ensure that there was no friction during the formation of the new work groups. The task forces' role was to work toward improvement in the standardized code sets for commodity and the other coding lists mentioned. The work group's role was to derive the *information structure* for data transmission.

In a short time, the greatest attention was with the work groups, and the influence of the theories of the older task forces became subservient. It then became apparent that the structure became the driving force and that the codes were addressed only as an item of detail when required in a specific structure.

Assessment: Building on the previous event, this event showed ***an enhancement of purpose***, since there was recognition that codes alone would not produce desired results, and that data structures had to be standardized as well.

3. 1975: TDCC's First EDI Standards Publication

One of the primary charter tasks of TDCC was to develop a program to facilitate the electronic interchange of information between industrial, service, and governmental organizations of the transportation community. The extremely broad scope of the problem and complexity of subjects to be addressed presented a wide range of alternatives relative to developmental approach.

This is designed to be a dynamic specification to be modified and adjusted as necessary to ultimately reflect the real needs of industry. The validity of the specification can only be proved through test and evaluation. Its applicability and utility will be proved by adoption and use.

Assessment: Documenting the result of the previous two events and introducing concepts for dynamic specification, real needs, and basis for use are ***milestone events.***

4. 1976: TDCC's General Systems Specification

Imagine—inbound transactions recorded for action in seconds after they are released by the originator—with no paperwork or intervening people ... Getting operational data so early that planning is no longer an estimation process ... The elimination of clerical transcribing errors ... Current status reports even when the source of information is another company ... Positive control over operational information from origin to destination—from the time of ordering raw materials until payment for delivered finished products ... An information system adaptable for expansion as your needs and capabilities change ... A single computer "window" to the world—a single set of computer programs to interface your system with the system of any other company—on any business subject"

Assessment: Creating a list of possibilities represented ***enhancement of purpose***, since some of the list items were not included in the original purpose.

5. 1976-77: American and European Views

In the U.S., whenever we introduced a new data element, we determined its length by finding out what length was used in present computer programs at TDCC-member companies. Europeans determined length by how much room was allocated on a form for a particular element. Thus, if half a page width was allocated, the corresponding data element length specification was set at thirty-five, considering ten characters per inch and seventy characters per line of a typed page.

TDCC's approach was quite different. The theme was, 'I (the company providing the data] will send you (the company receiving the data) whatever data you require. It will be in a *standardized format that a computer can process.* It will be sent directly from my computer to yours. It will be error-free. It will be timely.' The receiving company's theme was, 'Fine. I will send you an acknowledgment from my computer to yours after my computer has checked that all of the data is error-free and you have indeed sent all of the data I require.' No mention is made of documentation formats.

Assessment: International EDI discussions were ***milestone events***, since a single worldwide EDI standard is in everyone's best interest.

6. 1978: Enter ANSI and ASC X12

In 1978, the American National Standards Institute (ANSI) approved a motion to add an Accredited Standards Committee (ASC) for EDI. The name given to the standard was X12, since ANSI used "X" to designate a communications standard, and "12" was the distinguishing number from other communications standards.

Some "driving forces" behind this movement were:

> Ed Bronder of U.S. Steel reported that the steel industry already had an EDI standard that they called COMPORD and which was satisfactory from the point of view of defining steel industry requirements for specifying and purchasing steel. He was looking for a way to possibly use this standard imbedded in a broader standard, and to work under ANSI rather than TDCC. The reason for this, he said, was because the steel industry had recently finished fighting allegations of collusion by steel companies and did not want any steel company EDI meetings to be considered any endeavor other than standards activity.
>
> George Klima of Super Valu said that his company had proprietary formats for EDI in purchase order and invoice applications, but his company was interested in a public standard for EDI because they did not want to have to maintain their own standard, considering all of the ramifications for documentation and training of the users.
>
> Burt Millard of P&G said that his company was interested in a broadly based standard because it viewed participation in several proprietary standards as having a potential negative effect on P&G considering maintenance, operation, and quality control of the different standards."

Assessment: Although TDCC was chosen to coordinate the associated technical tasks for this movement, Credit Research Foundation was appointed secretariat for the standards activity. This represented a ***change in direction***, since control shifted. It also ***meant a change in scope***, since many more industries were now open toward EDI because of ANSI's involvement.

7. 1980: Grocery Industry's A.D. Little Study

The overall study objective was to "… evaluate the economic and technical feasibility of replacing the present [in 1980] manual and paper-based information flows among food/non-food manufacturers and distributors with an integrated electronic data communications network. The report addressed the economic and technical issues, and predicted that with a 50% EDI transaction penetration, the industry had a potential to save $324 million per year."

The report recommended how the effort should be organized, that a standards-setting working group must be broadly represented, why and how a pilot project must be formed, and why the grocery industry should build on the EDI work already started in the transportation industry. The report also advised on a schedule with milestones and completion times. The proposed schedule addressed the issue of reasonable cost while meeting impressive objectives.

Assessment: Addressing information detail required by decision makers in a major industry, providing guiding principles for subsequent implementers, and recognizing the similarities for technological development across industries, this event was ***a milestone achievement*** that kept the U.S. EDI focus on track and set an example for other industries. Although the TDCC started with a multiple industry concept, this event also indicated ***a change in scope***, since it greatly broadened the multi-industry considerations for EDI and brought it to a higher level.

8. 1984: JEDI Agreement

The Joint EDI Committee (JEDI) was created in 1984 to correct a situation where TDCC and X12 committees were assigning conflicting elements of definition and identification for critical items in the EDI standards documentation.

It took two years to correct the situation.

Assessment: The fact that this event even occurred indicates there was definitely ***a regression*** during development. Given the regression, completion of this event was ***a milestone achievement*** since without it, the standardization process would have faltered.

9. 1985: An EDI Service Industry Takes Shape

There are four primary components of the EDI service industry: addressing products and services for communications, software, consultation, and financial EDI expertise. There are other important components like encryption and authentication services, specialized publications, EDI outsourcing services, EDI education, and EDI research.

Assessment: This industry, by 1985, was routinely providing services at competitive prices, enabling cost-effective EDI solutions for many companies and making it possible for companies not previously automated to become members of the EDI community. This was truly ***a milestone achievement***.

10. 1986: Unnoticed

Consultant Ian Finch traveled from the United Kingdom to the United States on an assignment to assess U.S. acceptance of EDIFACT as a standard. About 1986 after a suggestion to do so by Dan Ferguson of the EDI Group, he talked with Buddy Bass and Ralph Notto on the subject. Bass and Notto said that a single worldwide EDI standard was in everyone's best interest, that there were already a significant number of users of both the U.S. X12 and the European TDI standards, and that this needs to be addressed in the EDIFACT definition.

"What would you do?" he asked.

"Take all transaction structures and definitions that are used or *definitely* planned to be used in both X12 and TDI and their derivatives, *wrap* them inside EDIFACT header and trailer segments, and call the result *EDIFACT*," was the reply. "Then define a migration path from this to a new EDIFACT version to be coordinated for release at an agreed time in the future," they continued. The idea was to define EDIFACT in such a way that most current standard EDI users were already in the EDIFACT community. A second motive for the suggestion was to initiate a process for erasing non-required detail from the standard.

Assessment: Since this item was never carried forward, is does not fit any of the assessment categories in our list. However, serious discussions about ways to eventually make the EDI community more inclusive and mutually beneficial among all its members are ***a milestone achievement*** each time they occur.

11. 1987: General Motors/First Chicago EDI/EFT Pilot

The payment process was completely automated with EFT/EDI. In one step, GM made all payments electronically. Multiple options were provided, considering the technology status at banks and supplier companies. All communications between GM and the banks were encrypted and authenticated EFT/EDI and via point-to-point dial-up connections. Payment dates, from a payee's viewpoint, now changed from being estimated dates to dates certain.

Assessment: Bringing EFT into the same reengineering environment with EDI and introducing encryption and authentication with EDI processes was ***an enhancement of purpose*** and ***a milestone achievement***, since these additions added management of money via increased control, increased security, and change in cash flow estimating from empirical methods to dates certain as potential benefits of EFT/EDI.

12. 1989: First International EDI Congress

Following keynote speeches by five proactive people in EDI definition and implementation, this event was reported in the 1989 *EDI Forum* issue as "The EDI Standards Debate." Was this in fact a "debate," since it was only five keynote addresses without any rebuttals? In the sense of the formal program, it was not; in the sense of discussions in the halls following that five-speech session, it was. Thank Marshall Spence of Canada for introducing an International EDI Congress as an annual event where people from all over the world came together to report progress and to argue for their positions on the nature of EDI and the corresponding importance of this for their countries and companies within their countries.

Jeff Sturrock of Texas Instruments, chairperson of the North American EDIFACT Board, told about the many different data standards his company must use and what he sees evolving with EDI syntax.

Colin M. Hill, manager, EDI Contingency and Planning, Mitsubishi Motors Australia Ltd., spoke about the need for EDI in Australia and how they expect to evolve toward a common standard.

Ray Walker, chief executive of SITPRO and UN/EDIFACT rapporteur for Western Europe, listed six challenges for establishing EDI in the world community and described where we stand in relation to these challenges.

Earl J. Bass, chairperson of ASC X12, vice president of EDI Inc., and one the original developers of EDI standards in 1975, explained the process in place for X12 for coordinating development with EDIFACT and said that the initial X12 coordination with EDIFACT did not follow proper procedures for consent of the users, but that controls are now in place to ensure this in the future.

Joseph G. Carley, Jr., president of EDI Integration and the person responsible for developing the strategy used during EDI's inception in 1973-6, disagreed with the current direction of EDIFACT. Carley argued that the status of the present (1989) EDI user community of 10,000 companies and the effect of EDIFACT on their currently functional and stable EDI operations is not desirable.

Assessment: Beginning an international EDI congress with such openness, conflicting views, and still with all key people supporting *international* cooperation was ***a milestone achievement***, since there was still considerable support or use for national and company-proprietary EDI standards in 1989. The international EDI congress became an annual event with continuing openness for discussion of progress and issues.

13. 1990: Norman Barber's "Beyond Connectivity"

During the late 1980s, when others were struggling to understand how to implement EDI, Norman F. Barber, president of Cornerstone, an EDI professional services organization, was analyzing research findings and statistics and reflecting on his own findings to determine what companies should do relative toward realizing the ultimate promise of EDI. He published his analysis and recommendations in a 1990 *EDI Forum* treatise on 'Implementing EDI Beyond Connectivity.'

He said that there are three distinct stages of EDI implementation: computer-to-computer, application-to-application, and peer-to-peer.

Considering all three stages, he said that the implications are: skills must change, responsibilities may shift, patterns of communication may be altered, transaction processing time is decreased, number of transactions increase, work relationships with trading partners may change, and new organizational structures may evolve.

Assessment: Norman Barber's definitive work came at the time in which many companies were ready to use EDI in their process reengineering schemes, which was ***an enhancement of purpose***. His work was also ***a milestone achievement***.

14. 1994: Internet

In the early 1990s, companies did not consider that EDI and the Internet belonged in the same environment. By 1994 attitudes began to change. Typical use of the Internet at that time was to implement Web-based forms, which companies expected their non-EDI-capable suppliers and customers to use for data exchanges with the "host" company. These suppliers and customers were on one "side" of the Web forms. The other side had software that accepted EDI formats from the host, and converted that to the web form—conversely for incoming data. There were no standards for construction of these forms among hosts. The scheme offered hosts the benefit of extending their reach with EDI. The scheme was of less benefit to the others, because it required manual Internet interaction and subsequent data entry to get information into their own computers.

In the early years of the Internet, companies did not employ it for transmitting EDI-formatted data. However, the academic community did use the Internet for that purpose with use of the File Transport Protocol (FTP) or Simple Message Transfer Protocol (SMTP). The SMTP technique uses attachments to email transmissions. The messages are directed to an EDI software system rather than to a person, and the files are encrypted for security reasons. The results were, and continue to be, very satisfactory. Companies began tests with business transactions and these same techniques by year 2000.

Assessment: Use of the Internet to connect via EDI to any place world wide, with rapid access to the receiver, and with minimal cost for transmission is ***a milestone achievement.***

15. 1996: EDIFACT

Work on the United Nations standard EDI For Administration, Commerce and Transport (UN/EDIFACT) progressed during the late 1980s. Country attitudes toward a UN EDI standard were favorable, since that put all participating countries on an equal footing with regard to standards development and maintenance. There was considerable interest in this worldwide. There were also arguments—not about importance, but structure. A "debate" on this was included at the First International EDI Congress in 1989. There was talk about U.S. countries migrating from X12 to EDIFACT by the early 1990s. Use of X12 continued to grow while use of EDIFACT began to grow. By 1996, EDIFACT included 137 message types (subjects) in its detailed specification. Nevertheless, it will take new software developments to complete any total migration.

Assessment: Publication of 137 standard message specifications in complete detail to enable worldwide data interchanges on subjects important in world trade and for use in process-to-process, computer-to-computer, company-to-company environments is a significant ***milestone achievement***. The list grew to 158 standard messages by 1999.

In the late 1990s, General Motors stated that it would increase its use of EDIFACT.

16. 1998: Use of Expert Opinion

Accredited Standards Committee X12 has several standing subcommittees that provide expert input and analysis for major functions like finance, purchasing, and transportation. Also, a technical assessment committee uses all types of experts to evaluate proposed changes to the EDI standards.

The following 1998 email shows an example of the role of expert opinion on a particular subject. The reference in this case is X12 831 ("Application Control Totals: Developing a Business Practice"). The expert is Richard Bort. This example was chosen in reference to maturing purpose because it describes how security and control in EDI/EFT processes protect against fraud in ways superior to what was previously possible. However, the real meaning of the new process has to be understood before the benefits are received

(Dick Bort was a member of the ASC X12 Finance Committee at that time [and for a total of eleven years], and is the author of the *Handbook of EDI*—published by Warren, Gorham & Lamont and updated through 2000—as well as other books and articles on electronic commerce.)

The purpose of the 831 is to transmit totals associated with a collection of like transactions.

Assessment: Incorporating other technologies in EDI/EFT processes, seeking expert opinion for developing a best business practice, and using email to reach out to a focused group represents another example for ***enhancement of purpose***..

Email Contents

From: Richard Bort
To: [List from ASC X12 Finance Subcommittee Members]
Cc: Larry Marocco
Date: Thursday, June 18, 1998 6:25 PM
Subject: 831 Usage

This is in response to Larry Marocco's June 17 missive, "We need some help on developing a business practice for the use of the 831 with regard to a functional group (batch) of 820s [Payment Order/Remittance Advice transaction sets]." [He then described a scenario in which the functional group of 820s was out of balance with the control total in the related 831.]

Thank you, Larry, for raising this issue. You asked for the "best practice" for this situation, which would be to require authentication or encryption of all 820 originations. Anything short of that is not a "best practice." Let me move my soapbox into view here because this whole topic is troubling. Then, perhaps the answer to your question will become obvious.

Soapbox: The 831 is merely the electronic equivalent of an adding machine tape. Anyone who ascribes more credence to it than that is kidding himself. The 831 is not an acceptable substitute for the use of cryptographic security surrounding the transmission of payment orders (820s).

Just because the total in the 831 agrees with the total in the batch of 820s does not mean that the batch doesn't contain an error or hasn't been tampered with. It only means that the dollar totals agree.

For example, suppose the 831 total is $15,000 and is supposed to consist of three payments of $6,000, $5,000, and $4,000. But a bad guy intercepts the package, changes the amounts to $14,800, $100, and $100, and changes the destination account number on the $14,800 transfer to his own account at the same destination bank?

The originating bank would obliviously process the batch of 820s because the 831 total agrees with the batch total, despite the fraud. Even if the interloper only changed the destination account number on one or more of the payment orders without changing any of the amounts, the 831 would not catch it. Only by using cryptographic authentication or encryption would the alteration become known.

Moral to the Story: Do not rely on the 831 to protect against error or fraud in originating payments. Only cryptographic authentication or encryption can do that. If you choose not to require crypto methods, then you must recognize the risk that the originating bank is undertaking, especially in view of UCC Article 4A.

Conclusion: I would assume that the originating bank that decides to rely on the 831 control total anyway would have a written agreement with the originator as to how to handle such an out-of-balance condition. I would also assume that the agreement would instruct the bank in an out-of-balance situation to:

a) Suspend processing of the batch of payment orders until the batch and the 831 agree; and

b) Advise the originator/customer immediately of the out-of-balance condition and request that the originator correct the situation.

If the 831 and functional group of 820s are out of balance, then obviously the process should be suspended until the error is discovered. Without knowing whether the batch is defective or the 831 control total is incorrect, the bank would have no authority to act.

Then, if the accuracy of the batch of 820s is confirmed, the originator needs to re-send a corrected 831. If the batch of 820s is not correct, then that batch must be rejected and a new, corrected batch re-sent to the bank.

I hope this sheds some sense on the situation. Best regards.

Dick Bort, Bort & Company, Inc.

Summary

Twenty assessments were assigned in this chapter, because four of the sixteen events identified had dual evaluations.

Considering these topics, *enhancement of purpose* occurred five times—1973, when the data structure as well as the contents were part of the standardization discussions; 1976, when the list of reasons for doing EDI increased to include processes not doable without EDI; 1987, when the General Motors/First Chicago EDI/EFT pilot created the link between EDI and EFT and introduced encryption and authentication into EDI processes; 1990, when the focus on EDI shifted to "Beyond Connectivity" and EDI's role in process reengineering, and the late 1990s when use of experts in focused EDI communities becomes available electronically.

There was one *regression* in 1984 when TDCC and X12 made conflicting specifications. That was corrected over a two-year period.

Assessment	Tally
Enhancement of purpose	5
Regression	1
Complete change in scope	3
Milestone achievement	11

Three *changes in scope* included starting the movement in 1968, the EDI relationships with ANSI and ASC X12 beginning in 1978, and the grocery industry's increased emphasis on cross industry coordination in 1980.

Finally, eleven *milestones* were reached:

1975: TDCC's first EDI standard was published.

1976-7: American and European EDI views were understood.

1980: Grocery industry's A.D. Little study gave reasons for doing EDI and instructions on how to get it started.

1984: JEDI agreement resolved issues between TDCC and ASC X12.

1985: An EDI service industry was formed and included data networks, EDI software, consultants, and electronic funds transfer experts.

1986: An unnoticed event about how to make EDIFACT inclusive of existing EDI standards helped those involved to adjust their work to accommodate EDIFACT without impacting current users.

1987: General Motors/First Chicago EDI/EFT pilot expanded the EDI and EFT communities to include each other.

1989: First International EDI Congress provided an international forum for reporting progress and for explaining differences.

1990: Norman Barber's "Beyond Connectivity" treatise explained concepts and principles to use for reengineering.

1994: Internet and EDI were both recognized as components of *eCommerce* that could work together or independently, dependent on requirements of a user community.

1996: EDIFACT standard included detailed specifications for 137 standard EDI messages.

In general, and for over a quarter century, these events were anticipated from the beginning, as was stated in the 1975 publication: "It must be precisely understood that the development effort reflected in this specification and the list of names and companies provided in ["Participants in Planning and Work Groups, 1975" and "Companies and Organizations, 1975," Appendix II] cannot be interpreted to mean U.S. industry has approved the concept, validated requirements, or signaled as intent to be committed in any manner or form. This is, as stated before, designed to be a dynamic specification to be modified and adjusted as necessary to ultimately reflect the real needs of industry. The validity of the specification can only be proved through test and evaluation. Its applicability and utility will be proved by adoption and use."

ATTITUDE AND PURPOSE

"Purpose" is fulfilled in different ways depending on the attitude of a participant. Three common attitudes relative to EDI are described in this topic—domineering, flexible, and compliant. To provide some insight for this, the EDI Group's report on *The Real Facts of EDI in 1997*[59] *references a survey that reports 55% of spokes*[60] *do EDI because their principal customer or supplier said they must. The reference is in response to the question, "What is the most important reason for your firm to continue doing EDI?" For mid-level compa-*

[59]Daniel N. Ferguson, "The Real Facts of EDI in 1997," *EDI Forum*, Volume 11, No. 1, pages 18-25,The EDI Group, 1998.

[60]The EDI group classifies companies as EDI hub, mid-level or spoke. Hubs are the drivers.

nies, the main reasons are competitive advantage (26%) and cost savings (24%). The hubs are driven by improving customer service (16%), competitive advantage (16%), and cost savings (14%). With EDI, according to the survey, hubs experience 40% cycle-time improvement, 30% error reduction, and $5.00 average cost savings per transaction.

Attitudes

The attitude classifications—domineering, flexible, and compliant—are based on the author's experiences and observations during the period 1975 to 2000. An understanding of these different attitudes is important for understanding the characteristics of the EDI community of users.

Domineering

Companies in this EDI attitude group have an understanding of the potential for EDI to favorably impact their companies' results relative to their objectives, took a proactive stance, and forcefully got many of their trading partners to participate with them. They required use of specifications they provided for mapping data to EDI formats. In many cases, they also required use of a specific network service or direct dial to the proactive company's computer. The choice on the part of the trading partner (if the trading partner was a supplier) was to do EDI this way or lose the proactive company's business.

Some in this group even imposed penalties on their trading partners for deviating from the performance expected from them. For example, a trading partner having an error in three successive transmissions would have to pay a sum of money (like $500) that may be withheld from an invoice payment. Other types of deviations included not performing data communications at prescribed intervals, not upgrading to a new standards version by a set date, etc. These were considered "errors" in the EDI processes and are different from errors in product quality, quantity delivered, and date of delivery.

Viewed from the perspective of an EDI software company, a typical scenario was: one of these trading partners calls a software company's sales department. In a somewhat concerned tone of voice, he or she says, "My best customer said that if we don't start doing EDI with them, we will lose their business. We never heard of EDI. They said that you would be able to help us. Can you help us?"

> **P&G**: Procter & Gamble
>
> **DoD**: U.S. Department of Defense
>
> **UCS**: Uniform Communication Standard [Grocery industry EDI standard, compatible with X12]
>
> **X12**: ANSI EDI standard
>
> **EDIFACT**: United Nations standard EDI For Administration, Commerce and Transport
>
> **EDI Software**: Software used to translate to or from EDI formats and to invoke related functions like data communications.
>
> **EFT**: Electronic Funds Transfer
>
> **Data mapping software**: Software used to relate internal application data with external data such as EDI

An EDI software sales representative answers, "Yes." Price and delivery dates are given along with other information about training and what equipment is required for the software to work. The sales person asks for the order, which may be received during the same telephone call or by fax or mail. All of the EDI software providers knew about these domineering companies and their requirements. Indeed, they had to pass on-line tests in order to be on the recommended list of software providers. Besides EDI software, they also had to provide communications and application software.

Make no mistake about it: without the domineering companies, it is not likely that use of EDI would have increased as quickly as it did, if at all. In that sense, a service was provided. The proactive company was rewarded by achieving increases in control, accuracy, timeliness, and cost reduction. Their trading partners were rewarded with renewed commitment for sales from the proactive companies.

The domineering companies were always corporate giants or government agencies. They worked within the boundaries of the EDI standards, but each established their own guidelines for data mapping between application systems and EDI formats. Sometimes, an industry set these guidelines. However, some domineering companies interpreted industry guidelines differently from each other. Some EDI software companies specialized in providing EDI solutions for only one industry like the automotive industry or the retail sales industry. Both industries have some members in the domineering class.

As important as it was to find successful ways to get EDI started, the domineering technique also had its downside. It is one matter to insist on certain actions from smaller companies that need your business. However, even corporate giants have other corporate giants as important trading partners. It is a different matter to impose a corporate will on a non-flexible peer. The result may be delay or no progress at all.

Giant vs. giant examples:

1) The author's company had supplied EDI software to Wal-mart in the mid-1980s. During a meeting there, a Wal-mart representative said that the system was used for transportation transactions, but the company preferred using its own proprietary (non-standard EDI) system for sending purchase orders. He said that they were having a problem getting P&G to participate with them.

That's easy," was the reply, "the buyer always wins."

Not when the seller is P&G," was the response. "P&G said EDI with either X12 or UCS standard. Take your choice," he said. The discussion went on to reveal that P&G was too important a supplier to Wal-mart, and therefore P&G was the stronger partner for dictating how these translations would be facilitated. Some weeks later, the author discussed this with Burt Millard of P&G.

He confirmed that what was stated at Wal-mart was correct. He said that P&G had previously conformed to different proprietary EDI systems of sixteen of their customers. He said that they concluded that P&G could not afford that kind of "efficiency" with a growing number of non-coordinated but similar software requirements and the inevitable impact on software maintenance and trained staff. That led to P&G's support and participation in the X12 and UCS movements.

2) Two large insurance companies that were natural trading partners did not do EDI with each other because of differences in data mapping for insurance transaction sets.

3) Some U.S. Department of Defense (DoD) EDI initiatives were subsequently disbanded because of insufficient participation from likely trading partners.

The ability of the EDI software companies to respond to the rigid requirements of domineering companies with competitively priced off-the-shelf prices for trading partners indicates that some flexible software techniques are possible. Rigidity, therefore, is not a requirement for progress. In fact, rigidity is a deterrent in the long run. Further, the early software EDI companies were mostly small start-up companies formed by entrepreneurs who sensed a need for a product. These companies later added flexible EDI data mapping software to their product offerings. Of course, available EDI software products support all versions of a standard and a company could use such software to communicate with several to many companies, including domineering and non-domineering trading partners. Also, many use the same software product for both X12 and EDIFACT standards.

In the near term in the twenty-first century, it will be in the domineering companies' best interests to evaluate their software capabilities and techniques, and to make adjustments to be more flexible. If this cannot be accomplished internally, outsourcing this task or retaining expert consulting support may be considered. The alternative is slowing down the rate of progress and associated benefits. Rigid software techniques, in the long run, will also make software maintenance more costly.

Flexible

Companies in the flexible EDI attitude group are similar to the domineering group in many respects, but they are not rigid. They may also have entered the EDI community because a member of the domineering group requested it. Consider the position described for P&G relative to quitting its support for proprietary standards. Consider the approach taken by Texas Instruments as reported at the First International EDI Congress. Consider the work of the grocery industry that included defining details on an industry rather than individual company basis and also their decisions relative to inter-industry coordination as well.

> P&G was flexible but only toward a non-proprietary standard; Walmart preferred to require that their trading partners use their proprietary standard, but P&G was strong enough to say, "No!" This resulted in Walmart also accepting the public standard.
>
> Texas Instruments was driven toward converting to EDI to the largest extent practical, and was flexible to the extent that they participated in many different public standards worldwide.
>
> The grocery industry was flexible—cooperating with TDCC and ASC X12 to achieve a common EDI syntax and set of rules, and sponsoring an industry convention for choices within the standard.

Further, this flexible group also includes corporate giants that used purchased off-the-shelf EDI software rather than develop their own. George

Klima at Super Valu, for example, said it was not cost-effective to develop EDI software for use at only one company. For similar reasons, his company was also the first to commit to using a VAN for EDI data communications.

Finally, this group was most likely to have EDI startup reasons like "improving customer service" or "customer/supplier request." In time, they also recognized other important reasons like "quick access to information" and "accuracy of data," since these two reasons are required for the first two, and all four reasons together lead to cost savings and competitive advantage.

Compliant

This attitude group is almost always in the customer/supplier request group of beginning EDI participants. These companies participate because an important trading partner requested (or strongly suggested) that they do so. Many companies begin EDI this way. If any subsequently sense other benefits from the effort, they may join the flexible class and become proactive with broadened interests.

This group includes mostly small to mid-sized companies that sell products used by larger manufacturers or retailers. These companies may sell a part used in automobiles, a specialty grocery product, or a particular type of clothing, for example. Their corresponding trading partners may be an automobile manufacturer, a large grocery chain store, or a national retail merchandize store. Such a single customer is extremely important to the success of the compliant group, and doing as that customer asks is in their best interest, even when they are asked to become EDI-capable.

Summing It Up

EDI started from the belief that there must be better ways to exchange data among companies and organizations than those methods used in the 1960s. This was a strong belief, but not universal. George Klima, for example, reported that likely participants told him, "We will never see EDI, our kids will not see EDI, and their kids will not see EDI." or "We considered EDI, but it did not look feasible to us."

Still, the belief persisted among influential people. The first milestone to complete a standards manual occurred because almost everyone involved believed that a standard was necessary for success. Then after several more years, companies began getting practical results or benefits.

Insight from the grocery industry and the A.D. Little Report pointed out that doing this would decrease operating costs for each participating company. This will happen, they said, because error rates will diminish or disappear, faster access to information will lead to better management decisions, control over operations will tighten, and people will need less time for clerical tasks and can use the time for process improvement.

More and more industries and more and more companies and organizations became EDI-proactive. Other companies participated because they felt that they had no other choice. In time, even they experienced benefits.

Some companies and governmental organizations took on a domineering role and forcefully enticed others into becoming EDI-capable, so the EDI growth rate increased rapidly. The EDI community became sophisticated in terms of scope of subjects covered in EDI standards, number of these subjects used by a single company, and volume of data transmitted. Skilled people in companies now included EDI professionals.

An EDI service industry grew in less than fifteen years from zero to several billion dollars in sales per year.

> **EDI:** Electronic Data Interchange
> **EFT:** Electronic funds Transfer

Purpose was enhanced over time: link the EDI processes to EFT processes, increase security by including encryption and authentication in EDI processes, use EDI as one of the building blocks for process reengineering.

All of this required technological advances like chips with more and more speed, larger memory modules, faster modems, sophisticated software, standardization, and skilled people.

Purpose will continue to mature. Look for attitude changes, EDI service industry changes, and corporate process changes. Look for more interaction between Internet and EDI technologies.

The results reported are good. The future looks good.

7. Mentors

"Give me ten men who are stout-hearted men,
And I'll soon give you ten thousand more."
Oscar Hammerstein, *The New Moon*

FROM VISION TO REALITY

'Ground Rules'

Steadfast in their belief and firm in their commitment were several people in leadership roles who inspired the rest of us to "dig deep" within ourselves for an understanding of exactly what was the goal. Then with that, and armed with the skills and experiences each of us brought to the endeavor, we were to forge "something" that would lift world communities to new plateaus, offering broad advances based on a compassionate understanding of the results of our work and the usefulness and quality for any tools or procedures we created or discovered.

Make no mistake about it. The goal was *not* to invent Electronic Data Interchange—EDI, as it is known today. We never had such a term as "EDI" at the beginning of the project.

There were goals, however, but they were stated in terms of effects to be achieved: elimination of inter-company paperwork, absolute accuracy, timeliness for key processes, complete control over repetitive processes, protection of the databanks of individual participating entities from each other and invasions from outside, cost reduction, and catalyst to stimulate ever increasing customer satisfaction.

EDI is the result of *these* goals. It had its own requirements in order to have been labeled as successful. It had to be related to a broadly-based standard, it had to be modular in its design, it was required from the beginning to be a "living" standard always subject to careful updates, it had to be controlled, it was always meant to be a standard and never meant to be merely only a pattern, it had to be able to interface with other technologies that permitted each technology (like data communications, software, and related hardware) to mature at its own pace without requiring other interfacing technologies to mature at the same time. The EDI component had to be able to transparently incorporate enhancements of interfaced technologies. Thus, when a new communications alternative like the Internet became available, the communications process in some EDI environments may have changed, but on a scheduled determined by pairs of trading partners rather than by the entire EDI community in lock-step.

Sparks

Dan Ferguson and Ned Hill included in their founding issue of *EDI Forum* a section on EDI pioneers. The people selected for recognition in that issue were Ed Guilbert of TDCC, George Klima of Super Valu, Joe Carley of TDCC, Don Trafford of SITPRO, John Nelson of Missouri Pacific Railroad, and Richard Cook of the NWAD. Bill Plumb was added to this chapter's list, although his story appeared in later *EDI Forum* issues. All seven had unique interacting roles in the path toward EDI's beginning and future successes.[61]

The founding issue also included a personal story by Paul Olson, confessing how he got his company to be the first to enter the EDI service industry.

And also included was Connie Robinson's story about what was involved to get the metals industry into the EDI community.

These stories are the focus for this chapter.

Another section indicating how the EDI community recognizes some of its members closes this chapter. It is a follow-up story about Joe Carley, two people he led, and how the three worked together.

---

[61] See also "ED Pioneers," page 203.

PERSISTENT, DEDICATED, AND VISIONARY

Edward A. Guilbert

Ed Guilbert

Ed Guilbert at various times has been identified as the "father" or "grandfather" of EDI.

Describing the importance of Ed Guilbert as president of TDCC, Joe Carley wrote:[62] "The organization would not have survived without Ed, since the activity was on the brink of disaster with only $10,000 in the bank when Ed assumed his responsibilities. Further, it is extremely doubtful another organization would have materialized to take TDCC's place within a reasonable time." Joe emphasized that he seriously doubted that a different organization would have demonstrated equal or even similar breadth in conceptual vision. In the final analysis, he said that it was the conceptual vision that made it possible to formulate what became known as the U.S. EDI standards. Joe continued in the article with, "There was an audacious, *we can pull it off* attitude prevailing in TDCC back in 1973 when I joined the staff. Because of sound historical experience, the TDCC board of directors expressed serious doubt as to the feasibility of our proposal to attack the four transportation modes concurrently with an objective to establish single-standard message syntax. Reservations aside, however, they were intrigued by the idea and gave us the go ahead to try it. We were not very vocal about it at the time, but we believed our real objective was to design for ultimate inclusion of the buying, selling, and banking levels of trade activity in the concept. Of course, to express such an attitude to a group of transportation organization directors would have more than raised eyebrows in those days."

Joe said that the concept worked because the TDCC board established a fundamental course of action: "*We do not want to put our business data into a central public database.*"

Such databases had advocates in the early 1970s. That concept was to have all the inter-company relevant data stored in a centralized computer system somewhere in the country where those who had the need and authority to know could provide it or access it. That concept made many people nervous, because they did not want what they considered to be pri-

---

[62]Quoted paragraphs are from Joseph G. Carley Jr., "Ed Guilbert: EDI Pioneer," *EDI Forum*, Founding Issue, page 98, EDI Group, Oak Park IL, 1988.

vate data to be stored and managed in a public place available to competitors and to the government. Ed Guilbert fought for companies to maintain control of their own data that they would send directly to others that had a need to know. Are the business-to-business (B2B) concepts being forged on the Internet a return to the central public database concept? Not really, but perhaps the B2B innovations may be a combination of both centralized and diverse schemes. The keywords are "***our** business data*" and what they imply. To them, "*our*" meant what belonged only to an individual company. In that regard, Ed's vision is still valid.

Joe Carley's description of how Ed managed whatever funds were available was colorful but correct:

> **TDCC**: Transportation Data Coordinating Committee
>
> **AAR**: Association of American Railroads
>
> **ATA**: American Trucking Associations
>
> **B2B**: Business-to-business
>
> **DISA**: Data Interchange Standards Association

It was Ed who kept his eye on the ball. He found and applied the glue and pins to hold the organization together, pinched pennies until they cried, danced around the AAR and ATA political thorn bushes to keep their modest but essential contributions coming in, and flawlessly catered to the shipper members and their technical representatives to hold on to annual dues and company names. He worked hard to obtain supplemental, lifesaving contracts with the Department of Transportation, and charged around the country in his sales suit speaking to any group that would listen about how the world was going to do business in the future. Not many really believed him in those days, but they enjoyed his energetic, eclectic presentations. Many have seen him literally throw fifty or more dollar bills at the audience to make his point—and then make sure he got every dollar back before he left. Externally, people saw Ed Guilbert as a mission-driven apostle who could infect with his fantastic energy, enthusiasm, and optimism. Back at the office, I saw him as someone who was continually concerned with his ability to retain the support of his directors; whether there would be attendees and exhibitors at the forum; managing tensions between staff personnel and members of the technical development groups; and always concerned with the need to assure the financial viability of TDCC. Joe's description of Ed's background sheds light on Ed's qualifications:

EDI: Roots from the Berlin Airlift!

In showing the connection between the success of the Berlin Airlift in 1948-49 and the successful launch of EDI in 1975, Tony Seideman wrote about why and how the airlift began and why Maj. Gen. William H. Tunner was chosen to lead the endeavor.[a]

"Tunner tapped Maj. Edward Guilbert to be his traffic manager. The highly regarded Guilbert would be responsible for managing every aspect of the cargo—coordinating its movements, loading it, unloading it, sending it to the right sector of the city, and accounting for its whereabouts. Even as he struggled to keep his cargoes in the air, Guilbert made efforts to improve the movement of goods.

"[Guilbert] and his staff had already conceived of a way to deliver ten tons a minute, around the clock. Guilbert had realized that under the airlift's intense pressure, *information* about cargoes was as important as the cargoes themselves. Yet in his operation the paperwork simply couldn't keep up with products in motion." ... "He decided that the key to success was to transmit the information ahead of the airplanes. Furthermore, the information would have to be broken down into a simple, universal code, so that everyone involved would know exactly what everyone else was talking about. The reports could not be open to interpretation.

"Thus the concept of electronic data interchange—one of the most powerful and least visible technologies of the information age—was born. In today's business world true electronic data interchange (EDI) uses one standardized electronic language to report on the movement of goods from the point of sale to the main store system, letting a supplier know the exact status of its inventory at any given time. Put simply, EDI facilitates better distribution."

Note the 1949 focus: Importance of timely *information* and simple *standard* universal code!

Top: Col. Ed Guilbert, U.S. Air Force [1950]; Ed Guilbert at the U.S. Department of Transportation, [about 1960]—Photos courtesy of Fran Guilbert.

a. Quoted paragraphs are from Tony Seideman, "What Sam Walton Learned From the Berlin Airlift", Audacity, Vol. 4, No.3 Spring 1996, pages 52-61, published by Forbes and American Heritage, New York.

> I could prove the Ed Guilbert success was no accident by reviewing his record in the Berlin Airlift, where air transportation history was made; in the Hungarian Airlift, where he facilitated an easy transition from Europe to the U.S. for the refugees; at the Military Traffic Management Command, where he had the gall to implement filing of household carrier tariff tenders in IBM card format in lieu of paper; as a special aide to the first Secretary of Transportation, where his mission was to help establish the Department of Transportation; and in the Military Airlift Command, where, among numerous firsts, he pioneered hot food on the troop transports. I know, because I was either there or nearby in each case.

Add to that from the author's experiences, "Ed was always a joy to work with and always on top of any situation."

Ed Guilbert died from cancer in 1973. Before that, Joe Carley and Ralph Notto talked with him one evening at Walter Reed Hospital. We went over what he had started in EDI. Ralph compared it with his having had the good fortune to be a young mathematician when the computer industry began in the 1950s. He said that today's youth can look forward to long productive careers in electronic commerce, partially because of Ed's pioneering work, and especially because of Ed's success in motivating business leaders into understanding new concepts and becoming proactive toward *eCommerce.* That night, Ed said that he and Paul Lemme proposed that we receive the annual award given by the Data Interchange Standards Association (DISA). He was sorry that he and Paul were not successful. After Ed's death, the award name was changed to the "Edward A. Guilbert EDI Professional Award," and it is presented annually for "Outstanding Contributions to the Advancement of EDI." Joe Carley, Buddy Bass, and Ralph Notto received the award jointly in 1995. Ed would have been at least as pleased as the three of us were.

Two days after the visit at Walter Reed Hospital, Ed's son Peter Guilbert called to say that Ed had died. We think of Ed often. Even while writing about this seven years later, it is difficult to hold back a tear.

Joe Carley wrote:[63]

> The death of Edward A. Guilbert on May 16, 1993 in Washington, DC signaled the end of an era—an era uniquely characterized for twenty years by Ed's spirit, energy, ethics, personality, and persistence. The fruits of that

---

[63]"Joseph G. Carley Jr.," *EDI Forum*, 1993 Issue No. 2, page 59, EDI Group, Oak Park IL, 1988.

era remain with us today and will continue to influence events throughout the future of the EDI user and vendor community. The one thing all of us in EDI can agree on is that the EDI foundation established at TDCC under Ed Guilbert's leadership was a significant accomplishment.

Ed Guilbert with Buddy Bass and a Korean group participating at the 1988 TDCC Forum—Young-Kook Kim, Hak Jung Lee, Ed, Buddy, and Soo Hong Noh.

True, hundreds of people had a hand in defining and setting up the EDI conceptual foundation. Progress only became feasible, however, when the TDCC staff constructed the necessary bridges among the diverse and complex community of EDI users. The disparate professional backgrounds of the people who became involved as potential users during the initial years presented a formidable barrier to collective understanding of the EDI concept—a barrier that was finally overcome by the creation of the EDI *language.*

Ed Guilbert looked upon the TDCC mission as a challenge and an opportunity to accomplish something important for the future. He was correct—but it wasn't easy. EDI presented new technology barriers to overcome. It demanded changes to the internal cultures of all user organizations.

The TDCC effort faced many political minefields through which Ed had to navigate, at the same time keeping the momentum of the project at just under Mach speed. In spite of the hurdles and barriers confronting the effort, Ed Guilbert's tenacity, courage, determination, experience, and skills enabled him to overcome all obstacles to the TDCC mission.

I knew and/or worked with Edward A. Guilbert for forty years, and I witnessed his performance in many endeavors. I was not surprised that he would undertake the *impossible mission* of TDCC as the final contribution in a long lifetime of constructive enterprises. I was also not surprised that he succeeded.

I salute him, with great respect and admiration.

George Klima

George Klima

From a different perspective, George Klima of Super Valu was also a "mover and shaker" toward EDI. While Ed Guilbert approached the EDI from a perspective of interacting industries and a joint industry-government sponsorship, George Klima's strength of purpose came from corporate and grocery industry visions.

That the work of Ed and George should somehow meet was both wonderful and inevitable. George talked about this in an interview with *EDI Forum:*[64]

EDI Forum: Did you look to other EDI standardization efforts that were underway at that time?

Klima: Yes. To try to move our own efforts forward more rapidly we looked into several standards being developed by other organizations. We talked to the drug industry but discovered they had different needs and did not place the same value we placed on fast message delivery and message acknowledgement. We felt their approach would not work well for the grocery industry. We visited with the people at the Transportation Data Coordinating Committee (TDCC), but their approach was too informal to satisfy our needs at the time. We also looked into the generic standards being created by ANSI X12 and even participated with them in the initial stages. Progress, however, was too slow, and the standards were too generic to suit our objectives. We also felt a need to establish more controls dealing with how the data would be sent and how responses should be made.

[64] *EDI Forum*, Founding Issue, "EDI at Super Valu: An Interview with George Klima," pages 97-98, EDI Group, Oak Park IL, 1989.

Finally, the grocery industry agreed to form another task force to review the development of EDI. I became a member of that task force. One of the first things we did was commission another cost/benefit study. This time we commissioned the consulting firm Arthur D. Little (ADL) to conduct the study. As in the earlier studies, the direct store delivery aspect of EDI was not examined.

***EDI Forum*:** The results?

Klima: They confirmed our earlier study that found significant benefits to EDI. They computed that the industry could save some $300 million if one-half of our documents were replaced by EDI transactions. The benefits were shown to accrue to all parties, not just the distributors. However, because not everyone in the industry uses UCS standards, it suggests, people are not unanimous about those conclusions. Based on the positive results of the ADL study, the industry task force proceeded with the job of making EDI happen throughout the grocery industry.

The task force agreed that a single industry standard would be developed. The acronym 'UCS' was born. At this point the so-called "Super Valu standard" being used by Super Valu and other firms was rejected because it could be seen as being too proprietary.

Klima: We turned again to the TDCC, which had been successful in developing a number of different standards for the transportation industry. They had the experience behind them. The task force commissioned ADL, as our independent consultant, and Kraft, as industry coordinator, to look carefully into the TDCC standards. They recommended adoption of the TDCC syntax and the task force concurred. By adopting TDCC syntax as a basis for UCS standards, the effort was probably moved ahead by at least a year. The UCS project moved into the development stage under the management of Touche Ross and Co. When the project moved to the pilot stage in 1982, TDCC was selected to manage that phase of UCS."

ADL: Arthur D, Little Consulting Firm

UCS: Uniform Communications System (Grocery industry name for EDI standard)

EDI: Electronic Data Interchange

TDCC: Transportation Data Coordinating Committee

***EDI Forum*:** How did the UCS standards evolve?

George stated explicitly the real driving force toward development of EDI:

George Klima had a worldwide vision toward the value and significance of EDI. The photos from top, left to right: Maria and George Klima taking a break from an EDI conference in Munich; George in Norway following another EDI conference; George [left center and bottom] in England with a friend following their escape from Communist Czechoslovakia in 1949; and George near the Grand Canyon contemplating [in his words] "the chasm between talk, reality and practicality of EDI application in a business environment."

I feel that the obsession with technology and lack of understanding of EDI benefits are the main contributors to the slow adoption and expansion of EDI. This was not the project direction I was looking for but it was a start. It enabled Super Valu to take advantage of the business benefits of EDI.

***EDI Forum*:** What were some of those opportunities?

Klima: Most of those firms using EDI were just transmitting data from one point to another, just replacing paper documents. That was what some of us were already doing back in 1962. At Super Valu, in the meantime, EDI led to the development of new internal systems, processes, and concepts utilizing EDI to improve productivity and decision-making. We computerized many processes, such as purchase orders and invoices. But we went further and developed transaction sets for many other documents, such as item maintenance, price lists, promotion announcements, and promotion announcement confirmations. These led to whole new concepts, like having our suppliers maintain our product databases. Because of such innovations, EDI enabled us to significantly reduce overhead expenses at Super Valu.

***EDI Forum*:** What lies ahead for EDI?

Klima: It is my hope that the industry will begin to address 'Phase II' of EDI. By that I mean recognizing the significant business opportunities EDI provides. I don't think many firms have fully realized what these benefits are. When that happens we can then start addressing the next frontier made possible by EDI—file and information integration. By this I mean that EDI will let firms integrate files and information both between and within firms. When the industry reaches this phase, then the real benefits and the real advances will emerge.

In four letters to the author, George presented his own summary of events and identification of companies and people involved in early EDI movements.

Paul Olson wrote in the 1988 pioneer article for George:[65] "The world-class individual standard for excellence in EDI implementation was shaped over the last decade by George Klima. He turned his firm into the premier showcase for the U.S. grocery industry's Uniform Communication Standard (UCS) program. In fact, no corporation, worldwide, can match the magnitude of EDI partnerships, degree of internal

[65] Quoted paragraphs are from Paul L. H. Olson, "George Klima: EDI Pioneer," *EDI Forum*, Founding Issue, page 99, EDI Group, Oak Park IL, 1988.

systems integration, savings, improved supplier relations, and customer service of Super Valu Stores, Inc., a $9.4 billion grocery wholesaler/retailer headquartered in Eden Prairie, Minnesota.

More than 1,400 vendors via 100 brokers and 200 manufacturers exchange EDI transactions daily with all sixteen divisions of Super Valu Stores. Payments are approved from paperless invoice notification. A single automated systems audit of UCS transaction pairs saves the company $6,000 per day. Scores of supplier meetings, seminars, and telephone conferences over the years have bonded business alliances, thereby providing lower-costing, consistently available, and fresh grocery goods to consumers.

In the mid-1970s, Klima was tapped by senior management to incorporate UCS into day-to-day business practice. Having led successful major systems development and implementation projects for office automation and micrographics, he was the confident choice for the UCS project. His twenty years of experience with manufacturers' promotions, accounts payable applications, buying systems, inventory control, and retail systems at the firm provided valuable insight into the practical, operational application of UCS.

As chairman of the UCS Standards Maintenance Committee during the development of the Uniform Communication Standards, he traveled extensively to promote and explain the use of UCS.

"Numerous articles authored by Klima have appeared in the *Wall Street Journal*, *Barrons*, *Datamation*, *CIO*, *Technology Strategies*, *Journal of Commerce and Industry*, and industry-specific periodicals including *Progressive Grocer*, *Supermarket News*, *Serviceline*, *Food Broker Qurterly* , and *NAWGA Review*. Titles like *Taking the Chaos Out of Ordering*, *EDI and Retail Strategy*, *UCS: Perfecting Communication*, *UCS: The Bandwagon Begins to Roll*, and *Why UCS?* reflect a practical and strategic understanding of EDI. In addition, he delivers more than two-dozen speeches, seminars, and presentations each year in the U.S. and Canada, and regularly hosts business executives from European and Pacific Rim countries. In early 1989, he will retire from Super Valu Stores after thirty-six years of service. He plans to set up an international consulting and speaking practice from dual residences in the U.S. and Italy.

Joseph G. Carley, Jr.[66]

> For electronic data interchange, he was a man for the time. The challenge was to organize participating companies into using new ways of exchanging information. The concept included computer-to-computer, database-to-database, and application-to-application considerations. The complications were data exchange between peers (rather than master/slave as was a common concept at the time), unlike equipment, unlike system software, unlike application software, a multitude of options for communications protocol. He met the challenge.
>
> Joe Carley did it.
>
> The time was 1973 to 1975. The place was the Transportation Data Coordinating Committee in Washington, DC. The result was the United States Electronic Data Interchange (EDI) standards—1975 version. The ultimate result is a worldwide EDI movement with thousands of participating companies and organizations—cross-industry and international.
>
> Joe Carley and Ed Guilbert worked very closely together. The EDI concepts and standard survived, grew, and eventually flourished because of Ed Guilbert's leadership and talent for motivating large groups of people and because of Joe Carley's ability to take a large complex problem and organize it into understandable and manageable *chunks* that enabled many people to be contributors at the same time.

What Joe Carley, Ed Guilbert and the others did is reported in the section of this book entitled "The Scheme and the Issues."

The education, skills, and experiences Joe used are an indication of why he could see the "big picture" so easily.

"He is a graduate of Southeastern Louisiana College, BA degree in music. He led his own jazz band during and after college. World War II interrupted his music career and brought him into the Air Force. He was a pilot and also trained pilots.

After the war, he returned to jazz music. But then he was interrupted by the Korean War, and was called back into active duty for the Air Force. After that war, he decided to stay in the Air Force. This led to other educational experiences sponsored by the Air Force: Master's work in Systems Science and Technology at American University, Air Forces' Advanced Officers Transportation School, graduate of Chicago School of Advanced

[66] Quoted paragraphs are adapted from Ralph W. Notto, "Joseph G. Carley, Jr.: EDI Pioneer," *EDI Forum*, Founding Issue, page 96, EDI Group, Oak Park IL, 1988.

Transportation, graduate of United States Army Command and General Staff College, officer and pilot training, and training in computer sciences.

At TDCC, Joe Carley served as director of operations for programs and systems. He exercised decision authority in recruiting the technical staff for TDCC. He is credited by numerous industry participants for visualizing a workable solution and approach towards achieving a single data standard for United States industry. The EDI standards (a term established by Joe) are a significant result of his organizational and coordination capabilities as well as his long experience in supervising systems development.

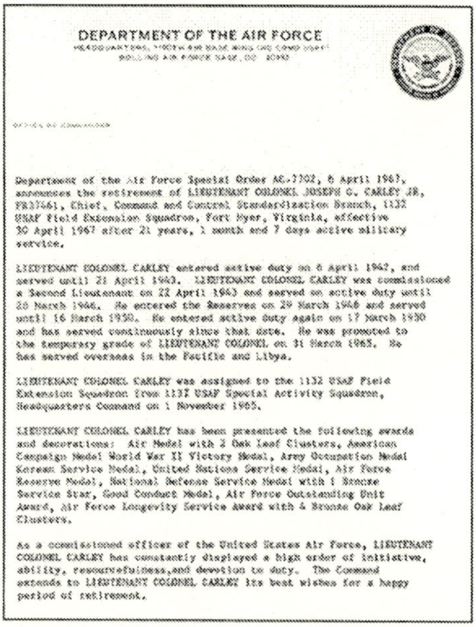

DEPARTMENT OF THE AIR FORCE

Department of the Air Force Special Order AC-7302, 6 April 1967, announces the retirement of LIEUTENANT COLONEL JOSEPH G. CARLEY JR, FR37661, Chief, Command and Control Standardization Branch, 1132 USAF Field Extension Squadron, Fort Myer, Virginia, effective 30 April 1967 after 21 years, 1 month and 7 days active military service.

LIEUTENANT COLONEL CARLEY entered active duty on 6 April 1942, and served until 21 April 1943. LIEUTENANT COLONEL CARLEY was commissioned a Second Lieutenant on 22 April 1943 and served on active duty until 28 March 1946. He entered the Reserves on 29 March 1946 and served until 16 March 1950. He entered active duty again on 17 March 1950 and has served continuously since that date. He was promoted to the temporary grade of LIEUTENANT COLONEL on 31 March 1965. He has served overseas in the Pacific and Libya.

LIEUTENANT COLONEL CARLEY was assigned to the 1132 USAF Field Extension Squadron from 1137 USAF Special Activity Squadron, Headquarters Command on 1 November 1965.

LIEUTENANT COLONEL CARLEY has been presented the following awards and decorations: Air Medal with 3 Oak Leaf Clusters, American Campaign Medal World War II Victory Medal, Army Occupation Medal Korean Service Medal, United Nations Service Medal, Air Force Reserve Medal, National Defense Service Medal with 1 Bronze Service Star, Good Conduct Medal, Air Force Outstanding Unit Award, Air Force Longevity Service Award with 4 Bronze Oak Leaf Clusters.

As a commissioned officer of the United States Air Force, LIEUTENANT COLONEL CARLEY has constantly displayed a high order of initiative, ability, resourcefulness, and devotion to duty. The Command extends to LIEUTENANT COLONEL CARLEY its best wishes for a happy period of retirement.

Joe retired from the United States Air Force as a lieutenant colonel and command pilot with 8,000 flying hours in fighters, bombers, and transport aircraft, and with over 400 hours of combat time. During his Air Force career he served in numerous command, director, and supervisory roles.

He is credited as being the *father* of the Air Force Integrated Command and Control System (AFICCS)."

Joe has a Commendation Medal from his military career. He has an Outstanding Citizenship award from the Governor of Maryland for work with young people.

Prior to joining the TDCC, Joe served as director, Command and Control Systems for the Bunker Ramo Corporation and, in addition, supervised East Coast marketing for the company. While with Bunker Ramo, he conceived and caused the initiation of design work on integrated display systems. He also initiated work on unit level local area network systems designed to directly support operations where people, things, and time had to be controlled, and where upward reporting (organizationally) was a necessity. The latter concept was essentially a source data automation concept where upward reporting was to be a by-product of operations.

Joe Carley had distinguished music, military and business careers. From top, left to right: J. *Gaines* Carley and his Orchestra [1948]—Shirley Cress in this photo is now (year 2001) Shirley Carley and CEO of EDI Integration Corporation (EIC); Joe with his clarinet [1950]; Joe, President of Creative Jazz Composers with Trumpeter Clark Terry [1975]; Air Force Lt. Colonel Carley [1967]; Joe as Director, Command and Control Systems for the Bunker Ramo Corp. [1971]; and President Joe Carley of EDI, Inc. with Hak Jung Lee of Data Communications Corporation of Korea [1987]—(Joe Carley was subsequently a founder and president of EIC.)

Following his work at TDCC, Joe was one of the organizers of EDI, Inc. and was its president during its first six years (see page 98). He subsequently founded EDI Integration Corporation.

Joe Carley's educational, music, military, business, teaching, and community experiences all contributed to his success in helping to establish EDI as national and international standards and as the cornerstone for significant change in data communications methods worldwide.

Don Trafford

While there was an EDI initiative in the United States in the 1970s, there was another in Europe at the same time. There was dialogue between EDI people on both continents; some of it was formal at meetings in Geneva, and some was informal at offices where these people worked. At one of these informal meetings in the TDCC office, Don Trafford from the U.K. had some influence on frequently used data element specifications (see "Forcing a Coordination Issue," page 59).

Don worked to coordinate the two initiatives. In particular, he worked to influence the U.S. to accept the European specifications. Initially he was partially successful, since leaders from the U.S. and European groups stayed apprised of each others work; years later with the introduction of the United Nations EDIFACT standard, he had additional success since coordination was executed on a worldwide scale, including the U.S.

This was possible because in spite of the differences between U.S. and European EDI standards, there were also similarities: EDI data structures in the U.S. included transaction sets, segments and data elements as information units; the corresponding structure in Europe included messages, segments, composite elements, and data elements. Transaction sets and messages were equivalent in purpose, since they addressed particular subjects like "purchase order" and "invoice." Both the transaction set and message structures were composed of segments and used similar rules for processing segments. The main specification difference in the two structures was the composite element that was defined to include two or more data elements. The U.S. people thought that it complicated software development; the Europeans thought that it simplified message design. After several years, composites also were included in the X12 standard, and they are used in the EDIFACT standard.

There was also a difference in purpose that explains why it took over ten years to come up with EDIFACT as a worldwide EDI standard. The U.S. wanted EDI to help eliminate paperwork; Europe needed an intermediate step that facilitated standard ways to transmit data so that required documents could be printed at the destination of international shipments.

Ray Walker wrote in 1988:[67]

> Quite simply, Don Trafford is one of the technical giants of the international EDI scene. For nearly twenty years he has striven toward the goal of common international standards and in particular, has made a major contribution to the development of syntax.
>
> Don started his working career in 1948 joining the British telecommunications carrier, Cable and Wireless, and was quickly emerged in this developing industry. He spent considerable time overseas, often in the rather remoter parts of the world, before returning to the U.K. on a permanent basis in the mid 1950s. In 1965 he joined the U.K. National Data Process Service (subsequently part of British Telecom) as a senior systems analyst and in 1968 transferred to the London Airport Cargo EDP project known as LACES as a senior analyst in the real-time systems development team. LACES became the first successful real-time cargo clearance system in the world and was the pioneer of many of today's clearance systems.

LACES: London Airport Cargo EDP project
EDIFACT: EDI For Administration, Commerce and Transport
SITPRO: Simplification of International Trade Procedures Board
EDP: Electronic Data Processing
UN/ECS: United Nations/Economic Commission for Europe
MERCATOR: First ever international EDI project
ODETTE: European Automotive EDI initiative
TDI: Trade Data Interchange
ISO: International Standards Organization

> In 1971, Don was seconded as director of EDP to the newly formed U.K. government agency SITPRO (the Simplification of International Trade Procedures Board) which had been established to cut through the documentary and procedural red tape of international trading and speed up both the delivery of goods and the payments for them. He soon realized that if computers were to be successfully used in this area then a strategic solution would have to be found which allowed incompatible computers to transfer transaction data to each other. Further, that solution would need to be independent of hardware, software, medium of transfer, and the particular application.

[67] Ray Walker, "Don Trafford: EDI Pioneer," *EDI Forum*, Founding Issue, page 101, EDI Group, Oak Park IL, 1988.

Under his leadership SITPRO began to tackle these problems, and by the mid 1970s EDI strategy had been proposed and accepted. In 1978, SITPRO published the first European rules for variable format trade data interchange, which consisted of syntax and data element directories. Subsequently, these rules lead to the Economic Commission for Europe (UN/ECE). Despite its name, UN/ECE is a worldwide body and not just European. The standard is known as GTDI, and is still the basis of many U.K. EDI applications including those of the TRADACOMS community that now (1988) has over a thousand users. Recognition of his technical strengths in EDI came with his appointment as a rapporteur (expert) to the UN/ECE.

Don also anticipated the user's need for software to support the standards and the likely emergence of microprocessors, and his work in this area subsequently allowed SITPRO to produce world-class software to facilitate international trade.

On behalf of the European Commission, Don directed the first ever international EDI project, known as MERCATOR, that was the forerunner of the European Automotive EDI initiative, ODETTE.

In 1984 he led the UN/ECE team that enhanced GTDI and produced an EDI standard, TDI, which was unanimously accepted by all European countries. This standard was about to be processed by the international standards organization (ISO) when the UN took the JEDI[68] initiative that has led to the EDIFACT standard.

Don has been a key player in the development of the EDIFACT standards (particularly the syntax which became an ISO standard in 1987). He is widely recognized on both sides of the Atlantic for his technical knowledge, his objectivity, and his ability to accept the logical argument of other EDI experts. Although Don left SITPRO in April 1986 to form his own consultancy company, he has continued to be very involved in the EDIFACT developments and is currently the chairman of the EDIFACT West European Technical Assessment Group.

In 1987, in recognition of his services to international trade, he was made an Officer of the British Empire (OSE) by Her Majesty the Queen—the first ever award made to anyone involved in EDI in the U.K.

Don is fifty-eight and married with two children and is known for his sharp sense of etiquette and his dashing sense of dress. In his spare time he is a keen fan of the distinctly English game of cricket and in his early career

[68] This is not the same "JEDI" reported on page 78.

was considered to be good enough to play professionally. Clearly cricket's loss has been EDI's gain!

William D. Plumb

Bill Plumb[69] was an EDI pioneer who was successful with industry EDI standards before the national and international inter-industry standards became available. Nevertheless, he took early positions in the broader standards and successfully transformed his company to be one of the worldwide leaders in the EDI service Industry.

Bill Plumb

His story:

Bill Plumb [right]on an outing in Japan as guests of Global VAN Japan, hosts of an EDI seminar in Tokyo in 1989. With Bill are fellow speakers Phyllis Sokol and Dave Dodge of ORDERNET and Ralph Notto of EDI Inc

.Bill Plumb as executive vice president of EDI Group[70] and president of the ORDERNET International Division at Sterling Software, Inc., was the executive most responsible for defining the product mix that has become typical of the principal EDI network service offerings. The distinguishing features of this mix are broken down into four primary areas—communications services, enabling software, shared applications, and professional services

ORDERNET pioneered the trading community concept of EDI, as opposed to the *hub and spoke* trading partner concept. In 1982, for example, it began working with the American Hardware Manufacturers Association (AHMA), which in

[69] Quoted paragraphs are excerpts from three *EDI Forum* articles: "William D. Plumb," 1992 Issue, No. 4, pages 47-48; "Interview with Bill Plumb: EDI Entrepreneur Extraordinaire," 1992 Issue, No. 4, pages 50-56; "A Dedication to William D. Plumb, EDI Pioneer," 1995 Volume 8, No. 1, page 72.

the late 1970s had tried, and failed, to bring up a system called EAGLE within their industry. ORDERNET resurrected EAGLE, launching it in late 1982 in the U.S. and Canada simultaneously. Along the way, ORDERNET picked up endorsements from not just the hardlines and pharmaceuticals industries, but also fourteen different trade associations, a crucial part of its trading community approach.

Next, in late 1983, ORDERNET joined the grocery companies' environment with that industry's major trade association—the National American Wholesale Grocers Association (NAWGA)—to affect a pilot on behalf of its members, mostly medium-sized to smaller grocery wholesalers. Moving forward from there, ORDERNET got involved in other aspects of the grocery industry—retail, then transportation, financial EDI, and discrete manufacturing.

Bill said that ORDERNET has been successful because of a focus on vertical industries and business solutions; not just selling technology, because we have a helluva lot of good Midwestern work ethic too.

Bill moved to England and brought that Midwestern ethic with him. His purpose was to revitalize the ORDERNET International Division.

He worked to expand further in the U.K. and on the continent while keeping responsibility for ORDERNET business in Canada, and leveraging ORDERNET's relationship with Global VAN Japan to get into the Japanese domestic market and Southeast Asia. Under Bill's direction, ORDERNET continued to reinforce its strong position in the U.S. EDI market and globally.

From essentially a one-man operation in its early days, ORDERNET grew over the years to become one of the top two EDI network services and the top provider of EDI translation software."

Excerpts from the interview:

EDI Forum: To begin, recount for us the history of ORDERNET.

Plumb: To understand the history of ORDERNET, you have to understand the background of a few other companies. My background is in the distribution area. For example, immediately prior to coming to a company in Columbus called Management Horizons, I was director of operations for a large multi-division drug wholesaler in Philadelphia called The Drug House. Prior to that, I held a variety of line management jobs for a

[70] "EDI Group": Not the same organization as *The EDI Group*, publisher of *EDI Forum*.

major grocery retailer in the Philadelphia area. I managed distribution centers, buying, data processing, labor relations, and so on.

In 1972, when I was at The Drug House, we were deciding whether or not to beef up our then IBM 360/30 in-house computer, or in today's vernacular, to outsource it. The reason we'd even contemplated outsourcing was that Management Horizons came to us and said, 'Hey, we've got a shared-resource, major data center, with parameter-driven and customized applications. You can tie into us from a dedicated leased line, have all your processing done here, get back your printouts, submit jobs on punch cards, and all that kind of stuff.' So I decided to outsource with Management Horizons.

As we got further into the project and implemented a couple of divisions on this new, state-of-the-art system, I became enamored of the company. It not only had very strong systems and a deep understanding of distribution, but also a consulting and, frankly, an academic bent to it. As a result, in 1974 I left The Drug House and joined Management Horizons as vice president of market development. First thing, I was put in charge of the user groups of—guess what?—the grocery and pharmaceutical industries. As I organized the user groups, the customers I had known from my years in the pharmaceuticals industry said, 'Look, you're essentially creating the purchase order from the records we send you—we get it back, we print it, we sign it, and we mail it. So why don't you just go to the data center in Columbus and transmit directly to the manufacturers?' I agreed, and we started transmitting purchase orders electronically.

Some years before I had been on an industry committee that developed the industry's electronic standard for the purchase order. It was simply a header and a spread card image for code and quantity and a trailer, and a freeform record, and that was it. So, using that, we went out to five or six manufacturers on behalf of this customer base, which at that time consisted of thirty-two different drug wholesalers in the U.S. and Canada.

As often happens, the mental light bulb clicks on while you're taking a shower. I thought, "Well, if this is good for my customers, it's got to be good for the whole industry.' So I embarked upon essentially a two-year sales effort to convince the major trade associations that this offered real value to their membership. I finally succeeded with three of them: the National Wholesale Druggists Association (NWDA), the Drug Wholesalers Association, which has since become part of NWDA, and the Pharmaceuticals Manufacturers Association. Then I consummated the internal sale—convincing people that this could be a business—which was just as hard if not harder than the external sale. Finally, I named it ORDERNET and launched the thing in September of 1978.

Bill continued in the interview to describe the origin of Management Horizons, "What had happened was that Management Horizons had sold its subsidiary, MHDS (Management Horizons Data Systems), to Citibank. Citibank in turn divested itself of MHDS and sold it to Informatics General Corporation in July 1977. When I went to market with ORDERNET, it was a small business unit within Informatics General Corp."

Regarding when ORDERNET first started, Bill added, "I was doing literally everything: I was selling over the phone, I was getting people tested, I was working the trading partners, as we now refer to them, I was calling companies saying, 'Good news—now you've got somebody to transmit to, etc., etc.' It was very much a one-man show, notwithstanding some part-time help, which is how things went until mid-1979."

He said that ORDERNET was successful because it always focused on business solutions, not just on selling technology.

Also from the interview:

EDI Forum: If you could change any one thing in the world of EDI to increase its acceptance and use, what would that be?

Plumb: At the risk of sounding a bit shrill, there is one thing I'd like to address. I've been to enough EDI conferences and quasi-EDI conferences of late to observe, as you probably have, that everybody now has a shingle out with *EDI* on it, regardless of what their business was before. If you're a lawyer, now you can be a lawyer with EDI expertise. If you're a business consultant, now you can be a business consultant with EDI expertise. If you're an applications development outfit, now you do that, but with added EDI expertise. While many of the people are well meaning, and everybody's got a right to make a living any way they can, I think some of it is actually slowing down the EDI process.

Classic example: about three years ago, at an EDI conference in Washington, I attended a session billed as EDI-oriented. A lot of our customers were there—Fortune 50 companies—so I figured I'd better go. I'll leave the name of the company unmentioned, but what it turned out to be was a front for a consulting firm that was trying to understand logistics, having consulted in financial and similar areas. This consulting firm had a customer whose business was in the logistics area. During a consulting engagement with the customer, it had tripped across EDI, and now it was positioning itself as a consulting firm in the logistics area. Their message was that you absolutely had to engage in extensive consultation before you got into EDI. So the net message was, spend $100,000 with us on long-term consulting, redo your applications and procedures and all that kind of stuff, and then, sir, you're ready to go out and buy a $2,500 PC product and start doing EDI. It was absolutely nuts.

In that audience there was a palpable chilling. It scared the hell out of them. The consulting firm did it intentionally to grind its own axe, and it did not serve those companies well who were there to find out how they could get going quickly on EDI. Unfortunately, I'm afraid there's an element of this in the EDI market.

EDI Forum: So the consulting company was telling these people not to do EDI but to *study* EDI for two years, give us all this money, and then maybe you can do it …?

Plumb: Exactly. And I think there are enough quality companies out there like ORDERNET and our competitors, all of which are very mature and very straightforward and can guide any company through what's required for EDI. I mean, we've got something like 8,000 customers in some form or fashion, GE's got a few more, IBM's got a few, so presumably all of us have satisfied our customer base. And I don't think you need a major consulting firm coming in and clogging up the works.

EDI Forum: And what you're saying about everybody having their EDI shingle out is that everybody and their mother want to be an EDI service provider—although I guess that's a good sign in a way, it means there's a lot of interest in and need for EDI, or else people wouldn't be responding in this way.

Plumb: Well, it depends. If someone's out there really adding value, fine. There's a lot of really good software companies, there's a lot of good service providers, there's a lot of good consultants, and there's probably a lot of good attorneys. I mean, we use our attorneys.

But I think there are also some people who benefit by slowing down EDI—lawyers, for instance. They often throw the fear of God into you. They say have you considered this in your contract; have you considered that in your contract?

For example, I attended an industry group meeting of a particular research firm. They actually had one of their staff members advising users to develop their own agreements for software licenses. At that, the software vendors in the audience, me included, went *nuts.* The industry already has standard boilerplate language that's totally acceptable for buyer and seller in terms of warranties and confidentiality and everything else. If a vendor had to negotiate a license every time it sold its software, I mean that could *chill* the industry. And I'm not talking about just EDI in this case; I'm talking about the whole software industry. So if someone has a particular axe to grind, it isn't always harmonious with rapid growth of EDI.

EDI Forum: An axe to grind or an axe to sell?

Plumb: Yes. A Plumb axe, to be precise.

Dedication

The *EDI Forum* dedicated its Volume Eight, Number One issue to Bill Plumb after learning that he had died of cancer at his home in McLean, Virginia on January 14, 1995. The dedication stated that he was one of the most energetic and successful executives in the EDI vendor community.

John Nelsen

Credit John Nelson for definition of the format of EDI segments, including data, header, and trailer segments. First offered in the mid-1970s, that segment structure is still in use today without changes, except for the addition of composite elements as an information unit. This work was essential in that it provided the generalized structure used for all of the 297 transaction sets listed in "Transaction Sets 1999," on page 267 of this book. In turn, that led to the feasibility of generalized EDI software at off-the-shelf prices offered by competing EDI software vendors.

In 1988, Buddy Bass wrote about this contribution:[71] "One of the prime movers and shakers in the world of electronic data interchange is John Nelsen of the railroad industry. He was involved in that first gathering of users in 1973 where it was determined that the only useful computer-to-computer exchange of information regarding business transactions had to be all encompassing and complete. With that charge, John Nelsen went back to his office at the Missouri Pacific Railroad and, with the help of his company associates, developed the concept of dividing the document or transaction into logical information segments and data elements. In addition, due to the demand for total and literal information in the transaction, this design included the concept of variable length segments and data elements. This

71 Earl J. Bass, "John Nelsen: EDI Pioneer," *EDI Forum*, Founding Issue, page 100, EDI Group, Oak Park IL, 1988.

provided the means for the sender to furnish total transaction information as it appeared on paper documents and allowed the receiver the freedom to translate the information into his own system. This required format and content without concern for the sender's system capabilities. This concept has weathered the test of time and is the very basis for all EDI applications, including the generic transactions of X12 and the international applications being developed under the EDIFACT syntax structure.

John was also instrumental in pursuing the development and implementation of the EDI concept within the railroad industry. In fact, the railroads were the first organized industry group to formally adopt the new EDI standards as the official standards for all applications within the railroad industry. This occurred with a resolution adopted by the General Committee of the Data Systems Division of the Association of American Railroads in 1978. It was the year that two railroads, Conrail and the Missouri Pacific, provided the first ever demonstration of EDI. They demonstrated how EDI worked for Waybill Data Exchange for shipments moving between the two carriers. From this early beginning the railroads have become one of the most active industries using EDI, developing a wide range of applications and a large community of participants. As of January 1, 1989, the railroads have mandated EDI for waybills as the formal means of supplying information on the shipments interchanged between carriers.

John Nelsen provided exceptional leadership in the development and maintenance of EDI standards. He has been involved with the TDCC Standards Maintenance Committee since its inception and is currently the chairman of that group. He also has been involved with the ANSI X12 processes of standards development and maintenance, and he is the current chairman of the Transportation Project Team and the vice chairman of the Technical Assessment Committee.

John has worked for the railroad industry for over thirty years. He started with the Southern Pacific Railroad in the late 1950s and culminated with his retirement from the Union Pacific Railroad in December 1988. He started his career working in the switching yards in Los Angeles. Later he became the manager of the administrative support of that terminal operation. In the mid 1960s, John joined the joint Southern Pacific and IBM team that developed and implemented the first online freight car management system in the rail industry. In addition to his significant contribution to the functional design of the system, he was responsible for the development and management of the education and training program in support of the implementation of the Total Operations Processing System (TOPS) on the Southern Pacific.

Early in 1971 John went to work for the Missouri Pacific Railroad, which later was merged into the Union Pacific. He held the position of an internal railroad consultant and provided support to system users. John was a major contributor to the functional design of Transportation Control System (TCS), the railroad's premier freight car management and scheduling system. In fact, he was responsible for the empty car distribution and freight car scheduling applications. During his tenure with the Union Pacific, John has been a major contributor and has provided leadership in the industry's efforts to standardize data processing applications in a variety of areas besides EDI. But he is best remembered as Mr. EDI in the rail industry.

Richard Cook

While the author knew and worked with the previous six pioneers portrayed at the beginning of this chapter, he never met Richard Cook. That is because Dick's work specifically addressed the healthcare industry and preceded the availability of the EDI standards that resulted from the TDCC work. Years later, the healthcare industry also migrated to the X12 standard. Nevertheless, EDI on an industry level is an enormous achievement as indicated by the quantitative analysis provided by Bill Plumb in the following EDI pioneer article:[72]

> By any measure, Richard C. Cook was the true pioneer and implementer of EDI in the healthcare industry. Prior to his retirement in 1984, as director of operations and research for NWDA (National Wholesale Druggists' Association), Dick had established and directed a NWDA Business Systems Committee. By 1971 this committee had developed, as a start, an automated order entry system between drug wholesalers and their suppliers. The committee consisted of nine members who had the data processing responsibilities in their respective companies. Six of these executives were from drug wholesaling companies, while three were from pharmaceutical manufacturing.

[72]William D. Plumb, "Richard C. Cook: EDI Pioneer," *EDI Forum*, Founding Issue, page 97, EDI Group, Oak Park IL, 1988.

At that time the NWDA active membership consisted of 140 drug wholesalers operating 418 distribution centers in forty-eight states, plus the District of Columbia and Puerto Rico. NWDA's associate membership of 303 included most of the pharmaceutical and health and beauty aid companies in the country.

These 443 companies relied heavily on Dick Cook to research and develop means to: improve bottom line profitability by utilizing state of the art computer capabilities in electronic data flow; reduce the alarming increases in paper flow and resultant human errors between the wholesalers and the manufacturers; and develop a data line that would work in all directions between the manufacturer, wholesaler, and retailer (independent and chain) to provide better services to the ultimate customer.

NWDA: National Wholesale Druggists' Association
NDC: National Drug Code

A major advantage held by the industry was the in-place use of the National Drug Code (NDC). This all-numeric nine-digit code provided unambiguous product identification for almost all items handled by the wholesalers.

Within one year of its inception, the NWDA Business Systems Committee under Dick Cook's leadership had developed a series of eighty column cards providing all relevant purchase order information. Most of these cards contained fixed fields for items, quantities, company code, ship to locations ... there were also several free form cards to provide special shipping instructions.

Bergen Brunswig and Eli Lilly tested the computer-to-computer order entry system and developed the software required to handle the document flow. By the end of 1974, the program had been debugged and was operational between these companies.

During this period, Dick had the committee develop an EDI directory which listed mainframe computers and major components by wholesaler and manufacturer location. This served to identify potential interface problems. However, 90% of all companies had IBM mainframes.

"With active campaigning on Dick's part, a number of the major NWDA members joined the system on a one-on-one basis, but progress was too slow.

Recognizing in 1978 that many of the smaller NWDA members did not have the time or capabilities to interface individually with many other companies, Dick led the committee to look for a better solution.

After an in-depth look at about a dozen computer service companies, the committee selected ORDERNET Services, a division of Sterling Software (formerly Informatics) to jointly develop an order entry clearinghouse.

This system was rapidly successful, with more than one hundred wholesaler companies becoming linked with the top forty or fifty pharmaceutical, toiletry, and health and beauty aid manufacturers within the first two and one-half years of operation.

How did this early effort in electronic data interchange (EDI) work out? It was Dick's responsibility to find out.

The investment in inventory represents well over 50% of drug wholesalers' assets, so the savings of time in manual order preparation, mail time, and manual order receipt at the other end causes a savings by allowing a reduction in the level of inventory.

The day's sales in ending inventory in 1972 were 59.45%, while by 1987 it was down to 51.70%. Wholesaler sales in 1972 were $6.2 billion and had grown to $19.5 billion in 1987.

Operating expenses reflecting many technical advances, including bar code scanning and, in particular, greatly expanded EDI network capabilities, have substantially reduced the manpower requirements and dramatically lowered costs. In 1972, operating expenses for NWDA members as a percent of net sales were 11.47%; in 1987 they were down to 5.28%.

Today the industry stands on the brink of major new advances in data and funds transmission. It is now even possible for a price increase introduced by the manufacturer this morning to be sent to the wholesaler and be entered into the drugstore pharmacy computer by this evening.

As an industry, healthcare is still ahead of the pack in terms of EDI utilization and proliferation among suppliers and wholesalers. And it continues to expand. This, in my judgment, is a direct result of the foresight, conviction, tenacity, and breadth of perspective Dick Cook consistently exhibited as a true EDI pioneer.

Paul Olson

In a very interesting story that included reflection on what was running through his mind at the time, Paul Olson wrote about why and how he got his company into EDI.[73] He also gave a forward look of what effect

[73] Indented paragraphs are from Paul L. H. Olson, "Confessions of an EDI Pioneer," *EDI Forum*, Founding Issue, pages 103-108, EDI Group, Oak Park IL, 1988.

the proliferation of EDI will have on productivity gains in your business. The story is excellent in both content and style.

Some excerpts from that story:

> A wise person observed, 'An expert is someone who thinks he is not an expert.' Labels are dangerous, particularly when engaging in self-labeling. Pioneers blaze trails for others to follow. I was asked to give account as a pioneer in the field of EDI. I am not sure I qualify as one. You be the judge.
>
> Three major dynamics drive up the value of information—globalization of business trade; technological advances and declining costs of communications and computing; and reliance on information for personal convenience and corporate competitive advantage.
>
> The world-at-large changed significantly in the last decade. Technology shattered barriers to defensible competitive strategies. Low cost labor and aggressive international marketing by developing countries reaped the benefit of domestic deregulation. The relatively stable and predictable corporate world is a part of the past. Gone is the era of passively sustainable excellence.
>
> Business practices are changing. Today's challenge is to manage the change in an orderly, responsive manner. It is an artful science. Listen to a business manager. How does he intend to achieve excellence and sustain a competitive advantage?
>
> *We've had to do it. We had customers... requesting Electronic Data Interchange ... if we didn't do that, we were going to walk away from hundreds of millions of dollars a year .they want acknowledgment electronic ally, they want us to send them shipping information electronically, invoice them electronically, they want to pay us electronically.*
> —Paul Jones, GE Plastics Group
>
> The conduct of business is fundamentally to buy and sell. EDI is the conduit for business conduct. Not yet, you say. Yes, already. Pioneers paved the way for EDI. They brainstormed ideas, analyzed paper-based practices, drafted new standards of conduct, experimented, piloted, shared the vision, and kept the dream alive. Only the size, the spokes, and the use of the conduit are changing. Pioneers are innovators, not implementers. Today, the implementers are jumping on the EDI built by the pioneers. The contribution of the implementers will be recognized when it is agreed

that EDI is the norm for business conduct. It won't take one hundred years. It will take just a few more beyond 1988.

My prediction is hedged. It has no quantitative support. It is a qualified and highly empirical viewpoint. Technology acceptance curves indicated that EDI acceptance and production usage, as a norm, would occur after 1995.

The more complex the technology, the longer it takes to accept. EDI, as an integral part of everyday business conduct, is extremely complex. It is perhaps the most important strategic battleground for obtaining, maintaining, and improving competitive advantage in the 1980's and 1990's. It will require money, time, and energy to implement.

Furthermore, EDI stretches the human mind in determining how to embed electronic processing into the organization. It requires enormous amounts of planning, interpersonal communication, and perseverance to practice it practically and profitably. The pioneers of electricity, the telephone, the automobile, the airplane, and the computer surely never imagined how long it would take for their inventions to become an everyday part of our society.

What's the hedge? It depends on the understanding of the 'perils of exploration' and a willful and progressive response to the signposts for adventurers established by the pioneers. Listen to an EDI pioneer. If you do EDI, your business will dramatically reduce incremental costs and expand market share. And someday, the productivity gains in your business will be credited to the proliferation of EDI.

IPaul's prediction for the EDI service industry was: "Information exchange products and services designed for corporate and individual user markets, worldwide, is a significant and strategic business opportunity."

In 1981, Paul was a branch manager for a time-sharing industry company, Tymshare. He explained the reasons for his initial interests in EDI:

> **ISD**: Information Systems Department
>
> **UCS**: Uniform Communication Standard (Grocery Industry EDI standard)
>
> **Tymeshare**: A leading company in the time sharing industry in the mid 1970s
>
> **OnTyme**: An email service provided by Tymeshare
>
> **Tymnet**: Tymeshare's wholly owned public network

In September 1981, I was introduced to a potential revenue opportunity for our branch to become involved in using

Uniform Communication Standards (UCS) to facilitate the purchasing process between a grocery store's computer and a manufacturer's computer. At the time, the computer time-sharing business was entering the classic 'decline' stage of the product/market life cycle. There was a malaise in the company and the branch personnel were pleading for new products to sell. This sounded like electronic mail with a twist to me. We were already selling and supporting an electronic mail product, OnTyme®, so I decided to call on a current customer to offer this UCS service as a new product.

Rarely do you hit gold on the first strike! David Graves, an ISD director at General Mills, not only knew about UCS, he had helped develop UCS. General Mills utilized a number of our products and services and our business relationship was solid, so I proposed a project to develop a UCS Tymshare product. He explained that General Mills had decided to support the UCS effort, but not participate in its thirteen-member pilot. Though disappointed in General Mills' decision not to partner with us, I had his encouragement to pursue a relationship with members of the UCS pilot.

Before leaving General Mills that day, he provided a brief summary of the document format and communication standard. As I drove back to the office, my thoughts were on my next step—calling the pilot companies. However, I puzzled over two features of the communication standard. The standard required computer systems to dial each other at 2400/2780 bisynchronous protocol and make the connection without a network level login. I wondered if it was technically possible or permissible for Tymeshare's wholly owned public network, TYMNET®, to enable a connect without a login. The '2400/2780 bisync' meant nothing to me.

At David Graves' suggestion, I contacted the president of a computer service bureau that served one of the UCS pilot companies, Paul Lemme. He showed great interest in third-party network services. Paul used TYMNET for customer access to his service bureau and believed he could use it for UCS communications. I proposed modifying the OnTyme electronic mail product to move UCS purchase orders and invoices. Paul candidly remarked, 'You don't understand UCS.'

For the next month and a half I researched the UCS standards, studied TYMNET communications technology, and met with or called several Tymshare employees to discuss how to build and support a third-party network service for UCS.

Another key question should have been, 'Is there a business case for launching the service?' The cost of communications cited in the Arthur D. Little report was a benchmark for calculating costs. Ten cents a document—the cost of a pay phone call at that time—was too conservative an estimate to justify a significant investment. However, figuring out how to make money was low on my list of priorities. The most important challenge was to build a product and sign a contract. The entrepreneurial spirit was the driving force. UCS represented leading-edge technology; it offered a pioneering opportunity. The challenge of managing change was exciting!

Several of my internal contacts expressed interest in the project. We clearly knew we lacked management authorization. We had no budget for software, software development, or personnel. Yet, within weeks we assembled a remote team of people consisting of a network manager, a data center supervisor, an equipment procurement administrator, and our branch technical staff.

By early October our team was functioning on an ad hoc basis and I felt comfortable that our product would be in place on December 22—the *live date* established by the UCS pilot companies connecting to Paul Lemme's service bureau. Telephone lines and modems would be installed to handle the 2400/2780-bisync protocol within TYMNET. A special code was developed and would be installed and tested in a slot on a TYMNET engine thereby enabling a network login bypass. Switching software would be written and installed in a specially configured IBM 3330 partition in order to sort and deliver the *mail*. In early December, Paul Lemme received my commitment to adhere to the schedule.

When Paul Lemme called me at 10:00 a.m. on that cold morning on December 23, his conversation was short and terse. His message was clear: either deliver the UCS network service by 4:00 p.m. that day or forget about any chance of securing a contract with him, and for that matter, doing any network business in the grocery industry. Furthermore, if I was unable to deliver the system on that day, Paul would have to admit to the chairman of Sales Force Companies, Marsh Blackburn, that he had misled him. He would also have to apologize to the management of their UCS pilot partners, George Klima of Super Valu and George Garrett of Dow Chemical. These were specific instructions from vacationing Marsh Blackburn. My integrity and the integrity of several others were at stake.

Paul went on to explain how attempts to change the situation were not successful until finally placing attention toward an unordinary participant:

A young sixteen-year-old played an important role in the history of EDI. He loved computer technology and understood it. Disliking the way his microcomputer operated, he dismantled it, made a hardware modification, and reprogrammed the operating system. In 1981 he was helping at Tymeshare's office by producing presentation graphics and running customer overnight jobs. Brent Geske became an integral player in the success of the first EDI transmission.

Brent Geske arrived at the office at 3:30 p.m. and we discussed the UCS problem. He suggested that he log into the Dallas Terminal host, draw the file into our Texas Instruments Intelligent Terminal (the forerunner to the microcomputer), and then log into Paul Lemme's DEC 20/20 in Chicago. It made sense, and since we had no other alternative, I told him to try it.

At 3:45 on December 23, 1981, we showed positive confirmation on our system that the file from Quaker Oats had been received by the Sales Force computer. Brent Geske was a hero. The challenge of initiating the first EDI transmission had been met. Paul Lemme was notified at his home just before 4:00 p.m. He never inquired regarding the production status of the service and no explanation was offered. Our remedy was unorthodox, but integrity was restored.

In his "Confessions" article, Paul Olson included a list and descriptions of eight useful-to-know "Signposts for Adventures." The (1988) list:

"EDI is more than a concept, and commitment is key to its success.

"Standards are not yet standard.

"Mainframe translators in business application systems are vital.

"EDI champions will accelerate the use of EDI.

"MIS [management information systems] organizations should be (but are not) leading EDI implementers.

"EDI is a business partnership decision.

"EDI saves—but it also costs.

"EDI is a system that bridges across every business function."

Connie Robinson

In 1988, Connie Robinson was president of the Consensus Bureau and a member of the Data Interchange Standards Association (DISA) staff. She was previously technical director for EDI standards development in the metals industry EDI project. In an article about the history of EDI development in that industry,[74] she described a five-year project by member companies of the Aluminum Association and the American Iron

& Steel Institute that led to a 1986 publication of a three-volume set of EDI implementation guidelines for the metals industry. She wrote, "The availability of this documentation has triggered a wave of EDI implementation projects this year [1988] among metal producers and their distributors, customers, and suppliers."

After announcing the five-year result, Connie continued with questions:

> Why has it taken so long? What does it take to *do* EDI? What is it that all these companies have been waiting for? "Why have the member companies of the Aluminum Association supported an EDI program every year for the last six years?
>
> The identification and resolution of several major obstacles to the implementation of electronic data interchange technology shaped the course of the Aluminum Association's EDI program from its inception in 1981 to the present. Not all of them were under the total control of the Association or its member companies, but all of them will be recognized as common to any attempt to introduce EDI technology into any sector of American industry. They are lack of information about the technology, lack of national standards for EDI suitable for use in the industry, and lack of standardized industry nomenclature and computer codes for product description.
>
> What kicked off an investigation of EDI at the Aluminum Association in 1981 was the threat of a new customer requirement. Beverage-can manufacturers began to press their aluminum sheet suppliers for more timely order status information. They went so far as to request direct access to their suppliers' computers to get it.
>
> The situation that makes order status information critical in the aluminum industry is probably not much different from that in other industries where bulky, custom-made products are the rule rather than the exception. An aluminum producer cannot always sell from stock, since many types of aluminum products are made-to-order and not generally held in inventory. Typically, aluminum producers schedule production and shipment anywhere from 'immediately' to as much as six weeks out from receipt of order. Many customers who buy primary aluminum and semi-finished aluminum products further process the material before it is sold to the end user. Without up-to-date order status and shipment information from their suppliers, it is difficult to schedule processing and promise shipment to their own customers.

---

[74] Indented paragraphs are from Connie Robinson, "What Does It Take to Do EDI?" *EDI Forum*, Founding Issue, pages 109-112, EDI Group, Oak Park IL, 1988.

Aluminum suppliers understand the truth of the old axiom, *what the customer wants, the customer gets.* But how to satisfy this customer demand was, at first, considered individually by each aluminum producer. Obviously, none of the companies was willing to let a customer have access to his computer system, so some producers installed computer terminals in the offices of their best customers and created a special database that could be accessed through the terminal. This entailed hardware acquisition, creating special databases, keying in current information, maintenance, installation, and training at the customer's office, and other expenses. The cost was justified by the perception that they had the customer locked in and the customer was happy.

Yet, when customer offices began to fill with dumb terminals, good for nothing but one highly specialized function, each requiring a different entry method and special training, and used daily for only a few minutes, customers began to wonder whether it was worth it. When they stopped using the terminals altogether, the producers could not see a return on their investment. Not only that, but there were still other customers who did not get this special treatment—what about them?

Some producers tried a different approach. They acquired computer hardware enhancements and protocol converters to make them compatible with their best customers' computers and wrote special programs for each customer's computer system. Others looked for less expensive ways to accommodate this customer request. They found that some industries had endorsed a third-party service bureau, where the bureau would provide computer-based data interchange and either resolve incompatibility problems between computer types or recommend a particular brand of hardware. They also learned that convincing a whole industry to go onto one system was very seldom successful. Some aluminum companies invested in facsimile machines or used telex equipment to get the speed and convenience of a system that eliminated postal delays and telephone calls. But FAX, though it was faster, was still paper-intensive and did not solve the problem of keying errors. However, it was apparent that none of these approaches could do the whole job to everyone's satisfaction. A solution that would work for the entire industry seemed to be what was needed.

The Aluminum Association, Inc. is an industry-wide trade organization representing over seventy companies and virtually all the primary producers of aluminum in the United States, leading manufacturers of semi-fabricated aluminum products, and principal foundries and smelters. It supports technical, statistical, marketing, standards, and educational programs, among others; but like many other trade associations in 1981, it did not have a standing program to handle computer-related industry issues. When its member companies suggested that an industry-wide approach to telecommunications might help them solve the customer communication issue, the Association agreed to appoint an ad hoc task force to explore possible solutions to the problem.

As the committee set out to educate itself in telecommunications technology (no easy task), it discovered two relevant pieces of information that, in the end, made all the difference to the program. First, the steel industry had been involved in EDI for several years already and had some valuable information and experience to share. And, second, the American National Standards Institute had accredited a committee, called X12, responsible for setting standards for electronic data interchange.

The ad hoc committee talked to representatives at the American Iron and Steel Institute (AISI), in Washington, DC. In 1978, its Committee on Systems Communications published two sets of documents to provide steel customers and suppliers with the information they needed to utilize EDI for computer ordering of steel. The first is a series of nomenclature handbooks that recommend standard nomenclature relative to steel mill products. The handbooks also suggest a logical sequence for entering order information to make it easier to identify the data on documents. Thus, all companies doing business in the steel industry could use the same language to describe all the industry's products, whether they were communicating on paper, via FAX, telephone, or computer—in text or in code. The EDI portion of the system is called COMPORD, for computer ordering, and it provides formats, codes and instructions for programming transactions for computer transmission.

Connie's (a) thorough (g) list of why ANSI X12 was exactly what the ad hoc committee was seeking is significant in that it emphasizes the need for a standard which affects many parallel requirements like hardware independence, security, standard support products at competitive prices, cross-industry coordination, standards maintenance, software simplification, and cost reduction.

When the aluminum ad hoc committee held conversations with the X12 Committee to discover the purpose and objectives of the national standards, they soon realized that the national standards for EDI offered exactly what they were looking for. Electronic data interchange under the ANSI standards has these benefits: a) installing X12 EDI software does not necessitate changes to computer hardware; b) security is not a problem; c) users can write their own software or purchase software and/or a service bureau, depending on their own business needs, from an established EDI software/services market; d) national standards for EDI can be used across industries and are not created by or for just one segment of the business community (so suppliers as well as customers could be accommodated with a single system); e) each industry or company with a material interest in the standards can, through maintenance procedures, affect the content of the standard in order to make it usable; f) with national standards in place, an aluminum company can create just one program and use it for all its trading partners; and g) EDI has the potential to dramatically lower the cost of doing business.

However, as the committee was to discover, finding X12 and *doing EDI* are not, unfortunately, the same thing.

Connie continued with the topics :Organizing and Planning," "Standard Nomenclature," "Modifications to X12 Standards," and "Joint Metals Committee." The Committee faced the issue of how to get the metals industry to implement the national standards for EDI without losing the economy of the standards, and posed the question: "How many companies would interpret the national standards differently from each other?"

She then emphasized: "The need to face this new chore was underscored by the fact that aluminum and steel serve many of the same customer markets. Without specific guidelines to tailor the standards, the whole metals industry would be back to a Tower of Babel."

She concluded with:

What does it take to do EDI? Several kinds of documentation are helpful: the national standards, industry standards, and implementation guidelines. It may not take long to get one's hands on it now, but the process of creating them can certainly be lengthy.

Each industry facing the challenge of implementing EDI should include some consideration of information/education, standards and industry nomenclature, and EDI guidelines for implementation at the industry level during its early planning stages.

To get what it takes to do EDI and enjoy its benefits will require of each industry a major commitment of sometimes scarce resources to a fairly new and barely understood technology. There are few shortcuts, but good planning and good information are a good start toward good national and industry standards.

DISA GRANTS HONORS

> **DISA**: Data Interchange Standards Association
> **ASC**: Accredited Standards Committee
> **X12**: Name of the U.S. EDI standard
> **EDI**: Electronic Data Interchange
> **EC**: Electronic Commerce

In 1995, the *EDI Forum* reported on the DISA awards presented at an ACS X12 meeting in Seattle that year.[75] DISA began presenting awards in 1991. In the following text, Rodger Cadaret, chairman of the DISA Board of Directors at that time, explained the origin of the awards. About 2,000 people attended the meeting.

This section is presented in two parts—the reported 1995 presentation, and identification of other DISA award recipients during the 1990s.

The 1995 Meeting

> ***EDI Forum*:** Buddy Bass, Ralph Notto, and Joseph Carley receive the Edward A. Guilbert Professional Award. It took DISA and Roger Cadaret to render Joe Carley speechless.
>
> **Editor's Note:** Buddy Bass, Ralph Notto, and Joe Carley have enjoyed distinguished careers filled with rare moments that shimmered through the EDI and EC communities. As they forthrightly shaped the industries, they hurdled obstacles to make electronic data interchange a form of daily business exchange, and watched their pioneering efforts not only mushroom in popularity, but also develop into electronic commerce. Sometimes high-spirited, sometimes the teacher, always loyal to their cause, Bass, Notto, and Carley made a difference by spreading their enthusiasm for their creations. The DISA proceedings follow, as well as what Carley said, and what he would have said if he hadn't been too choked up to take his prepared speech out of his pocket.
>
> **Cadaret:** The first business item for me this morning is one of the greatest pleasures of my career and my involvement in EDI and electronic commerce activities. As the chairman of the board, I am privileged to be the one to award the 1995 Edward Guilbert EDI Professional Award.

---

[75] Indented paragraphs in this topic are from *EDI Forum*, "DISA Grants Honors," Volume 8, No. 2 (1995), pages 72-77, The EDI Group, Oak Park, IL.

Roger Cadaret addressing the 1995 DISA meeting; seated are Charles Baggett [keynote speaker], Joe Carley,

Since 1991, the DISA Board of Directors has annually recognized individuals that have over many years distinguished themselves as outstanding EDI professionals. The first recipient of this award was a gentleman named Edward A. Guilbert. The world lost Ed in 1993. The name of the award was changed in his honor. Some of you knew Ed personally; many of you have heard of him and know that he is credited by many as being the father of EDI. Well, as any mother knows, being a father doesn't mean you deserve all the credit, or even most of it. In fact, Ed's role may have been better characterized as mid-wife and nurturer for EDI. He facilitated its birth and nurtured it for eighteen solid years. He was the ultimate proud father of EDI and the ultimate promoter.

This year the award committee has chosen to go a bit behind the scenes and in just a few minutes you will each meet the inventors of EDI. They are seated to my left. Their names are Joe Carley, Ralph Notto, and Buddy Bass.

Let me tell you a bit about the EDI invention story in the words of Ralph Notto, the closest thing to an EDI historian we have found yet.[76]

[76] Indented paragraphs of others referenced by Roger Cadaret are enclosed in single quotes.

'The time was 1973 to 1975. The place was the Transportation Data Coordinating Committee in Washington, DC. The challenge was organizing the companies to use new ways of exchanging information. The concept included computer-to-computer and application-to-application considerations, data exchange between peers rather than master/slave, which was so common at the time. That was the goal. Things like dissimilar equipment, system software, application software, and a multitude of options for telecommunications protocols complicated things just a bit. The result was the United States Electronic Data Interchange Standards, 1975 version, which ultimately resulted in a worldwide movement with many thousands of cross-industry companies participating.'

Just look around the room today.

Now, I want to share with you a short glimpse of what was involved in the invention of EDI. Ed Guilbert, at the time president of TDCC, had appointed Joe Carley to be the director of systems and programs for TDCC. He in turn told Carley to hire Ralph Notto and Buddy Bass as consultants. Again, in Ralph Notto's words:

'Standards work had begun years earlier in 1968. It moved slowly at first. The theory was that agreement was needed for common codes and everything would fall into place. Well, codes were completed for commodity, location, carrier, patron, and packaging information. Agreement on codes was reached, but falling into place was not happening. Something else was needed.

'The TDCC was sponsored by the Department of Transportation with a grant to develop a proposal for standardization, and at the first meeting of the standards committee, the objectives were stated by Ed Guilbert: 1) To develop a set of standards for electronic interchange of data between companies, and 2) to invent a living standard, one that was organized to accommodate change as the needs of the users changed.'

In the words of Joe Carley, 'A major factor in our planning strategy was to insure that standards would be open-ended. We were fundamentally going to attack the entire interface requirements under a single concept. In short, we were designing the universal packing crate for shipping data to discrete locations.'

Ladies and gentlemen, these pioneers coordinated the effort of numerous volunteer committees and they virtually manufactured consensus. For those of you who have been involved in the X12 standards development process, you would love their methodology. They controlled all communications between committees, kept all committees separated, and, working with each committee, they told them which consensus was shaping-up.

Masterful, gentlemen, masterful. Thank God we were guided by their genius.

Here is a glimpse of the EDI world at that time, again, in the words of Ralph Notto:

'In 1975, the American Trucking Associations representative argued strongly for the character limit for segments. A seventy-character limit, because tens of thousands of Teletype and Telex machines were in use.'

Yeah, Teletype and Telex machines.

'Unfortunately, this seventy-character limit would make it awkward to see some of the desired effects. But in 1975 (as you will remember was nine years before the microcomputer revolution), participants in the standards wanted it explicitly clear that small companies would not be excluded.'

Those are the times in which this work took place. We have to consider these historic times and, what are their individual efforts? We have only a glimpse of their individual roles, but we do know that in any team effort, it is impossible to single out any one individual. Here is a glimpse at the roles these individuals played. Joe Carley, the boss, in Ralph Notto's words:

'Joe, I discovered, was a master at taking an enormously complex problem and organizing it in such a way that many people could work on it at the same time. Numerous industry participants credit Joe for visualizing a workable solution and approach to achieve a single data interchange standard for U.S. Industry. The EDI standards, an acronym established by Joe, are a significant result of his organizational capabilities and experience.

'Ralph Notto,' according to Joe Carley, 'was most adept at converting concept to reality in terms of systems. Ralph approached us with a proposal to develop a new language to define the standards. He proposed that we call them transaction sets, and recommended that line items be data segments, which would contain data elements. Ralph also developed his card computer. He used a card file to store established functional relationships between data elements. It was during this period that we began to identify generic data elements, with qualifier codes to specify meaning. It was not long before Ralph said, "I can convert the card file to a set of computerized tables that will define each transaction set and all of its elements.'

Nothing of the kind existed before 1975.

'Buddy Bass's role was to invent the structure for the standards documentation with respect to ease of use, inter-industry coordination, and conformance to syntax. After three weeks on the job, working with the standards committees,' says Ralph Notto, 'Buddy came in and said he had completed the EDI standards book. After three weeks, the work groups had not yet finished their definitions; but Buddy had put the book together with the material available, and a plan to update it as work progressed. It contained all of the chapters. The first use of mandatory, conditional, and optional, terms appeared in Buddy's book. These ideas were introduced to the work groups and adopted. He also developed reference designators. It is no coincidence that current EDI standards are similar to Buddy's original book.'

Now, let's meet our inventing heroes. I'm going to introduce these gentlemen one at a time to you. You will be able to go away and say you met the inventors of EDI. We are going to ask them to make a few remarks.

I'm going to start with Buddy Bass and ask him to come up in just a minute. In more recent years, Buddy has served the ANSI X12 organization in many capacities. He was chairman of the Technical Assessment Committee, chairman of the Data Dictionary Coordinating Committee, served on the Standards Maintenance and Rules Committee, Version Release Task Force, Publications Task Force, and ultimately he was the chairman of X12 for two years. He was U.S. delegate to the UN Working Party instrumental in an international effort. He also served on the board of directors of DISA. While Buddy was the chairman of X12, he paved the way for unification of all EDI standards under the X12 banner. Now, in the spirit of audience participation, I am going to ask for your help. We are going to welcome Buddy up to the podium, but you have to understand: this is a very important day in Buddy's life. We can't tell you how old he is, but it is rumored that today is the first day of his eighth decade. So, if you would all participate and help me welcome Buddy on this day, happy birthday dear Buddy, happy birthday to you!"

Bass:

Thank you, Roger, for those flattering words. This feels like the night of the Academy Awards, when ten people run up to the stage to share an Oscar. But don't worry. Unlike those winners, I won't thank my grandparents for immigrating to the United States. However, a major thank you does go to Ed Guilbert and my two co-recipients, Joe and Ralph.

Ed hired Joe more than twenty years ago, and then Joe hired Ralph and me. We all helped to systemize and document the first EDI standards in 1975. We continued developing and maintaining the standards and assisted in the formation of X12. Sometime after X12 was formed, Joe, Ralph, and I left Ed's non-profit organization to form an EDI software company. I have been corporate representative to X12 since its inception. The two years I spent as chairman of X12 were personally very gratifying. Besides attending regular X12 meetings, I attended meetings at the UN in Geneva, international meetings in Europe and Canada, Goodwill meetings in Australia, New Zealand, and Japan; and, of course, ANSI headquarters in New York. When I chaired the X12 meetings, I also brought up my three-part credo for successful standards making. The most important part was when you come to the X12 standards meeting, leave your corporate hat at home and wear your industry hat. Come to negotiate and compromise, and don't push your own company's systems and procedures, and that way we will end up with the best standards, and your company will be well served. Obviously, they listened, for the X12 standards are good standards. In fact, if they weren't, you wouldn't all be here today.

Twenty years ago we didn't even have one network that would transmit out messages. Companies had to dial in to get their electronic mail. Today there are many full-EDI networks. Advances such as electronic commerce, the information superhighway, and Internet came along. Just last week there was an announcement of a break-trough of electric superconductivity, which dramatically changed the computer industry. Tomorrow there will be new scientific and business breakthroughs. The dedication and perseverance of all X12 members will adapt EDI standards to all business requirements, both national and international. Efficiency and reliability will become the important factors. Since X12 has been involved with the international standards in EDIFACT, I believe the X12 members are now wearing both their company and industry hats under their country hat, and are producing standards ideal for the entire country.

I am glad I was a part of the EDI process for the last twenty years, and I intend to continue to advance EDI in the future. Again, I want to thank the committee for this recognition."

Cadaret:

Buddy, congratulations. Next, we will meet Ralph Notto. As I said, Ralph is the closest we have to an EDI historian. His writings are terrific, and you will find them in more and more places. Carley says that most people work to live, but Ralph Notto lives to work. In addition to his TDCC EDI invention/contribution, he has done significant EDI consulting work in the U.S., Canada, and overseas. He authored a white paper and was one of the coordinators for the resulting Korean/North American EDI Pilot. He was a North American representative for the UN/EDIFACT Joint Technical Group in 1990, and has done a lot of technical writing related to EDI. A brilliant man, Ralph has degrees in mathematics and economics, and minors in journalism, education, history, and statistics. Please help me welcome Ralph Notto."

Notto:

You know, I always wondered if anyone read these history articles, and I am really pleased that you did so well with it. You get an 'A' in history this morning, Roger. Buddy said he wasn't going to thank his grandparents for immigrating here. Well, in my case, I'm a first-generation American. From immigrants I knew, I gained an early appreciation of history, and all of us here today are making history by beginning a new industry—the EDI industry, or the electronic commerce industry if you want to look at it that way.

How many times in history do people even get a chance to do this? I thought *that this has got to be recorded.* So I made an offer in 1987 to Dan Ferguson, who said he was going to start a journal called *EDI Forum*. Now that was twelve years after 1975 when EDI started. I said I would like to write a series of six articles describing from my point of view the most significant events toward the formation of EDI, and its becoming generally accepted. He said OK, and I did in fact write the article that Roger was reading from. It was twelve years after the fact when I wrote it, and it was done from memory, but also in conversation with the people who were there at the time. It was my intent to name names. There are other names in the article besides Ed Guilbert, Joe Carley, and Buddy Bass. In fact, the article has a subtitle, 'A Cast of Hundreds.' That is a little bit of an overstatement, but there were about 180 people who participated from various companies in the production of those standards.

I would like to just take a minute to tell you what those [nine] issues were in 1975, and compare them with issues today, and tell you why it is significant that you take time and look back in history. " (See "The Scheme and the Issues," page 25.)

Cadaret:

Now I am going to introduce the boss. In fact, I finally refer to this gentleman as the old warhorse. The first time I met Joe Carley was in a hotel in Chicago. It was a break at a conference. He walked up to me and said, 'Is your name Cadaret?'

I said, 'Yes, sir.'

He said, 'I heard about you and want to check you out and see if you know what you're talking about.' What a greeting. This is one of the most fascinating, straightforward gentlemen I have ever met in my life, and I just love it. Let me tell you this: he is a jazz musician who had a band, and his music career was interrupted by World War II and the Korean War, and I found out just this morning he was also involved in Vietnam from the Pentagon. He retired from the Air Force as a lieutenant colonel and command pilot with 8,000 flying hours. Along the way, he picked-up five U.S. Air Force medals, numerous campaign ribbons, and an accommodation medal.

You will notice he is a very tough guy. But please, remember he received an outstanding citizenship award from the governor of Maryland for his work with young people. Oh, by the way, he invented EDI.

Joe, please come meet the people.

Carley:

Well, I had an hour and thirty minute speech, but these guys took so much time. I am holding a special meeting this afternoon at 4:30 in this room. And if you want to hear the really important stuff, please come back. If not, I will be over in my room, watching TV probably.

First of all, I want to express my gratitude to DISA for having me come out today. I was more than surprised when Roger called me. In fact, I became slightly emotional, and he mentioned that during the conversation. The reason I became so emotional was it came as a total surprise. I was sitting in my office getting ready to go home. It was 4:30 in the afternoon. Low and behold, it was Roger on the phone and he was laughing like hell. I guess he was remembering Chicago. I don't remember Chicago, but I can't remember further back than two years. So he said, 'Listen. When we introduce you, you will give a speech and be able to say anything you want.' I spent a lot of time Sunday afternoon writing me a two-page speech. Then there was his offer of the chance to say anything I want. Well, anybody who was in Vancouver knows that you shouldn't offer me that. [See 'Joseph G. Carley, Jr.,' page 69]

So, I appreciate it because Roger is a courageous and generous man. Now, I would like to say one other last minute thing here. When I got the call, the next person I heard from on the subject of this meeting was Bill Myers. I have been working with him for years—since way back in the Economic Commission for Europe meetings—and I know Bill. When he coordinates something [this meeting], it is really coordinated. In the process, I met Connie Shaw. It is a class act, and I appreciate it. I am going to skip the rest of this. We have an important man who is going to speak (Charlie Baggett). But if you want to be here at 4:30, I will see you later.

And from Carley's pocket ...

When Roger offered me the chance to speak on any topic he revealed himself as a politically courageous and fair-minded man.

The specific orientation of this presentation was prompted and strongly stimulated by a random Internet message, addressed to no one in particular, which arrived on my desk a few weeks ago.

Before telling you about that, I would like to cover two categories of milestones: those I am pleased to have experienced, and those I wish had not happened.

Now, under the good items is what I call my opening milestone, which was the decision by the transportation industry to form TDCC in 1967. This decision foretold of major changes in direction collectively by the airline, motor carrier, railroad, ocean carrier, forwarder, consolidation, and shipping industries. It ultimately impacted all forms of trade at all levels simply because it was a joint effort instead of the normal individual industry approach. At that time, all of the industries mentioned were represented in the Transportation Association of America (TAA). The TAA was reportedly the largest transportation association in the world. In my opinion, the primary function of the organization was to maintain a significant transportation lobby in Washington, DC.

The change in direction originated at a major meeting of TAA in 1965 or 1966. The final result was the demise of TAA as an organization, and that was in about 1976. At that meeting, a senior representative from Chrysler Corporation challenged the value of the TAA role as a lobbying function. This individual wanted some form of activity initiated that would promise increased operating efficiency in the TAA membership companies.

The Chrysler official said that all companies represented in the room were highly computerized and many had invested heavily in nationwide data communications. He reportedly argued that communications systems throughout the industry could not easily interconnect. He said that database structures and operating data were grossly incompatible, and Chrysler prints out 5,000 computer-generated orders daily for auto windshields and mails them to Pittsburgh Plate Glass, for example. He said they, in turn, print computer-generated invoices and mail them to Chrysler to cover purchase orders. Now I'm going to quote what I remember him saying: 'We send checks through the mail to cover the invoices we receive. Our checks are turned over to PPG's bank as a deposit. The banking system processes our checks, and our bank debits our account. Finally, our checks are returned to us where we hold them in storage for seven years. I believe it is silly for us to own all of these electronic systems and continue to operate through an intensive paper mill to do business with one another. I think it is time for us to do something to electronically alleviate the situation.'

Something was done. Action was taken to form an analysis and planning team of representatives from Chrysler, E.I. du Pont, Union Carbide, Conrail, Ford Motor Company, Missouri Pacific Railroad, the American Trucking Associations, and American Airlines, among others. In 1966, a small analysis team was sent to Rehobeth Beach in Delaware for a few days to develop a high-level plan. The recommended course of action of the analysis group was for the transportation industry to form a special intermodal technology center with a single mission: solve the procedural and electronic incompatibility problems!

The initial plan was to make the new technical center a part of the TAA. However, that plan was aborted in favor of an independent organization with its own staff and board of directors. The resulting organization was named the Transportation Data Coordinating Committee (TDCC). It became actively operational in 1968 with Colonel Edward A. Guilbert as its president.

The second major milestone, of course, was my decision to join TDCC in March of 1973. Before joining the TDCC staff, I occasionally visited with Ed Guilbert to recall old times and to monitor progress on the TDCC mission. The project strongly interested me because it somewhat paralleled other assignments I had worked on in United States Air Force Command and Control Systems and, after my retirement from USAF, with Bunker Ramo Corporation. I felt I might make a worthwhile contribution some day.

The opportunity to make a contribution presented itself in 1973. I found it necessary to resign from Bunker Ramo on a Friday in mid-March. On the Monday morning following, I called Ed Guilbert and told him I was available and wanted to go to work at TDCC. Ed invited me down to Washington, DC to have lunch with him, and the next day I was at work at TDCC.

The third milestone is represented as a psychological condition which contributed significantly towards the development of the EDI standards. At the root of the condition was the work environment always associated with Edward A. Guilbert. After seven years, it was a pleasure to again be working with Mr. Guilbert. The years I was assigned to the 21st Air Force of the Military Airlift Command were among the most enjoyable of my USAF career. Mr. Guilbert was one of the reasons. I had gained considerable respect for him by observing his methods as a member of the 21st Air Force headquarters staff, and I felt that if I succeeded in obtaining a position with TDCC, I would be given almost free rein to perform my responsibilities.

My relationship with Mr. Guilbert was as I predicted: I was able to function almost without interference. In those days, no one knew what would result from the effort in TDCC, so having the functional and technical freedom to explore various strategies was essential to finding one that would work.

The development of the EDI concept is what I call the fourth historical milestone. The first task I faced upon joining the TDCC staff was deciding what was going to be my first task. I felt that the development of an overall concept was a high priority item that should be followed immediately by a strategy for implementation. However, research and analysis had to precede those steps before we could find out what already had been done and what the parties concerned were currently pursuing.

Research revealed considerable evidence of serious work at improving operational efficiency by the separate transportation industries (air, motor, ocean, and rail). There were published visions of a paperless U.S. trade environment. Some concepts were more advanced because they suggested that overall improvement of the business information environment was an essential objective for the future.

We found some very constructive efforts underway in the nation's railroads, which were establishing one-on-one electronic links with shippers using proprietary data formats. The motor carrier industry had an active program, but it was less aggressive in the collective sense than that found in the rail and air transportation modes. The ocean carriers (U.S. flag carriers) similarly had electronic programs underway, but they were heavily oriented towards independent, internal operations.

An important conclusion of the status review was a forecast for a future of continued electronic incompatibility if each carrier industry insisted on employing unique and independent approaches. Competition stimulated a trend toward uniqueness, which was carried beyond the possibility of achieving market advantage. The combined factors of pride in industry and in member organizations described the fundamental nature and character of the trade industry at that time.

Thus was the general state of things when TDCC was placed in active operation. We became convinced that most of the parties participating in, or *tracking* TDCC activities were in a mood to jointly work towards the objectives for which the technical center was formed. Some company representatives were probably participating primarily to deflect unwanted change; but the majority were involved with a purpose and a long-term commitment.

The TDCC effort attracted attention because it brought a new promise for the future in business operations. It was an opportunity to permanently relegate to history the many failed efforts of the transportation industry to establish standard paper forms and simplified procedures. Those experiences created a considerable number of cynics and doubters who expressed their opinions on whether the TDCC endeavor would succeed.

Even members of the TDCC board of directors appeared to be cynical at times. For example, when I presented our plan to the board to establish a single data interchange standard, some members clearly stated their doubts about the plan. They used, as their basis for doubt, a three-year coordination effort between Missouri Pacific and CONRAIL to standardize on a single paper form to be used by the two companies at the St. Louis (rail) gateway. The effort failed; nevertheless, the board gave us a vote of support and authorization to proceed.

What we did not tell the board was that the same standard we had in mind would also work for trade at all levels, including international trade. (It is estimated that 90% of the trade value in the U.S. is related to the invoice level of transactions. The transportation function accounts for the remaining 10%.) In 1974, we concluded that expanding the single standard concept to encompass the manufacturing and financial environments was inevitable.

By the end of 1973, we had arrived at a course of action. The board had restrained any inclination to perform design work through policy. This greatly reduced possibilities for coping with unnecessary pressure on the technical staff. In fact, the single admonition passed to Mr. Guilbert was that TDCC did not want to place customer, transportation, tariff, and product value data in any public central database. Our primary strategic objective would therefore be to greatly reduce or eliminate the use of paper-intensive data communications methods for the conduct of inter-company business. The most logical solution was going to be the primary use of electronic methods as a substitute for paper communications. Once those objectives were established, the TDCC staff was postured for commencing with actual definition and development.

The award of a $75,000 contract to TDCC by the Department of Transportation (DOT) is by me the fifth major milestone in the development of EDI standards. First, it enabled me to expand our technical staff. Secondly, it provided TDCC with a much-needed financial boost. After the TDCC Board had approved our plan, we approached the DOT Office of

Facilitation to request funding consideration. This action was taken because the DOT was requesting TDCC's support at meetings of the Economic Commission for Europe (ECE). The European representatives were discussing electronic methods in their meetings. They were also placing pressure on the U.S. delegation to establish some form of joint activity in trade facilitation with the ECE.

The addition of Ralph Notto and Earl Bass to the TDCC staff was the sixth major milestone in the history of TDCC. Those two additions were the most important reasons why I was able to successfully perform and complete my responsibilities there, and for the development of the EDI standards.

Shortly after Notto and Bass joined the staff, we began identifying the characteristics and philosophies on which the standards would be founded. For example: 1) The standard would be user controlled both during development and after implementation; 2) A management structure would exist solely to serve the users (this management structure would be denied any form of directive power and would not be able to pose a danger of potential takeover power grabs); 3) The technical design would be open-ended; and 4) The standards would be placed in the public domain. In addition, we came to realize that there was a need for new definitions and new terms of reference to describe the structure of the electronic message that would become the centerpiece of the planned standards. Therefore, transaction set and data segment are among the new terms that have become a permanent part of the standards lexicon. I credit Ralph and Buddy as the people primarily responsible for recognizing the need and for creating most of the new definitions." [Author's note: John Nelson of Missouri Pacific Railroad was the originator of the *segment* concept of EDI.]

Probably the least operationally important of the new terms of reference is the term 'EDI,' which I selected to colloquially identify the X12 standards. It is now a reference that has proven to have the most 'staying power' of any term originating in TDCC. It enjoys common international use by the media and users alike.

Publication of the first standards document must be identified as a major milestone—in this case, the seventh milestone. We entitled the document *The United States Electronic Data Interchange (EDI) Standards*, and it was published on July 15, 1975. The only question we had was whether industry would accept what we had developed. On the date of publication, one of us said, all we have to do now is wait for the other shoe to drop! The rest is history.

The eighth milestone proved how universally and flexibly EDI standards could be applied. The political barrier to expanding application of the standards to environments external to the transportation industry was dissolved by the grocery and warehouse industries. After a careful study of their options, these industries collectively adopted EDI as their standard for electronic data interchange. TDCC was contracted to help develop the grocery and warehouse transaction sets.

Probably the most important milestone, the ninth milestone, is the significant action taken by industry during the initial period EDI standards were evolving. That action was a decision to move the standards under the ANSI wing. Although this decision caused considerable pain for Mr. Guilbert, he and I both knew that it was an inevitable decision. A joint effort was undertaken by TDCC and personnel representing ANSI to realize the concept. Once the responsibility was moved to ANSI, a new momentum and energy was released within the United States. The result was phenomenal growth in implementations and rapid expansion in the number of industries to become involved.

This point in my story leads to the second category of milestones—those that I would have preferred not to have happened. The first not-so-good item was the decision to agree to adopt EDIFACT as the international standard. I will not repeat my criticism contained in my Vancouver speech [page 69], but I still maintain that the X12 managers at the time were strongly influenced by European and United Nations politics, not by the merit of the system. However, I accepted and will support the decision without further complaint. In fact, my company's translator system will process EDIFACT messages.

The next negative milestone came in the form of a decision by DISA to *trash* the X12 standards in 1997. I received a call from a representative in the motor carrier industry asking if I would support the motor carriers in their effort to overturn the X12 *sunset* decision. I informed the caller that I was a vendor and tried not to interfere in user standards matters. I also told him that I had absolutely zero influence in DISA and X12 matters. I agreed with him that the UN/EDIFACT people were obviously now in control of X12 and would use every means at their disposal to *sink* X12. I wished him luck. The next thing I heard from the gentleman was that the motor carriers had only been able to push things out in the future for a time. Several months later I noted that DISA was going to declare X12 to be a non-ANSI standard. In other words, X12 would have no standing either in ANSI or in DISA.

The next call I received was from someone in the healthcare industry. The person was also soliciting my support for their plan to launch a revolt. I advised the individual to make sure that he approached the problem with very strong support in terms of the number of users agreeing with his cause. Most people now know that the healthcare people managed to overturn the plan through an aggressive floor fight.

Then came the final straw. Several months ago, I received a message via the Internet that was not addressed to anyone in particular. The message made reference to the healthcare floor fight and reported that there was quiet action being undertaken to change the voting rules so that no organization would be able to overturn any DISA decision in the future. The message also warned that the rule change was going to be *buried* in language that would not be easily detected until the decision was made.

This development caused me considerable distress. Has anyone researched this subject to the point of determining why such strong uncivil efforts are being undertaken to *push* EDIFACT down the throats of U.S. industry? What would it cost to force the U.S. business environment to adopt EDIFACT and discontinue X12 after millions of dollars have been expended to launch EDI activities? Since when did the dollar volume of international trade exceed the amounts represented by U.S. companies trading within the boundaries of the U.S.?

If this kind of conduct continues in DISA, then I would be inclined to recommend that U.S. industry setup a separate X12 organizational structure and invite the UN/EDIFACT U.S. personnel to continue to operate in the basement of UN politics and to cease interfering with U.S. progress in EDI.

Regardless of my response to the above distractions, I was highly impressed with the overall 1995 forum in Seattle. I am also deeply indebted to DISA and particularly to Roger Cadaret for the honors bestowed on me at the DISA Forum. Thank you.

Between the Lines

The introductory comments by Roger and the speeches by the award recipients said something about each of them. Buddy was methodical, non-political, and gifted with a capability to make concise and unambiguous explanations. Besides the technical aspect of his work, Ralph was just as interested in the history of what was going on and sensed the importance of recording it. (In fact, in his prior studies of history, he regarded that many recorded on-the-scene stories are spellbinding.) Joe "pulled no punches." He was organized, had a keen sense of mission, and he knew how to work with large groups and still accomplish objectives.

The text also says something about Roger and the situation relative to working in a standards movement. Some of his comments reveal that he has experienced how difficult it is to achieve consensus, not that it is impossible—but sometimes it takes much longer than one thinks is necessary.

Roger also told the crowd of 2,000 attendees about these three award recipients: "This year the award committee has chosen to go a bit behind the scenes and in just a few minutes you will each meet the inventors of EDI." Even given that 1) Roger himself is a major contributor to EDI and *eCommerce* and knows very much about what is going on in that endeavor, 2) the award recipients played key roles leading toward success of the endeavor, and 3) the recipients greatly appreciated the recognition, the author sticks to his thesis that the work was accomplished by "A Cast of Hundreds" as reported in Chapter 2. These people are named in other chapters of this book and in the appendix, but there were even more people indirectly and directly involved: there were those involved with the social and legislative events decades ago—G.I. Bill, civil rights, women's rights—that contributed toward creating a multitude of very educated people who were necessary to bring about the scientific, engineering, and entrepreneurial events required to achieve the electronic and communications miracles required for *eCommerce*; there were those executives in the private sector and governments who understood the need for EDI even before it was defined, and contributed staff and funds for its development and experiment; there were those in the academic community who, over a period of four decades, had the insight to adjust the curriculum to include training and discussion for relevant courses that are now a foundation for *eCommerce*; and there were those who came after the definition of EDI, like the consultants and entrepreneurs named in chapter four, who made EDI practical.

Award Recipients, 1991-1999

The Edward A. Guilbert EDI Professional Award is given to one or more persons each year by the Data Interchange Standards Association (DISA). The DISA award was changed to its present name after the death of Ed Guilbert in 1993. Candidates for this award are evaluated on the scope, duration, and quality of service toward the advancement of EDI and EDI standards. Candidates are nominated by DISA members.

The recipients through year 1999 were:

Year	Recipients	Reference
1991	Edward A. Guilbert David L. Torma	*Edward A. Guilbert*, page 156 *Dave Torma*, page 248
1992	Clifford R. Buys	*People, Affiliations and Other Issues* [Issue 7], page 28 TDCC Advanced Systems Planning Group, page 256 TDCC Shipper/Motor Carrier Work Group, page 258 Electronic Payment System Subcommittee, page 261 TDCC Board of Directors, page 262
1993	Burton F. Millard	*Burton F. Millard*, page 233
1994	Ken Hutcheson	E. I. du Pont Fourth Chairperson of ANSI X12
1995	Joseph G. Carley, Jr. Earl J. Bass Ralph W. Notto	*The 1995 Meeting*, page 181
1996	James J. Muenz	*Jim Muenz*, page 234
1997	Hans Wieting	*Citing*, page 30 *TDCC Shipper/Forwarder/Ocean Carrier Work Group*, page 259
1998	Harriet J. Rusk	First President, Data Interchange Standards Association (DISA)

Year	Recipients	Reference
1999	Lee Barrett	Chairperson, ASC X12 N Committee [Insurance and Health Care] While chairperson of X12N, Lee was also one of the original members of the Workgroup for Electronic Data Interchange [**WEDI**], which resulted from a 1991 federal forum of health care and insurance industry leaders convened to determine how health care administrative costs could be reduced and to streamline health care administration by standardizing electronic communications across the health care industry. WEDI was initiated in 1992. The WEDI vision was of a health care industry that would conduct all business electronically, using one set of standards. X12 was recommended as the standard to use, and a steering committee was formed in 1992 to bring about EDI as a routine means of conducting business between payers and providers by 1994, and extend the full benefits of administrative automation across the health care industry by 1996. Using the strength of X12N, Lee helped to facilitate the redefinition of 450 different electronic claim formats to a single [EDI] format.

8. Consequence

"The decisions that bear most closely upon
the well-being and expectations of the individual
are those that engage the well-being and expectations of all."

Gerard Piel, *The Acceleration of History*[77]

SUMMING UP

In December of each year during the period 1970 through at least 1988, Ed Guilbert of TDCC was host at an EDI Forum in Washington, DC. He spent a significant amount of his time during the year preparing for the event, concentrating on a theme, getting speakers, and motivating people to attend. About 1984, the keynote speaker at the forum was a futurist who evaluated how the EDI endeavor was progressing in comparison with other (completed) endeavors of similar complexity. The futurist said that we were doing well, and we would probably reach our goal of significant participation within twenty years of publication of the first public EDI standard (1975). Some of us groaned quietly. Anticipating this, the speaker followed with, "Given an endeavor of EDI's complexity, you would expect that the period would be twenty-five years, so you are doing well." His assessment was correct, since there were about ten thousand active EDI participants by 1989, and the community was growing rapidly. By comparison, the Internet did not begin to find its way into corporations until about 1993.

What was done? We were challenged to invent *electronic commerce* and tasked to implement a major component of it. The goals were stated in

---

[77] *The Acceleration of History*, page 369, published by Alfred A. Knopf, Inc., 1972.

terms of effects to be achieved: elimination of inter-company paperwork, absolute accuracy, timeliness for key processes, complete control over repetitive processes, protection of the databanks of individual participating entities from each other and invasions from outside, cost reduction, and catalyst to stimulate ever increasing customer satisfaction.

This chapter addresses the evidence and the social impact of what has happened.

EVIDENCE

Expectations

Evidence that something significant has happened is presented in previous chapters based on: 1) Quotes from articles in *EDI Forum—The Journal of Electronic Commerce*–articles written by insiders in a company or organization and approved by those companies before release; 2) quotes from other articles and publications written by participants, and published by a responsible committee; 3) conclusions reached by the EDI Research division of the EDI Group based on surveys and statistical evaluation of the responses to survey questions; 4) writings by the author published in *EDI Forum* during the period 1988 through 1998; and 5) experiences of the author shared with other people in the EDI endeavor during 1975 through 2000.

Those in 1975 who laid the basis for this work were possibly putting their careers at risk, because many in industry thought that the goals could not be accomplished in our lifetimes. Fortunately, there were also enough capable people who with their corporate sponsors were not afraid to attempt. They started developmental work already convinced because of earlier experiments and experiences.

Why did they do it when even the convinced understood the many obstacles to success? The rewards from success were thought to be significant, while choosing continuation of processing punch cards, printing, and mailing reports and documents, and tracing and correcting errors hardly seemed like an exciting future.

Still, it took at least five years from the date of publication of the first U.S. EDI standard until we began to witness significant actions toward operational EDI. It took another three years after that before we believed that EDI had reached "a point of no return."

The estimated *U.S.* EDI population was 100 sites (companies) in 1984 and 8,000 by 1989, an average growth rate of 140% per year over five years. The 8,000-population figure in 1989 grew to over 347,000 EDI locations by 1999, an average growth rate of 46% per year for the ten-year period.

The estimated *world* EDI population was 10,000 sites in 1989, including the U.S.

Although continuance of significant EDI growth is expected, it does not seem likely that the pace will be as rapid as in the past. In any case, the rate of growth will be determined by continuing demands on trading partners by large corporations that have included EDI as one of the building blocks in their process reengineering schemes; demands on companies by governments as they expand the scope of governmental EDI initiatives and drive toward complete elimination of paperwork; moves in the academic community as they complete the conversion to EDI for transmission of student transcripts among colleges and universities to also include transmissions to secondary and elementary schools and to potential employers of their students; initiatives in countries relatively new in EDI as they aggressively pursue means to remain competitive and to address service issues important for foreign customers; implementation of EDI plans in major industries (like healthcare) that have been working several years to employ EDI implementation conventions on an industry-standard basis in all companies—large and small; aggressive actions by the financial community as they clearly understand their role in facilitating EDI becoming a unilateral (rather than forced) decision as pointed out by Craigg Ballance—a long time leader in financial EDI; innovations in the technological community that will continue to make all of this even more practical with user-friendly and cost-effective improvements; and significantly more use of the Internet for sending and receiving EDI-formatted data—nationally and internationally.

The EDI growth rate may be slowed down by situations like the continuing XML vs. EDI competition. But also in 2002, those working in XML and EDI are beginning to recognize that each has a role as pointed out in an *Electronic Commerce World* cover story, "Companies combine the thirty-year-old technology with emerging business process integration systems, XML, and the Internet to improve business processes within and between enterprises."[78] The issue's cover also states, "Old tech reemerges as a backbone for e-business."

---

[78]Michael S. McGarr, "Transforming Business Processes with EDI," *Electronic Commerce World*, Vol 12, No. 4, pages 22- 29, May 2002.

Was EDI responsible for the unemployment increase during years 2001 and 2002? The statistics in Table 8-1 show otherwise, since unemployment was decreasing in both number of persons and unemployment rate while the total employment increased during 1997-2000, years of significant EDI expansion. .

Table 8-1. Employment Facts During EDI's Rapid Growth in 1997-2000 Compared with 2001-2002

Date	Unemployed persons	Unemployment rate	Total Employment
Sept. 1997	6.8 million ↓	4.9% ↓	129.7 million ↑
Sept. 1998	6.3 ↓	4.6% ↓	131.9 ↑
Sept. 1999	5.8 ↓	4.2% ↓	133.6 ↑
Sept. 2000	5.5 ↓	3.9% ↓	135.2 ↑
Sept. 2001	7.0 ↑	4.9% ↑	135.2 Same
Sept. 2002	8.1 ↑	5.6% ↑	135.2 Same
Source: U.S. Department of Labor, Bureau of Labor Statistics Web site: http://stats.bls.gov/schedule/archives/empsit_nr.htm#1998			

In 2001 and 2002, total employment remained the same as in 2000, but the number of unemployed increased by over one million persons each of those two years. It is likely that EDI continued to grow during 2000-2001, since one of EDI's benefits is cost reduction. The implication, then, is that something else caused the unemployment, like 1) the "over exuberance in the stock market," as suggested by Federal Reserve Board Chairman Alan Greenspan in a report to Congress in the late 1990s, that led to significant amounts of money prematurely invested in new ventures, causing a rapid increase in total employment that followed with a rapid decrease when hopes for success of a significant number of the new ventures did not materialize; 2) dishonest financial disclosures by a critical number of very large corporations as reported in the general and business news during 2000-2002, resulting in the layoff of tens of thousands of employees in the companies; and 3) the effect of the of the events of September 11, 2001, on travel-related industries that also lead to similar layoffs

Results Measured and Observed

Some motivations summarized by the EDI Group in 1994 were: "Companies that are driving EDI do it for the 40% cycle-time improvements, 30% error-rate reductions, and $5.00-per-document-converted cost savings."

The transportation and grocery industries were early in the use of standard EDI. Their motivation stemmed from goals for improving operations while decreasing costs. Both industries in the 1970s were noted for profit ratios averaging between one and two percent of sales. Both had significant logistic challenges, and both considered timeliness a factor in customer satisfaction.

A quick search on the Internet in December 2000 showed twenty-six trucking companies out of forty-nine tracked had profit margins (operating earnings) averaging more than 5% over a five-year period; eleven of the twenty-six had over 10% profit. A similar search showed eighteen railroads out of twenty tracked for the same period had over 5% profit; fifteen of these had over 10%.

While we do not know how much of the profit change, if any, is directly due to EDI, we do know that companies generally experienced significant increases in productivity during the 1990s. Further, we know that productivity gains are related to availability of pertinent and timely information, dramatic reductions in error rates, and decrease or elimination of paper-intensive tasks. EDI was a major factor in all of these activities, so we can reasonably assume that EDI was one of the significant enablers for favorable changes in profitability. The transportation industry is a "heavy" user of EDI.

We also can reasonable assume that EDI is still this kind of enabler, since surveys show that the number of EDI sites worldwide is continuing to increase at a rapid rate.

The A. D. Little report for the grocery industry (1980) predicted that with a 50% EDI transaction penetration, the industry would have a potential savings of $324 million per year. By 1983, companies doing EDI were reporting that savings were significantly higher than initially predicted.

Some cost reduction and related results reported:

Apple Computer (1990) experienced reduction in operational transaction cost from $1.07 per purchase order before EDI to $0.27 after. This did not take into account further cost reductions expected from lowering inventory levels.

One of the revisions due to EDI and possibly at Sears (1990) was that store floor space allocated to inventory would become only 20%, compared with 50% before.

George Klima of Super Valu said (in 1989): "Most of those firms using EDI were just transmitting data from one point to another, just replacing paper documents. That was what some of us were already doing back in 1962. At Super Valu, in the meantime, EDI led to the development of new internal systems, processes, and concepts utilizing EDI to improve productivity and decision-making. We computerized many processes, such as purchase orders and invoices. But we went further and developed transaction sets for many other documents, such as item maintenance, price lists, promotion announcements, and promotion announcement confirmations. These led to completely new concepts, like having our suppliers maintain our product databases. Because of such innovations, EDI enabled us to significantly reduce overhead expenses at Super Valu."

(George Klima's reference to "improve[d] decision-making" is especially significant, since it infers that, based on his company's experiences, information can be derived from data that passes through an EDI system, and this information is useful for executive and operational decision-making purposes.)

San Jose State University reported in 1995 that paper costs of $18 to $36 per student transcript could be reduced to $1.50 per transcript.

About Productivity:

What effect do you believe all of this has on productivity? Why does the number of jobs increase while productivity increases so dramatically? This productivity gain/job increase phenomenon has occurred consistently since the computer industry began in the 1950s. By the early 1960s, *experts* were predicting that the bubble would burst, and jobs would be scarce. It never happened. It is not happening now. Productivity gains permit a company to assign tasks never assigned before because of limited resources. Completion of these tasks results in product enhancements, improvements in customer service, and increased reliability. Increased sales follow. More people are added to the workforce, and product demand increases. New innovations surface, and new companies appear. Still more people are added to the workforce.

About Win/Win Scenarios:

In the long run, expect that coercion to do EDI will diminish as the EDI community grows and performs flawlessly, since EDI objectives are to operate timely and error-free in win/win scenarios, with or without coercion.

"An early well-attended course in EDI, 'Principles of EDI,' included a segment about restructuring payment agreements between buyers and sellers in win/win scenarios where both sides received substantial gains.

EFT: Electronic Funds Transfer

"Many exciting things began to happen in the business world after EDI and EFT processes were linked. Terms of sale were reengineered in a 'win/win' exchange between the buyer and supplier, permitting prompt payment on dates-certain by the buyer and more favorable discount terms offered by the supplier.

About Reengineering:

The significance of early EDI consulting and system installation activities is that the concept of a single cross-industry EDI standard became firmly entrenched in participating companies, and the potential of EDI as one of the enabling tools for subsequent reengineering was beginning to be understood by the user community.

Publication of *Implementing EDI Beyond Connectivity* was a significant event in EDI history, because it offered organized thought processes required when analyzing the *pre-reengineering* situation in any company, and provided a *must read* paper for those assigned to process-reengineering teams.

The idea was not to automate with new standards, equipment, and services what we were previously doing; the idea was to question what we were doing in light of what was now available. This is called *reengineering*.

What was learned? Significant change is not easy. Executive attention has benefits. Imagination is an asset. EDI environments facilitate reengineering; the most dramatic benefits are associated with reengineering. However, designs relevant to the EDI/Web-based form choices need to be addressed with broad system engineering principles, considering total impact on all participants and the value of consistency and standardization. Customers benefit from the better service and product reliability that follow.

SOCIAL IMPACT

The Wall

TDCC: Transportation Data Coordinating Committee

In the TDCC *Concept* document, Joe Carley wrote how conveyance of business information in the 1970s was dependent on the telephone and postal service, and this limited communications to voice, typed documents, or hand-written notes. He observed that these restrictions imposed a "wall" around each company's computer, so the information flow between trading partners had to follow time-consuming steps before EDI became an option. The sending company had to print a document, package it for mailing, apply postage, and mail it. The receiving company had to route the packaged document to the intended recipient, open it, mark it up if necessary, and send a form to the key punch department to record the event for entry into the receiving company's computer system.

If relevant information from the other company were required more quickly, the telephone would be used to obtain whatever status information was currently available. However, this verbal information did not always find its way to both trading partners' computer records.

Of course, some companies did much better than that. Airline reservation systems, for example, showed that companies within an industry could work together to solve common information problems and develop useful standards. Yet most companies continued to keep their computers behind "the wall" as they drudgingly followed the tedious steps imposed by communications limitations. On top of that, smaller companies did not even have computers, since the PC would not be introduced for another decade. The only significant upgrade to hand-written and typed documents was hand-marked updates to printed forms distributed between companies.

Did "the wall" come down? Did companies eventually do what we asked them to imagine: "A single computer *window* to the world—a single set of computer programs to seamlessly interface your system with the system of any other company—on any business subject!" EC Research indicates that a half million companies have at least started![79]

Internet's Effect

The Internet and EDI are both components of *eCommerce*. The scope of the Internet is enormously significant, and while some of its techniques compete with EDI, cooperation makes more sense than competition when data-oriented communications flow is between *processes* at two different companies.

> **VAN:** Value Added Network
> **FTP:** File Transfer Protocol
> **ISP:** Internet Service Provider

Examples: 1) Internet business-to-consumer environments can efficiently link retailers with the public. However, the supplying company also needs to be notified of any retail purchases. The retail companies, in turn, need to communicate with carriers and their suppliers. Many, if not most, of these companies prefer EDI-formatted communications, which are efficient, can be automatically edited by the receiver, and are already linked to internal processes reengineered using EDI as one of its components ... and these are supplemented with a component that includes retry, audit, and guaranteed delivery mechanisms built into the interface applications. The 1999 Christmas rush and subsequent poor delivery results for these retail web environments were due, in part, to the lack of the EDI connection. This issue is now better understood, and is being addressed. 2) "During its first twenty years, EDI-formatted data was transmitted via VANs or via private point-to-point connections or dial-up connections. EDI is a data-formatting standard. To be of any use, the data must be transmitted, but the EDI and communications standards are independent of each other and mature independently. Therefore it was easy for EDI processes to adapt to the Internet for data communications." 3) VAN communications prices for transmitting EDI were initially established by setting rates that favorably competed with postal costs. As the volume of characters transmitted greatly increased, the communications cost became a serious consideration. EDI, however, can now be transmitted over the Internet, company-to-company, by an Internet feature known as File Transfer Protocol (FTP), or as an attachment to an email message. In either case, encryption is an

[79] EC Research: "2000 EC Article Library and EC Research Sample Reports," Faulkner & Gray EC Research, Compact Disk Version 2000.6.

option when privacy is required. 4) Given that a company already has an Internet service provider (ISP) as most companies now do, the Internet offers a cost-effective means to transmit EDI-formatted data anywhere in the world. (In such transmissions, the sender is generally an EDI software application system in one company's computer and a similar system is at the receiver's site. Further, the two companies are not required to buy EDI software from the same vendor, since EDI is a standard. The software prices are therefore set by competing companies and are also cost-effective.)

Another View

Dr. Y.T. Lee

Dr. Y.T. Lee of Seoul, Korea invited four Americans in 1987—Joe Carley, Dan Petrosky, Jim Oravec, and Ralph Notto—to be the speakers at the first EDI Forum in Korea. At a meeting with him and his top management (he was chairman of Data Communications Corporation of Korea at that time), he said that he observed that the American small-company entrepreneurs were the backbone of our democracy. Korea did not have the equivalent of this, he said, because a large corporation "owned" all of the small companies that supplied it and any small supplier who ever tried to sell to other companies would never sell to any of the large companies again. He thought that EDI might start to change that.

In the week we were in Korea, October 1987, Koreans voted for their new constitution. It was printed in its entirety in the *Korean Times*, an English-language newspaper available during the flight to Korea. Ralph

Notto studied all of it, and saw a clear relationship between the meaning of the constitution and Dr. Lee's statement.

Later in the week, Notto asked his American colleagues what they thought of what Dr. Lee had said about "American small entrepreneurs were the backbone of our democracy" and "EDI might help Korea to offer a more open environment for small entrepreneurs." None of them recalled that Dr. Lee said that. In 1991 in Korea, Notto again had lunch with Dr. Lee and asked him if he said what Notto thought he had said.

"Absolutely," Dr. Lee said.

Dr. Lee's insight indicated that EDI may also address a significant social issue, and *eCommerce* and EDI's role in *eCommerce* are *that* important.

Challenge and Consequence

For a quarter century, the author participated with hundreds of others working to lay EDI and *eCommerce* foundations, paving the path toward achievement of predicted benefits. Each person's work was done in a spirit of service to company, industry, country, world, and each other. It was a privilege for any of the participants to be a part of this.

We thought that EDI was a standards issue that required for its implementation the use of data communications, computer, software technologies, and associated facilities and equipment. We also thought that EDI was a business issue, because it has a direct affect on timeliness, control, accuracy, and efficiency. All of these affect customer satisfaction and corporate profitability.

Dr. Lee suggested that EDI might also impact social issues. As of this writing, more than a decade has passed since Dr. Lee's statement. During that decade, EDI has favorably impacted productivity and customer satisfaction worldwide while not having adverse affects on job satisfaction and corporate success. In fact during this period, productivity, profitability, and salaries increased while unemployment decreased and many tedious tasks were eliminated. Dr. Lee is correct; EDI is indeed *also* a social issue.

Appendix I

"People worked at this in a spirit of service
to company, industry, country, world,
and to each other."

Into the Future, page 1

ED PIONEERS

EDI Forum Selections

Collecting stories about the men and women who made EDI happen began in 1987 when Dan Ferguson and Ned Hill decided to publish the *EDI Forum.* The founding issue introduced the pioneer articles with:

> Many of the people we have interviewed on EDI in the past several years have commented that the same issues seem to return again and again over the years. Articles on historical topics in EDI offer up the lessons learned by EDI pioneers as well as recognize those pioneers for their contribution to EDI. We believe that recording and compiling the history of EDI will accelerate its growth in the long run as well as add a measure of respectability to EDI that we now see as lacking.
>
> In the founding issue we have included a personal story, one industry story, and we have profiled six people (of many) who clearly have had a profound effect on the development of EDI.
>
> There are undoubtedly many more individual and industry stories that deserve to be included in future issues. We encourage you to submit these stories as well as nominate individuals whom you feel deserve the special individual recognition as an EDI pioneer.

Included in that issue were stories about Ed Guilbert and Joe Carley of TDCC, George Klima of Super Valu, John Nelsen of Missouri Pacific Railroad, Don Trafford, who was with SITPRO[80] and subsequently a leader in the design and promotion of EDIFACT, and Richard Cook of National Wholesale Druggists' Association. Paul Olson told the story about his "initiation" into EDI and how his interest derived from his search for new products for a time-sharing service company to sell. Connie Robinson told of the reasons for and methods used to get EDI started in the metals industry.[81]

This group of eight pioneers started their EDI work in the early 1970s or before. By 1988, the founding issue publication date, their work and its significance was generally well known by people making a career in EDI. All eight plus Bill Plumb are the subject of chapter seven.

Dan Ferguson, publisher of the *EDI Forum*, met with his editors and consulting editors several times before the founding issue was published. Included in the discussions was a formal process for nominating pioneers: a person had to be recommended by one of the editors or consulting editors; the publisher and all editors discussed the reasons for each nomination; a majority of all editors had to agree for a person to be selected; and the editor responsible for nominating anyone that was selected also had to write the article.

Dan included a nomination form in the Founding Issue, inviting others to propose pioneers for recognition. He established three criteria to address on the nomination form. These were that the nominee exhibited pioneering leadership in the development of EDI, contributed to EDI significantly and over an extended period of time, and contributed to EDI in unique ways when compared to peers.

Additions

Not all pioneers were identified in *EDI Forum*. The list was limited by the amount of space allocated in the journal for the "History of EDI" department, including pioneer stories. Consequently, from the author's experiences, several other EDI pioneer stories are combined with the *EDI Forum* list in this section. All others named in other chapters or appendices of this book were indeed also EDI pioneers. There were still others, but our paths may not have crossed. George Klima wrote several letters[82] identifying EDI pioneers he knew in the early 1970s. His con-

---

[80] SITPRO: The Simplification of Trade Procedures Board, a United Kingdom Government agency.

[81] "Connie Robinson," page 256.

[82] "George Klima Letters," page 67.

cern was that he might have overlooked some he should have identified. The author shares his concern with reference to this section.

Significance

The intent in this appendix is to show the diversity of education, skills, and experiences used to create the EDI phenomenon. Look in these stories for examples of leadership, innovation, determination, vision, belief, dedication, technique, and results.

Information Source

For stories where the pioneer article was adapted from an *EDI Forum* article and the author is not indicated, the article was processed by an EDI *Forum* editor. For stories not having any reference, the article is based on recollections by Ralph Notto and may include requested information provided by the pioneer.

Ruth Andersen

Ruth Andersen, as a vice president of First Chicago Bank, led a team of consultants dedicated to implementing and promoting EDI in the mid-1980s. At the time, no other major commercial bank in the U.S. offered electronic data interchange consulting services as a cash management banking service, although National Bank of Detroit and several other regional banks were quick to follow. Under the consulting division leadership of Daniel Ferguson (page 110), Ruth's teams developed early analysis models for evaluation of financial EDI (page 119) and implementation of FEDI. Key clients included pioneering studies for General Motors Treasury and Owens Corning Fiberglass Corporation in 1987.

FEDI: Financial EDI

In 1989, Ruth joined EDI Group Ltd., responsible for education and market development in the U.S. and Canada. EDI Group specialized in education, research, and publications for EDI. As a member of ASC X12 Finance Subcommittee, she developed in coordination with other members the design of payment and financial EDIFACT messages during 1990-1994. In 1991, Ruth joined the newly formed firm of EDI Partners, Ltd. with Dan Petrosky, John Moriarty, and Jeffrey Kessler to focus on development of a nationwide EDI education service and international consulting practice. The tiny firm grew from initial EDI course offerings in two cities to sponsorship by thirteen universities in over twenty U.S. cities. As a senior consultant, Ruth also implemented EDI systems for over thirty U.S. and Canadian firms and government organizations during the 1990s. (In 1999, the independent firm of EDI Partners, Ltd. was acquired by Research Triangle Consultants, Inc. (RTCI) and is run as a separate division of RTCI.)

Ruth Andersen was one of the founding members of Greater Chicago EC Forum (formerly *EDI Forum*), a Chicago-based non-profit organization dedicated to the promotion and use of electronic commerce. Ruth served successive terms as president and vice president for that organization.

Ruth speaks at numerous national and regional conventions, including DISA, Treasury Management Organization, Financial EDI/EFT, and Investment Management Institute conferences. She has written articles and chapters for *Cash Flow Magazine*, *EC World*, *Computer World*, *The Journal of Cash Management*, *EC Forum*, *Business Credit*, and *Corporate Treasury Management Manual.*

Craigg Ballance

EFT: Electronic Funds Transfer

Craigg Balance with the Royal Bank of Canada (and several years later directing the EDI Group's Canadian operations) wrote several important articles for the *EDI Forum* relative to financial EDI in Canada and around the world. These were based on his experiences and analysis. Craigg was truly both an EDI and EFT pioneer.

Quotes from Craigg's articles:

> The New Canadian EDI/EFT Payment System," Craigg Ballance and Gail Kelso, *EDI Forum*, 1990 Issue: "One of the greatest challenges in business is to anticipate correctly and chart a course through opportunities–to be able to determine the appropriate and most successful course of action. This is particularly true when it relates to future or advanced applications of technology. The banking industry in Canada has generally been perceived as a reactive rather than pro-active business. Since January 1989, the Canadian financial community has been actively developing an EDI/EFT mechanism.
>
> Electronic Data Interchange at Royal Bank of Canada: Synergy Between Usage and Service," Craigg S.T. Balance, *EDI Forum*, 1992 Issue,

No. 1: "The Royal Bank of Canada has made an exceptional commitment to electronic data interchange, as both a user and a service provider. Its overall success with the technology is in large part attributable to the synergy it has exploited from this dual role in EDI.

Financial Electronic Data Interchange in Canada," Craigg Balance, *EDI Forum*, 1993 Issue, No. 1: "Canada is the largest trading partner of the United States, not only as a seller but as a customer. In fact, the combined trade between the two countries in 1988 amounted to more than $200 billion, with approximately $140 billion coming from Canada. This compares impressively with total trade with Japan of $90 billion in the same year. Not only are the trade environments of Canada and the U.S. intertwined, so too are the economies of the two countries. Even a portion of the electricity that the U.S. receives is of Canadian origin. In such a tightly integrated relationship, one would think that the penetration of electronic data interchange (EDI) and related technologies would be similar in both countries. In most relationships a 10% rule can be applied: Canada's population is roughly 10% of that of the U.S. (28,000,000 vs. 280,000,000), and most statistics correlate. This is not the case, however, with EDI. EDI has deeper roots and greater development in the U.S. than in Canada. According to research done in 1990 by the EDI Group, the larger and more mature American EDI market is helping to nurture ongoing growth in Canada's EDI marketplace.

Canadian Financial EDI: An Architectural Template for Future Banking Systems," Craigg Balance, *EDI Forum*, Volume 7, No. 1 (1994): "Canada boasts one of the premier financial EDI systems in the world. It could serve as a model for many other countries as they modernize their payments systems and respond to the new demands of the banking market.

Cross Border Payments in North America: A Challenge for the Trade Process," Craigg Balance, *EDI Forum*, Volume 9, No. 1 (1996): "To meet the new challenges electronic commerce is presenting for international trade, the Cross Border Payment Council last August finished drafting rules and developing an operating model now available to companies wanting to do business using cross border payments. A significant amount of work in defining the next step remains. Governing bodies, rules, participant's rights, and several other challenges have been discussed by the council, and probably will be discussed well into the next century. Optimists say this link between two of the world's most disparate banking environments will be the foundation for transacting business around the world more efficiently, cost-effectively, and quickly for both corporations and banks.

Can Chile, Ireland, and South Africa Teach the U.S. Anything about Financial EDI?" Craigg Balance, *EDI Forum*, Volume 11, No. 1 (1998): "We tend to think that since North America is the pioneer in electronic commerce technologies there is little benefit in looking at what other countries or regions have done. Even the World Bank commissioned a report in 1996 concluding that over half of all EDI in the world is being done in North America. So why would anyone want to look at other places and their experiences? Aren't the early implementers the ones who find all of the problems and therefore have all the answers? Not necessarily. Of course, there are some similarities that can be found when looking at how the EDI experience has evolved in other parts of the world. But there are also some significant differences. No matter where you look—on different continents or in different cultures—the key issues of value and usability are always what ultimately define success. What does this mean to the success or failure of financial EDI? It seems to suggest that there are commonalities in how the value of corporate electronic payments is defined, and that there are always new or different ways to accomplish that goal. Some of the reasons that latecomers to financial EDI have an advantage over the early adopters are: technology issues have been ironed out and are running smoothly, the technology costs less due to the emergence of competitive products, and there is a road map of *do's* and *don'ts* that has been created by the blood and toil of those who have gone before. Implementations tend to go better.

Jack Bartley

Quoted paragraphs are from EDI Forum, 1993 Issue, No. 4, page 60.

Jack Bartley is one of the EDI pioneers within the U.S. federal government. He has been a leader in advancing the maximum and consistent use of the technology within the government since the early 1980s.

DoD: US Department of Defense
EC: Electronic Commerce
EDI: Electronic Data Interchange

He is the founder and principal force behind the Department of Defense (DoD) Electronic Commerce Through Electronic Data Interchange (EC/EDI) Program. At DoD, he introduced the concept of electronic commerce, which dramatically expands the vision of EDI to embrace the electronic movement, end-to-end, of all information needed to conduct business. Built into this concept is the need to extend the benefits of EC/EDI to all trading partners, including small businesses. As a result of his efforts, DoD became the first agency to commit to full-scale implementation of EC both internally and externally with all of its 350,000 trading partners. In recent years, his concept of EC has become widely used in government and industry worldwide.

"His involvement in EDI was an outgrowth of projects that he initiated to implement bar coding, introduce smart card technology throughout DoD and modernize the interchange of DoD's (one billion per year) internal electronic business transactions. Early DoD EDI initiatives addressed procurement, finance, and transportation. Although these initiatives demonstrated the potential of EDI, they produced limited benefits. They involved few DoD activities, trading partners, or transactions sets. Implementations were local, diverse, and uncoordinated. Transactions were usually non-standard or industry-standard, and vendors dealing with multiple DoD activities had to contend with diverse implementation conventions.

Jack went to the ANSI X12 Committee for assistance with these problems. ANSI produced a report for him on the readiness of American industry to conduct business electronically with DoD. This report helped Bartley issue a policy that committed DoD to maximum use of EDI in all its business operations, adoption of a common EDI implementation approach, and a standard interface with industry to include the use of ANSI X12.

Within ANSI X12, Jack was a founding member of the government subcommittee. He was an active supporter of the use of business modeling, product data, interactive EDI, email-enabled EDI, and the harmonization of X12 with EDIFACT.

Earl J. "Buddy" Bass

Adapted from EDI Forum, 1991 Issue, No. 1, page 94, author Ralph Notto.

Earl J. 'Buddy' Bass has been a consistent force in the progress of EDI standards development since 197,5 when he participated in the industry work groups that defined the initial U.S. EDI standards. He defined the format for EDI standards documentation. He enhanced the concept for the table-driven computer program logic used in processing EDI. He contributed to the development of UCS and X12. He was the first chairperson of the X12 Technical Assessment Committee. He was the third chairperson of ASC X12. He has also contributed toward international EDI standards progress. He was an extremely busy and valuable individual during the growth of EDI standards.

When Buddy and the author first met in April 1975, we were both consultants to the Transportation Data Coordinating Committee (TDCC), and were working toward the first EDI publication. Within three weeks, Buddy said that he had completed the EDI standards book. 'Sure you did,' Notto said, entirely in jest. 'Really, I did,' he said.

And he had. What was remarkable is that the work groups had not finished their definitions at that time. Buddy put the book together with the material available with a plan to continuously update it as work group progress was made. The book included: introduction, specification structure, concept, communications, information structure, transaction sets, detail segments, data elements, and appendix.

The material he used was the result of work group meetings and writings by members of the TDCC staff and other consultants. The first use of the designations 'mandatory,' 'conditional,' and 'optional' appeared in Buddy's first book; the idea was then introduced to the work groups and was adopted.

At the same time, he also came up with the term 'reference designator,' which was used as a cross reference from data elements to segments and was defined as the segment identifier code plus a two-digit number indicating a data element's position in a segment. The need for the definition arose from the requirement that all information units in EDI be cross-referenced to facilitate accurate change when updates are required.

It should come as no surprise that current EDI standards documentation is very similar to that 1975 book.

Buddy's unique contribution to the table-driven computer programming logic was to devise a way to explicitly specify conditionality requirements for processing data segments. The result was elegant in its simplicity and exacting in its meaning. The technique he devised was to use a letter to indicate the type of condition followed by a string of two-digit numbers to indicate which data elements in a segment are involved. Thus, 'P0304' means that the third and fourth data elements in a segment are *paired*. The transmitted segment is valid if it contains both of those elements or neither; it is not valid if it contains only one. Similarly, 'R0203' means that at least the second or third data element in the transmitted segment is required for the segment to be correct. Other codes were used to indicate other conditional types. The codes were inserted into tables related to segment processing. As a result of this contribution, there was no ambiguity in meaning, and a significant EDI software task for editing was both generalized and simplified.

After 1978, Buddy has had such roles as systems consultant for the X12 standards committees, chairperson of the Technical Assessment Project Team, member of the 'B' subcommittee for X12 maintenance, chairperson of the Data Dictionary Coordinating Committee, member of the X12 Rules Committee, member of the Version/Release Task Force, member of the X12 Publications Task Force, member of the Joint EDI (JEDI) International Task Force, United States delegate to United Nations ECE Working Party 4 for UN/EDIFACT, member of the DISA Board of Directors, member of the X12 Executive Committee, and member of the North American EDIFACT Board (NAEB).

He was also a member of the original U.S. JEDI committee in charge of bringing the data and segment dictionaries of TDCC, X12, UCS, and WINS into alignment.

As chairperson of X12, Buddy paved the way for all these groups, as well as the U.S. role in UN/EDIFACT, to be under ASC X12 control. This unified all U.S. EDI standards under the ANSI banner.

Buddy was a cofounder, director and vice president of EDI, Inc.

Buddy's educational background includes an MEA (Engineering Administration) from George Washington University; a BA in Chemistry from the Catholic University of America; and graduate studies in biochemistry and computer science at George Washington University, University of Maryland, and American University.

Buddy's influence on EDI standards development has extended over a period of twenty years. He is richly deserving of EDI pioneer recognition because his broad view of the usefulness of the standards combined with his attention to detail has benefited all of us."

Joseph Bass

Joe Bass started his EDI career as the customer support person at EDI Inc. in 1984. Since the concept of EDI was very new to most users that year, Joe had to define the position based on random telephone calls from Telink users asking questions about EDI, Telink, setting up a PC computer, modems, VANs, acknowledgments, recovery, automatic operations …

Within a short time, Telink users formed a Telink user's group, and Joe was his company's representative at their meetings, interpreting their needs and passing requirements to his company.

He also used software tools his company developed to make EDI more practical for beginners, and in particular devised application screens so that users could manually enter transaction data to be converted to EDI format and transmitted. This was especially important in the mid-1980s when PCs were in their early stages of development, and EDI was being "forced" on companies by their major trading partners. In particular, some companies new to EDI had never had computers before, and many others that were computer-capable had systems (or software) never intended for applications like EDI. In the latter case, Joe's application screens permitted user's to rapidly become participants in EDI by manually entering required data until such time as the user's software applications were capable to interface directly to EDI.

Joe continued his innovated and service-oriented EDI career into the twenty-first century, including the coordination of the EDI implementation conventions for Electronic Research Administration (ERA). (ERA addresses the complete cycle of grant activity as computer-to-computer communication for proposal announcements, applications, award notification [or rejection], peer review, project accounting, and reporting.)

Michael S. Baum

Adapted from EDI Forum, 1992 Issue, No. 4, page 46.

Michael S. Baum, JD, MBA, deserves credit as the first American lawyer to bring attention to the legal aspects of EDI. He provided the early vision and energetic leadership behind several projects that have examined and offered resolutions to EDI legal questions.

He was responsible for initiating the first EDI-specific legal work by the American bar. He founded and chaired the American Bar Association's Electronic Messaging Services Task Force, which produced one of the earliest American reports on EDI legal issues, as well as the ABA's path-breaking Model EDI Trading Partner Agreement.

Michael proposed and chaired the first 'EDI and the Law' conference in the United States (1990), sponsored primarily by the Data Interchange Standards Association.

> **ABA**: American Bar Association

He also founded and chaired the ABA's EDI and Information Technology Division within the Section of Science and Technology. This division includes five EDI-related committees (Financial EDI, Global Data Networks, Information Technology Healthcare Informatics, Information Security, and Judicial EDI) whose projects have included the publication of a 'Model Electronic Payments Agreement and Commentary,' as well as initiating the development of the first ABA Resolution concerning information security and the legal efficacy of computer-based commerce. Additionally, Michael first proposed the creation of, and subsequently chaired, the Legal and Business Controls Task Group of ANSI ASC X12.

Michael is coauthor of *Electronic Contracting, Publishing and EDI Law* (Wiley Law Publications, 1991), a contributing author to *EDI and the Law* (Walden, ed., Blenheim Online, 1989), and the author of the first American articles on EDI legal issues. Michael is a member of the Massachusetts Bar, and is principal of Independent Monitoring, a Cambridge, Massachusetts consultancy specializing in the legal and security aspects of electronic commerce and Electronic Data Interchange.

Marcia Brodsky

Marcia Brodsky began her professional career in biomedical research. Eighteen years later, in 1986, having earned an MS degree in Computer Science, she made a career change and became a programmer for EDI, Inc., a producer of EDI translation software.

In her early days with EDI, Inc., Ms. Brodsky was assigned the task of expanding the communications capabilities of the software by adding interfaces to allow the communication of EDI data to many Value Added Networks (VANS). From 1986 through 1995, she produced about thirty communications interfaces to the VANS and to several large corporations for direct communications. She supplied technical and user documentation, as well as customer support for the more unusual situations. The application environment required that several communications alternatives (VANs and/or direct connections) could be employed by a single system.

Marcia presented her experiences and findings on EDI communications protocols to a DISA conference. The text of the presentation was published as "Communications Protocols for EDI," *EDI Forum*, 1991 Issue No. 1.

In the mid 1990s, Marcia changed her employment to Affiliated Computer Services/Government Solutions Group on a contract at the U.S. Department of Labor, Office of Workers' Compensation. The contract called for the automation of the processing of hospital and pharmacy bills. The X12 837 (Healthcare Claim) transaction set was used for the hospital bills, and the NCPDP 3A standard for the pharmacy bills. She received a technical excellence award in 1998 for the pharmacy project.

Another EDI effort at the Department of Labor involved implementing the X12 148 (Report on Injury, Illness or Incident) to automate the establishment of new federal workers' compensation cases. In 2000, she was a member of the team that received Vice President Gore's "Hammer" award for this effort.

In addition to the EDI projects, Ms. Brodsky has also been producing other electronic commerce applications for the Department of Labor.

Juletta Broomfield

Adapted from EDI Forum, 1992 Issue, No. 4, page 46.

Juletta Broomfield, as general manager of Tradelink Electronic Document Services Ltd. in Hong Kong, was closely involved in Hong Kong's efforts to establish a community EDI facility and managed Tradelink—a group of leading Hong Kong organizations set up in 1988 to develop, promote, and educate local businesses in the use of electronic trading.

Juletta then worked on full-time secondment from Hong Kong Bank, one of Tradelink's eleven shareholders. She was seconded by the Hong Kong Bank to the Tradelink project in June 1988, and was appointed as the Project Manager by the Tradelink Board of Directors in the same month. She then led the project management team, which consisted of secondees from Tradelink's ten other shareholders, for the following three and a half years. During this time, she played a leading role in coordinating the EDI study carried out by Coopers and Lybrand on behalf of Tradelink and the Hong Kong government. In addition, she developed and led a publicity campaign to raise EDI awareness in the Hong Kong business community, especially among the smaller, Chinese-speaking businesses, which comprise a large and important sector of Hong Kong's import/export trade.

Following on from the Coopers and Lybrand report, Juletta put together Tradelink's proposals to the Hong Kong government for a community-wide EDI service, leading to the establishment of SPEDI (the Shared Project for EDI), a government/Tradelink joint initiative. She was the natural choice as overall coordinator for SPEDI.

At the same time as she was preparing these proposals, Juletta was creating the first of what was to become an annual event—EDI Asia '89. Almost single-handedly, she has established EDI Asia as the Pacific Rim's premier conference and exhibition for electronic trading. Its reputation has spread far and wide, and it is widely reported on throughout the world; past attendees have come from North America, Europe, and Australia, as well as Asia.

Out of SPEDI came proposals for the Community Electronic Trading Service (CETS). At first, many so-called *experts* voiced opposition to SPEDI's recommendations, and it would have been easy for Juletta to advise the shareholders in Tradelink against any further investment in community EDI. Juletta persisted, however. She was able to engender the same determination in the project management team and the shareholders. She led the Tradelink team in continuing discussions with the government, culminating in 1992 with the government's commitment to CETS and its becoming a shareholder in Tradelink.

In recognition of her illustrious achievements, the Tradelink board appointed Juletta General manager at the end of 1991. In the early days, she had had to operate very much as a one-woman band, since the other members of the team were only part-time. Despite the inevitable loneliness that she must at times have felt, she never let this sway her from her goal—the introduction of the benefits of EDI across the trading community, to the overall benefit of Hong Kong Inc.

Dale Carley

Dale Carley designed and wrote a most comprehensive menu and automatic timer systems that were part of EDI Inc.'s early Telink product. These were especially significant since they were already in use by 1985, only two years after the microcomputers with Microsoft DOS software initially became available. The menu included the grouping and classification features of software menus in general use several years later. Also in Dale's work, and available from the menu, was a scheduler that permitted a user to specify for a year in advance on what days and times the EDI system should start its automatic operations for downloading data, translation to EDI, data communications, and uploading inbound data after translation form EDI. "Uploading" and "downloading" are with reference to interaction between application software and EDI software.

Beginning in 1988, Dale did the analysis for and wrote several significant application software modules to work with EDI Integration Corporation's Eagle product. These were put to use at several locations of the U.S. Department of Defense and several companies in the shipbuilding, apparel, and other industries. The Eagle system provided its users with complete integration of important components, including EDI, application modules, and financial EDI.

Dale is also an accomplished musician, and played trumpet in Count Basie's band for several years.

Edgar Chambers

Adapted from EDI Forum, Vol. 8, No. 2 (1995), pages 80-81.

Edgar Chambers, associate executive vice president of San Jose State University, worked to create an early, fully operational implementation of EDI technology in higher education.

Starting in 1991 with an early vision of EDI.Smart software from SCT Corporation, and using MCI's EDINET VAN service, he established San Jose State as a hub for trading partnerships across the bay area. Trading partners included junior colleges, community colleges, and East Bay high schools. Once the systems were operational, cost studies comparing paper to EDI processes revealed that paper costs of $18 to $36 per transcript could be reduced to $1.50 per transcript.

'We've proved that EDI works and is a real value,' Chambers said. 'Though EDI is a success at our current levels, the future is even more exciting. The electronic approach is much more volume, staff, and student-friendly than the paper approach.'

He continued, 'San Jose State is the alpha EDI site for the California higher education systems, and I believe it is inevitable that all one hundred two-year and four-year public institutions in the state will be EDI-ing someday soon.'

Pearleen Chan

Adapted from EDI Forum, 1993 Issue, No. 4, pages 60-62.

With a view towards achieving a national competitive advantage, since the early 1980s the Singapore government has championed the use of information technology (IT) on a national scale, in both the public and private sectors. In the public sector, the government launched a multi-million dollar Civil Service Computerization Program (CSCP) to introduce computers in every facet of government operations, across all ministries.

As the deputy general manager of the National Computer Board (NCB), Mrs. Pearleen Chan undertook the task of implementing the CSCP. Within five years, the use of computers had spread to all government ministries. More than 100 mainframe and minicomputers had been installed, more than 300 applications had been developed and implemented, and more than 500 IT professionals were actively engaged in further developing the CSCR.

In the mid-1980s, a national IT plan was formulated to build on this earlier work. It called for the integration of operations across the government and the private sector through national networks and sectoral applications in three areas—trade, medicine, and law. Under the ambit of the NCB, studies were conducted in each of these areas to map out plans for the application of information technology to enhance the productivity and efficiency of Singapore businesses.

TradeNet was the first of these sectoral applications.

Herbert Chereck

Adapted from EDI Forum, Vol. 8, No. 2 (1995), pages 80-81.

Herbert Chereck, registrar of the University of Oregon, led the University of Oregon's educational EDI initiative in 1992 by using SCT's EDI.Smart software and the Internet as the network service. He spearheaded a steering committee within the Oregon State System of Higher Education (OSSHE) to create a basic mission and launch educational, technical evaluation, and trading partnership development initiatives among OSSHE institutions.

The result of these initiatives led to active trading relationships between several schools in the state, including: the University of Oregon, Lane Community College, Portland State University, Oregon State University, Eugene School District 4J, Oregon Institute of Technology, Multnomah Education Service District, Portland Community College, and Clackamas Community College. As an example of the value and reliability of EDI to these schools, the procedure for mailing paper transcripts between Lane Community College and the University of Oregon was discontinued."

He said, 'It's not so much what EDI has done for any one individual school, it's what it has done for the whole state. In Oregon, there is pressure from property tax limits to reduce the size and cost of government.

'Seventy-three percent of our transcript exchanges are generated from instate students. We have taken a big step with this technology to improve the quality of a key student service while reducing the costs.

Daniel S. Codman

Adapted from EDI Forum, Vol. 8, No. 2 (1995), pages 78-79.

Dan Codman was a member of the grocery industry's EDI standards development team in the early 1980s, representing the American Can Company. He was an active participant in discussions involving all levels of detail. Not the ordinary type of detail generally considered, but foundation detail like how to represent monetary amounts in EDI data elements. Three methods were considered—accounting (use of parenthesis to indicate negative numbers), algebraic (use of the minus sign), and journal (use of the suffix "dr" or "cr" for debit or credit). Algebraic was chosen after all alternatives were thoroughly discussed.

Dan continued to be actively involved in the development of X12 standards as chairman of the X12C [Communications and Controls] Subcommittee. It is more than length of service to the EDI community that distinguishes Dan's activities in making EDI a preferred way of conducting business. Dan has been heavily involved in the core design activities that are at the heart of the EDI standards.

While a great deal of attention is often paid to the transaction set development activities in areas such as healthcare and government within X12, the design and control foundation for these activities is the responsibility of X12C. This subcommittee addresses issues such as communications standards for asynchronous communication, how VANs interconnect (XI2.56 Interconnect Mailbag Control Structures), and Internet linkage.

ANSI: American National Standards Institute
ASC: Accredited Standards Committee
X12: ANSI ASC X12—EDI
X12C: Communications and Controls Subcommittee
X12.56: Interconnect Mailbag Control Structures
X12.6: Application Control Structures
X12.254: Interactive EDI Control Structures
X12.58: Security Structures
X12I: Transportation Subcommittee
EDIFACT: United Nations standard EDI for Administration, Commerce and Transport

Dan and the subcommittee also addressed the architecture and design rules of the X12 standards, maintenance of the X12.6 Application Control Structures, issues of syntax related to the migration to EDIFACT—standard for Interactive EDI Control Structures (XI2.254), and standards for encryption and data security (X12.58 Security Structures)—critical for any use of the Internet.

Dan was a leader in the formation of the Transportation Subcommittee (X12I) and contributed to that group's effort to integrate the TDCC standards for motor, rail and ocean standards into X12. This was a significant milestone in X12 becoming a true inter-industry EDI standard.

What has distinguished Dan in the X12 process has been his leadership and his wisdom regarding the nature of EDI standards, as well as the process of setting the standards. Because of his experience in developing early industry standards, he has provided invaluable insight into what has worked and what has not worked.

He was also at the forefront of the EDI software industry that provides the translation software based on the X12 standards. Dan was a cofounder of the APL Group in 1983. (See "APL Group," page 97.)

It is Dan's length of service and his leadership and integrity that distinguish him as an EDI Pioneer. He has played a critical role in the evolution of EDI from its original focus on eliminating paper to becoming an enabling technology for business process redesign.

R. T. Crowley

R.T. Crowley

R.T. Crowley, vice president marketing and education at Internet Commerce Corporation (ICC) has over twenty years technical and managerial experience with companies involved in electronic commerce, initially in international trade and transport, and later with a variety of industries. Prior to joining ICC, Bob Crowley owned and operated C.W. Consultants, an EDI consulting firm until it was acquired by RTCI with RTCI further merging with ICC.

CESAC: US Customs Electronic Systems Advisory Committee
USCS: US Customs Service
ISO: International Standards Organization
XML: eXtensible Markup Language

Bob is active in many EDI projects around the world, including having served during 1993-95 as chair of ANSI ASC X12, the U.S. national standards body for EDI. He has served as a member of the U.S. Delegation to the United Nations on matters of electronic commerce and EDI, and has been a civilian advisor to the committee creating the U.S. government implementation guides for electronic commerce. He is the founder of the EDI standards committee for the ocean transport industry, as well as the U.S. Customs Electronic Systems Advisory Committee

(CESAC), advising the U.S. Customs Service (USCS) on matters of electronic commerce. He now serves as chair of the X12 Security Task Group, vice chair of ISO Technical Committee 154 U.S. Technical Advisory Group, and was one of the authors of the X12 technical report on the use of XML for conducting EDI.

A well-known speaker on EC and EDI, Bob has authored many articles and books on EDI. His book, *EDI–Charting a Course to the Future* is one of the best-selling books on the topic.

Lance Dailey

Lance Dailey is a former director of EDI for Sears, Roebuck and Co., where he formed the award winning team that implemented EDI with 4,800 trading partners. Prior to this EDI assignment, Lance held management positions in human resources, as well as accounting, buying, and store operations. With this background, the implementation of EDI at Sears was approached from a business point of view rather than as an information technology issue.

In 1993, Lance joined Vendor Logistics Services as director of operations and retail EDI specialist. VLS is an EDI outsourcing company with over 1,200 customers that were vendors to companies such as IBM, Chrysler, Sears, JC Penney, and Diamond Motors (Mitsubishi).

In 1995, Lance founded Customer-Focused EDI, Inc., a seminar and consulting company dedicated to electronic commerce technologies, with emphasis on EDI. Consulting customers represented companies from retail, telecommunications, pharmaceutical, healthcare providers, healthcare manufacturers, food producers, and Department of Defense.

In 1999, Lance became *eCommerce* process architect with the Kodiak Group, addressing the specific client business issues that must be addressed in implementing electronic commerce technologies with customers or suppliers.

Lance is invited to national and international speaking engagements every year. In addition to consulting with companies regarding *eCommerce*, he has designed *eCommerce* educational programs and teaches various courses regarding the business impact of *eCommerce* on the processes and philosophies of a company. He has published articles in *EDI Forum–The Journal of Electronic Commerce*, *Integrated Interchange*, and *Consumer Goods Manufacturer* magazine. He is the past editor and contributor to the "Retail Trends" column in *EC World* magazine. As a subject-expert facilitator, he has also worked with the Price Waterhouse Coopers EC Best Practices study.

William P. Farrell

Adapted from EDI Forum, 1991 Issue, No. 2, page 66, author William Plumb.

For many years the American Hardware Manufacturers Association (AHMA) had attempted to come to grips with EDI, for both its members and their customers. In 1978, the association spent two years laying the groundwork for the hardware industry's EAGLE system, which grew out of a computer order entry committee that explored the feasibility of an industry-wide system to link manufacturers, wholesalers, and retailers.

AHMA: American Hardware Manufacturers Association
EAGLE: Hardware industry EDI system
AHDS: American Hardware Data Systems

The first flight (or Kitty Hawk) of the EAGLE system was in 1980. That year, ten pilot warehouse distributors and manufacturers tested the concept of electronically transmitted purchase orders from distributors through a central clearinghouse to a manufacturer in the real world environment. EAGLE was an exciting development that held much promise for the industry; it was especially exciting for those men and women in the industry who donated their time, staffs, and energies to the preliminary testing phase. The ideas were sound, the tests proved conclusively that the benefits of what was to become EDI were real, and now it was time to put into place all the necessary mechanisms and relationships that would ensure long-term success for the hardware industry.

In 1981, AHMA formed a wholly owned subsidiary, American Hardware Data Systems (AHDS), and signed a license agreement with a firm to handle development, marketing, and processing for the hardware industry. Unfortunately, AHMA and AHDS experienced problems with that firm.

What could have ended as a major setback for the industry became an opportunity for Bill Farrell to rise above what could have been project-ending problems, and to exert his leadership over the entire hardware industry. Bill believed firmly that EAGLE was right for the industry and a benefit whose time had come, and that EAGLE could play a major role in assuring continued economic viability for hardware wholesalers, most particularly the smaller and middle-sized companies. Bill Farrell thus directed the search for a quality provider of EDI services and products, and in 1982 signed a long-term agreement with ORDERNET Services, which was then a division of Informatics General Corporation. Together AHMA and ORDERNET relaunched the EAGLE system. Because of the rapid advancement to application technology and communications capabilities, the relaunch was far more akin to a moon shot than it was to Kitty Hawk.

By 1983, nearly one hundred manufacturing and wholesaling firms had signed contracts and were testing the system. The first live purchase order was transmitted in mid-January of that year by Emery-Waterhouse in Portland, Maine to the Sterling Faucet Company in Schaumburg, Illinois, through ORDERNET Services. As is common with the evolution of most new technologies, there was a wait-and-see attitude prevalent in the industry. With the exception of a handful of firms, few wanted to take a chance on a new system with no track record.

Through Bill Farrell's drive and determination, however, 250 companies were using EAGLE by the spring of 1984. Farrell demonstrated the system at conventions and trade shows, and got other trade associations to add their endorsements to EAGLE. Many of these were associations on the distributor side, such as NWHA and SWHA. Others were representative of different segments of the manufacturing community. AHMA put together audio-visual presentations for in-house training; an EAGLE newsletter was created and innumerable press releases were sent out. These activities really did help achieve the desire of manufacturers to see more distributors on the system and distributors to see more manufacturers using EAGLE. Consistent with the definition of a pioneer, Bill Farrell truly helped open up a new line of thought and prepared the way for others to follow.

With many of the major firms signed up, AHMA had a decision to make: either to devote much of the energy involved in running all aspects of a trade association into a data processing operation by becoming a computer support operation, or to transfer the association's interest in the EAGLE system to Informatics General Corporation. Bill Farrell knew that it was time for him personally and for his association, the AHMA, to refocus their attention and energies on the much broader role of the AHMA. Bill accurately discerned that an EDI pioneer in the hardware industry was no longer needed. The EAGLE system had become a monumental success due to Bill's leadership; it was now time to turn over the day-to-day operation and the future success of EAGLE to someone else. Consequently, in 1985, AHMA's board of directors authorized the sale of its ownership rights to the EAGLE system to Informatics, which in turn was purchased by Sterling Software later that year.

AHMA had spent more than eight years and $750,000 for development and implementation costs associated with EAGLE. Although AHMA is no longer officially affiliated with EAGLE, the association still sponsors and endorses it within the hardware industry. While clearly many companies have moved to adopt the ANSI ASC X12 public standards, thus replacing some of the original industry standards developed by AHMA, Bill Farrell and his association continue to be staunch supporters of EDI for the hard-lines industry.

Bill Farrell, along with many others in the hardware industry, believes that the industry has merely scratched the surface in terms of fully taking advantage of the benefits of EDI. Bill continues to speak at industry meetings and has 'unofficially' moved from pioneer to EDI advocate for the entire industry while continuing his leadership role as president of AHMA. The growth in terms of number of customers, documents, and usage of EDI in the hardware industry is attributable to Bill's vision as a pioneer and constancy of purpose as an EDI advocate.

Daniel M. Ferguson

EFT: Electronic Funds Transfer

It is incredible how many *eCommerce* activities Dan Ferguson engages in, each of which is more than a full time occupation for most of us when performed at the intensity, quality, and content on a level with Dan.

His first EDI pilot in the mid 1980s was not only EDI, but EFT too. The EFT involved not only First Chicago, the bank he represented as vice president, but nine other large banks as well. The focal point was not just any company, but General Motors. The initial trading partners besides the banks were not just one or two General Motors suppliers, but all of them. The main transaction set used was not one off the shelf and tested, but the newly designed for this purpose 820 (Payment Order/Remittance Advice). And encryption and authentication were required during the pilot as well. All went according to plan, and billions of dollars in funds transfers are periodically transmitted routinely and electronically from General Motors to its banks via EDI/EFT and subsequent transmissions are made bank-to-bank to complete the funds transfer to suppliers' banks.

Following that, Dan founded the EDI Group with Ned Hill. He had a three-way focus: EDI research, EDI education, and the *EDI Forum—The Journal of Electronic Commerce.* All of these are referenced many times in this book. The *EDI Forum* was not just a magazine, but a journal with in-depth informative presentations of *eCommerce* subjects that are of intense interest to *eCommerce* professionals.

Even with this capacity for work, Dan is also dedicated to his family, and they spend quality time together at home, at a cabin retreat in upstate Michigan, and during occasional travels together.

For more about Dan Ferguson and his work, see "Plotting the Trend, U.S. and Canada," page 81; "Daniel M. Ferguson," page 110; "Financial EDI," page 119; "Drives for Experiences and Results," page 127; 11. 1987: General Motors/First Chicago EDI/EFT Pilot," page 146; and "Results Measured and Observed," page 197.

Albert J. Fenaroli

Al Fenaroli, manager of distribution operations at Union Carbide Corporation, was on the TDCC Board of Directors during the period when the first U.S. EDI standard was developed and published, 1974-75. He took an active interest in EDI development during the development of the standard, representing the interests of manufacturers who had need for timely delivery of commodities that had complicated transport requirements. Requirements for hazardous material, container type, cleaning specifications, and size needed to be included in transaction sets in addition to common transportation specifications.

Working on consulting assignments a decade later, Al Fenaroli and the author had an opportunity to work on a common project concerning the definition of new EDI system requirements relative to being able to order transport equipment for delivery of chemicals coast-to-coast. The process included an inquiry transaction set sent from the manufacturer to the carrier, inquiring on the availability of a specific kind of container and schedule. The carrier was required to reply within fifteen minutes, or the reply was ignored. "Why only a fifteen-minute window for coast-to-coast?" Al was asked.

"It's an issue about customer service," Al replied. "There are many opportunities to lose or gain time during the trip, so timing estimates for routine trips can be close to the plan, and the objective is to have a means to plan for arrival of these commodities, such that they do not have to be ordered too far in advance and storage will be required." Al Fenaroli was always steadfast in his determination to use EDI for transportation process improvement, defining how to make previously impossible tasks now doable with the support of *eCommerce* technologies. This is an early example of combining *operational* time-sensitive requirements with EDI transactions.

Robert Fisher

Adapted from EDI Forum, Volume 11, No. 3, page 81, 1998.

Robert Fisher, currently president and CEO of FORESIGHT Corporation, was part of the group at Sterling Software that gave us the GENTRAN family of software (he actually gave it that name [see "Sterling Software," page 103]). Ten years later he is still involved in EDI innovation. His new company, FORESIGHT, is a proven provider of state-the-art quality assurance tools for EDI development, and more recently, as an innovator in Web-based EDI.

> Bob was part of Sterling's operations for twelve years, working in their original business, the ORDERNET mailbox service. As a senior operations manager at Sterling, he helped the company establish itself as provider of basic mainframe translators. By the time he left in 1990 to launch a new endeavor with partner, William Kamerer, Sterling Software was enjoying great success with their EDI systems.
>
> FORESIGHT originally became well known for their EDISIM productivity products that have evolved into standard equipment in the EDI community. Since then, they have introduced additional products that provide increased support effectiveness for an organization's EDI management.
>
> Making EDI more accessible to non-EDI trading partners is the key to future EDI growth. Robert Fisher with FORESIGHT has already begun to take EDI business to a level that allows all parties to take part in EDI business practices now.

Kathleen E. Flynn

Adapted from EDI Forum, Volume 10, No2, 1997.

Kathleen Flynn of First Chicago (now Bank One) designed the original (1986) transaction set 820 (Payment Order/Remittance Advice). The significance of her design is that it addressed all of the requirements of the potential user groups and scenarios, considering payer's directive to its bank to send funds to the payee's bank, payer's transmission to the payee identifying the payment sent (if the payee's bank is not capable of sending this information), payer-bank's transfer of funds to the payee's bank if the payee's bank is not the same bank as the payer's, electronic funds transfer from the payer's bank to the payee's bank, and payee's bank transmission to the payee to inform the payee of the new funds and reconciliation detail.

The scheme made it possible for any company to convert its complete payment and reconciliation processes to EDI/EFT, even including payments to companies that were not EDI-capable. This was possible because the communications was between the payer and its bank, and an EDI/EFT-capable bank communicates with the payee's bank.

Kathy's work was first employed during the General Motors/First Chicago EDI/EFT pilot project in the mid-1980s, directly involving ten other banks.

Her design was of such quality that very few subsequent changes to the 820 were required as the concept was implemented on a national scale over the next decade.

Continuing into the twenty-first century, Kathy is developing Internet applications for large corporate, international, and capital markets.

The *EDI Forum* included the following in a 1997 article:

> The selection of Kathleen Flynn as an EDI pioneer proves once again that this prestigious award is conferred only on those who have made a difference in the world of electronic commerce. In addition to her numerous and valuable contributions to First National Bank of Chicago (Bank One), Flynn—more than any other single individual—was responsible for the initial development of the successful family of ASC X12 payment transactions.
>
> Flynn's ANSI experience dates to 1983 when she represented her bank at her first X12 meeting in Dearborn, Michigan, when the newly established finance subcommittee was organized. Because of her obvious abilities and desire to contribute to the success of this group, Flynn was quickly appointed to the key role of secretary. In this capacity, she was responsible for recording and distributing all committee minutes, preparation of meeting agendas, establishing and maintaining membership and attendance records, and resolving logistic issues ad infinitum. To place her secretarial accomplishments in the proper perspective, her responsibilities are currently filled by three individuals.

ANSI: American National Standards Institute

ASC: Accredited Standards Committee under ANSI

X12: ANSI EDI standard

UN/EDIFACT: United Nations standard EDI For Administration, Commerce and Transport

GM: General Motors

NBD: National Bank of Detroit

Not content with her duties as secretary, Flynn contributed her impressive technical skills as co-chair of the task group responsible for designing many of the X12 electronic formats currently flowing between leading financial institutions and their corporate customers. She also served as the finance subcommittee expert to the group developing electronic safeguards and contributed greatly to their ultimate design.

Flynn brought her strengths and abilities to the international arena when she served as one of the three initial U.S. representatives to the UN/EDIFACT Finance Message Group. She filled numerous roles during the formative stage of UN financial-message development. Flynn is a recognized and respected representative of the United States in the international UN/EDIFACT activity.

Flynn, as a vice president at First National Bank of Chicago, was first involved with financial EDI in 1985 when General Motors requested First Chicago to facilitate electronic payments using EDI. Flynn worked closely with GM and EDS on the business and technical design of the EDI payment system.

For the last twelve years, she has held various positions, including product management/development, consulting/technical sales and technical systems, for the purpose of developing EDI-EFT at First Chicago. Flynn was instrumental in the systems design and development of the EDI-BANX project where a consortium of banks developed a complete financial EDI network based on the GM system design. Currently, Flynn is the EDI product manager for the merged First Chicago NBD. Prior to joining First Chicago, she worked for International Harvester, Central Telephone and Utilities, Zenith Corporation, and the University of Chicago.

She has a bachelors degree in mathematics from the University of Illinois and an MBA from the University of Chicago.

Harry Gaples

Adapted from EDI Forum, Volume 9, No. 3, pages 95-96, 1996.

Harry Gaples successfully introduced Kleinschmidt, at that time a division of SC Corporation, to the data interchange industry in 1979 through its Shipper Assisted Message (SAM) program for the collection and distribution of Car Location Messages between shippers and railroads.

The company advanced into EDI by expanding the business to interchange TDCC, UCS, and WINS EDI standards in the early 1980s and further into processing of X12 EDI standards as they were defined and used by customers.

Under Gaples's leadership, the company developed a unique approach to supporting customer's entry to EDI by offering customized in-network programs to translate or convert among the data formats.

The company consistently supports its customer-oriented operation. In 1986, Gaples pursued a dream of owning his own business and purchased the division he was running, allowing him to continue his focus on customer service.

> **TDCC**: Transportation Data Coordinating Committee
>
> **UCS**: Uniform Communications System [grocery industry]
>
> **WINS**: Warehouse Information Networking Standard
>
> **X12**: American National Standard for EDI

One of his first objectives was to further motivate key employees by letting them share in the risks and rewards of the business. This was accomplished, in part, by selling 40% of the business to key employees who had worked at Kleinschmidt for at least five years. Another objective was to reward both hourly and salaried employees monetarily for outstanding performance. This was accompanied by a program that pays bonuses in January and July to employees with at least one year of service. The bonus pool to be paid out is based on a formula. The bonus each employee receives is based on subjective judgment. Over the years, employee productivity has increased and the bonus pool has become large. Six-month bonuses range from less than 10% to more than 100% of an employee's salary.

Everyone's personality includes particular quirks, and Gaples is no exception. He doesn't believe administrative tasks are beneficial. Management is, to a large degree, administrative, so Gaples works on minimizing it. He feels the same about paperwork. Job applicants who want to be managers are not considered for employment. Directing employees is considered bad form because it reduces employee's productivity.

Gaples defines quality as responsiveness with continuous, small improvements. For example, answering a phone call or writing custom software quickly is a demonstration of quality from a customer's point of view. Avoiding large changes is another example of quality, according to Gaples. Employees who are available while at home, work, or vacationing is another.

Customer service is likely to be better when employees are happy and employee turnover is low. Happiness, of course, is difficult to measure, but employee turnover is not, and turnover is low at Kleinschmidt. The company is, in many ways, like a family in that each child is different and siblings discover areas where each can excel, according to Gaples. With luck, the 'parents' do not discourage their excellence.

Gaples allows customers to drive Kleinschmidt. Under his leadership, employees do what customers ask, provided it can be done with the company's computers. Kleinschmidt is an EDI facilitator. Flat files and images are converted to EDI transactions. EDI transactions, on the other hand, can be converted to print images, placed onto a scanned-in customer form, and fixed to a trading partner. As a facilitator, Kleinschmidt supports all EDI standards and versions along with dial-in, dial-out, dedicated line, frame-relay, Internet communication, and a variety of communication protocols. Incoming transactions are processed as they are received and are either immediately transmitted to their destination or placed in a mailbox for later delivery.

In August 1995, Proctor & Gamble recognized Harry Gaples and Kleinschmidt employees for superior performance in customer service and support of its EDI program for more than ten years.

Under Gaples's direction, Kleinschmidt continued to expand and grow in EDI from new customers and growth in use of EDI by existing customers." (See also "Kleinschmidt," page).]

Rex D. Gavin

Adapted from EDI Forum, Vol. 8, No. 2 (1995), pages 79-80.

Rex Gavin spearheaded an ambitious and fruitful initiative at the U.S. Department of Housing and Urban Development (HUD) to use EDI as the catalyst for modernizing legacy systems. By focusing on production systems in HUD's Federal Housing Authority (FHA) mortgage insurance program, HUD's initiative energized the entire mortgage banking industry's commitment to EDI.

He was a special assistant in HUD's Office of Information Policies and Systems, the department's information technology center. In the spring of 1991, as the government drafted standards for its electronic business processes, which became known as Federal information Processing Standard (FIPS) 161, Rex's task was to evaluate and apply X12 and/or UN/EDIFACT standards to reengineer relevant HUD business applications. From a concept with no underlying infrastructure, the HUD EDI program blossomed into a successful operational entity that will benefit not only the FHA, but also every participant in the mortgage industry from homeowner to lender to secondary market underwriter to mortgage-backed securities investor.

Cyrus N. Grant

For more than a decade, Cyrus Grant was an *eCommerce* consultant with Thompson EC Resources and its predecessors, helping to develop EC market forecast models. He presented his findings at group presentations and in *EDI Forum* articles, always pointing out both the statistical facts and the implications. His worked helped EDI-user companies and EDI service providers determine trends and the reasons behind the trends. Ultimately, sharing this knowledge helped the EDI community to aggressively plan for dramatic growth.

Professor Cyrus Grant is chair of the Computer Science and MIS Department at Dominican University.

Ned C. Hill

Ned Hill was cofounder of the EDI Group with Dan Ferguson in 1987. They concentrated on three needs for the new EDI industry—education, a journal, and research.

Ned was eloquent in his presentation of win/win scenarios for combining the synergistic effects of EDI and electronic funds transfer (EFT) together. His concepts were precise, easily understood, far-reaching, interesting, sparkling with relevant humor, and laced with examples.

The significance of the EDI Group's contributions to the understanding and growth of *eCommerce* is enormous. It provided methodology, encouragement, facts required for successful implementation by members of the newly forming *eCommerce* community, insights into the real potential for this endeavor, camaraderie-building for *eCommerce* professionals, statistical research predicting trends useful for steering efficiently toward the future, and a journal for members of the community to use for sharing their experiences and findings with others in the profession.

Ned Hill is always interesting, both in his teaching and writings. For more than a decade and a half, and in addition to his teaching, he has written many of the *EDI Forum* articles based on his experiences and research.

Dr. Hill is a professor at Brigham Young University.

Patrick J. Hlubik

Pat Hlubik was on the UCS pilot project during the early 1980s, which involved thirteen companies charged with testing the adequacy of EDI standards and methods for the grocery industry. At that time, Pat was director of Staff Support Systems at Nabisco Brands, Inc. The project was an outstanding success. Pat was one of the first to comprehend and quickly employ the logic and programs of the table-driven software newly introduced by TDCC.

During the UCS activity preliminary to the pilot, Pat introduced the concept of the transmission header and trailer, which at that time was an addition to the EDI syntax and included the data elements for communications ID and password. Subsequently, he also led the development of the X12 transaction set 997 (Functional Acknowledgment). This is used by almost all EDI-active companies to complete the information loop relative to status of each EDI transmission between trading partners.

UCS: Uniform Communications Standard used by the grocery industry and compatible with TDCC and X12 EDI

WINS: Warehouse Information Networking Standard, also EDI compatible

Following the pilot, Pat worked with Gene Nelson of Dry Storage and Ralph Notto of TDCC to make the first draft of the WINS standard. Using techniques directly related to the table-driven software, but applied to documentation instead of operational EDI, the three completed the task in one week in 1982 while working at a computer terminal at TDCC. The new WINS standards manual, comprising six transaction sets compatible with TDCC and UCS, was readily accepted by the potential user community.

In the early 1990s, Pat became an EDI consultant with Capgemini.

John R. Hon

John Hon was a software consultant to TDCC and had the assignment in the early 1980s to write the first table-driven computer software for EDI, which referenced the TDCC tables. This was an especially difficult assignment, since the software was written in COBOL, which was not structured to conveniently program for such a level of generalization as that required for the table-driven computer programs required by TDCC. Nevertheless, John completed the assignment, and the software was used in the grocery industry's UCS pilot in 1982 and helped to facilitate that project's timely and successful conclusion.

In the mid 1980s, John worked with Paul Lemme, who became executive director at TDCC. They extended the scope and usefulness of the software, which had over 700 subscribers.

John joined EDI Integration Corporation (EIC) in the early 1990s where he implemented one of the earliest interfaces between EDI systems and the Internet FTP protocol and wrote application software required to implement EIC's user communities.

John B. "Jack" Hunter

Adapted from EDI Forum, 1991 Issue, No. 1, page 95, author Earl Bass.

The selection of Jack Hunter as an EDI pioneer verifies the long-held suspicion that some of the EDI initiators did not—and still don't—possess technical backgrounds. Since 1978, Jack demonstrated the skills that placed him in continuing officer positions in the X12 movement for over fifteen years. In addition, he has been a member of many technical groups, both X12 and UN/EDIFACT, and on the DISA Board of Directors.

In the fall of 1978, ASC X12 was getting started and Jack was completing his twenty-seventh year with the General Electric Company, serving as a consultant, corporate treasury operation. Following four years of wartime service in the U.S. Navy and a degree in accounting from George Washington University, Jack joined GE in early 1951. He began his career in what was then called the Business Training Course, an intensive three-year work/study training program designed to furnish an ongoing supply of financial managers to GE. Upon successful completion of the program, Jack was assigned to the corporate audit staff. After a three-year stint in this prestigious organization, Jack filled a series of financially related positions in various manufacturing, distribution, and corporate headquarters components. He developed expertise in distribution management and financial analysis. His work yielded major contributions to GE cost-containment programs.

Jack's entry into what subsequently became known as EDI dates back to the early 1960s, when he participated in electronic inventory replenishment programs for small appliances, consumer electronics, and electrical construction material. The goal then was the same as now—to reduce investment lockup in finished goods stocks and to lower the labor cost of the inventory replenishment process.

In Autumn 1978, when that fateful call for a gathering of people interested in electronic payments was issued by George Christie of the Credit

Research Foundation, GE assigned Jack Hunter to assess the potential of the concept and to represent their interests. [See "Involvement of ANSI in EDI and Development of X12," page 48.]

Out of that landmark 1978 meeting came the birth of X12. The actual chartering of X12 by ANSI occurred in 1979, with Ted Johnson elected as its first chair. As Jack recalls, the initial scope statement included the charge '... to provide standardization to facilitate inter-business/institutional electronic interchange of transactions ...' The key word was *standardization*. Jack and other initial participants in the preX12 effort were inexorably led to two conclusions: that out of the many proprietary formats in vogue at that time had to come one standard format that all would use; and the ultimate standard had to stem from a recognized consensus process. Thus, in Jack's mind, the merger of the EDI effort with the American National Standards Institute was not only a foregone conclusion, it was more importantly a most fortunate action for the future growth and acceptance of X12 standards.

Jack Hunter participated fully in those early decisive days as well as in all that followed since the launching of X12. Back in the days when X12 consisted of just four subcommittees, he served as vice chair of the invoice group. He then began a five-year tenure as chair of the group, which grew into the Finance Subcommittee, now the largest group in X12. In this capacity, Jack was instrumental in attracting the insurance industry, currently the fastest-growing segment of X12, to the ANSI environment.

Along the way, on December 31, 1985, to be exact, Jack retired from the General Electric Company. Without missing a beat, he began his second career on January 1, 1986, as a consultant, standards development, under contract to the General Electric Information Services Company (GEIS), a highly visible player in the EDI world.

Jack's sole responsibility to GEIS was to participate to the fullest possible extent in the development and maintenance of X12 standards. In essence, he served as a full-time loaned executive to the ANSI standards effort.

Jack's retirement from GE occurred at a fortunate time for the EDI world. X12 was on the threshold of dynamic growth, and the international effort, now known as EDIFACT, had begun its relentless move across the Atlantic Ocean. Jack attended the initial EDIFACT working session held in London in 1986. For several years, he participated in every joint rapporteur session since that first face-to-f ace meeting.

The stated goal of X12 is to isolate and eliminate existing syntactical and structural differences between X12 and EDIFACT standards. Actual compatibility between the two formats is scheduled to occur in 1994. Jack agreed with the objective of the goal, i.e., one standard used worldwide by all EDI players, but questioned its achievability by 1994.

'I was more positive a year ago as to an eventual marriage than I am today,' he commented, 'even though its desirability is becoming increasingly obvious.' Jack attributed his doubtfulness to what he perceives to be a growing dysfunction between the two standards. Of the two standards, Jack commented that while EDIFACT probably constitutes the more technically correct one, X12 is more user-friendly from an implementation viewpoint. 'And,' he hastened to add, 'users, not technicians, formed X12.'[83]

Jack has frequently demonstrated during thirteen years in EDI that he was more than willing to support his convictions with deeds. He emphatically stated his intention to push for compatibility in standards, using his participation in the EDIFACT and X12 technical assessment groups as the appropriate platform, but not to the detriment of either user group.

Abdel-Kamel Imadalou

Abdel-Kamel Imadalou, working at Adcognito in Montréal during the 1990s, was given the task to transparently integrate an American EDI software product into his company's AGAT.

AGAT was tailored for use by the advertising sector.

This involved translating all of the text used in the American product from English to French, and adding to the total package application new software specifically designed for advertising companies. The applications included the composition of reports interactively using source data extracted during data flows, so the information reported was always the latest available and relevant to the user's current interest.

Abdel-Kamel, a native of Algeria, has an engineering degree in computer science and a master's degree in mathematics. As of this writing, he is working as an Oracle DBA in Switzerland.

Gail Jackson

Adapted from EDI Forum, Volume 8, No. 2, 1995, page 79

Gail's diligence and commitment to advancing EDI led to the alignment of the X12 and EDIFACT standards. By monitoring their differences

[83] As of the year 2000, use of both X12 and EDIFACT are growing, but international cooperation and coordination are growing also.

and submitting change requests to each as appropriate, they are kept as similar as possible in an attempt to facilitate the eventual migration path to the international standard. She has been not only a leader but also an innovator in the advancement of EDI, both domestically and internationally.

Her accomplishments in the EDI industry are numerous, but perhaps the biggest feather in her cap is that she is one of three people in the world who authored the first draft of CONTRL, the EDIFACT equivalent of the 997 (Functional Acknowledgment).

Gail was a North American representative on the UN/EDIFACT Joint Technical Group in 1990. During a discussion on possible adoption and use of Functional Group segments for EDIFACT for similar purpose as for X12, Gail took a strong stance against adoption.

"Why," Ralph Notto asked privately during a break. "Your company is already expert in the use of this."

"I know," she replied. "But the discussion is about having a control segment optional. Either have it or don't have it!" This dialogue is an example of Gail's keen insight into the implication of such detail, and her use of this to influence the design of the standard.

In 1984, Gail was the president and cofounder of Supply Tech, Inc., whose EDI software subsequently became used in over forty countries and twenty-six industries.

Also in 1984, she joined the Automotive Industry Action Group AIAG) where she wrote the original implementation recommendation for the 830 (Material Release) and 856 (Advance Ship Notice) transaction sets.

Gail was elected vice chairperson of the full X12 committee in 1994. She was also very active in the development of UN/EDIFACT.

Kent Jamison

Adapted from EDI Forum, Volume 9, No. 3, pages 94-95, 1996.

Kent Jamison, a giant in the world of EDI and a former football player, was a driving force behind much of the development of EDI concepts and standards. The early days of EDI were adventurous and required a pioneering spirit. Kent's proactive leadership and foresight helped EDI to enjoy its current role in a global economy. Kent was practicing electronic commerce before today's buzzwords were even formed. Over the years, many have benefited from his firm and effective leadership.

Kent's career began at Yellow Freight Systems, Inc. in Overland Park, Kansas. He started in the computer room as a shift supervisor, was offered a position as a programmer-trainee and quickly moved into application development. Subsequently, he was promoted to manager and then director of Systems Development.

Yellow Freight was an early player in EDI and electronic commerce, and Kent was point man in that effort. As a programmer, he was called on to figure out a way to electronically exchange invoices with a large retail customer. Early on, he recognized the need for public development of those standards. He has been at the center of the action ever since.

Kent's introduction to the national EDI scene came in 1983 when he was named to the EDI Task Group of the American Trucking Association (ATA). In 1985, Kent was named one of the two representatives from the motor industry for the Transportation Data Coordinating Committee (TDCC). In 1986, Kent was named chairman of the task group.

In 1987, he spearheaded the effort to write the first *Motor Carrier EDI Implementation Guide.* Versions of the guide have proved to be critical success factors in EDI projects worldwide. In 1989, Kent continued his active role in the industry and was named chairman of the Motor Task Group for ANSI ASC X12. In addition to these leadership positions, he frequently spoke at DISA and ATA annual conferences and TDCC forums.

Kent is best known for his ability to build teams and form coalitions. This skill has been invaluable in the development of EDI standards. He is skilled in the art of persuasion and has a natural ability to derive consensus from chaos. Some have called him an EDI purist. He is a firm believer in single-purpose, unambiguous transaction sets. It takes much more work to develop the simple solution.

Kent never backed away from a challenge. He led a charge to redefine/ reengineer all motor-carrier transaction sets. The goal was to remove the ambiguity that crept into standards. This was fueled by less-than-truckload (LTL) carriers, truckload carriers, and small-package services attempting to use the same transaction set for different business needs.

Kent is a person of strong convictions. He is firmly grounded in his beliefs and he rarely wavers from those beliefs. EDI is often developed in the technology department, but successful EDI requires a blend of technology prowess and business expertise. The technology is easy. The ability to mobilize an entire corporation is hard. Kent was able to rise above the technology and garner support from the rest of the corporation.

During development of public EDI standards, he consistently stood for the rights of carriers in the product value chain. Kent built a strong network of allies among groups traditionally viewed as rivals. He supported the real stakeholders in the EDI partnership and looked beyond the perspective of just another vendor.

After twenty-five years at Yellow Freight, Kent Jamison took a position as MIS manager of Consolidated Freightways in Portland, Oregon, where he continued a leadership role in the world of EDI and electronic commerce."

John Kaess

Beginning in the early 1980s, John Kaess was a representative of Conrail at TDCC standards meetings. He quickly mastered the EDI concept on both the major conceptual and the detail structural levels. He was quick to point out any conflicts on the detail level, and was a consistent contributor toward accuracy of the detail.

For two decades, he applied his EDI expertise in development and maintenance of national and international EDI standards. He had several roles with the Pan American EDIFACT Board (PAEB) and the Accredited Standards Committee (ASC) X12.

After leaving Conrail in 1988, he has used this expertise to help other companies implement EDI solutions by developing and maintaining internal company standards, providing data mapping, and working with trading partners to coordinate successful EDI implementations.

John developed more than thirty new X12 transaction sets and three EDIFACT messages that subsequently became operational at user sites; coordinated maintenance activity between ASC X12 and TDCC; assisted the Automotive Industry Action Group (AIAG) and the Motor Carriers in modification of Motor transaction sets to accommodate AIAG needs; evaluated new EDI standards and maintenance proposals making recommendations for change when required to eliminate misuse of standards; and performed a long list of other essential EDI standards maintenance and enhancement functions.

Walter Keyes

Adapted from EDI Forum, Volume 10, No. 1, page 86, 1997.

Walter Keyes's contributions to the EDI industry date back to the early 1970s when he designed an integrated automotive release and shipping control system for a Detroit-based automotive supplier. A Walsh College graduate of accounting, Walt has worked in corporate accounting in the automotive industry from the start of his career.

> **OEM:** Original Equipment Manufacturer
>
> **AIAG:** Automotive Industry Action Group

In 1974, Alpha Stamping, a high-volume parts supplier, realized it was necessary to improve the tracking of its customers' orders. Using an IBM system, Walt designed software to better track part requirements and automate shipping. Using EDI to feed the system, his earliest work provided the ability to plan production and shipping, produce invoice documents, and feed this data into the company's financial and manufacturing applications. When Walt could not find anyone to code his design, he learned to program and developed an unusual Automotive Release/Shipping Control system. In 1983, Future Three Software, Inc. was created with Walt as president.

Early on, he worked directly with many automotive suppliers in implementing and converting fixed-format communication to variable-length EDI. In an effort to promote the use of EDI in the OEM supplier community, he began work with the Automotive Industry Action Group (AIAG). With Keyes leading the way, Future Three Software became one of the original companies to be EDI-certified by the AIAG.

His original design continued to grow, integrating some of the earliest ANSI X12 transaction sets directly into his release accounting and shipping system. Over time, interfaces were written to carry the electronic demand through the system and into the major manufacturing systems. What started as an X12 standard 830 (Planning Schedule) ended up as an 856 (Shipping Notification). Before the electronic data made its way back to the issuer, it would first travel through the system to create shipping documents, invoice papers, relieve inventory, and update accounts receivable, general ledger and manufacturing records. Walt pioneered this EDI integration, and many automotive supplier companies implemented his technology into their businesses.

In the late 1980s, he designed another system to deliver EDI updates to suppliers. Electronic Support System (ESS) was created for automotive suppliers, giving them the ability to receive updates to their Auto Release system 24 hours a day. With EDI transactions being mandated by OEMs at every turn, it became necessary to implement a way for suppliers to receive added EDI transaction set development at a moment's notice.

Under Walt's direction, his company grew to more than ninety-five employees, and it has appeared on the Michigan Private 100 Fastest Growing Companies list six times. In 1991, Future Three was the recipient of the Michigan Leading Edge of Technology Award. His EDI efforts were recognized in 1994 when Future Three Software was awarded a corporate achievement award from AIAG.

He continues to lead the efforts of the EDI industry and promotes the integration of data throughout the manufacturing systems of North America. Walter Keyes, a resident of Northville, Michigan, has been married thirty-one years and has two daughters. When not busy running his company, he enjoys an occasional round or two of golf."

D.K. Kim

DK Kim was a pioneer in introducing EDI into Korea. As one of the most well known leaders in the information technology industry in Korea, he played a pivotal role in developing and promoting data communication and information services, which at the time were both beginning in Korea. After joining DACOM in 1982 as one of the founding officers, he exercised his leadership in planning and launching various data communication and information services such as packet network, email, on-line information service, EDI, and many other services known as "VAN" at that time. All of these were all quite new to Korean industry.

D.K. Kim

Soon after learning about the implications of EDI (sometime around 1986), DK determined to aggressively promote this new technology and concept in Korea. First, he organized a great number of seminars and conferences, arranged to distribute many EDI publications, and set up education programs. The education focused on promoting EDI awareness and propagating its significance and implications to the Korean business society and the government sector. These were mostly sponsored by DACOM, but in many cases this was accomplished in close cooperation with the related industry associations, training institutions, and the government ministries. The EDI concept was first introduced in Korea by DACOM in 1987 and presented by the Yankee Group under the title Inter-Company Networks.

DK also spent many hours and days in speaking at seminars and meetings with the industry leaders, government officials, academia, and the press. He addressed its concept, implications, implementation methodology, and the social, business behavioral, and technological issues and standards.

As a managing director for DACOM in charge of data networks and services, DK initiated several very ambitious projects for EDI implementations. The first project, STEEL VAN, launched in 1987, connected POSCO and its buyers and dealers (encompassing at that time ten hosts and fifty-five PCs) and allowed them to exchange business documents and information about production schedules and order processing status. The second project, MOTOR VAN, for the automotive industry, was put into commercial service in 1989. Its initial operations, with KIA Motors as the facilitator, connected the KIA computer center with its thirty-nine suppliers' systems, which at at that time were transmitting ten business documents, including purchase orders. DK also directed the Korean/North American EDI Pilot Project initiated in 1988 with the support of EDI Council of Canada, EDI Inc., and Martin Marietta as the facilitator team. He also influenced the set up two other major EDI networks in Korea, KT-Net and KL-Net. These supported the trading community, government agencies, customs clearances, transporters, and port operators.

DACOM: Data Communications Corporation of Korea—The exclusive data communication services provide in Korea when DACOM was formed.

POSCO: A Korean steel company

KT-Net: Korean Trade Network

KL-Net: Korean Logistics Network

IT: Information Technology

DK also made his every endeavor to build up an EDI-based world in Korea and internationally as well by actively participating in such influential organizations and bodies as EDI Council of Korea as the first chairman, Korea Data Base Society as the chairman, EDI World Institute as a director of the board, the National Competitiveness Board of the President Office as a counsel, and many other trade associations and academic societies as the vice-chairman and a director.

For these contributions to the IT industry in Korea, he received two grand awards, one from the president of Korea in 1988 and the other from the Twenty-First Century Executive Club in 1991.

Alexander Kreithen

Alex Kreithen was one of the four consultants retained by TDCC during the period 1975-77 when the concept and definitive details of the EDI standards were being coordinated and documented. During that period, he often had the role of "consultant to the consultants" to pose questions and help the drive toward consensus. He is also noted as the author of the *TDCC Volume V—Communications.*

Alex was one of the founders and a vice president of EDI Inc., the first EDI software company to use PC computers during EDI pilot projects.

Hank Lavery

Adapted from EDI Forum, 1992 Issue, No. 4, page 47.

Hank Lavery, while senior manager with Peat, Marwick, Mitchell & Company in 1972, recognized the need for public EDI standards and assisted in the early review of the first draft of TDCC standards published in 1975.

In the late 1970s, as vice president of management systems and administration with Cooper-Jarrett, Inc., Hank designed and implemented internal systems that could provide data to shippers and receivers in standard TDCC EDI formats. Hank was a leading proponent of the rapid development and rollout of these motor carrier EDI standards, since they provided *electronic* answers to the problems of limited information system resources and a large variety of trading partners in the motor carrier community.

In 1979, Hank was recruited by TranSettlements, Inc. to bring an innovative freight settlement system to the marketplace. In the ensuing three years, the more rapid movement into standardized EDI between carriers and their customers overshadowed the technical success of this proprietary system. From this vantage point Hank recognized that the growth of standard EDI was being impeded by the lack of a translator. Customers had only one choice in the transportation area, and that was to use the TDCC EDI translator, which was essentially a *starter kit* to help companies begin EDI. He believed that the TDCC translator lacked much of the functionality that was required for an effective payback. [See 'TranSettlements,' page 104.]

With this in mind, Hank provided the creativity and technical and managerial direction to develop the first fully functional mainframe EDI translator, which was released in 1982 to a motor carrier on the West Coast. This translator supported TDCC, UCS, and WINS standard formats; in 1983 it was enhanced to support the growing use of ANSI X12 standards.

In 1981, as vice president of TranSettlements, Hank led the company into the EDI communications marketplace, developing the first operational value added network service for transportation transactions that complied with public EDI standards. With Hank at the helm, hundreds of motor and rail carriers were quickly introduced to the concept of interacting electronically with shippers, receivers, and freight payment service companies.

Paul Lemme

Adapted from EDI Forum, Volume 11, No. 1, page 98, 1998, author Ralph Notto.

Although the first EDI standards were published in 1975, it was not until 1983 when those committed to it believed that a 'point of no return' was reached. This meant that a large enough group of important companies had realized benefits from EDI implementations. They liked what they experienced. Many realized the potentially favorable impact on their companies from this type of standardization, if its use were expanded.

Paul Lemme was one of those who immediately understood the significance of EDI in relationship to: the inter-company data exchange cycles and scenarios; the degree of inter-industry interaction in these cycles; the effect of a unifying technology for implementation; the role of application software; the importance of timing, accuracy, and efficiency; and the modular requirements for EDI implementation.

Representing Sales Force, a food broker in the grocery industry, he spoke out often on these points at meetings leading up to the publication of the Uniform Communications Standard (UCS) and the subsequent Grocery Industry EDI Pilot Project. This occurred during the period 1979-1982.

Joakim Lundgren

Adapted from Chalmers Electro Trainnee Appointment Committee, 1990 Report, pages 57-59, Chalmers University, Göetborg, Sweden.

Joakim Lundgren (Jock) spent the summer following his graduate studies at Chalmers University in Sweden at one of the U.S. EDI software companies. He was given the assignment to use *table-driven software* concepts to create programmed instruction software for an EDI-user to quickly learn his new company's EDI software product.

He successfully completed his assignment. His report when he returned to Chalmers is interesting, since at the beginning of the summer of 1990, Jock had previously heard of neither topic, and his assignment involved both of these. His description of EDI and programmed instruction are quite interesting, since EDI was still considered as *new* in 1990.

In Jock's own words:

At last, May 30th, 1990. I have been waiting for this day for about one year! New York, New York here I come! Well, to be honest with you, I was not too excited about getting to New York. What I wanted to do was to get to Gaithersburg, Maryland, to work at EDI, Inc. I wanted to be on my own, far away from everything connected with Sweden, exploring the American way of working and living. I feel very satisfied with how both my way of working and living turned out."

EDI—the Concept

EDI, Inc is in the business of EDI (surprised?). EDI stands for Electronic Data Interchange and is kind of an administrative communication between companies. Instead of sending purchase orders and invoices by mail between companies [for example], computers do this. By using EDI, a lot of time can be saved. A really important concept when speaking about EDI is standards. To make any sense, companies with different software products must still be able to communicate with each other. In North America, a standard called X12 is used, while in Europe the EDIFACT standard is used. The standards are a well-defined description of how data should be sent between the trading partners. Today [1990], there is not too much EDI communication between North America and Europe, because of the different standards. There are two ways of adjusting this in the future. One way is to decide that only one standard is going to be used. The other way is to make EDI software able to handle both X12 and EDIFACT. EDI is still just a baby, but one thing is sure though—it is here to stay.

My Project at EDI, Inc.

When I arrived at EDI, Inc., it turned out that I was going to implement programmed instructions (PI) for their software product, TELINK. What on earth are PI, you may ask? Well, I did not know either when I first got there. Today I would say that PI's are a way of letting a person how a software application is functioning in its environment. That is, the computer is used as tutorial instrument, and the person who is to be taught has the feeling of working with the real product during his education. The teaching process should also contain questions after each moment. If the pupil seems to have understood *the lesson*, he may proceed, otherwise he gets additional instruction.

I am convinced that well-designed PI for a product could be very useful. Most software companies in EDI are pretty small and do not have the ability to concern themselves with the customers as much as they should. When a customer is buying a system, he needs to get it installed and then there is a break-in period when he has a lot of questions that need to be answered.

A well-designed PI can be used in multiple situations. It could be used to give a five-minute demonstration of the product to a customer but also to demonstrate the concept of EDI, which today [1990] is far from obvious to everybody. It could also be very useful in helping a customer make a quick installation, i.e. PI takes the user along a certain path in the system to make him do all the important set-ups. By using this feature the customer should be able to install his system pretty much by himself. The main purpose, though, should be to get the user so familiar with the system that he can use it without PI. 'All right,' you say, 'but most software products have really good documentation in their manuals, distributed together with the product.'

Why should the company spend a lot of time and money in doing this again? Here, it is important to consider PI as a complement to the manuals and not as substitutes. Manuals tend to be pretty technical and *dry* reading. They also often tend to give you a lot of words that are not really needed. You have to be sure that everything about the product is in there–but that is not what a lot of users want. They want to make a quick start-up in order to use the product for intended purposes. As time goes by they want to gradually learn more about the system. By using PI, the user can take the lessons he really needs at the moment. He is doing it from the keyboard, in the real environment, which makes him turn on a smile of recognition later on, when he gets back to this part of the system and is *on his own.*

For a lot of uncertain, non-technical users, this smile could turn into a grimace if he tried to understand everything when reading the manuals.

I finished my small project at EDI, Inc by doing a presentation for the staff. It was a really good experience to stand up in front of people, giving a presentation in English.

Howard W. McKenna

Adapted from EDI Forum, 1990 Issue, page 75, author Ralph Notto.

'Who is that person who speaks out so forcefully?' Ralph Notto asked of Joe Carley at an EDI meeting in April 1975.

'Howard McKenna of General Motors,' Joe said.

It was even that early in the formation of the EDI standards that Howard spoke with such conviction and instantly got attention and commanded a following.

Small wonder. He had an early insight into what EDI standards are all about. He showed the General Motors Fremont plant as an example to Ed Guilbert and Joe Carley. One motor carrier placed a computer terminal there so that GM had access to the carrier's computer with current status information about GM shipments. Not to be outdone, a competing carrier did the same. Of course, the equipment, operating instructions, and formats were different. Then the next competing carrier placed a terminal, and the next, and the next, and so on. This not uncommon scenario was an initial motivation toward EDI standards.

Howard's first EDI efforts were in 1970 with the design, implementation, and operation of a system that was one of the earliest attempts to exchange machine-processable data electronically across company boundaries. GM's vehicle delivery carriers were asked to report in a Teletype message to GM on the delivery to dealers of each vehicle. The message was variable length. It was structured according to syntax rules with data element and segment delimiters, and was parsed and edited by a computer without human intervention. An application program then processed the resulting records. This is identical to today's EDI concept. The carriers, located at approximately fifty sites throughout the United States and Canada, reported 25,000 vehicle deliveries per day. The accuracy rate was exceptional considering that the data was initially keystroked on 33ASR Teletype machines and transmitted over public and private Teletype networks.

The experience (blood, sweat, tears, and frustration) of that undertaking was an important preview of the TDCC work in developing EDI standards in 1973-1975. Howard was very active in both the motor carrier and rail carrier work groups, working closely with the TDCC managing and technical staffs. He was also an active participant in the TDCC Standards Maintenance Committee until 1987 and participated in the Users Work Group for several years. In addition, Howard contributed to the Joint EDI

(JEDI) efforts that synchronized the TDCC and ASC X12 data dictionaries and syntax rules. He was a member of the TDCC path-finding Advanced Systems Planning Group. Finally, he was one of the earliest implementers of the table-driven computer programming concepts for EDI.

During the early years of EDI development, Howard was a frequent speaker at the TDCC Annual Forum, and before various other transportation associations. In both 1988 and 1989, he received service recognition awards from TDCC and its successor, EDIA.

Prior to his involvement in EDI, Howard spent many years at General Motors in the fields of programming and systems analysis for both analog and digital computers, and in the field of general instrumentation use and maintenance. He wrote many technical papers and holds two patents covering binary clocks.

By 1990, Howard was EDI program manager for EDS, with responsibility to direct and coordinate the application of EDS information processing and communications technologies with the implementation of EDI across EDS's total customer base, which includes General Motors.

He began work at General Motors Corporation in 1953, upon his graduation from the University of Detroit with a BEE (Bachelor's of Electrical Engineering) degree. In 1958, he received his MBA from the same school.

Howard served in the United States Navy from 1945-1947 as an electronics technicians mate 2/c and retired as a major from the United States Air Force Reserves. His non-work interests include boating, travel, and family and church activities.

Howard has used his experience to help chart an early direction and form for the EDI standards, their purpose, and operational use. His leadership ability has helped ensure an EDI following and common focus. Howard McKenna is truly a man who has helped build the foundation for the EDI community as we know it today.

Burton F. Millard

Adapted from EDI Forum, 1990 Issue, page 76, author Ralph Notto.

Firm in his conviction and aggressive in his contribution, Burton F. Millard of Procter & Gamble is definitely a leader who has helped to form the characteristics of the EDI community.

Burt was a participant in the 1977 meeting between TDCC, Credit Research, and industry representatives who met to discuss automation of the order placement, billing, and payment process. In 1978, this evolved into a project called Business Systems Applications (BUSAP), which was the beginning of the expansion of the TDCC transportation EDI standards into other business activities. He is one of the few people who attended the initial committee meeting that spawned X12.

In 1979, this activity was transferred to follow American National Standards Institute (ANSI) procedures, and at that time was officially designated as 'XI2.' Burt attended the first official X12 meeting in October 1979.

In 1980, Burt became a member of the original Uniform Communication Standard (UCS) organization, which led the grocery industry into an early and very successful implementation of EDI on an industry-wide basis.

Burt maintained his membership and active participation in both X12 and UCS and was instrumental in making these two standards closely related as well as derivatives of the TDCC standards. Thus, X12, UCS, and TDCC have a common syntax, common segments, and common data elements. Burt focused on maintaining a common standard for TDCC, X12, and UCS, and the present status of the EDI standards maintenance reflects the effect of Burt's work. (Earlier in 1990, all of the North American EDI Standards groups—XI2, UCS, TDCC, and WINS—agreed to become part of the Accredited Standards Committee [ASC] X12 for standards maintenance and enhancements. This was, in effect, a formal declaration for organization of something that was previously carried out through determined effort by individual participants. Burt's earlier work had set the stage for this transformation.)

NACHA: National Automated Clearing House Association
EFT: Electronic Funds Transfer
CTP: Corporate Trade Payments
UCS Uniform Communication Standard (grocery industry EDI)
TDCC: Transportation data Coordinating Committee
ASC: [ANSI] Accredited Standards Committee
X12: American National Standard for EDI
WINS: Warehouse Information Networking
JEDI: US Joint EDI Committee
VICS: Subset of X12 used by the retail industry

Burt's involvement in EDI began in the late 1960s with implementation of bank transmissions of customer remittance data. Following that, several companies defined proprietary standards for electronic transmission of purchase orders. At first this seemed like a good idea, but Burt could foresee its ultimate effect on Procter & Gamble—namely that many of P&G's large customers would each define a purchase order standard, meaning there would be no coordination for items such as structure, format, data elements, communications, operating procedures, and maintenance. Some years later, for example, one of the owners of such a proprietary standard informed the author that Procter & Gamble had just said 'No' to proprietary standards, giving its customers a choice between only X12 or UCS. It was leadership like this and firmness of conviction that led to the strong surge in X12 and UCS participation, since the natural beginning base of participants was composed of those companies already engaged in some form of EDI and with the objective to increase EDI information exchange.

Upon his graduation from the University of California at Berkeley, Burt Millard joined the United States Army Intelligence Corps, where he served for two years. Burt then began his career with P&G, at first in the sales department. His experiences with P&G included management of sales/distribution/accounting offices, order-shipment-invoice processing, credit and accounts receivable, promotion payment, and systems. In 1981 and 1982, Burt managed P&G's participation in the UCS pilot implementation project. In 1990, he was EDI applications manager for P&G and served as the company's corporate representative for electronic data interchange.

Burt was a member of the NACHA Corporate-to-Corporate Systems Committee that developed corporate trade payments (CTP) formats for electronic funds transfer (EFT). He was vice chair of the Joint Electronic Data Interchange (JEDI) Committee, which served to bring TDCC and X12 together after a period of drifting apart, and which also served as the nucleus for the UN/JEDI[84] task group used for international EDI standards coordination and eventually evolved into EDIFACT. He served on the Steering Committee as well as on the Technical Standards Committee of the National Wholesale Druggists Association. He was a member of the American Logistics Association Task Group, which implemented EDI in the military resale system, and is a member of the TDCC/EDIA Standards Maintenance Committee.

Burt was a member of the Grocery Manufacturers of America Information Systems Steering Committee and Subcommittee Chair for EDI. He was a member of the Uniform Code Council EDI Advisory Committee, the Steering Committee for UCS, WINS, and VICS EDI activities. He was the chair of the UCS Maintenance Committee. He was also the chair of the Distribution and Warehousing Subcommittee (X12M) of ANSI ASC X12, a member of the X12 Steering Committee (X12X), a member of the Technical Assessment Subcommittee (X12J), and a member of the Finance Subcommittee (X12F).

[84]Not the same as the "U.S. JEDI" identified on page 78.

Burt's participation, sense of direction, and ability to lead others toward a common beneficial goal have helped EDI standards to be shared by a worldwide community."

Jim Muenz

Adapted from EDI Forum, 1989 Issue, page 90, author Dick Norris.

Jim Muenz has been a pioneer in making EDI work. In contrast to many of our other pioneers whose EDI careers date back to the early seventies, Jim did not come onto the EDI scene until 1980. It's not just a coincidence, however, that since that time EDI has really begun to be used rather than talked about, with the grocery industry being an especially active player.

Jim's early experience with systems development methods and database administration prepared him well for EDI, as it taught him the fundamental value of things like standards, data definitions, and properly articulated procedures for getting on with the design and implementation of systems and programs that can actually do the job. As a result, it is not surprising that he took an active role when he first served on the UCS Message Standards Committee, formed in 1981 to develop the original UCS draft transaction sets. These were first tested in an industry pilot program in which a number of grocery manufacturers and distributors took part. Kraft was an active participant, with Jim directing the company's effort.

In August 1982, the test program was completed and several of the UCS draft standards (the purchase order, invoice, and functional acknowledgment) were issued as operational standards. At the same time, the UCS Standards Maintenance Committee was formed as an ongoing entity with Jim as the first chairman. He served in this post until January 1989, when he retired from Kraft and joined the Uniform Code Council as EDI Technical Director.

Jim was a member of the UCS Direct Store Delivery Task Force and chairman of the steering committee that directed the UCS Communication Standards Study. Both of these activities have contributed to keeping the grocery industry in the forefront of EDI progress.

Jim's dedication to EDI business usage has been and will continue to be an important force in its further evolution and growth."

Gene A. Nelson

Adapted from EDI Forum, 1989 Issue, page 91, author Ralph Notto.

Gene Nelson, 'Mr. WINS.'

WINS is that part of the North American family of EDI standards called 'Warehouse Information Network Standard.'

At the grocery industry UCS meetings, Gene represented Dry Storage Corporation, a warehouse company serving grocery manufacturers for distribution in Chicago and other areas. Beginning in 1980, he participated in UCS meetings.

Gene is deserving of the title 'Mr. WINS,' however, because of the way the first draft of the WINS standard was created. While UCS, X12, and TDCC EDI standards were created during many seemingly endless committee meetings, WINS did not happen that way. Gene, Pat Hlubik of Nabisco and Ralph Notto met for one week in 1982 at a computer terminal at TDCC. By that time the software technology used for supporting the development and publication of the EDI family of standards had matured so that we were able to create standards diagrams and documents based on table technology. [see "Enabling Technology," page 30.]

Gene, for that week, was the ad hoc representative of warehouse companies. Pat represented grocery manufacturers, the natural trading partners of these warehouses. (Perhaps Pat is 'Uncle WINS,' but that is another story.)

At the time, all three men were experienced in UCS and use of the tables. Gene, with concurrence from Pat, stated the names of EDI transaction sets required. Then he said of each, 'It is similar to UCS transaction set X, but …' At the computer terminal, Ralph made a copy of the appropriate tables, modified the copies according to Gene's dictates, added a few new table entries required, and directed the computer to print the WINS standards volume, which contained six transaction sets, segment diagrams, data element dictionary, cross references within WINS as well as cross references to the other EDI standards, and a text that explained the standards.

The six transaction sets were 940 (Warehouse Shipping Order), 941 (Warehouse Inventory Status Report), 942 (Warehouse Activity Report), 943 (Stock Transfer Shipment Advice), 944 (Stock Transfer Receipt Advice), and 945 (Warehouse Shipping Advice).

The motivation for WINS was understood by a brief visit to Nelson's former company at Dry Storage. There, in a room of approximately 600 square feet, were terminal and communications equipment donated by about fifteen grocery manufacturers. Of course, each set of equipment and the accompanying manufacturer's instructions was different, because the grocery manufacturers never coordinated with each other in the pre-EDI era. The common scenario was that at a certain time of day, a manufacturer would send data messages to its terminal at the warehouse. The terminal was expected to be in a ready state and loaded with forms supplied by the manufacturer. A warehouse person took the completed forms and keyed the data into the warehouse's computer. The transfer of the information was important enough to the manufacturers that they bore the expense of the equipment, communications, and forms even though the average duration of a given transmission was only fifteen minutes per day per manufacturer.

It is amazing how little of the first WINS standard was changed during the resulting committee process. Several hundred companies in the United States and Canada were using WINS by 1990."

Vegard Nervik

> **ERP**: Enterprise Resource Planning software

Vegard Nervik is a co-founder of Emanio, Inc., and developed an EDI product that maps directly to application databases without requiring intermediate flat files and associated extra programming functions.

Vegard, chief technology officer at Emanio, has worked extensively with complex cross-application integration in highly heterogeneous data systems at Norwegian Telecom. He was responsible for several important data interfaces between Norwegian Telecom's ERP system and supply chain management system, and headed projects for performance testing of mission critical systems at Norwegian Telecom. Vegard also has significant experience programming ERP systems for the Scandinavian market. He worked as senior programmer at BAS Data AS, a Norwegian independent software vendor, where he went from junior programmer to head of special programming projects in less than a year. One of the special projects he headed was the integration of the ERP system with the Norwegian Customs and Excise for Norwegian Railways.

Vegard holds a master's in business and economics degree from the Norwegian School of Management, where he also worked as a research assistant in information technology strategy and information systems design. He has studied and worked in Southeast Asia and speaks five languages. (See also "Emanio, Inc.," page 99 and "XML—Is it the future?" page 92.)

Soo Hong Noh

Soo Hong Noh (Daniel)

Soo Hong Noh (Daniel) was an active member of a team assigned the task of introducing Korean business and government representatives to EDI in 1986. Part of his preparation for this included attendance at the 1986 TDCC/EDIA Annual Forum and Exhibition, Washington DC. His role was to meet and bond with some of the EDI experts at the forum, including Ed Guilbert and Joe Carley. On return to Korea, he was assigned by Dr. Y.T. Lee and DK Kim to work with Hak Jung Lee to organize an EDI conference in Seoul.

Daniel met EDI leaders at the 1986 forum and "bombarded" them with well-prepared questions. One of Daniel's "victims" was Ed Guilbert. Ed introduced Daniel to other people, but confessed later that he did that because even Ed had no answers to some of Daniel's important questions. The conference was held in October 1987, and included several hundred attendees looking for possible solutions to business, governmental, and technical issues.

Koreans work diligently to represent their country and to bond with others from other countries. Daniel was excellent in this respect. His interest in others as professionals and friends is readily understood and appreciated.[85]

Daniel had a consultant's role for the first Korean EDI projects, STEEL VAN and MOTOR VAN. These were similar in purpose to the U.S. steel and automotive industries EDI initiatives. The two projects laid the cornerstones for EDI penetration in Korea.

Daniel traveled extensively in the U.S. and Canada with Hak Jung Lee and Ralph Notto to talk with company representatives about the Korean/North American EDI Pilot project.

He spoke extensively and contributed papers describing his findings from EDI tasks he performed and EDI conferences he attended. His publications were printed in North America, Europe, Southeast Asia, and Korea during 1988 to 1993.

---

[85] An example is that he and the author have met on many occasions since 1987, both on business and for dinners with each other's family.

He was instrumental in the formulation of the EDI Council of Korea. Also, as a member of an initial group of thirteen EDI experts, he helped to establish the EDI World Institute, based in Montréal.

> **mCommerce**: Mobile Commerce—Electronic commerce over wireless devices.

In 1994, Daniel turned his main interests to the Internet, and joined Inet Inc. as managing director. Inet was then Korea's first and number one Internet Service Provider (ISP). Daniel has put his efforts in growing *eCommerce*, mCommerce, Internet-based education, and online content in Korea. As of this writing, he is country manager for $\mathbf{O_2}$ Korea (formerly British Telecom Wireless) and is completing his PhD program in international IT studies. He has a master's degree in computer science from Florida Tech (1985) and a bachelor's degree in business administration from Korea University (1984).

Mobile commerce is electronic commerce over wireless devices.

Richard C. Norris

Adapted from EDI Forum, Volume 10, No. 1, page 85, 1997.

Although his expertise encompasses a broad range of industries and EDI applications, one of Richard C. Norris's most significant contributions in the use of EDI technology has been through the grocery industry.

In the late 1970s, six grocery-industry associations united to investigate EDI for their industry through the A. D. Little consulting firm, and Norris was the principal investigator. [See "The Role of UCS and the Grocery Industry," page 36.]

The report covering the investigation was significant because it had a unifying purpose, was based on a thorough, objective investigation, presented a quantitative analysis of the effect of EDI, made far-reaching recommendations, and proposed a plan of action. The action proposal included development of the UCS standard based on TDCC's work with EDI for the transportation industries and implementation of a pilot project to test the standards in operational environments.

Norris's study, which was the beginning of significant EDI use in the grocery industry, evaluated the economic and technical feasibility of replacing manual and paper-based information flows among food/non-food manufacturers and distributors with an integrated electronic data communications network. The report also predicted that with a 50% EDI transaction penetration, the industry had a potential savings of $324 million per year.

The study not only established the feasibility of EDI but also laid down some of the key design features of UCS (Uniform Communications Standard), the industry's approach to EDI that has proven successful over the following years. UCS is now one of the most active EDI arenas in U.S. commerce, linking grocery and other retail-product manufacturers, distributors, and brokers to directly interchange transaction messages, such as orders, invoices, and promotional announcements.

> **UCS**: Uniform Communication Standard
> **TDCC**: Transportation Data Coordinating Committee
> **DSD**: Direct Store Delivery
> **DEX**: Direct Exchange
> **UCC**: Uniform Code Council
> **EAN**: European Article Numbers

Once UCS became actively used to handle transactions at the grocery supplier to warehouse level, the industry asked the consulting firm and Norris to investigate how it might handle direct store delivery (DSD) transactions. In the study phase, a new form of data interchange called DEX/EDI for Direct Exchange EDI was defined, permitting data transfer directly between electronic units of deliverer and receiver at the store back door.

Shortly thereafter, he was asked by the chairman of the ECR Executive Committee to assess and determine the best methods for linking the independent retail store into the food supply chain in order to enable these stores to be full participants in ECR programs. This project led to the formation of the Independent Retailer/Wholesaler Task Force of ECR, aimed at supporting the independent retailer more generally. The study focused on the proper roles for two different data interchange standards, UCS and SIL, and recommended the appropriate role for each to support industry supply-chain operations. These recommendations were subsequently accepted by the task force and incorporated into ECR and industry action programs.

As a consultant for over thirty-three years, Dick has been active in logistics management, mostly with Arthur D. Little, Inc. During this time, he has counseled a broad range of corporations concerning their supply-chain and related activities as well as the use of information systems and technology to support these business operations. He has been particularly active in the areas of EDI and bar coding.

Relative to bar coding, Dick has been especially active in the use of the various UCC/EAN bar coding systems and symbologies, and the role of bar coding and EDI in business process reengineering. He writes and lectures widely on EDI and bar coding and its use in business operations.

His work in EDI is based on a substantial practice in transportation, physical distribution, and materials management, serving clients in countries on five continents. Trade channels worked in include grocery, apparel, hand tools, automotive parts, and carriers in all of the transportation modes. Dick is a consulting editor for *EDI Forum: The Journal of Electronic Commerce.*

Richard Norris received his AB and SM degrees in engineering sciences and applied physics from Harvard University, and his ScD degree in electrical engineering and operations research from the Massachusetts Institute of Technology. In 1979, he participated in the Senior Executive Program of the M.I.T. Sloan School of Management. He is a member of the Council of Logistics Management.

Ralph W. Notto

Adapted from EDI Forum, 1991 Issue, pages 67-68, author Joe Carley.

Ralph W. Notto

Ralph Notto is one of the few persons in this world who can claim to be an *original EDI pioneer.* This assumes, of course, that we are referring to the original EDI standards that were officially published and named as *The U.S. Electronic Data Interchange (EDI) Standards* in 1975 by TDCC (Transportation Data Coordinating Committee). To say that Ralph made a *major contribution* towards the development of the standards would be an understatement. To credit him with making a major contribution and *quite a bit more* might be a better description of reality. The purpose of this article is to put the *quite a bit more* into proper perspective.

My sixteen years [by 1991] of a continuous working association with Ralph as a trusted and respected colleague began with a fifteen-minute interview at TDCC in 1975. Following is a short history concerning his selection as a member of the TDCC technical staff and some of the contributions he made while on the staff.

When I joined TDCC in 1973 to assume responsibility for systems and programs, the sole technical member of the staff was a transportation tariff-coding specialist. Upon joining the staff, I almost immediately began preparing a plan to carry out the single mission of the TDCC, which was to develop a method for interfacing unlike systems of trading partners at the data or operations level.

The next step was to establish a program-funding source. We found it in the Office of Facilitation in the U.S. Department of Transportation that, in late 1974, awarded a small *seeding* contract of approximately $75,000 to TDCC to facilitate the initiation of our plan (to develop transaction standards). As I recall, the contract required us to complete the work by April 1975. In January 1975, I decided that we needed additional technically qualified personnel to ensure that we could complete the task on time. With the above as background and the following as quantification, you will understand why I was able to decide in fifteen minutes that Ralph Notto fit the need like a glove.

Education and Experience: The first qualifying characteristic was Ralph's background. His bachelor's in mathematics (University of Minnesota), master's in business administration (Mount St. Mary's College), and further graduate work at the University of Minnesota in mathematics and statistics provided an ideal foundation for the work we had to perform. His broad experience in industry (plus a 'hitch' in the Marines), which covered almost every field of endeavor in digital systems, gave us a breadth of know-how that proved invaluable to our mission. He had designed major mainframe software systems, had significant experience in smaller systems, and had designed and implemented a transportation and communications network for on-line freight bill generation and collection.

Creating the Big Picture: An additional item was Ralph's experience and a preference that established a capstone for a successful, long-term technical and business relationship. A major factor in our planning strategy was to ensure that the standards would be *open-ended.* We were fundamentally going to attack the entire interface requirement under a single concept. We were determined not to address the problem in a piecemeal fashion–i.e., rail standards, followed by motor carrier standards, etc. Additionally, we felt that a set of standards to satisfy only the four transportation modes would be inadequate, since the serially oriented trade transaction information exchange environment effectively begins with the purchase order and ends with payment—not only for transportation services, but for goods and other attendant services as well. We had a strategy. It was Ralph who was most adept at converting concept to reality in terms of systems. This ability proved to be invaluable during the formulative stages of our work in developing the EDI *system.*

Defining a New Language: During the definition stage, TDCC formed 'work groups' through which we obtained direct member company participation. We separated the modes of transportation into shipper/carrier groups, i.e., Shipper/Motor, Shipper/Rail, Shipper/Forwarder/Ocean

... this organizational concept provided several advantages. It enabled us to focus on the needs of the differing characteristics, traditions, practices, and general operating and tariff policies associated with the services of the individual modal industries (domestic and international). It avoided the competitive tendencies, particularly between motor and rail, which we felt could detract from the primary objective of defining a single standard. Most importantly, this organizational concept enabled the TDCC technical staff to work towards common concepts in syntax, control, and convention while meeting the operational needs of the individual modes and, at the same time, encompassing the essence of the overall transportation industry. In short, we were designing the 'universal' packing crate for shipping data to discrete destinations.

The TDCC technical staff believed that the communication of digital data would free business from the constraints of paper-based information systems, in which space and time played a very large role in such decisions as the kind, amount, and size of data to be communicated. We believed that communicated transactions should provide sufficient processable information to enable the receiver to accurately and completely perform the requested service or action. We began to think about new terms of reference to broaden the flexibility and scope of user thought processes to facilitate enhanced requirements definition.

Ralph, following his natural inclination to always search for solutions, approached us with a proposal to develop a new *language* to define the standards. He proposed that, since we were addressing business transactions and sets of data defining the transaction requirement, we should call the messages we planned to develop *transaction sets.* He further recommended that we refer to a line of information in a transaction set as a *data segment*[86] within a transaction. Such data segments would be discretely identifiable and contain functionally related groups of data elements. Experience had shown that our users tended to think of the word *line* as a line on Teletype printouts or on paper forms. We decided to adopt his recommendations.

Further discussions during the meeting resulted in a decision to support a functional group concept wherein several functionally separate groups of transaction sets could be communicated in a single *batch* during a single communications session.

Scope of the Single Standard Concept: Two fundamental perspectives on EDI have evolved over the years. One perspective places primary focus on the systemic features of EDI as the *heart* of the EDI standards.

[86]With reference to EDI data structures, the term "segment" was first introduced by John Nelson.

According to this perspective, the data element content in any given transaction set reflects the user or operating requirement and is secondary in importance in terms of whether a standard exists. Any subject can be addressed by the content, but without a stable systemic environment to transport the operational data, there can be no standard.

The second perspective places primary and almost absolute priority on content, leaving the control, syntax, and convention characteristics as primarily a matter of software organization. The systemic features definitely become secondary in this case.

The TDCC technical personnel concentrated on the systemic features, which they considered essential for the development of a single standard. They depended on and worked with the user groups to get agreement on content. The user groups decided what subjects to address and participated in the definition of the data content. The technical personnel organized those requirements to fit into the systemic bounds of the standards.

Any of the TDCC personnel will, even today [1991], provide convincing argument that there is a single EDI standard that essentially encompasses the transaction sets developed by TDCC and by the grocery and warehouse industries, as well as those developed under the aegis of ANSI ASC X12. The baseline systemic features are the same in all examples.

"One of the people most responsible for the development of the TDCC perspective on what constitutes an EDI standard was Ralph Notto.

Designing for Maximum Flexibility: The key to designing for the future was centered on maximum flexibility, but with a strong emphasis on avoiding ambiguity in the organization of the standards format, which would serve as the transport mechanism for transaction data (this emphasis on avoiding ambiguity in definition was also to apply to transaction data content). The flexibility objective was to be achieved through table-driven technology, as opposed to *hard-coded* solutions. It was natural that I should ask Ralph during the employment interview how he felt and what he knew about table technology. I struck a responsive chord. Ralph was a strong believer in table-driven methods and provided quality examples of extensive experience in their use.

Conversion of Concept Objectives to System Capabilities: Ralph demonstrated that he had taken seriously the table technology matter soon after he came on the staff. Draft documentation preparation efforts were *cut-and-paste* affairs demanding seven days per week and daily *wee hours* of effort. Ralph also began developing what is now recalled by some as his *card computer*. He used a card file to store (*remember*) and establish functional relationships between data elements. It was during this period that we (mostly by Ralph in his card computer) began identifying the need for *generic* data elements with related qualifier codes to specify meaning.[87] For example, a single data element called *time* could be qualified with an accompanying data element to define the kind of time being addressed. Example: ETA [estimated time of arrival] is one of many qualifiers for *time*.

It was not long before Ralph approached me with the statement that (paraphrased): 'I can convert [the card file] to a set of computerized tables that will define each transaction set and all of the elements therein.' We had developed a concept that envisioned a set of tables as the core of the standards making it possible for application software (i.e., EDI translator software) to be developed to work with the tables. Similarly, we envisioned that maintenance software could be developed to support a table (standards) maintenance function and, hopefully, we would be able to use the same maintenance software to produce artwork to facilitate standards publications in book form. Ralph developed a maintenance support system, 'Bookgen,'[88] from which TDCC could produce computer hardcopy output simply by entering the name of the desired subject. For example, entering the word 'MOTOR' would result in output that would facilitate the publication of the latest version of the Motor Carrier standards book. The system was also used to maintain control over the change process.

While the above does not sound unusual in today's technological environment, nothing of the kind existed in 1975. Therefore, I feel secure in stating that Ralph created new and important technology that has left a lasting imprint in the EDI field.

Expansion to the Buyer/Seller Level: In 1979, the grocery and warehouse industries independently approached TDCC with proposals to adopt TDCC standards as their respective industry standards. Each contracted with TDCC for assistance in the development of their respective group of transaction sets. Ralph was assigned the responsibility to assist both industries. He therefore played a significant role in enabling the grocery industry to become the first major industry-wide buyer/seller effort to convert to EDI.

The Perennial Entrepreneur: There are two kinds of people: those who *work for a living* and those who *live to work*. I consider Ralph to be in the latter category. The *live to workers* are always searching for new things to do or for new environments that they can create and within which they can be

[87] It must be noted that Buddy Bass (page 297) and Ralph Notto shared an office at TDCC.

[88] "Bookgen" was done with Susan Reamer (page 250). Some years later when microcomputers were available, Susan enhanced this software to run on a Victor computer at TDCC.

productive. They give unselfishly of their time and talent in support of new challenges.

Such people are superb taskmasters. When given a goal and a target requirement, they always deliver completely and on time. They are meticulous in defining and interpreting requirements, and approach their work in a highly organized and disciplined manner. They maintain a calm and confident demeanor, and are always constructive in their relations with other people. Many people in this category are natural entrepreneurs. Ralph Notto is a true entrepreneur, and was at TDCC and is today [1991] a prime mover in this new industry, technology, and methodology called EDI.

Robert R. Notto

> **FTP:** File Transfer Protocol (Used for file transfers via the Internet)
>
> **SMTP:** Simple Message Transfer Protocol (Used in Internet email)

In 1984, when companies were just beginning to buy off-the-shelf EDI software, Bob Notto joined the software team at EDI Inc., and quickly learned the table-driven concept that was the technological basis for the company's products. In a very short time, he wrote computer programs that automatically created test data in two variations for all transaction sets. The variations included: a) minimal data required per transaction, and b) expanded transaction. From that, he created a job stream that tested the company's product for all variations. This job required several hours to do all of the tests and report any discrepancies. The result insured that his company's products completely complied with EDI standards for all transactions sets.

In 1991, he founded Notto Corporation, dedicated to EDI consulting. Besides specific assignments for his clients, he was also co-designer with Ralph Notto, Gregg Zuberbier, and Susan Reamer of *System*.EDI which introduced practical concepts like "Transaction Log," a wizard for creating Internet FTP and SMTP data communications interfaces for EDI transmissions, and a relational scheme for accommodating user preferences and trading partner variations.

In 2000, Bob joined the Kodiak Group as a consultant.

Lee Pittman

Lee Pittman of Future Three Software and an active member of the Automotive Industry Action Group (AIAG) has been a frequent writer for *EDI Forum*. His work and writings explain how "Evaluated Receipts

Settlement" has eliminated the need for invoices at major companies and industries.

Lee wrote,[89] "Evaluated receipt settlement, or ERS, is not just another acronym on the information highway. ERS provides a new paradigm in conducting business between buyer and seller. It may be integrated into business applications by using electronic data interchange, which lets new business practices emerge from that source.

> By adopting ERS, the potential savings may be substantial for both customer and supplier. The method also gives both a decisive advantage in the increasingly competitive business climate. ERS is defined as the process of using pricing and receiving information to eliminate invoices—both paper and electronic.
>
> The first thought that usually comes to mind for many people is: 'Are you crazy? There is no way the invoice can be eliminated! We need the invoice to pay our bills!' True, invoices have been needed to transact business. But no longer.

Lee's writings explain both the concept and results. For example, "ERS adoption has provided a look at how the customer's receiving person and the seller's shipping department rather than accounting department decide what the supplier will be paid."

Donald C. Reamer

Don Reamer joined EDI Inc. in 1984, and teamed with Susan Reamer to write software that enabled the company to automatically manage the tables used to define the EDI standards. This software processed electronic copies of the tables used to define the TDCC, UCS, WINS, and X12 standards to create a set of "logic" tables that the company used to drive its EDI software product, Telink. The tables were accurate with respect to the standards and addressed issues like Telink processing speed and maintenance. A by-product of this work was automatic creation of part of the Telink user documentation.

Another of Don Reamer's innovations was to build into the Telink software the capability to automatically create a trading partner profile record if one did not exist for an incoming transaction. This function is similar to

[89] Lee Pittman, "Eliminating the Invoice: A look at Evaluated Receipts Settlement," *EDI Forum*, Volume 11, No. 3, pages 82-88,The EDI Group, 1998.

adding a record to an email system's address book if one does not exist. Don's adaptation of this function in 1991 preceded (Internet) email's adoption by U.S. industry. The function permits accurate recording of the details required for identifying the source of EDI data and for manual addition of other information into the trading partner record.

Since 1984, Don Reamer has managed all facets of EDI product development—design, EDI software, data communications (via value added networks, point-to-point linkage, and the Internet in multiple types of transmission environments), data mapping, quality assurance, user technical support, and documentation

Prior to his introduction to EDI, Dr. Reamer was a research chemist. His research skills—insight into cause and effect, attention to detail, focus on objectives, documentation, sharing findings with peers—were successfully migrated to EDI environments.

Susan M. Reamer

Susan Reamer has been an independent EDI consultant since 1982. She designed and wrote the program BOOKGEN used at TDCC to construct and print EDI standards manuals with industry orientations. This was dramatic, since with only a few minutes at a computer terminal, an operator could specify a new industry EDI manual and print it, knowing that it was fully compatible with the TDCC, X12, and UCS standards.

At EDI Inc., she specialized in writing software used to manage the EDI standards data, facilitating timely conversion to new standards releases with utmost accuracy. At Ralph Notto and Associates, she wrote many of the programs used in a database-driven EDI software product, *System*.EDI. She has also been a consultant to EDI Integration Corporation and Artel.

Roy G. Saltman

Adapted from EDI Forum, 1993 Issue No. 4, pages 62-63.

> Roy Saltman, as a computer scientist at the National Institute of Standards and Technology (NIST), was involved with EDI since the early 1980s. At that time, NIST was called the National Bureau of Standards (NBS), and Saltman was the manager of the federal government's data element standards program. NBS management chose Roy to follow the progress of the ANSI X12 Committee as it standardized data elements for EDI.

By 1984, he was named administrator for the U.S. group participating in the International Organization for Standardization (ISO) Technical Committee (TC) 154. EDIFACT had not yet come into existence, and TC 154 was in the process of adopting as an international standard the European-developed Trade Data Interchange system. In 1984, Roy attended meetings in Geneva of the TC 154 committee and the related UN working group, and influential Europeans who wanted a truly international EDI system that would include the U.S. approached him. They requested, and Roy agreed, that the United States should host the next plenary meeting of TC 154 at NBS headquarters in Gaithersburg, Maryland. Saltman made the arrangements. Americans and Europeans wanting to start a universal EDI system were invited to attend.

The meeting of TC 154 at NBS was held in May 1985. At the delegates' dinner, Americans including Tony D'Anna of AT&T and Dennis McGinnis of North American Phillips met Europeans including Ray Walker of the U.K. and Etienne Dreyfous of France. They agreed to begin the Joint Electronic Data Interchange Working Group, or JEDI [not the same JEDI reported in chapter two]. (The movie, *Return of the Jedi,* was popular at the time.) The deliberations of the JEDI group hammered out the basic concepts of what became known as EDIFACT.

In the same period, Roy was making presentations on the advantages of EDI to influential groups in the federal government. These groups included the Departments of Defense and Treasury, and the General Services Administration. By 1988, Roy arranged for NBS to sponsor the first government-wide conference on EDI, and he began to consider a Federal Information Processing Standard (FIPS) on EDI. He developed the FIPS, and the Secretary of Commerce approved it in 1991. It requires government agencies to use the X12 standards for domestic interchanges and either the XI 2 or EDIFACT standards for international commerce.

Roy said that the benefit of the FIPS is that it has forced federal agencies to work with industry groups to adopt standard X12 formats for EDI rather than to unilaterally issue proprietary formats that would be more costly for everyone."

Fred Sauers

Adapted from EDI Forum, 1993 Issue No. 4, page 63.

For many, EDI revolves around the work of standards development and standards implementation. Justifiable praise goes to those early pioneers who brought us the standards we use today. However, there were other EDI pioneers who exhibited the same zeal for the technology, but who worked independent of the standards-setters.

Fred Sauers was one of those pioneers at Sears, Roebuck and Co. Starting as early as 1970, Fred fostered a proprietary network known as SENDEN. Fred did not develop the network's technical capabilities; instead, he was SENDEN's business proponent, shepherd, and evangelist. Sears initially built a network that was to be used only internally, so that retail stores could 'teletype' customer catalog orders to regional distribution centers. This network significantly improved customer service because it eliminated mail time and the errors caused by handwriting orders at stores and reading and keyboarding those orders when they arrived at the distribution centers. It was not too great a leap for someone to recognize that these same benefits could be shared with Sears's vendors. That was the genesis of SENDEN.

Fred was chosen for coordinating implementations with vendors.

Fred's method was always to get a full understanding of the business issues before tackling the technical issues. Once the [Sears] buyer made contacts with the appropriate people at the vendor, Fred then shielded the buyer from any of the technical issues that had to be settled. As the process progressed, it was common for Fred to come to understand the details of processing at the vendor better than the Sears buyer did.

The proprietary networks set the stage for the EDI we know today. At Sears, SENDEN opened electronic pathways into and out of computer applications. Today's EDI uses the same pathways. The proprietary networks also made business cultures begin to appreciate the fact that maybe there was a better way of doing business than shuffling paper. Pioneers like Fred chipped away at the old cultures without the benefit of national organizations, trade magazines, or press coverage.

When EDI industry standards became available, Fred Sauers embraced them with the same enthusiasm as he had embraced SENDEN. Fred's support and leadership laid the foundation for the current success of the EDI program at the Sears Merchandise Group.

Marshall Spence

Adapted from EDI Forum, 1990 Issue, page 76, author Gordon Jenkins.

I first met Marshall Spence three years ago when I was on an executive exchange from the federal government to a large Canadian bank. The bank had just discovered that they had to get serious about EDI; one of their first steps was to send me to meet a Marshall Spence, who was president of an association dealing with EDI.

Little did I realize that Marshall not only was president of the EDI Council of Canada (as he had already been for the five years of its existence by 1990), but also knew everyone and everything that was going on in EDI in Canada, no matter what sector or industry. Marshall's name is truly synonymous with EDI in Canada.

Marshall never stops, and if he does, it is to talk about EDI. He is not just converted to EDI; he is convinced EDI is the answer to Canadian governmental and business problems.

Marshall, however, has not just kept to *Canadian* EDI, no sir! He has been instrumental in starting EDI councils everywhere, from Australia and New Zealand to Europe. He has spoken from Yugoslavia to Scandinavia to Singapore. He was one of the keynote speakers in autumn 1990 at the EDI Asia conference in Hong Kong.

Prior to joining the EDI Council, Marshall spent eleven years with Nestle Enterprises Inc. in various senior managerial positions. Before joining Nestle, he worked for Dow Chemical for nine years, where he was responsible for their Management Information Business Systems. Marshall began his career in business systems with Chrysler.

Marshall has always been involved with systems and international organizations. In 1985, when the initial EDI pilot in Canada was completed for the food, pharmaceutical, and retail industries, the eight major sponsoring trade associations convened a one-day conference to inform Canadian industry leaders of the benefits derived from the pilot companies' use of EDI. The most optimistic projections were that, at most, about 100 people would attend; as it turned out, over 700 attended, and from this historic meeting on January 28, 1985, began not only the EDI Council of Canada, but also Canadian EDI in general.

After this meeting Marshall's EDI Council of Canada had fewer than twenty members, but membership began to grow at the rate of one or two per working day. Over the first five years this rate did not leveled off—memberships from corporations and individuals kept rolling in. By 1990, the EDI Council had over 700 members across Canada, due in no small measure to the missionary zeal of Marshall.

Marshall's energy, organizing ability, and enthusiasm are contagious! For example, he was a driving force in setting up the first International Congress of EDI Users in Vancouver in July 1989, where sixteen countries were represented from as far away as Korea and Italy. It was a tremendous success and was followed by the Second International Congress of EDI Users in San Francisco in July 1990. Without Marshall's drive and enthusiasm there probably would not have been a first congress!

In December 1988, Marshall spoke at the first Canadian Federal Government EDI Users Group. This group of government users has grown from eight federal departments and twenty-six people to more than eighty people and twenty-eight federal departments, agencies, and provinces. Without Marshall and the EDI Council of Canada's support, this Federal Government EDI User Group would have had difficulty getting off the ground. This is not an isolated case: Marshall has provided support, counsel, coordination, and enthusiasm for the EDI efforts of countless other industries, such as grocery, electronics, chemical, petroleum, banking, and transportation, to name but a few.

I have never seen Marshall refuse any opportunity to talk about EDI and its benefits: no company is too small, no distance too great. He has spoken not just in Canada to various Canadian users of EDI, but by demand, in other countries of what he calls the *EDI Village.*

Just recently [in 1990], for instance, Marshall returned from Europe, where he spoke in no less than five countries. He was a key driving force behind the establishment of the proposed International EDI Institute.

To keep up with Marshall is an effort, because he is speaking in Victoria, BC one day and Washington, DC the next, then flying home to Toronto to consolidate and coordinate Canadian EDI before he is off again.

Mr. Marshall Spence is truly 'Mr. EDI of Canada.' His enthusiasm and drive helped make Canada an international leader in EDI. He is an EDI pioneer.

Harold Stein

Harold Stein

After thirty years in public education as a teacher of mathematics and science and a junior/senior high school administrator, Hal Stein chose a new career path as the director of training when he joined the staff of EDI, Inc., an EDI software company. Using his education and management skills and experiences, he designed the curriculum and successfully trained users to skillfully use all of the functionality of an EDI system and in various ways to relate EDI to current processes and procedures in their companies.

Hal and Buddy Bass spent many hours at EDI, Inc. discussing the background of EDI standards development, both in its structure and implementation. A major topic discussed with Buddy and Ralph Notto was the future of electronic business.

Soon after his hire, Hal produced a curriculum designed to teach the application and the EDI standards. The original program included TDCC and X12 standards. A second course was designed for training in EDI standards.

Hal trained several hundred people in EDI and electronic business, people from companies, government, and universities such as: AT&T, Bank of Montreal, Bell Canada, Burlington Northern, EDI Group, Fannie Mae, Kia Motors, Martin Marietta, Oracle, SeaLand, U.S. Department of Defense, UNISYS, and the University of Dayton.

Hal Stein in his classroom with Hak Jung Lee, Young-Kook Kim, and Soo Hong Noh of the Data Communications Corporation of Korea

Hal left EDI, Inc. (then named Telink systems Inc.) in 1995, taking his EDI skills to Corporate Data Systems Inc. (CDSI), a government contractor with the U.S. Department of Labor. His first task there was to design a new transaction set that was to be used by federal agencies and their civilian contractors to obtain federal wages for multiple contracting services. The transaction set, 288 (Wage Determination), was introduced to X12 through the government subcommittee and was approved for publication in 1995 in version 003060. Hal received the 1997 Leadership Award from CDSI for his work in this task.

He received a second award related to Worker's Compensation Programs, where he created a data map from the 3a-pharmacy record, satisfying all federal requirements to move from paper-intensive processes to EDI. This allowed hundreds of national pharmacies and pharmacy chains to now use EDI to submit workers' compensation invoices to the U.S. Department of Labor for rapid and accurate payment.

Hal worked on the task group designing the transaction set 148 (Report of Injury, Illness, or Incident) introducing the requirements for federal workers' compensation incident reporting into the EDI standards.

His implementation conventions for 148 were submitted to almost all Federal agencies.

Hal received the "Hammer Award" for his role in the development of the EDI application for the U.S. Department of Transportation. The Hammer Award was created by Vice President Al Gore and is presented through the "National Partnership for Reinventing Government."

Gunnar Sundblad

Adapted from EDI Forum, 1989 Issue, page 92, author Henk van Maaren.

Twice a year, in March and September, the Working Party Four of the United Nations Economic Commission for Europe meets in Geneva, Switzerland. The Working Party Four is the organization where all developments of UN/EDIFACT undergo final scrutiny. The rapporteurs' report is to this body of roughly one hundred experts and, although it is not a custom to deviate from their recommendations, the verification process is taken quite seriously.

The name of this body is slightly misleading. the Economic Commission for Europe was established in the years after World War II as a platform to discuss issues of relevance for the revival of the European economies. All European countries, West and East, as well as the United States and Canada, are full members. A number of other countries, the Commission of the European Communities, and international trade organizations are observers. Nonetheless, many in the U.S. apparently feel that EDIFACT is too much a European standard, perhaps because of the name UN/ECE and the meeting place in Geneva.

In any event, it is fair to say that a small number of persons are veterans in this environment: they have been involved in the early developments of the UN/Layout key, the Trade Data Elements Directory, GTDI (the Guidelines for Trade Data Interchange) and later, UN/EDIFACT. Of them, Gunnar Sundblad of Stockholm, Sweden, is one of the most prominent.

During these meetings, Sundblad would switch regularly between the microphones of the Swedish delegation and the ISO organization. At some meetings, in fact, the number and variety of issues that Sundblad contributed to the discussions was so great that he could not manage to 'change seats' fast enough. He would then simply remain seated where he last was, ask for the floor, and start with, 'I am now speaking on behalf of ...'

In those days, Gunnar Sundblad was active both for the Swedish Standards Institute and for SWEPRO (the Swedish Trade Facilitation Organization). His activities span a wide range of standardization issues in information technologies, which explains his broad view and knowledge of many issues. He has played a major role in the DEDIST development in the early eighties, whereby the Nordic countries (Denmark, Finland, Norway, and Sweden) designed standard messages.

Despite his formal retirement from the Swedish Standards Institute, Sundblad has not slowed down. As chairman of the MAG (Maintenance Group) of the Western European EDIFACT Board—as well as other positions held for UN/EDIFACT—he seems to be even more involved in EDI than ever before. With his knowledge of the details of international EDI standards developments, Sundblad is the ideal person for the position on the EDIFACT Board."

Dave Torma

Adapted from EDI Forum, 1989 Issue, page 93, author Paul Olson.

Dave Torma of the 3M Company pioneered early ANSI X12 EDI standards. His commitment to excellence, patient arbiter style, and long-standing role on various subcommittees helped forge business and technical standards in two key areas: communications and controls. Technicians' contributions to business solutions are often trivialized and go unappreciated, but no one is more deserving of credit for the success of practical, workable EDI solutions than Dave Torma.

'It takes a certain person to function in standards committees,' said Ed Fischer, director of data and product support at 3M. Fischer requested Torma's assistance in exploring communications issues to support the physical interchange of business documents prescribed by the ANSI X12 organization. Fischer said that Dave is not a combative-type person, is very logical, does not get on emotional highs, and has a very good technical background and coordinating skills as well.

As a major supplier to firms in many industries and markets, 3M faced the challenge of supporting multiple proprietary EDI systems. Non-standard EDI solutions are expensive and difficult to manage. In 1981, Fischer enlisted the support of both Torma and Hal McDonald of 3M for the ANSI X12 organization. The goal was to develop national, generic standards designed to work across multiple industries.

Besides fostering a solid technical foundation for standards, Torma contributed to the development of a fair and equitable set of procedures designed to facilitate the development, review, revision, and approval of standards. He was, in Fischer's words, very instrumental in certain structural aspects of how the X12 committee was to operate.

Anthony A. Vallario

Adapted from EDI Forum, 1989 Issue, page 94, author Bill Plumb.

When innovators of technological achievements in the wholesale drug industry are mentioned, invariably the name Anthony 'Tony' A. Vallario is cited again and again. During his forty-year tenure as a data processing executive, Tony led his team of professionals at Bergen Brunswig Corporation and at the National Wholesale Druggist Association to the forefront of EDI technology. His work in this field has dramatically affected the manner in which companies in the healthcare industry do business every day.

Tony, often characterized as the 'Father of Data Processing' in the wholesale drug industry, began his career in December 1949 when he joined the Bergen Drug Company of Hackensack, New Jersey. Bergen merged with Brunswig Drug Company in 1969, forming the Bergen Brunswig Corporation. Following the merger in 1969, Tony accepted the position of vice president of corporate information resources and transferred to BBC corporate headquarters in California.

The EDI story began soon after his move when, in 1970, Tony founded the Business Systems Committee for the National Wholesale Druggist Association (NWDA). This committee of data processing professionals was the driving force behind the advance of EDI technology within the healthcare industry. As chair of the Business Systems Committee, Tony and his fellow committee members—including Richard Cook of NWDA, one of last year's EDI pioneers—conceived, developed, designed, and implemented a system of order entry that revolutionized purchasing and inventory control in the healthcare industry.

In 1971 Bergen Brunswig's initial ventures in electronic order entry were from its Clifton, New Jersey data center to its largest supplier, Eli Lilly in Indianapolis, Indiana. Bergen transmitted punched cards that used the National Drug Code numbering system to indicate the items and quantity to be ordered. The data represented in these cards was transferred electronically via dialup telephone lines to Eli Lilly's computer, which then produced a duplicate set of cards. Although it may seem primitive now, this procedure for electronic ordering was the predecessor for what has come to be known as EDI.

The next step in the evolution of electronic data interchange in the wholesale drug industry was taken by Tony Vallario and his data processing team at Bergen Brunswig in 1974 when PHASE, the industry's first automated order entry system, made its debut. In brief, orders were keyed into a hand-held terminal and sent via telephone to Bergen's computer.

In 1975, Tony's department initiated the next service in the advancement of EDI technology—TELEPHASE, a touch-tone voice response system that was designed and implemented in only ninety days. In 1975, even though the PHASE system worked, it was not totally reliable. The goal was to move to solid-state units, but the customers' needs had to be met with an interim solution. Tony's group selected a touch-tone telephone system. This alternative enabled retailers to place orders around the clock using a touch-tone phone and a toll-free number.

While customers were utilizing the TELEPHASE system, the Bergen Brunswig data processing group, together with the Aerospace Division of Singer Corporation, was planning and developing ULTRAPHASE, which enabled retailers to manage inventory and ordering via a portable terminal with an integrated optical reader for scanning Universal Product Codes. All of these innovations allowed Bergen Brunswig to fill orders twice as quickly as the industry average and cut inventory costs.

1982 saw the advent of personal computers as a major player in the development of order entry systems. To accommodate this advance in technology, Bergen Brunswig introduced COMPUPHASE, under Tony Vallario's direction. This innovation in EDI was a local pharmacy microcomputer system with proprietary software. In addition to record-keeping and ordering functions, COMPUPHASE introduced electronic claims transfer, which reduced the payment cycle on third-party prescription plans from the typical ninety days to as little as five days.

In 1986, Tony and his EDI team led the industry in the development and implementation of a system to monitor charge backs. The Bergen Brunswig electronic charge back system captures and reports the sales of hospital customers back to suppliers to obtain necessary funds and credit information.

In 1987, Tony's team further leveraged their EDI strength by sending invoices via EDI. That same year, they began implementing a corporate trade payment program.

Tony Vallario's leadership and commitment to technological advancements in the wholesale drug industry have not gone unnoticed. The August 1989 issue of *CIO Magazine* recognized Tony's achievements by including him in the roster of one hundred leading Chief Information Officers as selected by a leading panel of information technology experts.

In addition to Tony's service and contribution to the NWDA Business Systems Committee, he has worked very closely with the Federal Drug Enforcement Administration. He served in the U.S. Marine Air Corps and attended the Academy of Aeronautics School of Engineering. A graduate of the Executive Program at the UCLA Graduate School of Management, Tony has completed the Corporate Computer Resources Program through the Harvard Business School.

It cannot be denied that Tony Vallario is a true EDI pioneer. He has provided the leadership, commitment, and vision necessary to achieve the goals that made his company and the wholesale drug industry leaders in EDI technology.

Khai Vinh

Perhaps the first operational functional acknowledgment report software was written by Khai Vinh in 1984 for use in EDI Inc.'s early *TELINK* product.

Even with the limitations of PC software at that time, Khai's work included use of data dynamically available from EDI translation and communications software. It provided "on demand" and always current reports of the EDI activity considering transactions sent and received, acknowledgments sent and received, and whether or not acknowledgments were required. The report identified types of transactions by ID code and name, and trading partners by ID code and name. The report reported what was still "open." It included any error statements that may have been reported. In 1984, this capability was extremely significant, since trading partners were previously doing a considerable amount of follow-up work via telephone conversations and handwritten notes.

Prior to 1975, Khai had been chief accountant in a large Vietnamese bank. He has degrees in accounting and computer science.

Ray Walker

Adapted from EDI Forum, 1992 Issue No. 4, page 48]

Ray Walker has for many years advocated paperless trading–the application of EDI to the national and international order processing, distribution, and payment chains. In particular he has been indispensable in the development of the UN/EDIFACT standard. He was also the chief executive of SITPRO (the Simpler Trade Procedures Board), the United Kingdom's trade facilitation body, a government agency sponsored by the Department of Trade and industry.

In 1985, Ray was nominated by the United Nations Economic Commission for Europe (UNIECE) to co-chair the team that went on to create the new international standard for EDI, UN/EDIFACT. Then, he served for five years as the UN/ECE Western European rapporteur for UN/EDIFACT, responsible for coordinating developments in the eighteen countries of the European Community and European Free Trade Association. He worked energetically to promote both EDI and the use of global trade standards.

(See "Ray Walker," pages 65 and 118.)

Tom Warner

Tom Warner was on the EDI*NET "strike force" at MacDonald Douglas when the company began to aggressively market this value added network (VAN) service, which it acquired from Tymshare in 1984. Starting about March 1984, the company added about a hundred new clients to EDI*NET that year. Although MacDonald Douglas is in the aerospace industry, it reached out to all industries when looking for clients for its VAN service. The company contracted with EDI Inc to resell its EDI software, Telink. The combination—EDI*NET and Telink—made it possible to offer clients a quick entry path into the EDI environment.

Tom was a dynamic, but still mild-mannered, force for convincing companies that EDI and EDI*NET was for them. Once the activities started, installation was easy; the service was timely, cost-effective, and reliable.

But in spite of his competitive spirit and his success, Tom offered and forced implementation of a proposal that would greatly benefit the EDI user community. Several competing EDI VAN services had begun service about this same period. Usually, a company new to EDI chose the same VAN service as the "hub" with whom it would first communicate via EDI. As this non-hub company commenced EDI with other hubs, it was likely that each hub would require use of its preferred VAN. Tom thought that a better service would be for the VANs to communicate with each other, making it possible for a small user to be a member of only one VAN and the employment of multi-VAN environments be completely transparent to users. Further, he said that there should be no additional communications charges when this VAN-to-VAN linkage is used. Tom's company, MacDonald Douglas, was a leader in providing this service.

In 1990-91, Tom was a North American representative to the UN/EDIFACT Joint Technical Group, addressing issues relative to the globalization of EDI.

In the late 1990s, he encouraged the move toward adoption of implementation conventions of EDI standards on an industry, rather than hub, basis. He helped develop the convention for use by the aerospace industry.

> **VAN:** Value Added Network [used for transmission of EDI-formatted data]
> **EDI*NET:** The name of the MacDonald Douglas EDI VAN service
> **Hub:** A proactive company in the use of EDI that has a significant number of active EDI trading partners

Tom Warner has repeatedly worked toward making EDI implementation easier, thus helping to increase the size of the worldwide EDI community.

Sylvia Watkins-Castillo

While most other EDI pioneers were concerned with implementing EDI in their companies or creating innovative EDI products and services, the research by Sylvia Watkins-Castillo of the EDI Group was aimed at learning about how companies are using EDI and how the community of people that are in charge of the EDI activities in their companies view their work.

Regarding EDI coordinators, Sylvia reported, "As EDI escorts business into the next century, it is important to understand the role of the EDI/Electronic Commerce coordinator in the marketplace. An annual survey of coordinators, conducted by the EDI Group, Ltd., Oak Park, Illinois, examines their expanding role and what business is demanding of them as EC/EDI becomes more important to the marketplace.[90]

> **EC:** Electronic Commerce

[90] Sylvia Watkins-Castillo, Ph.D., "The 1997 EC/EDI Coordinator Job and Salary Survey," *EDI Forum*, Volume 10, No. 3, pages 18-24,The EDI Group, 1997.

Sylvia wrote:

The 1997 EDI Coordinator Job and Salary Survey is based on more than 1,000 interviews completed in the fall and winter of 1996 by persons responsible for designing, implementing, and managing the EC or EDI programs within their U.S. and Canadian companies. Through the study, a profile of the professional emerged.

The typical EC/EDI coordinator is male, forty-one years old, most likely holds a bachelor's degree in computer science or information systems, and is earning nearly $51,000 per year. He has probably been on this particular job nearly six years and has been working directly in EC for the past five years.

The one in four EC/EDI coordinators who are female are also forty-one years old, with a bachelor's degree and nearly as much experience in EC. However, they make only about 75% of their male counterparts' salary, or just less than $38,000 per year.

EC/EDI coordinators appear to be satisfied with their present job, and enjoying the challenge it presents. Employers' additional recognition of their contribution and the role of EC in the marketplace are making a difference in how coordinators perceive themselves and their jobs.

The EDI Group's research reports are used by both companies that use EDI to improve their processes and procedures and by companies that provide EC/EDI services and products to help in planning for service and product improvement.

Nicole Willenz-Gardner

Adapted from EDI Forum, 1992 Issue No. 4, pages 48-49.

Nicole Willenz-Gardner tirelessly devoted a decade of her young life to advancing the all-important work of establishing EDI standards, both within the United States and internationally.

In 1982 Nicole joined the National Industrial Transportation League and became the director of computer and systems development. From this post she worked with the various EDI standards groups in the transportation communities, including the American Trucking Associations and the Association of American Railroads' EDI standards development groups. Also in 1982 she founded TransComp, one of the first trade shows dedicated to showcasing EDI and computer applications in the transportation and distribution industry.

During the next two years, Nicole participated in the Joint Electronic Data Interchange (JEDI) effort to bring together the standards of the TDCC and the ANSI ASC X12 Committee, and she was asked to serve on the X12 Management Task Force. This task force helped to bring the ASC X12 committee into the future with the creation of a full-time secretariat, the Data Interchange Standards Association (DISA), and helped to modify ASC X12 to respond to its growing membership's needs. Nicole was selected as the first convener of the ASC X12 Transportation Project Team and was instrumental in persuading the transportation community to move closer to the user and industry groups operating under the banner of X12."

Early on, Nicole was involved in the emerging international discussions concerning the development of an internationally accepted EDI syntax. In 1985 the international work began to take shape, and Nicole became a key player in the development of the UN/ EDIFACT syntax. She became vice chair of the ASC X12 International Project Team and, she was part of the first official delegation to the United Nations Economic Commission for Europe's Working Party on International Trade Procedures and Facilitation (Working Party 4). Nicole also became chair of the UN/Joint EDI international transport group and was one of the creators of the International Forwarding and Transport Message Framework.

She participated in missions to New Zealand, Australia, and Singapore to promote UN/EDIFACT.

Nicole subsequently joined Price Waterhouse as a senior manager for EDI consulting and business process transformation."

Benson K. Woo

Adapted from EDI Forum, 1989 Issue, page 95, authors Bernell Stone and Ned Hill.

Men and women of courage and conviction—EDI pioneers, by our definition—often seem to be recognized for their accomplishments long after gray hair has set in; not so with Benson Woo.

Benson Woo was instrumental in implementing Electronic Data Interchange and corporate Electronic Funds Transfer (EFT) concepts at General Motors, which has set the stage for EDI and EFT in the automobile industry as well as for the rest of the major North American companies. Woo entered cash management when General Motors placed him in charge of worldwide banking and U.S. cash management in 1984. At that time, the American banking industry's only success in marketing high-volume corporate EFT was in the area of automatic deposit of payroll. For years, the U.S. banks had been attempting to broaden usage of relatively low-cost electronic payments by replacing paper checks for inter-corporate transactions, such as supplier payments. Still, U.S. corporations steadfastly clung to their paper checks. At best, during 1984, inter-corporate EFT was practiced in only a handful of companies on a highly experimental basis.

A computer systems analyst prior to joining GM in 1979, Woo was neither mystified by EFT technology nor blindly accepting of it. He saw that the existing EFT product to move monies electronically merely electrified the paper check, envelope, and stamp, and that this was unlikely to produce true economic savings for a corporate customer given the additional overhead of computer costs.

At the same time, it was fortunate that Woo happened to work in the auto industry, because the auto makers and their suppliers had, for a few years, been attempting to promote the use of electronic data interchange for purchasing, transportation, logistics, and other materials management activities. In fact, another GM employee, Roger Cadaret, was at the time president of the Automotive Industry Action Group, which was responsible for this effort. The AIAG had estimated that up to $200 per car in headcount and overhead costs could be saved if the complete EDI cycle were to be employed in the U.S. auto industry. Woo quickly saw the connection (or lack of connection) between electronic supplier payments and the rest of the repetitive order/billing/payment cycle.

In April, 1985, at the annual conference of the National Automated Clearing House Association, a banking EFT trade group, and later that same year in an article he wrote for the *Journal of Cash Management,* Woo helped introduce the financial community to the concept of electronic data interchange and explained why EFT without EDI on a stand-alone basis was uneconomical. Moreover, in those presentations he argued that promotion by the banking industry of inter-corporate electronic payments using a unique communications format incompatible with ANSI X12 standards, commonly used for electronic data interchange, inhibited potential cost savings.

Woo's solution for EFT also provided for greater security measures than paper checks in order to reduce computer payment fraud. He insisted on a combination of both manual procedural controls and technical encryption and computer authentication of electronic payment orders. Woo felt that one of the most important reasons U.S. companies had not embraced EFT was the unstated but real concern over the lack of security in financial EDI and corporate EFT. GM lawyers, auditors, and financial control staff agreed with him.

General Motors subsequently became the first major American corporation to use electronic payments on a production basis for the majority of its supplier accounts payables. Using a system supported by Electronic Data Systems (EDS), GM worked with the First National Bank of Chicago to lead a bank syndicate (composed of Chase Manhattan, National Bank of Detroit, Pittsburgh National, Citibank, Manufacturers-Detroit, Chemical, and Bank of America) in advancing a customer-driven, state-of-the-art corporate EFT system embracing EDI principles and tight security. Today, GM makes over $10 billion worth of payments per year electronically, and that number should grow in the years ahead.

Woo then received two promotions at GM. He first left his New York-based banking director job to become treasurer of a GM/Suzuki joint venture in Canada. In 1988, Woo left Canada to become treasurer of GM do Brasil, a General Motors' subsidiary with annual sales of U.S. $2.2 billion.

Benson Woo received his undergraduate degree from the Massachusetts Institute of Technology and his MBA from Harvard; his EDI Pioneer Award is made for the insight and courage he showed in creating a new solution for the use of EFT via EDI."

Appendix II

COMPANIES AND ORGANIZATIONS, 1975

The following companies were represented at the TDCC 1975 work group meetings:

Air Transport Association of America	IBM World Trade Corporation
American Airlines, Inc.	Instant Management, Inc.
American Bankers Association	International Minerals and Chemical Corp.
American Commercial Barge Line Company	ITEL Corporation
American Trucking Associations, Inc.	Lever Brothers Company
Association of American Railroads	Lykes Bros. Steamship Co., Inc.
Atlantic Container Line, Ltd.	Maritime Administration
Bethlehem Steel Corporation	Martin Marietta Aluminum
Boeing Computer Services, Inc.	McDonnell Douglas Automation Company
Boston and Maine Corporation	McLean Trucking Company
Branch Motor Express Company	Missouri Pacific Railroad Company
Cass Bank & Trust Company	National Motor Freight Traffic Association, Inc.
Chemical Leaman Tank Lines, Inc.	Norfolk and Western Railway Company
Chessie System	Penn Central Transportation Company
Combustion Engineering, Inc.	Phillips Petroleum Company
ComTrac, Inc.	PPG Industries, Inc.
Continental Can Company, Inc.	Republic Steel Corporation
Dart Containerline Incorporated	Schenkers International Forwarders, Inc.
Delta Air Lines, Inc.	SCL/L&N Railroads
Department of Transportation	Scott Paper Company
Diamond Shamrock Chemical Company	Sea-Land Service, Inc.
Distribution Sciences, Inc.	Sears, Roebuck and Co.
Dow Chemical International	Smith's Transfer Corporation
Dow Chemical U.S.A.	Southern Railway System
E.I. du Pont de Nemours & Company	Spector Freight System, Inc.
Eastern Express, Inc.	St. Johnsbury Trucking Company
Emery Air Freight Corporation	Standard Oil Company (Indiana)
Exxon Company, U.S.A.	Telenet Communications, Inc.
Ford Motor Company	The Atchison, Topeka, & Santa Fe Railway Co.
General Electric Company	The Chase Manhattan Bank, N.A.
General Foods Corporation	The Equitable Trust Bank
General Mills, Inc.	The First National Bank of Boston
General Motors Corporation	The Flying Tiger Line Inc.
General Motors Overseas Operations	Union Carbide Corporation
General Services Administration	Union Pacific Railroad
Grand Trunk Western Railroad Company	United States Lines, Inc.
Harper Robinson & Co.	United States Steel Corporation
Hemingway Transport, Inc.	Western Electric Company, Inc.

PARTICIPANTS IN PLANNING AND WORK GROUPS, 1975

The following lists indicate the diversity of companies and job positions represented during the creation of the 1975 EDI standards.[91] The companies are listed on page 264.

TDCC Advanced Systems Planning GroupLucien

H. Bliss, *Manager, Corporate Documentation*, United States Lines, Inc.

Clifford R. Buys, ***Director of Management Systems***, American Trucking Associations, Inc.

Edward C. Christ, ***Assistant Director, Market Research***, Penn Central Transportation Co.

Anthony J. D'Anna, ***Consultant***, Western Electric Co., Inc.

Donald E. Johnston, ***Director of Direct Access Operating Systems, Engineering & Operations Analysis Division***, Phillips Petroleum Co.

Howard W. McKenna, ***Manager, Information Systems***, General Motors Corp.

William F. McKenna, ***Manager, Systems Department, Transportation and Traffic Office***, Ford Motor Co.

Gary F. Paler, ***Vice President, Management Information Systems***, Spector Freight System, Inc.

Robert A. Petrash, ***Executive Director, Data Systems Division***, Association of American Railroads

James W. Woods, ***Manager, Traffic Systems, Information Systems Department***, The Atchison, Topeka, and Santa Fe Railway Co.

TDCC Shipper/Rail Carrier Work Group

James A. Bailey, ***Vice President, Management Systems***, Association of American Railroads

J. M. Bailey, ***Director, Customer Accounting***, Chessie System

Thomas L. Baldwin, ***Manager, Traffic Systems, Distribution Department***, Dow Chemical U.S.A.

---

[91] Also, refer to <Figure 1. TDCC Project Coordination Structure," page 5.

Charles R. Barton, *Data Coordinator*, Exxon Co., U.S.A.

D. L. Berry, *Superintendent Stations*, The Atchison, Topeka and Santa Fe Railway Co.

J. Neville Black, *Assistant to Vice President, Management Information Services*, Southern Railway System

T. E. Briers, *Assistant Director, Data Systems*, Chessie System

David H. Builland, *Transportation Industry Manager*, Boeing Computer Services, Inc.

Arthur E. Burbage, *Project Manager Stations, Systems Development Department*, Penn Central Transportation Co.

George E. Campbell, *Administrative Transportation Manager, Transportation Division*, Scott Paper Co.

Charles J. Celusnak, *Project Coordinator, Traffic Parts Division*, General Motors Corp.

George D. Coleman, *Manager, Routes and Divisions*, Southern Railway System

Geoffrey A. Cooper, *Transportation Analyst*, Bethlehem Steel Corp.

Gary F. Fox, *Systems Analyst*, Bethlehem Steel Corp.

Philip Fruchter, Continental Can Co., Inc.

Michael J. Greco, *Project Manager, Transportation Systems*, General Foods Corp.

Ronald F. Heemann, *General Traffic Manager*, Martin Marietta Aluminum

S. Terrell Hull, *Manager, Business Systems*, SCL/L&N Railroads

F. A. Hyland, *Deputy Comptroller*, Boston and Maine Corp.

Donald E. Johnston, *Director of Direct Access Operating Systems, Engineering and Operations Analysis Division*, Phillips Petroleum Co.

Donald E. LePard, *Systems Specialist Corporate Transportation*, Combustion Engineering, Inc.

Raymond R. Mask, *Auditor of Station Accounts, Accounting Department*, Norfolk and Western Railway Co.

Thomas O. McConnell, *Director, Customer and Car Accounting*, Southern Railway System

R. L. McKee, *Manager Agency Operations*, Union Pacific Railroad

William F. McKenna, *Manager, Systems Department, Transportation and Traffic Office*, Ford Motor Co.

John Nelsen, *Systems Consultant, Transportation Control Systems, Information and Control, Systems Department*, Missouri Pacific Railroad Co.

Ron Othick, *Manager, Agricultural Systems*, International Minerals & Chemical Corp.

Robert T. Patterson, *Manager, Stations and Car, Records Department*, Chessie System

Gerry Pauls, *Program Manager*, Boeing Computer Services, Inc.

Robert A. Petrash, *Executive Director, Data Systems Division*, Association of American Railroads

Bruce A. Rick, *Systems Analyst*, Diamond Shamrock Chemical Co.

Joseph E. Riley, *Systems Analyst*, Standard Oil Co. (Indiana)

Virgil Ronsberg, *Manager, Transportation Information Systems*, General Mills, Inc.

J. L. Ryan, *Superintendent Stations*, Penn Central Transportation Co.

J. M. Schellenberg, *Transportation Programmer*, Bethlehem Steel Corp.

Roger H. Simonsen, *Industry Development Manager*, Boeing Computer Services, Inc.

J. M. Tomme, *Assistant to Auditor of Revenues*, Atchison, Topeka, and Santa Fe Railway

Richard Warren, Lever Brothers Co.

Barry Wessler, *Director of Sales*, Telenet Communications, Inc.

Thomas Wisecup, *Distribution Analyst, Chemicals and Plastics*, Union Carbide Corp.

James W. Woods, *Manager, Traffic Systems, Information Systems Department*, Atchison, Topeka, and Santa Fe Railway Co.

TDCC Shipper/Motor Carrier Work Group

G. V. Alles, ***Systems Analyst, Industrial Chemicals Department***, E. I. du Pont de Nemours & Co.

Douglas D. Anderson, ***Associate Director, Payments System Planning Division, Research and Planning Group***, American Bankers Association

Robert S. Aronson, ***President***, ComTrac, Inc.

Eugene G. Banchansky, ***Assistant Traffic Manager Glass***, PPG Industries, Inc.

Gene Brock, ***Vice President***, Cass Bank & Trust Co.

David L. Brown, ***Director of Information Systems***, St. Johnsbury Trucking Co.

Fred J. Burke, ***Consulting Engineer***, Consultant to American Trucking Association, Inc.

Clifford R. Buys, ***Director of Management Systems***, American Trucking Associations, Inc.

Gordon J. Coleman, ***Operations Officer***, Equitable Trust Bank

Geoffrey A. Cooper, ***Transportation Analyst***, Bethlehem Steel Corp.

Anthony J. D'Anna, ***Consultant***, Western Electric Co., Inc.

Jerome L. Dempsey, ***Vice President and Director of Marketing***, Cass Bank & Trust Co.

Michael D. Doering, ***Manager, Online Computer Systems***, Smith's Transfer Corp.

Emile Caman Dona, ***Manager, Data Processing Systems***, Hemingway Transport, Inc.

Joseph F. Egan, ***Manager, Computer Systems***, Corporate Distribution Department, Union Carbide Corp.

Gary F. Fox, ***Systems Analyst***, Bethlehem Steel Corp.

Thomas R. Fugee, ***Executive Director, National Accounting & Finance Council***, American Trucking Associations, Inc.

David Grumhaus, ***Executive Vice President***, Distribution Sciences, Inc.

John Kreitner, ***Manager Projects, Corporate Traffic Consulting***, General Electric Co.

Lloyd J. Leveille, ***Assistant to the Treasurer***, Hemingway Transport, Inc.

Stuart Mathison, ***Vice President, Planning***, Telenet Communications

Walter May, ***Supervisor, Systems and Planning***, Republic Steel Corp.

Howard W. McKenna, ***Manager, Information Systems***, General Motors Corp.

Vernon Mendenhall, ***Vice President, Data Processing***, Chemical Leaman Tank Lines, Inc.

Kenneth R. Miller, ***Vice President, Management Services***, Eastern Express, Inc.

William G. Mitchell, ***President***, Eastern Express, Inc. (Gary)

F. Paler, ***Vice President, Management Information Systems***, Spector Freight System, Inc.

Gerry Pauls, ***Program Manager***, Boeing Computer Services, Inc.

Joseph E. Riley, ***Systems Analyst***, Standard Oil Co. (Indiana)

J. M. Schellenberg, ***Transportation Programmer***, Bethlehem Steel Corp.

Walter L. Schlenker, ***Consultant Corporate Finance***, General Electric Co.

Harold Schoger, ***Assistant Manager Systems***, Republic Steel Corp.

Ronald L. Shenk, ***Marketing Support Representative, Industry Systems Division***, ITEL Corp.

Roger H. Simonson, ***Industry Development Manager***, Boeing Computer Services, Inc.

Jesse E. Smith, ***Assistant Director of Revenue Accounting***, McLean Trucking Co.

Donald B. Snow, ***Vice President***, First National Bank of Boston

Ben Spina, ***President***, Instant Management, Inc.

P. W. Suggs, Jr., ***Manager Systems & Procedures***, McLean Trucking Co.

George W. Underhill, Jr., ***Manager, Freight Payment, Electronic Customer Services Division***, The Chase Manhattan Bank, N.A.,

George Vallas, Branch Motor Express Co.

Roger H. Simonsen, ***Industry Development Manager***, Boeing Computer Services, Inc.

Albert W. Wharton, ***Senior Consultant, Transportation & Distribution Department***, E.I. du Pont de Nemours & Co.

Gerald C. R. Wheatley, ***Assistant Vice President***, Yellow Freight System, Inc.

TDCC Shipper/Forwarder/Ocean Carrier Work Group

Armour S. Armstrong, ***Director, Office of Ports and Intermodal Systems***, Maritime Administration

Lucien H. Bliss, ***Manager, Corporate Documentation***, United States Lines, Inc.

Mrs. M. Brommund, ***Assistant Vice President***, E.I. du Pont Export Department, Schenkers International Forwarders, Inc.

Michael diGennaro, ***Manager, Systems & EDP***, Dart Containerline Inc.

Arthur C. Dittenber, Dow Chemical International, Inter-Area Distribution

Thomas W. English, ***Corporate Documentation Specialist***, Sea-Land Service, Inc.

Anthony Faillachi, ***Central Study Group***, General Motors Overseas Operations

James K. Greiss, ***Senior Distribution Analyst***, Transportation and Distribution Department, E. I. du Pont de Nemours & Co.

John M. Kaiser, ***Executive Vice President***, Harper Robinson & Co.

Eugene F. McCormick, ***Director of Pricing***, Lykes Bros. Steamship Co., Inc.

W. B. Rigdon, ***Director, Product Planning***, McDonnell Douglas Automation Co.

Joseph E. Riley, ***Systems Analyst***, Standard Oil Co. (Indiana)

Daniel Ross, ***Management Analyst, Office of Facilitation***, Department of Transportation

Gerry Pauls, ***Program Manager***, Boeing Computer Services, Inc.

Roger H. Simonsen, ***Industry Development Manager***, Boeing Computer Services, Inc.

Raymond J. Suesser, Jr., ***Manager, Systems Development***, Sea-Land Service, Inc.

Hans Wieting, Manager, ***Data Processing Department***, Atlantic Container Line, Ltd.

G. A. Trampler, ***Executive Vice President, Ocean Division U.S.A.***, Schenkers International Forwarders, Inc.

Wilhelm E. A. Wulf, ***Market Research Analyst, Pricing Division***, Lykes Bros Steamship Co., Inc.

TDCC Shipper/Forwarder/Air Carrier Work Group

Anthony J. D'Anna, ***Consultant***, Western Electric Co., Inc.

Arthur C. French, Jr., ***Director Service***, Emery Air Freight Corp.

Gerald J. Godbout, ***Director, Cargo Services***, Air Transport Association of America

Carl D. Hart, ***Director, Special Financial Projects***, Air Transport Association of America

William H. Kestas, ***Manager, Freight EDP Systems***, American Airlines, Inc.

Fred Linch, ***Manager, Computer Systems Department***, Flying Tiger Line Inc.

Miles B. Manchester, ***Special Assistant to Assistant Commissioner for Transportation & Public Utilities***, Federal Supply Service, General Services Administration

Earl K. McDonald, ***Manager, Traffic Services***, Sears, Roebuck and Co.

Terry C. McGaughey, ***Director of Facilitation***, Flying Tiger Line, Inc.

Gerry Pauls, ***Program Manager***, Boeing Computer Services, Inc.

John R. Pogue, ***General Manager Cargo***, Delta Air Lines, Inc.

Dean E. Richardson, ***Manager, Distribution Systems***, IBM World Trade Corp.

George Shipman, ***Air Freight Terminals***, American Airlines, Inc.

Richard S. Shreve, ***Manager, Cargo Administration***, Air Transport Association of America

Roger H. Simonsen, *Industry Development Manager*, Boeing Computer Services, Inc.

Clifford J. Stueck, *VP, EMCON Computer Systems*, Emery Air Freight Corp.

R. Michael Swift, *Assistant to Director of Service*, Emery Air Freight Corp.

Electronic Payment System Subcommittee

Douglas D. Anderson, As*sociate Director, Payments System Planning Division, Research and Planning Group*, American Bankers Association

Gene Brock, *Vice President*, Cass Bank & Trust Co.

Clifford R. Buys, *Director of Management System*s, American Trucking Associations, Inc.

Anthony J. D'Anna, *Consultant*, Western Electric Co., Inc.

Jerome L. Dempsey, *Vice President and Director of Marketing*, Cass Bank & Trust Co.

Joseph F. Egan, *Manager, Computer Systems, Corporate Distribution Department*, Union Carbide Corp.

Thomas R. Fugee, *Executive Director, National Accounting and Finance Council*, American Trucking Associations, Inc

Harry J. Krieg, *Chairman of the Board*, Cass Bank & Trust Co.

Donald E. LePard, *Systems Specialist Corporate Transportation*, Combustion Engineering, Inc.

Vernon Mendenhall, *Vice President, Data Processing*, Chemical Leaman Tank Lines, Inc.

Donald B. Snow, Vice President, First National Bank of Boston

George W. Underhill, Jr., *Manager, Freight Payment, Electronic Customer Services Division*, Chase Manhattan Bank, NA

George Vallas, Branch Motor Express Co.

Albert J. Wharton, *Senior Consultant, Transportation & Distribution Department*, E. I. du Pont de Nemours & Co.

TDCC Board of Directors

Samuel A. Alward, *Vice President, Management Information Services*, SCL/L&N Railroads

James A. Bailey, *Vice President, Management Systems*, Association of American Railroads

Donald B. Bolger, *Manager, Common Carrier Transportation Division, Transportation & Distribution Department*, E. I. du Pont de Nemours & Co.

Clifford R. Buys, *Director of Management Systems*, American Trucking Associations, Inc.

Walter H. Cramer, Jr., *Vice President Marketing*, Grand Trunk Western Railroad Co.

Donald S. Day, *Manager, Traffic Operation*, General Electric Co.

N. C. Dunn, *Traffic Manager, Supply Department*, Exxon Co., U.S.A.

Albert J. Fenaroli, *Manager of Distribution Operations*, Union Carbide Corp.

Thomas R. Greenleaf, *President*, Chemical Leaman Tank Lines, Inc.

Richard Haupt, *Director, Transportation and Traffic Office Supply Staff*, Ford Motor Co.

Richard H. Hinchcliff, *Executive Director*, National Motor Freight Traffic Association, Inc.

John C. Howard, *Vice President, Transportation*, Bethlehem Steel Corp.

William J. Klauberg, *Vice President East Coast Division*, United States Lines, Inc.

Edward G. Kreyling, Jr., *Vice President Marketing*, Southern Railway System

A. Jack Mayor, *Vice President*, Sea-Land Service, Inc.

Louis H. Meece, *Vice President*, American Commercial Barge Line Co.

James J. McNulty, *Chairman of the Board*, Emery Air Freight Corp.

William G. Mitchell, *President*, Eastern Express, Inc.

William P. Noonan, *Director of Transportation*, Western Electric Co., Inc.

William K. Smith, *Vice President*, General Mills, Inc.
Richard H. Steiner, *Vice President Marketing*, Flying Tiger Line Inc.
Kenneth L. Vore, *Vice President, Traffic and Transportation*, United States Steel Corp.

TDCC Staff and Consultants (1975)

Edward A. Guilbert, *President*
Joseph G. Carley, Jr., *Program Director*
Ralph W. Notto, *Systems Consultant*
Earl J. Bass, *Systems Consultant*
Alexander Kreithen, *Communications Consultant*
Thomas DesNoyers, *Director of Coding Standards*
Lester Probst, *Systems Consultant*
Gina Forrest, *Administrative Supervisor*

Appendix III

TRANSACTION SETS 1974

The first EDI standards publication included forty-two transaction sets. These pertained to air, motor, ocean, and rail transportation and to payment, administrative, and control information. Of these forty-two, sixteen were still in use by the year 2000, but may have been enhanced.

The original scheme assigned the identifiers as:

100 series—Air Transportation
200 series—Motor Transportation
300 series—Ocean Transportation
400 series—Rail Transportation
900 series—General Application
500 to 899—Reserved for other industries and general assignments

That scheme is no longer in use.
The purpose for the list is to indicate the extent of the 1975 publication.

Identifier—Title

104—Shipment Information (Air)
105—Container/Equipment Transfer (Air)
107—Shipment Information for Export Declaration (Air)
108—Shipment Information for Import (Air)
109—Shipment Information for Equipment/Delivery Order (Air)
110—Freight Details and Invoice (Air)
111—Freight Details and Invoice Summary (Air)

113—Inquiry (Air)
114—Shipment Identities and Status Reply (Air)
115—Status Details Reply (Air)
116—Repetitive Pattern Maintenance (Air)
204—Shipment Information (Motor)
205—Container/Equipment Transfer (Motor)
206—Shipment Pick-up Order (Motor)
207—Shipment Information for Export (Motor)
208—Shipment Information for Import (Motor)
210—Freight Details and Invoice (Motor)
211—Freight Details and Invoice Summary (Motor)
300—Reservation (Ocean)
301—Confirmation (Ocean)
302—Container or Specialized Equipment Pick-up Order/Cancellation (Ocean)
303—Cancellation (Ocean)
304—Shipment Information (Ocean)
305—Container/Equipment Transfer (Ocean)
307—Shipment Information for Export (Ocean)
308—Shipment Information for Import (Ocean)
310—Freight Details and Invoice (Ocean)
312—Arrival Notice (Ocean)
313—Inquiry (Ocean)
314—Status Details Reply (Ocean)
315—Status Details (Ocean)
316—Repetitive Pattern Maintenance (Ocean)
404—Shipment Information (Rail)
407—Shipment Information for Export (Rail)
408—Shipment Information for Import (Rail)
410—Freight Details and Invoice (Rail)
411—Freight Details and Invoice Summary (Rail)
416—Repetitive Pattern Maintenance (Rail)
900—Payment Authorization
901—Completed payments
995—Advisory Information
999—Acceptance/Rejection (Subsequently replaced by 997—Functional Acknowledgment)

TRANSACTION SETS 1999

The purpose for including the list is to indicate the different industries involved and the diversity of subjects addressed.

Identifier—Title

100—Insurance Plan Description
101—Name and Address Lists
104—Air Shipment Information
105—Business Entity Filings
106—Motor Carrier Rate Proposal
107—Request for Motor Carrier Rate Proposal
108—Response to a Motor Carrier Rate Proposal
109—Vessel Content Details
110—Air Freight Details and Invoice
112—Property Damage Report
114—Air Shipment Status Message

120—Vehicle Shipping Order
121—Vehicle Service
124—Vehicle Damage
125—Multilevel Railcar Load Details
126—Vehicle Application Advice
127—Vehicle Baying Order
128—Dealer Information
129—Vehicle Carrier Rate Update
130—Student Educational Record (Transcript)
131—Student Educational Record (Transcript) Acknowledgment

135—Student Loan Application
138—Testing Results Request and Report
139—Student Loan Guarantee Result
140—Product Registration
141—Product Service Claim Response
142—Product Service Claim
143—Product Service Notification
144—Student Loan Transfer and Status Verification

146—Request for Student Educational Record (Transcript)
147—Response to Request for Student Educational Record (Transcript)

148—Report of Injury, Illness, or Incident
149—Notice of Tax Adjustment or Assessment
150—Tax Rate Notification
151—Electronic Filing of Tax Return Data Acknowledgment
152—Statistical Government Information
153—Unemployment Insurance Tax Claim or Charge Information
154—Uniform Commercial Code Filing
155—Business Credit Report
157—Notice of Power of Attorney
159—Motion Picture Booking Confirmation

160—Transportation Automatic Equipment Identification
161—Train Sheet
163—Transportation Appointment Schedule Information
170—Revenue Receipts Statement
175—Court and Law Enforcement Notice
176—Court Submission
180—Return Merchandise Authorization and Notification
185—Royalty Regulatory Report
186—Insurance Underwriting Requirements Reporting
188—Educational Course Inventory

189—Application for Admission to Educational Institutions
190—Student Enrollment Verification
191—Student Loan Pre-Claims and Claims
194—Grant or Assistance Application
195—Federal Communications Commission (FCC) License Application
196—Contractor Cost Data Reporting
197—Real Estate Title Evidence
198—Loan Verification Information
199—Real Estate Settlement Information
200—Mortgage Credit Report

201—Residential Loan Application
202—Secondary Mortgage Market Loan Delivery
203—Secondary Mortgage Market Investor Report
204—Motor Carrier Load Tender
205—Mortgage Note
206—Real Estate Inspection
210—Motor Carrier Freight Details and Invoice
211—Motor Carrier Bill of Lading
212—Motor Carrier Delivery Trailer Manifest
213—Motor Carrier Shipment Status Inquiry

214—Transportation Carrier Shipment Status Message
215—Motor Carrier Pick-up Manifest
216—Motor Carrier Shipment Pick-up Notification
217—Motor Carrier Loading and Route Guide
218—Motor Carrier Tariff Information
219—Logistics Service Request
220—Logistics Service Response
222—Cartage Work Assignment
223—Consolidators Freight Bill and Invoice
224—Motor Carrier Summary Freight Bill Manifest

225—Response to a Cartage Work Assignment
242—Data Status Tracking
244—Product Source Information
248—Account Assignment/Inquiry and Service/Status
249—Animal Toxicological Data
250—Purchase Order Shipment Management Document
251—Pricing Support
252—Insurance Producer Administration
255—Underwriting Information Services
256—Periodic Compensation
260—Application for Mortgage Insurance Benefits
261—Real Estate Information Request
262—Real Estate Information Report
263—Residential Mortgage Insurance Application Response
264—Mortgage Loan Default Status
265—Real Estate Title Insurance Services Order

266—Mortgage or Property Record Change Notification
267—Individual Life, Annuity, and Disability Application
268—Annuity Activity
270—Eligibility, Coverage, or Benefit Inquiry

271—Eligibility, Coverage, or Benefit Information
272—Property and Casualty Loss Notification
273—Insurance/Annuity Application Status
275—Patient Information
276—Healthcare Claim Status Request
277—Healthcare Claim Status Notification
278—Healthcare Services Review Information
280—Voter Registration Information
285—Commercial Vehicle Safety and Credentials Information Exchange
286—Commercial Vehicle Credentials

288—Wage Determination
290—Cooperative Advertising Agreement
300—Reservation (Booking Request–Ocean)
301—Confirmation (Ocean)
303—Booking Cancellation (Ocean)
304—Shipping Instructions
309—U.S. Customs Manifest
310—Freight Receipt and Invoice (Ocean)
311—Canadian Customs Information
312—Arrival Notice (Ocean)

313—Shipment Status Inquiry (Ocean)
315—Status Details (Ocean)
317—Delivery/Pickup Order
319—Terminal Information
322—Terminal Operations and Intermodal Ramp Activity
323—Vessel Schedule and Itinerary (Ocean)
324—Vessel Stow Plan (Ocean)
325—Consolidation of Goods in Container
326—Consignment Summary List
350—U.S. Customs Status Information

352—U.S. Customs Carrier General Order Status
353—U.S. Customs Events Advisory Details
354—U.S. Customs Automated Manifest Archive Status
355—U.S. Customs Acceptance/Rejection
356—U.S. Customs Permit to Transfer Request
357—U.S. Customs In-Bond Information
358—U.S. Customs Consist Information
361—Carrier Interchange Agreement (Ocean)
362—Cargo Insurance Advice of Shipment
404—Rail Carrier Shipment Information

410—Rail Carrier Freight Details and Invoice
414—Rail Carhire Settlements
417—Rail Carrier Waybill Interchange
418—Rail Advance Interchange Consist
419—Advance Car Disposition
420—Car Handling Information
421—Estimated Time of Arrival and Car Scheduling
422—Shipper's Car Order
423—Rail Industrial Switch List
425—Rail Waybill Request

426—Rail Revenue Waybill
429—Railroad Retirement Activity
431—Railroad Station Master File
432—Rail Deprescription
433—Railroad Reciprocal Switch File
434—Railroad Mark Register Update Activity
435—Standard Transportation Commodity Code Master
436—Locomotive Information
437—Railroad Junctions and Interchanges Activity
440—Shipment Weights

451—Railroad Event Report
452—Railroad Problem Log Inquiry or Advice
453—Railroad Service Commitment Advice
455—Railroad Parameter Trace Registration
456—Railroad Equipment Inquiry or Advice

460—Railroad Price Distribution Request or Response
463—Rail Rate Reply
466—Rate Request
468—Rate Docket Journal Log
470—Railroad Clearance

475—Rail Route File Maintenance
485—Ratemaking Action
486—Rate Docket Expiration
490—Rate Group Definition
492—Miscellaneous Rates
494—Rail Scale Rates
500—Medical Event Reporting
501—Vendor Performance Review
503—Pricing History
504—Clauses and Provisions

511—Requisition
517—Material Obligation Validation
521—Income or Asset Offset
527—Material Due-In and Receipt
536—Logistics Reassignment
540—Notice of Employment Status
561—Contract Abstract
567—Contract Completion Status
568—Contract Payment Management Report
601—U.S. Customs Export Shipment Information

602—Transportation Services Tender
620—Excavation Communication
622—Intermodal Ramp Activity
625—Well Information
650—Maintenance Service Order
715—Intermodal Group Loading Plan
805—Contract Pricing Proposal
806—Project Schedule Reporting
810—Invoice
811—Consolidated Service Invoice/Statement

812—Credit/Debit Adjustment
813—Electronic Filing of Tax Return Data
814—General Request, Response, or Confirmation
815—Cryptographic Service Message
816—Organizational Relationships
818—Commission Sales Report
819—Operating Expense Statement
820—Payment Order/Remittance Advice
821—Financial Information Reporting
822—Account Analysis

823—Lockbox
824—Application Advice
826—Tax Information Exchange
827—Financial Return Notice
828—Debit Authorization
829—Payment Cancellation Request
830—Planning Schedule with Release Capability
831—Application Control Totals
832—Price/Sales Catalog
833—Mortgage Credit Report Order

834—Benefit Enrollment and Maintenance
835—Healthcare Claim Payment/Advice
836—Procurement Notices
837—Healthcare Claim
838—Trading Partner Profile
839—Project Cost Reporting
840—Request for Quotation
841—Specifications/Technical Information
842—Nonconformance Report
843—Response to Request for Quotation

844—Product Transfer Account Adjustment
845—Price Authorization Acknowledgment/Status
846—Inventory Inquiry/Advice
847—Material Claim
848—Material Safety Data Sheet

849—Response to Product Transfer Account Adjustment
850—Purchase Order
851—Asset Schedule
852—Product Activity Data
853—Routing and Carrier Instruction

854—Shipment Delivery Discrepancy Information
855—Purchase Order Acknowledgment
856—Ship Notice/Manifest
857—Shipment and Billing Notice
858—Shipment Information
859—Freight Invoice
860—Purchase Order Change Request Buyer Initiated
861—Receiving Advice/Acceptance Certificate
862—Shipping Schedule
863—Report of Test Results

864—Text Message
865—Purchase Order Change Acknowledgment/Request Seller Initiated
866—Production Sequence
867—Product Transfer and Resale Report
868—Electronic Form Structure
869—Order Status Inquiry
870—Order Status Report
871—Component Parts Content
872—Residential Mortgage Insurance Application
875—Grocery Products Purchase Order

876—Grocery Products Purchase Order Change
877—Manufacturer Coupon Family Code Structure
878—Product Authorization/De-authorization
879—Price Information
880—Grocery Products Invoice
881—Manufacturer Coupon Redemption Detail
882—Direct Store Delivery Summary Information
883—Market Development Fund Allocation
884—Market Development Fund Settlement

885—Retail Account Characteristics

886—Customer Call Reporting
887—Coupon Notification
888—Item Maintenance
889—Promotion Announcement
891—Deduction Research Report
893—Item Information Request
894—Delivery/Return Base Record
895—Delivery/Return Acknowledgment or Adjustment
896—Product Dimension Maintenance
920—Loss or Damage Claim General Commodities

924—Loss or Damage Claim Motor Vehicle
925—Claim Tracer
926—Claim Status Report and Tracer Reply
928—Automotive Inspection Detail
940—Warehouse Shipping Order
943—Warehouse Stock Transfer Shipment Advice
944—Warehouse Stock Transfer Receipt Advice
945—Warehouse Shipping Advice
946—Delivery Information Message
947—Warehouse Inventory Adjustment Advice

980—Functional Group Totals
990—Response to a Load Tender
994—Administrative Message
996—File Transfer
997—Functional Acknowledgment
998—Set Cancellation

UN/EDIFACT MESSAGES 1999

The following list contains 158 entries. The purpose for showing this list is to indicate the extent of definition coordinated by internationally oriented companies.

Identifier—Title

APERAK—Application error and acknowledgement
AUTHOR—Authorization
BALANC—Balance
BANSTA—Banking status
BAPLIE—Bayplan/stowage plan occupied and empty locations
BAPLTE—Bayplan/stowage plan total numbers
BOPBNK—Bank transactions and portfolio transactions report
BOPCUS—Balance of payment customer transaction report
BOPDIR—Direct balance of payment declaration
BOPINF—Balance of payment information from customer

CALINF—Vessel call information
CASINT—Request for legal administration action in civil proceedings mess
CASRES—Legal administration response in civil proceedings
CHACCO—Chart of accounts
COARRI—Container discharge/loading report
CODECO—Container gate-in/gate-out report
CODENO—Permit expiration/clearance ready notice
COEDOR—Container stock report
COHAOR—Container special handling order
COLREQ—Request for a documentary collection

COMDIS—Commercial dispute
CONAPW—Advice on pending works
CONDPV—Direct payment valuation
CONDRA—Drawing administration
CONDRO—Drawing organization
CONEST—Establishment of contract
CONITT—Invitation to tender
CONPVA—Payment valuation

CONQVA—Quantity valuation
CONRPW—Response of pending works

CONTEN—Tender
CONTRL—Control
CONWQD—Work item quantity determination
COPARN—Container announcement
COPINO—Container pre-notification
COPRAR—Container discharge/loading order
COREOR—Container release order
COSTCO—Container stuffing/stripping confirmation
COSTOR—Container stuffing/stripping order
CREADV—Credit advice

CREEXT—Extended credit advice
CREMUL—Multiple credit advice
CU.S.CAR—Customs cargo report
CU.S.DEC—Customs declaration
CU.S.EXP—Customs express consignment declaration
CU.S.PED—Periodic customs declaration
CU.S.REP—Customs conveyance report
CU.S.RES—Customs response
DEBADV—Debit advice
DEBMUL—Multiple debit advice

DELFOR—Delivery schedule
DELJIT—Delivery just in time
DESADV—Despatch advice
DESTIM—Equipment damage and repair estimate
DGRECA—Dangerous goods recapitulation
DIRDEB—Direct debit
DIRDEF—Directory definition
DOCADV—Documentary credit advice
DOCAMA—Advice of an amendment of a documentary credit
DOCAMI—Documentary credit amendment information

DOCAMR—Request for an amendment of a documentary credit

DOCAPP—Documentary credit application
DOCARE—Response to an amendment of a documentary credit
DOCINF—Documentary credit issuance information
ENTREC—Accounting entries
FINCAN—Financial cancellation
FINPAY—Multiple interbank funds transfer
FINSTA—Financial statement of an account
GENRAL—General purpose
GESMES—Generic statistical

HANMOV—Cargo/goods handling and movement
IFCSUM—Forwarding and consolidation summary
IFTCCA—Forwarding and transport shipment charge calculation
IFTDGN—Dangerous goods notification
IFTFCC—International transport freight costs and other charges
IFTIAG—Dangerous cargo list
IFTMAN—Arrival notice
IFTMBC—Booking confirmation
IFTMBF—Firm booking
IFTMBP—Provisional booking

IFTMCS—Instruction contract status
IFTMIN—Instruction
IFTRIN—Forwarding and transport rate information
IFTSAI—Forwarding and transport schedule and availability information me
IFTSTA—International multimodal status report
IFTSTQ—International multimodal status request
INFENT—Enterprise accounting information
INSDES—Instruction to despatch
INSPRE—Insurance premium
INVOIC—Invoice

INVRPT—Inventory report
ITRRPT—In transit report detail

JAPRES—Job application result
JINFDE—Job information demand
JOBAPP—Job application proposal
JOBCON—Job order confirmation
JOBMOD—Job order modification
JOBOFF—Job order
LREACT—Life reinsurance activity
MEDPID—Person identification

MEDREQ—Medical service request
MEDRPT—Medical service report
MEDRUC—Medical resource usage and cost
MEQPOS—Means of transport and equipment position
MOVINS—Stowage instruction
MSCONS—Metered services consumption report
ORDCHG—Purchase order change request
ORDERS—Purchase order
ORDRSP—Purchase order response
OSTENQ—Order status enquiry

OSTRPT—Order status report
PARTIN—Party information
PAXLST—Passenger list
PAYDUC—Payroll deductions advice
PAYEXT—Extended payment order
PAYMUL—Multiple payment order
PAYORD—Payment order
PRICAT—Price/sales catalogue
PRIHIS—Pricing history
PRODAT—Product data

PRODEX—Product exchange reconciliation
PROINQ—Product inquiry
PRPAID—Insurance premium payment
QALITY—Quality data
QUOTES—Quote
RDRMES—Raw data reporting
REBORD—Reinsurance bordereau

RECADV—Receiving advice
RECALC—Reinsurance calculation
RECECO—Credit risk cover

RECLAM—Reinsurance claims
REMADV—Remittance advice
REPREM—Reinsurance premium
REQDOC—Request for document
REQOTE—Request for quote
RESETT—Reinsurance settlement
RESMSG—Reservation
RETACC—Reinsurance technical account
RETANN—Announcement for returns
RETINS—Instruction for returns

SAFHAZ—Safety and hazard data
SANCRT—International movement of goods governmental regulatory
SLSFCT—Sales forecast
SLSRPT—Sales data report
SOCADE—Social administration
SSIMOD—Modification of identity details
SSRECH—Worker's insurance history
SSREGW—Notification of registration of a worker
STATAC—Statement of account
SUPCOT—Superannuation contributions advice

SUPMAN—Superannuation maintenance
SUPRES—Supplier response
TANSTA—Tank status report
VATDEC—Value added tax
VESDEP—Vessel departure
WASDIS—Waste disposal information
WKGRDC—Work grant decision
WKGRRE—Work grant request

Printed in the United States
26371LVS00001B/61-69